JEWISH MAGIC AND SUPERSTITION

Courtesy of the Jewish Theological Seminary Library, New York

POPULAR MEDIEVAL AMULET TO PROTECT THE MOTHER AND CHILD AGAINST ATTACK BY LILIT DURING CHILDBIRTH.—FROM *Sefer Raziel*, AMSTERDAM, 1701.

JEWISH MAGIC AND SUPERSTITION

A Study in Folk Religion

JOSHUA TRACHTENBERG

Martino Publishing
Mansfield Centre, CT
2013

Martino Publishing
P.O. Box 373,
Mansfield Centre, CT 06250 USA

ISBN 978-1-61427-407-0

Cover design by T. Matarazzo

Printed in the United States of America On 100% Acid-Free Paper

Jewish Magic
and
Superstition

A Study in Folk Religion

Joshua Trachtenberg

Behrman's Jewish Book House
New York
1939

TO MY PARENTS

DEBORAH AND SIMON TRACHTENBERG

FOREWORD

TO UNDERSTAND a people—and through it, humankind—is to see its life whole. This has been a peculiarly difficult task where Jews are concerned, for the vision of the world has been obscured by darkly bias-tinted spectacles. If, on the one hand, Christological and anti-Semitic prejudices have revealed only an infamous horde of blasphemers and parasites, on the other, a historical perspective limited by Scripture has disclosed an exalted band of prophets, hounded and persecuted as prophets must be for their vision and temerity. Between these two extremes—which have alike doomed Jews to the unhappiest of careers—a normal people, with all the faults and virtues of humanity, has pursued its normal course through history, however abnormal were the conditions against which it struggled. This is perhaps the greatest achievement of Jewry, that in the face of an environment as perennially hostile as any people has had to confront, it has still maintained its balance, it has remained a normal member of the human family—even to owning, along with its peculiar virtues and faults, the common aberrations of the human race.

The Jewish people did not cease to live and grow when the New Testament was written. The two thousand years since have seen a steady expansion and development of its inner life. New religious concepts were advanced, the old were elaborated, and always the effort has been to make these something more than concepts, to weave them into the pattern of daily life, so that the Jew might live his religion. This was the sadly misunderstood "legalism" of Judaism. But alongside this formal development there was a constant elaboration of what we may call "folk religion"—ideas and practices that never met with the whole-hearted approval of the religious leaders, but which enjoyed such wide popularity that they could not be altogether excluded from the field of religion. Of this sort were the beliefs concerning demons and angels, and the many superstitious usages based on these beliefs, which by more or less devious routes actually became a part of Judaism, and on the periphery of the religious life, the practices of magic, which never broke completely with the tenets of the faith, yet stretched them almost to the breaking-point. If we call these "folk religion" it is because they expressed the common attitude of the people, as against the official attitude of the Synagogue, to the universe.

The rabbis sought to eradicate these practices, or at least to transmute their offensive features. But their efforts met with only indifferent success, and they were often obliged to accord the elements of this folk religion a grudging recognition and acceptance. "Better is it that Israel should sin unwittingly than consciously break the law."

In this respect the history of Jewish thought runs parallel with that of all peoples. Everywhere the common folk has existed on an intellectual and spiritual plane all its own, and it is only in the most recent centuries that true science and religion have made inroads into folk conceptions of the universe and brought them closer—if only a little—to what we call our modern, rationalist viewpoint. In Jewish scholarship this phase of folk religion and folk science has been sorely neglected. The tendency has been to impute to the Jewish people as a whole the ideas of a few advanced thinkers, to investigate philosophy and mysticism and law, the cultural and religious creations of the intellectual élite—valuable studies which, however, provide no insight into the inner life of the people themselves.

This book offers a contribution to an understanding of folk Judaism, the beliefs and practices that expressed most eloquently the folk psyche—of all the vagaries which, coupled with the historic program of the Jewish faith, made up the everyday religion of the Jewish people. It must be emphasized, however, if that should be necessary, that it depicts but this one phase of Judaism, a not altogether legitimate phase; the other has been described in many competent and sympathetic works.

The material here presented is culled from the literature of Germanic Jewry (described in the Note About the Sources)—the Jewry of Germany, Northern France, England, Austria, Poland, which constituted culturally and historically a single community—from the eleventh century through the sixteenth. It is with reference to this period that the terms "medieval" and "Middle Ages" are employed throughout the book. The cultural history of North European Jewry began to unfold only in the former century, though the community was in existence long before, and it retained its medieval aspect through the sixteenth century, and considerably later in some places. However, the year 1600, or thereabouts, has been selected as *terminus ad quem,* for during the succeeding century the so-called

Lurianic *Kabbalah,* emanating from Safed, introduced a variety of new mystical elements and emphases, and also at about this time the center of Jewish life was shifting toward the east, where it came increasingly under the influence of the Slavic cultures. Until about 1600 the North European community remained fairly homogeneous, and Germanic.

But we must perforce reach back to earlier periods for a complete presentation of the subject; the Bible, and predominantly the Talmudic and Geonic tradition, exercised a profound and determining influence upon medieval Jewish life. It would be vain to attempt an evaluation of medieval Jewish magic and superstition without according due weight to the older sources from which much of it derived. (It should be noted that the Talmudic period is usually considered to have closed at about 500 C.E.; the Geonic extended through the eleventh century.) And it may be added that the material here presented still possesses a certain contemporaneity. To quote Marvin Lowenthal, "Orthodox Jewry as the western world knows it today is to a great extent the heir, when it is not the creation, of German Jewry." A study of Germanic Jewry in the Middle Ages discloses the origin and significance of many present-day practices.

Biblical superstition and magic have been thoroughly investigated by a number of scholars; the Talmudic period also has been carefully, if not so intensively, examined; the Geonic period, unfortunately, has received much less attention. As for Northern Europe during the Middle Ages, a single pioneering chapter, very remunerative but necessarily limited, in Moritz Güdemann's *Geschichte des Erziehungswesens und der Cultur der abendländischen Juden* has had to suffice. The present work, I trust, will help to fill the gap in our understanding of the medieval Jew.

Jewry has been divided into two large groups, the *Sephardic,* representing the culture of Southern Europe (Spain, North Africa, Italy, and latterly the countries of the eastern Mediterranean), and the *Ashkenazic,* emanating from the Germanic lands and today constituting the mass of Jews in Europe and the Americas. The distinction is largely superficial, for fundamentally they were at one in their adherence to a common tradition and law, and there was an accelerating interchange of ideas and literatures which kept them united within the embracing folds of Judaism. But differences are to be noted, differences in cultural tone which clearly reflect their environments. The Jewry of the Moslem lands produced the flowering of

Jewish philosophy and poetry and science and mysticism. The North produced Talmudists—and a burgeoning superstition and magic. Throughout this book runs the thread of the remark in *Sefer Ḥasidim*, "As the Gentiles do, so do the Jews." The notion that the ghetto Jew of medieval Europe was completely shut off from the temper of his age is false. The *people* were in daily contact, and the ideas and movements that swept Europe invaded the ghetto as well. The Jews were an integral part of medieval Europe and their culture reflected, as in a measure it influenced, all the forces operative in the general culture of the period. This was especially so in Germany—and nowhere more notably than in the folk beliefs that constitute the commonest denominator between peoples. Jewish superstition and magic represent another view, from a hitherto unexploited angle, of medieval Europe.

Finally, I hope that the readers of this book will find in it some little contribution to our knowledge of the history of thought—not of Jewish thought alone, but of human thought. For superstition and magic are universal and uniform in their manifestations, and constitute an important chapter in the progress of man's ideas; those minor variations that appear here and there are but reflections of the infinite variety and ingenuity of the human mind. Professor Lynn Thorndike has made an exhaustive and rewarding study of the *History of Magic and Experimental Science* in medieval Europe, as one aspect of the history of thought. I may express the wish that this present book be regarded as a humble appendix to his work.

The reader's attention is called to the list of Abbreviations and Hebrew Titles, and the Glossary of Hebrew Terms, appended at the end of the text, which may facilitate the use of this book.

There remains the pleasant duty of acknowledging many obligations. I am greatly indebted to Professors Salo W. Baron and Lynn Thorndike of Columbia University and Professor Louis Ginzberg of the Jewish Theological Seminary who have read the manuscript and offered many helpful suggestions. My thanks are also due to Professor Alexander Marx and the staff of the Jewish Theological Seminary Library for their ready aid in utilizing the rich collection of that institution; to Mr. Louis Margolis, who so graciously assumed the heavy burden of preparing the index; and to the members of my congregation, *Brith Shalom*, of Easton, Pennsylvania, who provided me with the leisure to pursue this work, and ensured its publication. To my wife belongs my deepest gratitude; she has a greater share in this book than I can acknowledge.

TABLE OF CONTENTS

TABLE OF CONTENTS

JEWISH MAGIC AND SUPERSTITION

1

THE LEGEND OF JEWISH SORCERY

The anomalous position of the Jew in the modern world is but a latter-day version of the fate that has dogged his footsteps ever since he wandered forth among strange and hostile peoples. In no time and place, however, was his status—and his plight—so manifestly unique as in medieval Europe. The essence of that uniqueness lay in his ambiguous relationship to the Christian society in which he led his precarious existence, on the one hand influenced by all the objective forces which molded his environment, on the other, shut off from that environment by insurmountable walls of suspicion and animosity. His wilful persistence in his religious and cultural "difference" from the intolerant Christian civilization of the day, the dogmatic enmity fostered by the Church, his minority status coupled with an effective economic competition with his non-Jewish neighbors, all these combined to create an attitude of envy and hatred. But these alone do not tell the whole story; we must admit a further element into the psychological complex which determined the attitude of Christian toward Jew—an element which today has lost its force in the composition of anti-Semitism, but which in the Middle Ages loomed very large. For it contributed the emotion of fear, even of superstitious dread, in an age when superstition was the prevailing faith not alone of the masses, but of many of their leaders as well.

Sorcery was a very real and terrifying phenomenon in those days, and many medieval Christians looked upon the Jew as the magician *par excellence*. The allegiance to Satan, attributed to Jews with an insistence that almost drowned out its true implication, was not merely a form of invective or rhetoric. Satan was the ultimate source of magic, which operated only by his diabolic will and connivance. Christian writers make it quite clear that this is the connection to which they refer.[1] Secular and religious authorities took action time and again against the Jews expressly on this count, and the Inquisition occasionally availed itself of the charge to get around the restrictions of ecclesiastical law which excluded the Jew from its legitimate hunting grounds.[2]

The masses also were quick to seize the opportunity afforded by this accusation, and mass attacks upon the Jews frequently followed the levelling of the charge. To cite but one instance: the most violent mob assault upon Jews in England, which overwhelmed every major Jewish community and took a tragic toll of martyrs, had its inception at the coronation of Richard I in London on September 3, 1189. On that occasion a Jewish delegation bearing gifts and pledges of allegiance was driven from the palace, publicly accused of having come to cast their enchantments over the newly crowned king, and was set upon by the crowd; the outbreak spread rapidly through the city and the land, took more than half a year to spend itself and left in its wake a trail of horrible butcheries.[3] Such manifestations, in greater or lesser degree, were the usual concomitant of a like accusation.

The striking feature of the Christian apprehension of Jewish sorcery is that it adhered not to certain specific Jews, who had aroused it by their actions, but rather to the entire people, *en masse*. Consequently every innocent Jewish act which by its strangeness laid itself open to suspicion was considered a diabolical device for working magic against Christians. The custom of throwing a clod of earth behind one after a funeral brought a charge of sorcery in Paris, in the early years of the thirteenth century, which might have had dire consequences if a certain Rabbi Moses b. Yeḥiel had not succeeded in persuading the king of its utterly harmless character.[4] The practice of washing the hands on returning from the cemetery aroused the same suspicions of sorcery and provoked some bloody scenes.

So onerous did these recurrent accusations become that the rabbis of the Middle Ages found it necessary—forced to this step, no doubt, by Jewish public opinion—to suspend some of these customs. In the case of the clod-throwing, though "many were obliged to disregard the usage for fear that the Gentiles would accuse them of sorcery," custom was proof against fear. But in other instances fear triumphed. The mourning rites of "binding the head" and "overturning the bed" lapsed during the Middle Ages for this reason. In Talmudic times fear of the same accusation had led Jewish authorities to excuse the head of the household from the rite of "searching out the leaven" on the eve of the Passover in places owned in common with a non-Jew; during the Middle Ages there was a strong but unsuccessful agitation to suspend this rite altogether, even indoors, "because we have Gentile serving-girls in our homes" who might spread the alarm. In Provence, however, the ritual cleansing of the public oven in preparation for Passover baking was neglected "because of the Gentiles' suspicion of sorcery." When a fire broke out in a Jewish house its owner dared expect little mercy from the mob, for he was a sorcerer seeking to destroy Christendom, and his punishment was commonly simultaneous with his crime. The rabbis of the time were therefore unusually tolerant about violations of the prohibition to put out fires on the Sabbath and on the Day of Atonement. At the slightest danger they set this prohibition aside, "for this is a matter of life and death, since they accuse us and persecute us." We read of a lamb, slaughtered in fulfillment of a ritual obligation, which was cut up and buried secretly in sections, "so that the matter may not become known and they say, 'it was done for magical ends.' "[5] To such measures were Jews driven by fear of arousing the suspicions of their neighbors.

Jews were stoned as sorcerers. But it needs little knowledge of human nature to believe that the very vice became a virtue when Christians themselves had need of a little expert magic on the side. If Jews were magicians, their every act a charm, then their magic devices could aid as well as harm. R. Isaac b. Moses of Vienna, in the thirteenth century, tells that once when he was in Regensburg over a holiday, "a Gentile who had much power in the city fell dangerously ill, and ordered a Jew to let him have some of his wine, or he would surely die; and I gave this Jew permission to send him the wine (although it was a holiday) in order to prevent trouble, though there were some who disagreed and forbade this." Apparently Jewish wine possessed occult healing powers; perhaps this Gentile had in mind wine that had been blessed by Jews. It would be interesting to know how effective the cure was but R. Isaac carries his anecdote no farther.

The *mezuzah* (a Biblical inscription attached to the doorpost) was also an object of suspicion, and at the same time, of desire. That it was regarded as a magical device by Christians we know, for a fifteenth-century writer admonished his readers to affix a *mezuzah* to their doors even when they occupied a house owned by a non-Jew, despite the fact that the landlord might accuse them of sorcery. Indeed, the Jews in the Rhineland had to cover over their *mezuzot,* for, as a thirteenth-century writer complained, "the Christians, out of malice and to annoy us, stick knives into the *mezuzah* openings and cut up the parchment." Out of malice, no doubt—but the magical repute of the *mezuzah* must have lent special force to their vindictiveness. Yet even Christians in high places were not averse to using these magical instruments themselves. Toward the end of the fourteenth century the Bishop of Salzburg asked a Jew to give him a *mezuzah* to attach to the gate of his castle, but the rabbinic authority to whom this Jew turned for advice refused to countenance so outrageous a prostitution of a distinctively religious symbol.[6]

In the field of medicine in particular was the reputed Jewish magical skill called upon to perform miracles. According to the popular view, demons and magic were often responsible for disease, and medicine was therefore the legitimate province of the sorcerer. Jewish physicians, though by no means free from the general superstitious attitude, were among the foremost representatives of a scientific medicine in the Germanic lands. Their wide knowledge of languages, the availability of Arabic-Greek medical works in Hebrew translation, their propensity for travel and study abroad, their freedom from the Church-fostered superstition of miraculous cures, relics, and the like, these often conspired to make of them more effective practitioners than their non-Jewish competitors. Paradoxically, their scientific training, such as it was, made them superior magicians in the popular view, and every triumph of medical science enhanced the Jew's reputation for sorcery.

This accounts for the popularity of Jewish doctors in Northern Europe throughout this period, despite stringent Church prohibitions, constantly reiterated by popes and synods (Vienna 1267, Basel 1434, etc.), and the caveat of the clergy that these Jews would turn their magic against their patients. But who would risk his life in the hands of an inferior Christian physician for the sake of theological doctrine when a powerful Jewish doctor-magician could be called in? In 1657, when a Jewish doctor was given permission to practice in the city of Hall, in Swabia, the clergy epitomized the medieval clerical position in a public statement: "Es sei besser mit Christo gestorben, als per Juden-Dr. mit dem Teufel gesund worden"! But this pious preference was reserved for whole moments; when the issue was joined the ministrations of Satan were not rejected. For those who are interested there are lists of Jewish physicians practicing in Northern Europe during the Middle Ages. We know of most of them only because their names have been preserved in Christian documents, recording their services to Christian rulers and prelates, their receipt or loss of privileges, or the occasional tragic reward of their efforts. For if the patient risked his life when he called in a Jewish doctor, that doctor also risked his when he rolled up his sleeves and set to work. If his ministrations were successful he was a magician and might expect to be treated as such, with fear and respect, and active animosity; if he failed, he was a magician, and could expect to be called upon to pay promptly for his crime. The first Jewish physician we hear of in the West was one Zedekiah, court physician to Emperor Charles the Bald toward the end of the ninth century, magician, of course, as well as—or because?—physician. He marked the type to the end: accused of poisoning the Emperor in 877, he no doubt suffered the appropriate punishment.[7]

Another form which the charge of sorcery took was the recurrent accusation against Jews during the Middle Ages of feeding poisons to their enemies. Not alone were physicians accused of poisoning their patients, but Jews in general were considered especially adept in this art. In the Rhineland, in 1090, we learn of Jews dealing in various drugs and salves, and since the exotic elements of the medieval pharmacopœia were imported from the East, we may surmise that during this period such items were part of the regular stock in trade of Jewish merchants. We hear rather often of Jewish trade in drugs, throughout the Germanic lands. But drugs and poisons were almost synonymous terms to the medieval mind—and to the equation we may add sorcery as well. "Poisoning was for a long time closely associated with sorcery and magic. Mysterious deaths might be attributed to the one or the other, and both purported to employ occult and sensational forces of nature. The same word was used in the Greek and in the Latin language for poison and sorcery, for a drug and a philter or magical potion. The fact that men actually were poisoned supported the belief in the possibility of sorcery, and this belief in its turn stimulated excessive credulity in poisons which were thought to act at a distance or after a long lapse of time. . . . Popular credence was strong as to the possibility of wholesale poisoning." [8]

When, in 1550, the Polish king Sigismund Augustus demanded of Ivan IV (the Terrible) that he admit Lithuanian Jews into Russia for business purposes, by virtue of former commercial treaties between the two countries, Ivan replied, "It is not convenient to allow

Jews to come with their goods to Russia, since many evils result from them. For they import poisonous herbs into our realms. . . ." Luther wrote, "If they [the Jews] could kill us all, they would gladly do so, aye, and often do it, especially those who profess to be physicians. They know all that is known about medicine in Germany; they can give poison to a man of which he will die in an hour, or in ten or twenty years; they thoroughly understand this art." If there is high praise hidden in these words it was wholly unintended. In 1267 Church councils at Breslau and Vienna forbade Christians to purchase foodstuffs from Jews, for these were likely to have been poisoned—a sample of the kind of legislation this belief occasioned. In the middle years of the fourteenth century thousands of Jews (and also lepers) were massacred, accused of having plotted wholesale murder by poisoning wells. Such charges and mass persecutions preceded, in fact, the Black Death, dating back, in France, to 1320.[9]

These accusations, general in character, stemmed logically from the view of the Jew as sorcerer. They were accompanied by other charges, which indicate that he was accredited with the more particular skills of medieval sorcery. During the early Christian centuries the Church had been rocked by the controversy over the doctrine of transubstantiation. But the popular mind, thrusting subtleties to the wind, had driven straight to the main point, accepting that dogma in its furthest literalness. The rôle which the host, the body of Christ, played in popular superstition and magic throughout the Middle Ages was already evident as early as the fourth century; what more natural than that the Jews, magicians and enemies of Christianity, should be charged with utilizing the wafer of the Eucharist in their own diabolic schemes? The absurdity of attributing to Jews an acceptance and utilization of this most un-Jewish of dogmas never occurred to their accusers. The record is replete with accounts of mutilations of the host by Jews—and, of course, the attendant miracles and persecutions. But direct attack upon the body of Jesus was apparently too simple and gross a procedure to satisfy the crafty Jews, and they frequently resorted to a more recondite method of wreaking their venom upon the Christians and their Lord. Annually, if we are to believe the reports, they would fashion from wax an image of the founder of Christianity, and by their magic art transmit through this image to its model and his followers the pangs and tortures they visited upon it.[10]

This last is a form of the famous image magic known and used universally. By sticking pins into, or burning, or otherwise mutilating an image of one's enemy it is believed that he will be caused to experience in his own body the effects of such action. Christians did not hesitate to impute to their Jewish neighbors frequent resort to this technique, not only, as we have seen, with respect to the body of Christ, but of their Christian contemporaries as well. In 1066, for example, the Jews of Treves were accused of having made a waxen image of Bishop Eberhard, which, after having it baptized by a priest whom they had bribed, they burned on a Sabbath (!) ; is it necessary to add that he promptly fell ill and died? [11]

Of all the charges against the Jewish people the one that has enjoyed the hardiest tenacity and the utmost notoriety, and has produced the direst consequences, is the ritual murder accusation. In its popular version it foists upon Jewish ritual the requirement of Christian blood at the Passover service. The subject of much study and infinitely more polemics, its absurdity has been conclusively established, but the true nature of the accusation has never been made sufficiently clear.[12] The legend as we know it has experienced several redactions. In its pristine form it was the product of ancient superstition—and of the idea of the Jew as sorcerer.

One of the most pervasive beliefs was in the great utility for medicinal and magical purposes of the elements of the human body. Medieval magic is full of recipes for putting to occult use human fat, human blood, entrails, hands, fingers; medieval medicine utilized as one of its chief medicaments the blood of man, preferably blood that had been freshly drawn, or menstrual blood.[13] The ritual murder accusation was the result of these beliefs.

There is on record at least one accusation against a Jew, dating from the thirteenth century, of despoiling a servant girl, whom he was said to have drugged, of some flesh which he intended to put to a magical or medicinal use. This was the motive which was believed to have prompted many assumed ritual murders. One of the first medieval references to this accusation, made by Thomas of Cantimpré early in that century, attributed the need for Christian blood to the widespread Jewish affliction of hemorrhages (some later accounts changed the malady to hemorrhoids), which could be cured only by the application of this blood. The Jews of Fulda (Hesse-Nassau), accused in 1235 of murdering five children, are said to have confessed that they did so in order to procure their blood for purposes of healing. Matthew Paris's contemporary account of the alleged crucifixion of Hugh of Lincoln by Jews in 1255 ascribed to them the intention of using the boy's bowels for divination. To skip a century and a half, in May, 1401, the city council of Freiburg (in Breisgau) wrote to Duke Leopold requesting the total expulsion of the Jews from their city, the foremost count against them being that they periodically slaughtered a Christian child, for "all Jews require Christian blood for the prolongation of their lives." The only Christian statement on the ritual murder charge against the Jews of Tyrnau in 1494 explains their need of this blood on several grounds: "Firstly: they [the Jews] were convinced by the judgment of their ancestors that the blood of a Christian was a good remedy for the alleviation of the wound of circumcision. Secondly: they were of the opinion that this blood, put into food, is very efficacious for the awakening of mutual love. Thirdly: they had discovered, as men and women among them suffered equally from menstruation, that the blood of a Christian is a specific medicine for it, when drunk. Fourthly: that they had an ancient but secret ordinance by which they are under obligation to shed Christian blood in honor of God in daily sacrifices in some spot or other." As late as the beginning of the eighteenth century it is reported that in Poland and Germany tales were told and songs sung in the streets "how the Jews have murdered a child, and sent the blood to one another in quills for the use of their women in childbirth."

It is evident from these instances that the suspicion of magic was behind the accusation of child murder. There is no mention of the Passover, of kneading the blood into the unleavened cakes, or drinking it at the *Seder* service, all of which are late refinements. The records of the early accusations are meaningless unless viewed against the background of medieval superstition. A modern writer who has made a careful study of Christian magic and witchcraft, and who proves himself as credulous and superstition-ridden as the period he examines, expresses exactly the medieval view, which is his as well: Jews were persecuted "not so much for the observance of Hebrew ceremonies, as is often suggested and supposed, but for the practice of the dark and hideous traditions of Hebrew magic. Closely connected with these ancient sorceries are those ritual murders. . . . In many cases the evidence is quite conclusive that the body, and especially the blood of the victim, was used for magical purposes." Montague Summers, the writer of these lines, believes this "evidence" implicitly! If a present-day Catholic can so blindly accept the truth of these accusations of the use of Christian blood by Jews for magical purposes, how all-compelling this "evidence" must have been for his medieval predecessors! [14]

Most of the charges levelled against the Jews fit into one or another of these categories. The surprising thing is that the specific crimes of sorcery of which Jews stood accused were in the end so limited in nature. Or perhaps this is not so surprising when we consider that these accusations derived not from observed acts of Jews, but from the general picture of "sorcerer" which the Church crusade against sorcery and the later witch-cults painted so vividly. Prior to the inception of the Inquisition in the thirteenth century, excesses attributed to sorcery had been punished by the secular authorities simply as criminal acts. When the Church undertook to stamp out sorcery it branded its practitioners as devil-worshiping anti-Christians.[15]

Sorcerers and witches, brought before the bar of the Inquisition, were accused of, and confessed to, the adoration of Satan, the desecration of the host and other consecrated objects, the sacrifice of infants, cannibalism, the use of human ingredients, particularly blood and fat, in their salves and potions, effecting the death of their enemies by means of waxen images baptized in their names, poisonings, all the details of what came to be a stereotyped catalogue of crimes. One cannot fail to notice especially the constant recurrence of the charge of child sacrifice in these trials, and the importance of human blood in the witches' ritual; these were apparently the most distinguishing elements in the technique of the sorcerer and the witch, as disclosed to popular view by the campaign of the Church. We need but recall the famous trial in 1440 of the Marshal Gilles de Rais, aid and associate of Joan of Arc, at which he was accused and convicted of murdering several hundred children whose blood and bodies he employed for magical purposes.[16] It is these charges that determined the character of the sorcery propaganda against the Jews.

The Middle Ages inherited a tradition of Jewish sorcery from the ancient world. A host of popular magical works was attributed to Solomon and other fabled Jewish masters. Juvenal's jibe that the Appian Way swarmed with fortune-telling Jewesses who would "sell you any sort of dream at cut prices" was the kind of information that was bound to make and retain its impression, and bear a numerous progeny. Then too, it must be borne in mind, medieval Christians never had more than a very imperfect acquaintance with the language, the religion, the customs of the Jews who made their home among them; and what information concerning their Jewish neighbors they did possess was as often as not incorrect and misleading. Jews, consequently, remained an unknown and mysterious folk. Their very strangeness was a suspicious element, and the weirdest legends about them found ready currency among a people given to an easy credulity and the crassest superstition. Nor did the mistrust and animosity which the entire background of medieval Christendom fostered against the Jews serve to lessen the effect of their strangeness.

It need hardly occasion surprise, then, that to this despised anti-Christian nation (the crusade against heresy, inaugurated in the thirteenth century, ascribed diabolic rites to some of the heretical sects as well, and this, too, may have influenced the popular view), already tarred with the tradition of magic, was attributed the entire list of goetic practices publicized by the Church as the infallible marks of sorcery. The accusations came in time to be part of a pattern which repeated itself *ad infinitum.*

But if more varied charges did not enter the record, we may be certain that they existed in the mind of the people. Clearly, if the Jews were such skilful magicians, their art was not limited, they must be acquainted with all the more usual devices to which the ordinary sorcerer turned his hand. We have evidence, if meager, that this was so—evidence which pathetically discloses the Jewish side of the matter. Luther recounts an anecdote of a Jew who proffered to Count Albrecht of Saxony an amulet which would make him immune to all weapons of attack. Albrecht forced this Jew to take his own medicine: to test the efficacy of the amulet he hung it about its donor's neck—and ran him through with his sword!

A curious parallel to this tale indicates the tragic use to which this reputation for sorcery could be put, and the tragic necessity which prompted such a use. During the Chmielnicki pogroms of 1648-1649 a young Jewish girl of the city of Nemirov was carried off by a Cossack. Preferring a fate of her own choosing, she offered him a similar amulet. " 'If you have no faith in me,' she assured him, 'test it by shooting at me. You cannot harm me.' Her credulous captor, not doubting her word, fired straight at her and she fell dead, for the sanctification of the Holy Name, and to preserve her purity. May God have mercy on her soul!" concludes the pious chronicler of one of the bloodiest pages of Jewish history.[17]

2

THE TRUTH BEHIND THE LEGEND

JEWISH MAGIC

THE LEGEND of the Jew as sorcerer supreme was of Gentile making, fashioned after the latest pattern of the up-to-date thaumaturge, but like most ready-made fables it fitted the truth none too closely. For if Jews were not the malefic sorcerers that Christian animosity made them out to be, they still possessed an ancient and honorable tradition of magic which had been solicitously nourished until in the Middle Ages it reached its highest stage of development. Sheltered from Christian eyes by secrecy and the impenetrable wall of a strange tongue and an even stranger mystical vocabulary and method peculiar to itself, there flourished in Jewish circles a magic lore as extensive and potent as any known to the non-Jewish world, yet markedly different in character and technique.

The Biblical allusions to the practice of magic indicate a widespread acquaintance with its manifold forms at an early time, but this can hardly be called "Jewish" magic. It was merely a reflection of the superstitions of the Canaanites, re-inforced by importations from Babylonia and Egypt. Even the Talmudic period, reaching to about 500 C.E., did not yet produce a distinctive amalgamation of the various strands of tradition that led into it, duplicating in large measure the eclecticism of Hellenistic-Gnostic magic, which it itself influenced. Thus we find ensconced in the Hebrew lore beliefs and practices emanating from the entire Mediterranean world: representatives of ancient Babylon and Egypt nestled against Græco-Roman specimens, newer Egyptian developments, entering by way of the Hellenistic recension, hobnobbing with the latest Chaldaic doctrine, as exemplified in the Babylonian *Gemara*. Not until the Geonic age, which succeeded the Talmudic, do we find the beginnings of a definitely Jewish magic. It was in this period that Jewish mysticism, influenced to a considerable degree by Gnostic thought, took shape, though its origin undoubtedly goes back to the earlier period.

"Theosophy has always evinced a strong affinity for magic," wrote Prof. George Foot Moore. Searching out the secret springs of the universe, the mystic brings to light awesome and puissant truths, which his more practical and brazen confidants feel promptly impelled to profane for their own greater glory and might. Geonic mysticism opened the portals to a higher wisdom—and a more potent magic. Combined with the older eclectic lore this evolving theurgy bloomed luxuriantly in the Germanic lands, whither its most secret mysteries were transported and incautiously revealed to the gaze of initiate and tyro alike. This magic may properly be denominated "Jewish"; for all its more or less assimilated foreign elements, and its general similarity to the Gnostic-Jewish system imperfectly known to non-Jews as the *Ars Notoria,* it remained distinctive in its basic emphases. To be sure the details of magical practice are too hoary and universal to admit of fundamental modification. Only in its general tone, the impression left by the whole, can a system of magic be distinguished from others; its details are the *lingua franca* of superstition. In this sense we may characterize medieval Jewish magic as distinctively "Jewish." Its fundamentals were indigenous. But the intensification of superstition among non-Jews that accompanied the attack of the Church upon sorcery was not without its influence in bringing to fruition the latent potentialities of this Jewish mystical-magical lore. "Wie es sich christelt so jüdelt es sich auch." German-Jewish magic attained its richest proportions in the thirteenth century, with the school of Judah the Pious. At the same time many beliefs and practices, as well as technical terms, were assimilated from French and German folklore, making a strong impression without, however, affecting the essential quality of the Jewish doctrine.[1]

THE MAGICIAN

Who was the Jewish magician? What sort of person engaged in this profession, if profession it was? We can do no better, to gain our first impression of the craft, than to inquire into the character of its practitioners.

The orthodox picture of the sorcerer discloses some malevolent, dark creature, shunning the ways of men, haunting the black hours of the night, poring over his foul brews and his infernal paraphernalia, consorting with weird, frightful spirits, forever plotting mischief and destruction. Or the night-riding witch, associate and consort of demons, reveling in lewd satanic orgies, blighting man and beast and herb with her evil glance and her fiendish spells, cannibalistic murderess of innocent infants. Such are the conceptions that our western literature and tradition have popularized. The late medieval witch-craze, fostered by the heresy-hunting Inquisition, helped to fasten this picture upon the popular imagination, so that the word inevitably conjures up the image.

Though there is not a single unequivocal report of a professional Jewish sorcerer or witch, thus defined, in Jewish or Christian records, we may safely assume that some Jews did not hesitate to emulate the accepted model. The sources indicate that Jews were at least acquainted with methods of inducing disease and death, of arousing and killing passion, of forcing people to do their bidding, of employing demons for divinatory and other purposes. The belief existed, among Jews as among Christians, that sorcerers possessed the power of altering their shapes and roaming the woods and alleys in the form of wolves, or hares, or donkeys, or cats, and of transforming their victims into animals. We find accounts of the magician's power to project his soul to far-distant places, there to perform an errand, and then return to his comatose body. The common medieval beliefs that magicians (and their bewitched victims) may be recognized by the fixed, immovable stare of their eyeballs, and that their power remains with them only so long as their feet are in contact with the ground, are to be found in Jewish writings as well. Indeed, one Jewish author suggested without a smile that for this reason the only way to deal with sorcerers is to "suspend them between heaven and earth"! [2]

The popular notion of the witch, which was in the making as early as the eleventh century, is likewise reflected in the Jewish sources, but the use of such terms as *lamie, broxa* and *estrie* to describe the witch and her activities indicates the non-Jewish origin of the concept. We read in thirteenth-century works of witches with disheveled hair who fly about at night, who feed on the blood and flesh of infants and adults, who are accompanied and aided by demon familiars, who assume animal forms to carry out their nefarious designs. A story in *Sefer Ḥasidim* is a replica of dozens found in non-Jewish works: a man was attacked by a cat which he fought off;

the next day a woman appeared, badly wounded, and asked him for bread and salt to save her life. In 1456 the German, Johann Hartlieb, told a similar tale of a cat which attacked a child and was driven off and stabbed by the child's father; a woman was later found with a wound in the same place. Jacob Sprenger related as a recent occurrence in a town in the diocese of Strasbourg, that a laborer, attacked by three enormous cats, beat them off with a stick, and was subsequently arrested on a charge of brutally beating three ladies of the best families in town. Menaḥem Ẓiyuni, in his commentary on the Bible written in 1430, displayed his knowledge of the full-blown witch doctrine: "There are men and women," he wrote, "who possess demonic attributes; they smear their bodies with a secret oil . . . and instantly fly off like the eagle over seas and rivers and forests and brooks, but they must return home before sunrise; their flight follows a predefined course from which they cannot deviate. Anyone who trespasses upon their meeting place is likely to suffer grave harm. . . . They transform themselves into various animals, and into cats." These are typical details of the medieval witch-cults. Menasseh b. Israel favored the explanation that witches can change their forms because Satan, whom they worship, "fashions around their bodies the simulated forms of animals . . . the proof lies in the fact that when the paws of a pseudo-wolf are amputated the witch or magician appears minus hands and feet." His comment that "it is well known that all sorcerers and witches make a compact with the demons and deliver their souls over to them" is the leit-motif of medieval sorcery.[3]

Though these ideas, taken over bodily from Christian superstition, occur from time to time in Jewish works, most writers make it clear that they have not Jews in mind when they advance them. "There are men and women" who do these things, but not Jews specifically. Yet some writers were prepared to admit that Jews, too, might be engaged in such activities. If the precentor prays for a sick witch, one should not respond "Amen"; if certain women are suspected of cannibalism a warning of the punishment that will be meted out for such crimes should be pronounced *when they are present in the synagogue;* when an *estrie* who has eaten children is being buried one should observe whether her mouth is open, for if it is she will persist in her vampirish pursuits for another year unless it is stopped up with earth. These remarks imply that Jewish communities suspected the presence of witches in their midst.[4]

But a study of the Hebrew sources, and of the factors that influenced the development of Christian magic, creates the conviction that this picture of the witch and the sorcerer was an exotic graft on the main stem of Jewish tradition, that the Jewish magician was of another sort altogether. For one thing, the literature paints Jewish magic and its practitioners in totally different colors. But even more telling is the fact that the peculiar characteristics attributed to European magic effectively prevented the enrolment of the Jew in its service, while the availability of an equally potent yet respectable Jewish technique rendered it unnecessary to turn elsewhere.

Jews were *ab initio* excluded from the medieval fraternity of sorcerers and witches because these were commonly branded as members of heretical anti-Christian sects. In their organized form the witch-cults employed various blasphemous burlesques of Church rites in their own ritual, blasphemies to which sorcerers were also addicted, and which in themselves were accredited with magical potency. These could have no meaning for Jews. Further, medieval witchcraft and sorcery were based upon a perverted worship of Satan, according to popular belief, and individual warlocks were supposed consciously to accept the suzerainty of the Power of Evil and to operate through an appeal to his aid. Jewish magic, to the contrary, functioned within the framework of the Jewish religion, which naturally excluded any such association, real or fancied, with the arch-opponent of God. This reputed central feature of European magic, from which it derived its special character, was entirely foreign to the Jewish mentality, not only on theological grounds, but even more on folkloristic, for the figure of Satan as a distinct personality was very faint, almost non-existent, in Jewish folklore. The entire literature does not disclose a single instance of a magical act which depended upon submission to the devil himself, or his intercession, for its execution.

The primary principle of medieval Jewish magic was an implicit reliance upon the Powers of Good, which were invoked by calling upon their names, the holy Names of God and His angels. This simple dependence upon names for every variety of effect obviated resort to all the other magical acts with which the non-Jewish tradition has familiarized us. The magician who could produce wonders by the mere utterance of a few words had no need of the devious "business" of his non-Jewish colleague. It was the absence of the satanic element and the use of these names, that is, the employment of God's celestial servants, which stamped Jewish magic with a generally far from malevolent character, for the angels could not be expected to carry out evil commands and thus contravene the essential purpose for which their good Lord had created them. And it was this principle, too, which kept Jewish magic securely within the bounds of the religion, and prevented it from assuming the rôle of an anti-religion, as its Christian counterpart did. Magic was proscribed by the Church, and hunted down by the Inquisition, not because it was magic, but because it made a mockery of the Christian faith, and became a powerful anti-Christian force. It was a rival of the Church, with its own peculiar doctrine and ritual. Jewish magic during this period never strayed from the fold, observing closely the tenets of the faith, merely extending and elaborating certain accepted principles, so that, as we shall see, the magician remained a pious and God-fearing Jew.

There were, of course, deviations from the general rule. Demons as well as angels were sometimes called upon to do the Jewish sorcerer's will, both were ordered to do harm, and presumably obeyed, and many of the devices employed universally in magic were used by Jews along with the evocation of spirits. But these were deviations and not the customary procedure, and their infrequency and subordinacy tend to prove the strength of the rule. The deep impression which the *Kabbalah* made upon later Christian magic is indicative of the distinctive character of the Jewish theory and praxis, for it was recognized and touted as a novel and profound departure from earlier methods.

Now to revert to our original question: Who was the Jewish magician? According to ancient Jewish tradition, which was heartily seconded in the Middle Ages, women are inordinately prone to the pursuit of the magical arts.[5] Yet, however true this dictum may once have been, their activity in magic proper was now narrowly restricted by virtue of the esoteric and learned base of that magic.

Man asserted his supremacy by relegating to himself, along with all the other prized pursuits of this life, the big-game of magic. Knowledge of the names, through which Jewish magic worked, was inaccessible to women, for it required not only a thorough training in Hebrew and Aramaic, which most of them lacked, but also a deep immersion in mystical lore, from which they were barred.

Evidently what the authorities had in mind was that women were the spearpoint of the forces of superstition, that it was they who propagated the bizarre notions upon which the popular imagination fed, that they were the fountainhead of all those household recipes and remedies and whispered charms with which medieval Jewry was plagued—or saved. In this respect they were undoubtedly correct, for learned rabbis did not hesitate to sit at the feet of ancient crones when a pain in the eyes or head gave them no rest, and many of the prescriptions retailed by the popular literature make a bow of acknowledgment to womankind. We must regard women, then, as the folk-magicians, healers of wounds, prescribers of love-potions, but in no sense "witches." Jewish women never attained an importance in magic at all commensurate with the prominence of their sisters in the witch-cults.

Nor was Jewish magic the exclusive skill of the "magician"—it is hazardous to assert even that there were such people as magicians, by profession. One may define the Jewish magician as a scholar by vocation, a practitioner of the mystical-magical arts by avocation. Every mystic, properly trained, could practice magic as a side-line. Indeed, the dangers of invoking the spirits without an adequate education in mysticism were frequently stressed, and the possessor of esoteric traditions and writings was sternly counselled to keep them hidden from the common glance, lest they be misused, and to pass them on only to a select circle.[6]

Early mystical and magical lore was successfully guarded by a limited oral transmission. The secret lore of the German school, founded by the Kalonymides, who removed to the Rhineland from Lucca in the tenth century, was first written down in the thirteenth by the followers of Judah the Pious, among whom Eleazar of Worms was outstanding both for his prolific pen and the depth of his learning. Jewish life had turned more and more inward, as relations with the Christian world grew more difficult, and intensive study of the Talmud had become almost its sole intellectual pursuit. The result was that religious emotion, stifled by an exclusive emphasis upon hair-splitting technicalities in interpretation and observance of the law, finally burst its casuistical bonds, as has so often happened, and sought a free and ecstatic outlet in the luscious green fields of theosophy. This inner need was the prime incentive for the popularization of mystical doctrine that began at this time, concurrently in Germany and in Spain. But the German *Kabbalah* never attained the theoretical depth of its Spanish counterpart, nor did it exert so much influence.

A word about the *Kabbalah* and its relation to the subject-matter of this book: Properly used the term denotes the vast theosophical system elaborated in Southern Europe during the Middle Ages on the basis of ancient tradition. The so-called German *Kabbalah,* essentially a *Ḥasidic* or "pietist" doctrine, had intrinsically little relation to this system, being rather a short-lived excursion from the main line, and in the brief space of a century it was overwhelmed and lost in the intricacies of the greater doctrine. Two broad types of *Kabbalah* have been distinguished in Jewish tradition, the "theoretical" *(Kabbalah 'Iyunit),* which is *the Kabbalah,* and the "practical" *(Kabbalah Ma'asit),* which is really a misnomer, for the magical practice that it denoted had little enough to do with *Kabbalah,* even in its purest form, the invocation of names, and moved farther and farther away as it embodied a hodge-podge of ancient and medieval, Jewish and foreign elements. While Kabbalists themselves limited the term to name-invocation, in popular usage it was generic for the entire corpus of Jewish magic.[7]

"The Germans, lacking in philosophical training, exerted all the greater influence on the practical *Kabbalah,* as well as on ecstatic mysticism." Their school stressed the inner significance and higher mystical values of Hebrew words and letters—going to the extent of counting the words in the prayer-book so that none might fall out or be altered—and the rôle of *Kavvanah,* a profound concentration upon these inner values, in bringing to fruition their mystical promise.[8] Here we have the heart of the teaching concerning magical names, which, while adumbrated in the Talmud and developed in the Geonic period, reached its choicest and richest flowering in the doctrines of this school. What was put in writing became the common property of all who could read—and many who did not understand professed to be able to perform miraculous deeds by the bald repetition of what was written. The common fate of popularizations befell this mystical learning: the would-be experts flourished, oblivious of the bitter censure of the truly learned. So we may say that every Jew whose desire led him thither essayed a little magic in a small way. But it was generally recognized that only a minor portion of the mystical lore had found its way into books; much of it still remained private, jealously guarded property. The keepers of this treasure were the great magicians of the Middle Ages, in the public imagination at least, not because they were magicians, which is an unavoidable paradox, but because they were the supreme masters of the learning of which magic was an incidental offshoot. This is why such figures as Samuel, father of Judah the Pious, Judah himself, Eleazar of Worms, Eliezer b. Nathan of Mainz, heirs of the Kalonymide lore, and even such non-mystics as Rashi and his grandson R. Tam, Yehiel of Paris and his pupil Meir of Rothenburg, renowned for their Talmudic scholarship, stand out in the legends as the greatest miracle workers of the period.[9]

FORBIDDEN AND PERMITTED

It is this paradox, and the generally legalistic approach to the subject, which make medieval Jewish discussions of magic so unprofitable. The medieval writers sought to hew close to the Talmudic line, and adhered to the rabbinic classification at a time when it was essentially obsolete. As a result the generic terms usually applied to the magic arts, *kishshuf* and *lahash,* occur in a dual sense, sometimes to record the condemnatory verdict of the ancient law books, and again to designate the less reprehensible contemporary forms. The purpose of the medieval observations on the magic arts, we must bear in mind, was not to describe them, but to determine the degree of guilt attached to them, in accordance with Talmudic law. In conformity with the usual legal propensity for rehearsing precedents, the Talmudic definitions and distinctions were usually repeated verbatim, shedding little or no light upon the current varieties and forms.

The Bible had pronounced an unqualified condemnation of sorcery. The Talmud, while maintaining this fundamental attitude, pursued its customary function of clarifying and classifying Jewish law, and so broke up the all-inclusive category of sorcery into several divisions, establishing varying degrees of guilt. Two main types of forbidden magic were distinguished: that which produces a discernible, material effect, by means of "the performance of an act," and that which only creates the illusion of such an act or its effect (*ahizat 'ainayim,* "capturing the eyesight") ; or, as a further observation defined them, the one operates without the aid of demons, the other requires their assistance. The practitioner of the first type merits the Biblical penalty of death; the second is forbidden but not so punishable. Still a third kind of magic, "permitted from the start," involved the use of "the Laws of Creation," a term which was later interpreted to signify the mystical names of God and the angels.[10]

So stated, the distinction between the first two is far from clear and precise, and was hardly understood by the medieval writers. As Eliezer of Metz wrote, "I questioned my teachers about this but they gave me no satisfactory reply." They spoke often of a forbidden "magic" in the narrow and technical Talmudic sense of the performance of an act, "taking hold of a thing and manipulating it," or the performance of "enchantments." Yet this proscribed "magic" did not include the other forms: the "invocation of angels," the "invocation of demons," and the "employment of names," which they regarded as distinct divisions, at the least more acceptable, and by some, expressly permitted and even employed. About the permissibility of employing names and angels there was no question, for the Talmud had legalized their use, but the invocation of demons was generally considered less praiseworthy. Jeroham b. Meshullam wrote: "The codifiers differ with regard to demon-invocation. Ramah [Meir b. Todros Halevi Abulafia] wrote that it should be categorized as forbidden 'magic' and some of the other jurists agree with him but still others consider it permissible as in nowise belonging to the category of 'magic' acts." R. Eliezer of Metz held that "invoking the demons to do one's will is permitted from the outset, for what difference is there between invoking demons or angels? . . . An action may not be characterized as 'magic' unless it consists of taking hold of a thing and manipulating it, that is, if it is the performance of a deed, or an incantation that does not include an invocation of spirits, but invoking demons is permitted *ab initio*."[11] It is evident that medieval authorities regarded the category of "magic" as altogether distinct and different from the others, and correctly so, but I know of only one clear-cut statement of the principle of difference, by Moses Isserles. The counterfeit type of magic also appeared often in the discussions.[12] It provided a convenient dodge to get around the legal difficulties and cast a halo of respectability about the current forms, whose effects were described as not real at all but entirely illusory. But this road, too, was not quite smooth, for the Talmudic explanation that illusory magic is the work of demons arose to crowd angel- and name-magic off the right-of-way. In short, the Talmudic classification plagued the efforts of medieval codifiers to bring the law into relation with contemporary procedures. Yet, from a practical standpoint, they succeeded in effectively excluding from the proscribed "magic" all the forms current among Jews.[13]

Moses Isserles brings us closer to an understanding of what the forbidden "magic" was. "The roots of the [magical] arts are three," he wrote, "God, science, and nature. . . . From God comes . . . the power to invoke the heavenly princes by means of the holy names; the scientific root may be illustrated by astrology, by which a man can foretell the future, make talismans, and subdue the spirits and the powers of the stars and the like; on natural elements depends the effectiveness of the various types of magic, all of which consist in bringing out the inner nature of things, whereby an expert may perform deeds strange in appearance. . . ." This classification is not definitive, for Isserles failed to include the demonic "root" of magic; his inclusion of astrology, however, which was well known in Talmudic times but did not enter into the central discussions of magic, is significant of the place of that science in particular and the divinatory arts generally in medieval magic. But it is his last category that interests us particularly here. The "inner nature of things" is one way of describing the most primitive and widespread subject of magical activity. It is universally believed that all things are endowed with occult virtues and powers, that they possess mutually sympathetic or antipathetic qualities, and that it is possible to "step up" magical currents from the particular to the general, and down again from the general to the particular, by the simple manipulation of natural objects, which is the commonest form that magic takes. Frazer, studying the practices of primitive peoples, classified them under two heads, homœopathic or imitative, and contagious; "both branches," he wrote, "may conveniently be comprehended under the general name of sympathetic magic, since both assume that things act on each other at a distance through a secret sympathy." And again, "This belief in the sympathetic influence exerted on each other by persons or things at a distance is of the essence of magic." [14]

It is characteristic of magic that with the advance of religious thought and the recognition of a spirit world, it tends to move closer to religion, and to depend increasingly upon the spirit forces of religion for its effects. The rabbinic authorities set their face against all practices that smacked of Israel's heathen origins, and prominent among these was "the performance of an act" *without resort to supernatural aid,* which was for them the forbidden "magic" to be punished by death. Their opposition was not to magic generally, but to this particular "idolatrous" form; the use of angels, names, and even demons, involving an appeal to the supernatural and a recognition of the supremacy of God, was admitted past the barrier on sufferance, but the first type was rigorously excluded. It was this distinction which the medieval writers sensed and voiced negatively, without fully comprehending it, for the ancient bitter struggle against "idolatry" had long since been won, and the distinction had lost its force. Medieval Jewish magic depended almost entirely for its success upon the spirits and names; sympathetic devices persisted, as we shall see, but their rôle was regarded as secondary and incidental to that of their theologically more acceptable successors. Here we have a striking difference between Jewish and Christian magic in the Middle Ages. While the latter frankly recognized and employed the occult forces inherent in nature, recipes employing these forces slipped into Jewish practice by the back door, so to speak, disguised as *bona fide* invocations of the spirit world.

Now we can understand why such categories as good and bad, white and black magic are foreign to Jewish thought. These distinctions are concerned with the purpose of the magic act, while Jewish discussion centered around the method, and the legal attitude toward it. I do not mean, of course, that rabbis had no interest in the ends toward which magic was pursued, that a "legal" technique could be used criminally with their approbation. They often expressed disapproval of even the legally recognized methods just because they might be harmfully applied, and strenuously objected to placing mystical information in the hands of people who were not to be trusted with it. But the scholarly and pious character of the student of mysticism and the essentially religious nature of Jewish magic ensured a minimum of misuse of this lore. There was never any question that the immoral practice of magic was not countenanced by Judaism and therefore the discussion could remain on a legal plane. However, Jews were acquainted with this prevailing non-Jewish classification, as is indicated by the effort of Menaḥem Ẓiyuni and others to interpret the word necromancy: "'Nigromancia' is a combination of two words, *nigar* [Hebrew], 'gathered together, collected,' like water that has been stored up, and *mancia,* the name of the incense that magicians burn to the demons; but I have heard another explanation, that *nigre* means 'black,' and this is why the Germans call it *Schwarzkunst.*" As an example of *nigromancia* he cited "those who offer up their sperm to the spirits or demons with appropriate incantations." [15]

"IT IS BEST TO BE HEEDFUL"

The popular attitude toward magic and superstition, leaving aside the legalistic approach, recalls an incident that illustrates it perfectly. A teacher of mine, out for a stroll, was suddenly confronted with a black cat from which he shied away nervously. One of his students, observing this, twitted him, "You're not really afraid of a black cat, Professor!" "No," he replied indignantly, "of course I don't believe in such nonsense. But there's no harm in being careful." He might have been quoting *Sefer Ḥasidim:*[16] "One should not believe in superstitions, but still it is best to be heedful of them." This qualified skepticism was the farthest advance toward the modern spirit on the part of the religious authorities; the masses, if we may judge from the innumerable superstitions that were cautiously honored, took that qualification earnestly to heart.

The *Zeitgeist* overpowered even the most rationalistically inclined of the rabbis. The Jewry of Southern Europe owned several daring spirits who uncompromisingly stigmatized magic and superstition as "folly" and "untruth," but in the Germanic lands none dared go so far, though a few singled out one or another phase of magic for their contempt, or proved themselves free of one or another supersition by their actions. The authorities, whose religious convictions and position obliged them to voice at least half-hearted disapproval, could do no more than threaten the practitioners of magic with disaster. They would be punished for their acts, whether by the spirits whom they had momentarily enslaved, or by the wrath of God. According to some, it was the prevalence of superstition and magic among the Jews that delayed the redemption of Israel from exile. One opinion had it: "If you see a Jew who apostatized neither because of love nor through compulsion, you may know that he or his parents engaged in sorcery."[17] Sometimes the rabbis sought to counteract the influence of traditionally received techniques by arguing that they were no longer applicable, "for it is known that nature varies from place to place and from time to time," or on the ground that the requisite skill had been lost. Often they tried to soften the impact of superstitious practices by re-interpretation, by injecting religious meaning into them.[18] But the validity of superstition and magic was universally accepted, and the very rabbis who deprecated them were often obliged to condone them also. Moreover no matter how violently they condemned popular misapplication of mystical teachings they were obliged to admit that the "permitted" categories of magic, especially the invocation of godly and angelic names when practiced by adepts whose learning and piety could not be doubted, were in consonance with the religious tenets of Judaism and could not be denied. It was this acknowledgment that underlay the fatal inconsistency of religious opinion; the camel's nose once inside the tent, its entire hulk could no longer be excluded. One can hardly blame the masses for their unhesitating acceptance of the truth and power of magic. Whatever faith in an all-powerful God may have taught them to the contrary, the common people believed in the might of the magician and stood in awe of him. "If anyone quarrels with a sorcerer he has brought his death on himself." [19] The addiction to superstition and magic of the German pietists and mystics became a byword in the south of Europe and scandalized more than one pious Spanish-Jewish writer.[20]

Yet we meet at the same time, recognition of a profound psychological truth, far in advance of the spirit of the age: "Superstitions can harm only those who heed them." [21] It requires more courage and skepticism than the Middle Ages could lay claim to (or than we can boast even today, for that matter) to be free of the yoke that superstition and magic saddle upon the credulous masses. The material gathered in this book is the most telling evidence of the inadequacy of mere proscription to countervail ignorance and the blind "will to believe."

In the succeeding chapters we shall examine first the beliefs concerning the spirit world (Chapters III-VI), which were fundamental to superstition and magic, and the powers ascribed to what we may designate as the magic word, namely, the names of God and the angels, and the word of God enshrined in Scripture (Chapters VII-VIII), which were the most potent tools of magic. Chapters IX-XIII contain a description of the various elements that constituted the actual practice of magic, including a discussion of medicine. The concluding chapters (XIV-XVI) are devoted to an examination of the divinatory arts, among the most popular of magical exercises.

3

THE POWERS OF EVIL

THE MIDDLE WORLD

AT THE basis of Jewish magic lay the belief in a vast, teeming "middle world," a world neither of the flesh nor altogether and exclusively of the spirit. Demons and angels, to be counted only in myriads, populated that world; through their intermediacy the powers of magic were brought into operation. The most frequently employed terms for magic were *hashba at malachim* and *hashba'at shedim,* invocation and conjuration of angels and demons. The peculiar rôle of the angels, heavenly counterparts of all earthly phenomena, as well as the direct servants and emissaries of God, closest to His ear, rendered powerful indeed the man who possessed the secret of bending them to his will. The demons, on the other hand, invested with all the fearsome potencies that a still primitive, animistic folk-imagination could conjure up, were equally capable of making the fame and fortune of those who could exert a magic power over them.

Talmudic Jewry owned a highly elaborated demonology, distinguishing between classes and even individuals, with a wealth of detail concerning the nature and pursuits of the evil spirits. Its elements grew naturally out of the fertile popular imagination, convinced as it was of the reality of the spirit world, and fortified by a rich tradition drawn largely from the folklores of Egypt and Babylon and Persia. This lore served a dual need: it conveyed the power of control, and at the same time of self-protection. But the rabbis were generally opposed to demon-magic, and though they were not so severe with it as with sympathetic magic (some of the most distinguished Talmudic authorities themselves had recourse to it at times), they frequently expressed their strong disapproval. Even in the Middle Ages a few rabbis were ready to permit it, but the ancient strictures against a method which is "forbidden but not punishable by death" had taken effect. The intensification of the religious spirit that had proceeded through the intervening centuries produced a feeling that the demons had no proper place within Judaism, though they could not be ousted and the widespread fear of them persisted. Traffic with the "spirits of uncleanness," as they were often called, was repugnant to the Jew, who regarded them as inimical not alone to mankind, but to the pursuit of the religious life. The great development of name-magic, on the other hand, crowded out the earlier form. Invocation of demons, therefore, occupied a very minor position in medieval Jewish magic. The demons were employed almost exclusively in divination.

Jewish demonology, consequently, experienced little inner development during the Middle Ages, but clung closely to its early forms, and new departures were mainly borrowings from French and German sources, which in itself is an indication that the estimation of demons in magic had depreciated. Interest in the evil spirits centered mainly about their malevolent nature and implacable enmity toward man, and hence about the need and the best methods of protection against them.

Hardly a murmur of doubt do we hear of the existence and reality of the evil spirits. The Talmudic literature, both the *Aggadic* folklore and the *Halacha,* accepted their presence as axiomatic.[1] We may readily understand then, how it is that in the Middle Ages a people fed on this literature no longer questioned. The *Kabbalah,* indeed, accorded the demons an integral rôle in a cosmic design in which the right and the left are the opposing currents of pure and impure powers filling the world and dividing it between the Holy One and His Adversary. In all of medieval Jewry there were few who raised their voices against this superstition. Some Karaites vigorously repudiated such beliefs, and characterized them as "merely human imaginings." Maimonides and Ibn Ezra took a similarly strong stand. But these were citizens of southern, Mohammedan lands. Not a word to this effect do we hear in the north of Europe. Our literature takes them as much for granted as did the Talmudic. Certain works, especially from the school of Judah the Pious, reveal their activities on almost every page. Rashi repeated the Midrashic comment that "every living thing" represented in the ark included even the demons.[2]

If we are to believe Moses of Tachau,[3] Ibn Ezra paid dearly for his hardihood in denying the existence of demons. "Ibn Ezra wrote in his book," he says, " 'Of a surety there are no demons in the world!' . . . Verily he erred in this matter, for they were ever at his side . . . and indeed they themselves proved their existence to him. I have heard from the people of *Iglant* [England?], where he died, that once when he was travelling through a forest he came upon a large band of black dogs who glared at him balefully; undoubtedly these were demons. When he had finally passed through their midst he fell seriously ill, and eventually he died of that illness." This incident was apparently evidence enough for R. Moses, though we may question whether, if it occurred, it sufficed to convince the doughty Ibn Ezra.

Menasseh b. Israel, writing in the middle of the seventeenth century, summed up the thought of the Middle Ages when, after demonstrating to his own satisfaction that demons do exist, by calling into service proofs on the threefold basis of tradition, reason, and the senses, he cited a long list of appropriate passages from Jewish literature, and concluded, "The opinion of all Jewish authorities is that the Biblical references to spirits are to be taken literally." He lightly brushed aside the Maimonidean strictures against such superstitions with the familiar objection that their author had been "seduced" by the philosopher's predilection for the testimony of reason and experience, to the damage of his piety and faith in revelation.[4] Menasseh b. Israel was expressing not his own opinion but the judgment of Jewish folk-belief.

TERMINOLOGY

It may not be amiss if before we proceed to a consideration of the features of this demonology, we devote a few lines to the nomenclature employed in our literature. The terms most frequently met with are those made familiar in the ancient literature of the Jews: *mazzik,* from a root which means "to damage, destroy"; *shed,* an obscure word which occurs in the Bible in the plural,[5] and which in the Talmudic literature acquired the exclusive sense of "demon"; and *ruaḥ,* "spirit," often *ruaḥ ra'ah,* "evil spirit."[6] These words were not at all differentiated in our period, though a rather academic attempt was at times made to distinguish among them on the basis of Talmudic statements. In general, however, these three terms were used indiscriminately in a generic sense, and were often employed interchangeably in a single paragraph. An effort at schematization, which produced a list of ten categories of demons to balance a similar angelic list, introduced seven additional terms, which found little place in the general literature. One of them, however, *lilin*, regarded as the plural of Lilit, "night-demons," used in the Talmud, occurs fairly often, sometimes as *liliot*.[7]

I may also mention here the *malache ḥabbala*, "angels (or demons) of destruction," who made their initial appearance in the Talmud, and who were not absent from the medieval scene. Their names end with the letter *peh*, we are informed. The fact that the titles of the daily synagogue services, the eighteen benedictions, the prayer *Yoẓer Or*, and the grace after meals do not contain this letter, was cited as proof that prayer serves as a protection against these destroying angels.[8]

The Lurianic *Kabbalah* brought into common currency an old but little used term, *kelippah*, originally "scale, husk, skin"; occurring in the earlier mystical works and in the *Ẓohar*, this word rarely appeared in our literature. Its Lurianic popularization, reflected in the writings of the famous Polish mystic, Isaiah Horowitz (1555–1630), marked the beginning of a new development in Jewish demonology which is outside the scope of this study.

These traditional terms were used only to designate the general phenomenon. It is of interest to inquire why none of them acquired a specialized sense in our period, to single out those differentiated demonic types which people the folklore of all nations. The explanation is not far to seek. The Hebrew of the Bible and the prayers, while familiar to most Jews, was not the vernacular; nor did the Talmud, which so strongly colored Jewish life, provide Jewry with a spoken tongue. Words lifted from these sources entered into the everyday language of the people, to be sure, but their very antiquity and traditional meanings made it difficult to squeeze them into new molds. They sufficed as generic terms, but to designate the specific, the differentiated, the peculiarly contemporary, the Jews turned to the vernacular for their nomenclature. Specialized types of demons were not wanting in medieval Jewish folklore, but they appeared under their non-Hebraic names, words borrowed from the German and the French. This interesting subject, shedding so much light upon the question of non-Jewish influence on Jewish belief and superstition, will be presently considered.

THE GENESIS OF DEMONS

The number of demons in the world was prodigious. One Christian census estimated them as somewhat more than one for each person on earth. Our sources spurn such conservative figures; their number is uncountable, the simple unit employed in referring to them is no smaller than the myriad.[9]

The question of the origin of this demonic horde naturally agitated the medieval mind. It was of especial interest to the Jews, for in a world altogether fashioned *ex nihilo* by the Creator of all things, the demons alone have no recorded birthday; the first chapter of Genesis is silent concerning them. Talmudic tradition, however, provided the clew which was followed in the Middle Ages. On the first Sabbath eve, at twilight, as God was putting the finishing touches to His great work of creation, He turned His hand to the construction of these beings, who, though included in the plan of things as they were to be, might well be left for last. He had not progressed beyond the fashioning of their souls, however, when the hastening Sabbath overtook Him, and He was obliged to cease His labors to sanctify the first day of rest. So it is that the demons have no bodies, but are constituted wholly of spirit.[10]

But this explanation did not suffice to still all doubts, and a medieval rabbi,[11] during the course of a disputation with a renegade Jew, appended an interesting codicil to this theme. There remained yet another category, unaccounted for by the rabbinic theory and known to Jews under their non-Jewish names (R. Jeḥiel, our disputant, mentioned specifically the *lutin* and the *fae*), which possessed both soul and body. These obviously required something more than the traditional explanation. This R. Jeḥiel provided. He utilized a rabbinic legend to the effect that during the 130 years after the expulsion from Eden, when Adam was parted from Eve, he had relations with female demons who bore him demonic offspring, to account for this corporeal group which the Talmudic rabbis didn't know. The spirits whom we know as the *lutins* and *faes* are the children of Adam by this unnatural union, said R. Jeḥiel.

We read also of still another demonic category, whose members were created afresh daily out of the ranks of the most recent tenants of the grave. It is not altogether correct to hold, as some students have, that in the popular conception the spirits of the dead roamed the world as specters and vampires, recruits to the demonic armies.

On the contrary, the spirits of the dead were believed to remain in close contact with the living, retaining their old interests, and often performing signal service for their relatives and friends who still inhabited this earth in the flesh. Provocation, it is true, might stir them up to strike back at their enemies. But in general the dead were not regarded as malevolent; rather were they seen as wistful, harmless shades haunting the graves which shelter their bones. The spirits of the *wicked,* however, do become *bona fide* demons, and it is these that constantly replenish the demonic ranks. So vicious were they believed to be that special warnings were posted against them; wounds which they inflict can be cured by no human means, but their healing rests in the hands of God alone.[12]

I may add that the idea, so frequently encountered in Christian writings, that the demons are the gods of the heathen, is to be found in medieval Jewish works as well.[13] But it played no part in the popular belief.

It should be noted, finally, that in all this the demons, evil as they were, remained the creatures of God, subject to His will and respectful of His divinity, and actually subservient to the angels.[14] We have here no dualism; even the Kabbalistic mysticism which divided the universe between two opposing forces of good and evil, did not oust God from His position of overlordship. The German mystics, immersed in a deep piety peculiar to themselves, did not for a moment countenance any such heresy, and nowhere in the literature of Northern Europe do we find a suggestion of the autonomy of the demon world.

ATTRIBUTES AND FUNCTIONS

In what guise were these demons visualized? Altogether invisible to men, though the more acute sensitivity of animals responded to their presence,[15] it is not to be wondered at that the prevalent conception was as vague and undefined as these creatures themselves.

The rabbis of the Talmud had long since postulated certain demonic attributes which remained constant during the Middle Ages. "The demons, in accordance with their origin, are between angels and men. They have wings like the former, and move about from one end of the earth to the other, and know what will come to pass; but, like the latter, they eat and drink, propagate their kind, and die." "They see but are themselves invisible." In consequence of their lack of bodies they cast no shadow.[16] These characteristics, whose Talmudic authority permitted no questioning, were the constant features of the medieval conception. A few new details were added but they were not, I am afraid, of much help in making the evil spirits more readily recognizable.

Rashi, for one, attempted a degree of differentiation on the basis of several Talmudic remarks. Among the "various kinds of demons (*mazzikin*)," he wrote, "*shedim* have human forms, and eat and drink, like men; spirits (*ruḥin*) are completely disembodied and formless; *lilin*, which are possessed of human forms, also have wings." The rabbinic view, which was applied generally to the entire demon world, presented difficulties to the logical mind. A fifteenth-century authority essayed an explanation of how it was that these creatures of spirit could simulate man in certain respects. Their eating and drinking is, according to him, nothing more than a licking or lapping up of fire, water, air, and slime. Their decease, again, is not to be understood in our mortal sense; "when they dry up [from lack of these sustaining substances] they return to their primordial state; this is the manner of their death." But our author's ingenuity gave out in the matter of propagation; here he was forced to accord them physical shapes: "When they copulate they are possessed of bodies, but they will not unite in the presence of a third demon, or of man."[17]

There is little more to be said about the appearance of these evil spirits. One source attributed to their non-existent heads—hair! "Male demons have hair on their heads, but the females have none. This is why Boaz placed his hand on Ruth's head [when he awoke to find her at his feet]. When he discovered that she had hair [he knew that this was no demon] and asked, 'Who art thou?' " Demons, however, may temporarily assume physical shapes. There is in the folklore of the Middle Ages, as indeed of all times and all places, no definite and impassable line of demarcation between the worlds of man, of beast, and of spirit. Angels and demons may become men and animals, men may be transformed into cats or wolves or hares. We have already beheld the spirits embodied in the skins of dogs; Boaz apprehended a demon taking woman's shape. A medieval legend relates that a demon which had laid plans to enter the body of a certain pious rabbi transformed itself into a hair, which the rabbi was expected to swallow with his food.[18] Their stock of disguises was infinite. Many of the demons we encounter in medieval literature have conveniently masked themselves in human or animal bodies, so that they may make their appearance in the flesh. The test by hair is the only clew we are afforded against their evil designs, and even here half the demon world is immune.

Like the angels, the demons have especial posts and functions; when, for instance, a man has suffered an attack at the hands of one, he and his family must forever avoid the place where the attack occurred, for the demon is posted there awaiting another opportunity. Nor should one imprison the demons, who are everywhere, by shutting the doors and windows of a house tightly. Their paths of ingress and egress are prescribed, along with their functions, and to impede their freedom of movement is to invite their displeasure. Far wiser is it to pierce a small hole in door or window and thus enable them to move about freely.[19]

Demons frequented uninhabited places, deserts and forests and fields, as well as unclean places. Privies especially were believed to be haunted and the Talmud prescribed special incantations invoking the protection of guardian angels in these places. This prescription was frequently repeated by medieval authorities, but there is evidence that the dread attached to privies had worn off, and the incantations, if recited, had degenerated into mere formal vestiges of a traditional usage. The explanation was that the privies of Talmudic times were located outside of the villages, in the fields, whereas medieval privies were closer to home, within the settled area.[20]

The connection between demons and uncleanness was made to serve important hygienic ends. Evil spirits, sometimes called "spirits of uncleanness," and once identified by the name *bat melech,* rest upon unwashed hands, contaminate foods handled with them, and endanger the lives of those who eat such food. Seven occasions which require a ritual washing of the hands (which destroys or dislodges the demons) were enumerated; most important among these was upon arising in the morning, for the night creates a special susceptibility to spirit contamination. Even on *Yom Kippur* when no ablutions might be performed, the hands must be washed in the morning. Touching the eyes, ears, nose and mouth with unwashed hands spells trouble; no doubt it was feared that the evil spirits would enter the body through these orifices. (*Plus ça change plus c'est la même chose;* if, in speaking of infection, our vocabulary is more "scientific," the sense remains the same.) The demon of uncleanness, entering the eyes, could cause one's glance to have a devastating effect upon the innocent passer-by; it might even be responsible for the loss of one's memory, and ultimately complete loss of mind.[21]

Humans who established their homes on a spot already pre-empted by spirits were in a parlous way. The demons are jealous of their property rights and their privacy, and resent intrusions. Once a group of Jews, who had settled in a previously unoccupied place in Hungary, noticed that their death-rate had suddenly risen markedly. They fasted and prayed but to no avail. One day the head of the community met a large band whose leader sat astride a lion, using a snake for a bridle. He realized at once that these were no ordinary men, but demons. Their chief demanded the immediate removal of the trespassing Jews, for his spirit followers had previously selected that spot for a meeting-place. Needless to say they obeyed with alacrity, and their death-rate became normal once more. This incident explains why certain houses are very unlucky for their inhabitants, one after another dying off for no apparent cause. The only remedy in such a case is to move far away, where the demons who have been provoked by the intrusion cannot get at them. Pious deeds, fasting, prayer, usually so effective, are of no help.[22]

The best plan, of course, is to observe proper caution before establishing oneself in a new home. One should not erect a house on unoccupied land; but if he does he should certainly not construct it of stone (for a stone house has an air of stability and permanence that is sure to irritate the demons). Even a house of wood is suspect under these circumstances. If the new house is on the site of an old one the builder must be careful to place the windows and doors in the same positions they formerly occupied, for the local demons whose habits have become fixed, are bound not to be enamored of the innovations. Finally, it is wise not to move into a new house at all, but to sell it if one can. If this proves unfeasible, it must be left uninhabited for a time, or some skeptical friend must be prevailed upon to occupy it. People were actually paid to live in new houses! [23]

The general rule was that bad luck clings to a place or a person or a family—because once the spirits have chosen them for their special prey they cannot be shaken off. A house or a city in which children die young, a family that has been frequently bereaved, a woman whose husbands do not survive, all must be avoided like the pest. To illustrate the strength of this belief in the tenacity of misfortune I may cite this tale: A woman who had become barren came to Judah the Pious for counsel; the mystic should succeed where medicine was powerless! He told her that nothing would help, except that she be forgotten like a corpse moldering in the earth. To carry out his prescription he had her children place her in a grave and then had armed men, hired for this purpose, make a sudden attack upon them so that they were frightened and ran away, completely forgetting their mother. She arose out of the grave, newborn, and in short order proved the efficacy of the remedy. The symbolic interment and rebirth freed her from the misfortune that was her lot in what had now become her previous existence.[24]

Demons consort in the shade of trees, and in shadows cast by the moon. In fact, children who are moon-struck display symptoms that point definitely to the demonic source of their illness: their alternating chills and fevers are due directly to the fact that the demons who inhabit moon-shadows are compounded of fire and hail. *Sefer Ḥasidim* reports that upon a certain tree there were to be noticed drops somewhat like candle-drippings. When a man wished to cut this tree down he was warned by a sage, "Beware that you do not bring about your own death! Don't even shake that tree! For if you anger them they will certainly do you harm. In this tree the *liliot* foregather." Nut trees in particular were to be shunned as the meeting-places of the spirits.[25]

A special connection exists also between the storm-winds, tempests, whirlwinds, and the evil spirits. The home of all is in the north, which indeed is the source of all evil.[26] One writer even domiciled the demons in Norway, which to him was the farthest edge of the north.[27] This almost universal belief in the close relation between demons and storms was expressed in the idea that thunder and lightning are the bolts which the demons, aligned in two hostile camps, discharge against one another during a storm. Certain men are peculiarly susceptible to harm from these bolts, and can be healed only by magic.[28]

"JEWISH" DEMONS

Our discussion, devoted thus far to the general aspects of medieval Jewish demonology, does not exhaust the subject. Certain demonic types stood out from the undifferentiated mass, and to these we must turn our attention before we may consider the picture complete.

Among "Jewish" demons and spirits, that is, the vast horde which the Middle Ages inherited with the Talmudic tradition, there are few indeed that possess any individuality, any definitely distinguishing characteristics. Those few who in Talmudic times were sufficiently personalized to be accorded the distinction of a name, naturally survived into the Middle Ages, but in attenuated form. The tendency was to repeat the Talmudic characterizations, but with a mechanical air, as though rehearsing a lesson rather than describing a living, terrifyingly contemporaneous phenomenon. We do not find in the field of demonology that exuberance of invention which characterized medieval Jewish angelology—the reasons being, as I have suggested, that the magical utility of demons had depreciated, while a full-blown non-Jewish folk demonology lay ready at hand to be assimilated into Jewish folk-belief. Satan himself, king of the underworld, though he made frequent appearances in the moralizing literature of the period, possessed none of the vividness, the immediacy of his Christian counterpart. He was little more than a word, a shade whose impress on life was real enough, but whom one could hardly hope to identify from the vague, colorless comments about his person and activity. Quite probably he stood out more clearly in the popular conception than in the literature (he was not a personage of theological import, as in medieval Christianity) ; but that conception did not impress itself so deeply on the folk-mind as to find its way into the literature as well. Satan in medieval Jewish thought was little more than an allegory, whose moral was the prevalence of sin.[29]

The tendency to push into the background those demons that are named in the Talmud, to deny them an important rôle in the contemporary demon world, is demonstrated by the comparatively few references to them, and by the nature of these comments. The demon Shibbeta, for example, who strangles people, and especially children who eat food touched by unwashed hands—not one of those "spirits of uncleanness" already mentioned, but an individualized spirit which rests upon foods and is dispelled only by washing the hands prior to the handling of the foods—this demon no longer frightened medieval Jewry. "The reason why people no longer observe the precaution of washing before feeding their children is that this evil spirit is not to be found in these lands." This attitude was applied to many of the Talmudic superstitions which lacked the element of contemporaneity. As a later writer naïvely put it: the explanation of the neglect on the part of late authorities of many of the early superstitions is that "the nature of man has changed since those early days." He adduced as proof that "there are many things against which the *Gemara* warns us as being fraught with great danger [from the demons], but we have never seen nor heard of anyone who suffered harm from disregarding the Talmudic warnings." It was not that the belief in demons was weakening; rather, a host of modern spirits had displaced the ancient ones.[30]

Keteb Meriri, which according to the Talmud is most harmful at noon, and especially during the hot summer months, undoubtedly a personification of the sun's heat, made his momentary appearance during the Middle Ages. *Sefer Ḥasidim* reports that a group of children on their way to school one noon were suddenly confronted with this demon; all but two died, the fortunate ones surviving only after a severe illness. Even more evanescent is the rôle of Ashmedai, the "king of demons," and of Igrat, the Talmudic "queen of demons," and her mother Maḥlat. These and others appear only as names standing out momentarily from the midst of a horde of unidentified spirits.[31]

Alone among the spirits known through Jewish tradition, Lilit retained her position during the Middle Ages, if indeed she did not strengthen it by virtue of the closer definition of her activities. Originally a wind-spirit, derived from the Assyrian *lilitu,* with long disheveled hair, and wings, during Talmudic times the confusion of her name with the word *layil,* "night," transformed her into a night spirit who attacks those who sleep alone. Laylah appears also as the angel of night, and of conception. Out of the assimilation to one another of these two concepts grew the view that prevailed during the Middle Ages. Though Lilit and the popularly derived plurals, the *lilin,* and the *liliot,* appeared often in nondescript form, merely as another term for demons, as when we are told that the *liliot* assemble in certain trees, the *lilits* proper possessed two outstanding characteristics in medieval folklore which gave them distinct personality: they attacked new-born children and their mothers, and they seduced men in their sleep. As a result of the legend of Adam's relations with Lilit, although this function was by no means exclusively theirs, the *lilits* were most frequently singled out as the demons who embrace sleeping men and cause them to have the nocturnal emissions which are the seed of a hybrid progeny.[32]

It was in her first rôle, however, that Lilit terrorized medieval

Jewry. As the demon whose special prey is lying-in women and their babes, it was found necessary to adopt an extensive series of protective measures against her. The line of development of this type of Lilit from the rabbinic concept is not altogether clear. We seem to have here a union of the night demon with the spirit that presides over pregnancy, influenced no doubt by the character of the Babylonian Lamaššu, and the *lamiae* and *striga* of Greek and Roman folklore. While it is incorrect to assume that this type of demon was an invention of post-Talmudic Judaism, there can be no question that, its sources reaching far back into the past not only of Jewish folk-belief, but of that of neighboring peoples as well, the fully rounded concept is not met with before the Geonic period, when it made its appearance in Aramaic incantations of about the seventh century and in the *Alphabet of Ben Sira,* a work composed in Persia or Arabia some time before the year 1000. It is in this region that one might expect to find traces of old Babylonian beliefs, as well as the *ghoul* of the Arabian desert, influencing Jewish folklore. In Europe the persistence in various forms of the *lamia* and *striga* in the local non-Jewish superstition served to preserve and accentuate this feature of the Lilit concept.

According to the earliest Jewish literary version of the legend, Lilit, Adam's first wife, left him after a quarrel; in response to his plea God dispatched three angels to bring her back, but she refused to return, in consequence of which one hundred of her children were doomed to die daily. "Let me be!" she commanded the angels, when they overtook her. "I was created only to weaken children, boys during their first eight days [i.e., until circumcision], girls until their twentieth day" [perhaps a reminiscence of an earlier initiatory rite for girls]. Elijah Levita in referring to this legend wrote, "I am loath to quote it at length, for I don't believe it at all." But his coreligionists did not share his skepticism, as he himself admitted when he proceeded to describe a popular measure of protection against Lilit: "This is a common practice among us German Jews," he confessed.[33]

"FOREIGN" DEMONS

It constitutes a rather significant commentary upon the close cultural relations prevailing between medieval Jewry and its neighbors, that the Franco-German names of so many spirits were assimilated into Jewish folklore. Since our literary sources are the product of the intellectual and spiritual leaders of the times, whose scholarship and official position must have served to accentuate their natural predilection for the traditional ways and beliefs of the Jewish past, the easy and unquestioned acceptance of these non-Jewish elements is indicative of the hold they must have gained upon the popular imagination. By the eleventh and twelfth centuries some of them had already become part of the Jewish demonology. But the occurrence of French, German and Latin names and terms became especially notable only in the thirteenth century. There can be no doubt that the rise in Jewish superstition generally, and especially in the belief in demons in this period, was a reflex of the spirit of the times.

Most often mentioned were the *estrie,* the *broxa,* the *mare,* and the werwolf.[34] The transliteration into Hebrew of these names is often confusing, and the description of these creatures even more confused, but it is not difficult to recognize in them their non-Jewish prototypes. So intimately had they entered into Jewish folklore that it was possible for some writers to identify them with those original demons whose souls were created on the eve of the Sabbath, when the press of time left them in a bodyless condition. According to one source, *estrie, mare,* and werwolf are to be included in this category; others, however, would exclude the *mare,* which possesses both body and soul.[35]

It is difficult to determine whether the *estrie* was regarded as a true demon, or as a witch; it was described, sometimes in the same source, as both. Included among the incorporeal spirits, it was none the less also a woman, a flesh-and-blood member of the community. In either guise her character was that of the vampire, whose particular prey was little children, though she did not disdain at times to include grown-ups in her diet.[36] The sense of these passages appears to be that she is an evil spirit who adopts woman's form and spends her life among men, the more readily to satisfy her gory appetites. The equation of the *estrie* with the *broxa* leads one to believe that she was best known in her human form.

The *estrie* had the faculty of changing her shape as she willed, and of returning to her original demonic state when she flew about at night. A certain woman, who, it transpired, was an *estrie,* fell ill and was attended during the night by two women. When one of these fell asleep the patient suddenly arose from her bed, flung her hair wildly about her head, and made efforts to fly and to suck blood from the sleeping woman. The other attendant cried out in terror and aroused her companion; between the two of them they subdued the demon-witch and got her back into bed. "If she had succeeded in killing this woman she would have preserved her life, but since her effort was thwarted she died." These creatures sustained themselves on a diet of human blood, which preserved their lives when they were desperately ill. If an *estrie* was wounded by a human being, or was seen by him (in her demonic state), she must die unless she could procure and consume some of his bread and salt. A man who was attacked by an *estrie* in the shape of a cat and beat her off, was approached by the witch the next day and asked for some of his bread and salt. When he was innocently about to grant her request an old man intervened and scolded him sharply for his generosity. "If you enable her to remain alive, she will only harm other men." If the precentor, during services, offers up a prayer for the health of a sick woman who is known to be a vampire, the congregation must not respond with an "Amen!" When a *broxa* or an *estrie* is being buried, one should notice whether or not her mouth is open; if it is, this is a sure sign that she will continue her vampirish activities for another year. Her mouth must be stopped up with earth, and she will be rendered harmless.[37]

According to one source the *mares* are creatures which consort in forests in groups of nine, for if there were ten of them Satan would seize the tenth one; they do no harm to humans. The more authentic version, however, is that the *mare* is a being which rests upon man while he sleeps and deprives him of the power of speech by grasping his tongue and lips and choking off his breath, so that he cries out fitfully. It is the *mare* which is responsible for nightmares (here we have the word incorporated in our own speech and folklore); in French the phenomenon is known as the *cauche-mare*.[38]

The werwolf is a sorcerer, or a demon which inhabits the earth in man's form, but which at will assumes the shape of a wolf and attacks and consumes men. Like his feminine counterpart, the *estrie,* he requires human blood in his diet—another version of the vampire.[39]

We read of other familiar spirits as well.[40] The *kobold* makes its appearance in a thirteenth-century manuscript, a demonic homunculus which mimics and echoes man's voice in order to bewilder him, and which is used by ventriloquists. Another work of the same century tells of a "tiny demon called a *wichtchen*." [41] The spirits which dwell in waste places and attack men who are up alone at night were naturalized in Northern France and renamed *faes*.[42] "Many of these are to be found among us," lamented one pious rabbi, referring specifically to the *faes* and their associates the *lutins* (or the *nuitons* [43]), the hobgoblins which play such a prominent rôle in French folklore; nor was their German counterpart, the *alp* (elf) missing.[44] The watersprite, the *nixe*,[45] and her sisters, the sirens,[46] also put in an appearance. Genii were the familiars of witches and sorcerers, and the dragon became a demon with unusual attributes.[47] A blow struck by a man can have no effect upon the dragon; only a child from his own loins can wound him. When he is within a man's house he is harmless, but no sooner does he depart than the house goes up in flames. Thunder and lightning he dreads, and if he can he flees from them into a human habitation, where he is safe. Once a dragon cohabited with a princess who bore him a son. He confessed that he feared none but his own child. When the boy was grown to man's estate he was induced by the king to kill his dragon-father, and taking him unawares one night smote him a mortal blow. The demon begged that the blow be repeated, for strangely enough, one wound could kill him, but a second would save his life. His son, however, refused him this courtesy, and the dragon promptly expired, a consummation which proved rather embarrassing, for his body swelled until it had to be cut up into bits and carted off in a great number of wagons.

The familiar name for the Sabbath-loaf among German Jews, *Barches* or *Berches,* and the distinctive, plaited appearance of the bread, have led some scholars to suggest that we have here a Jewish version of an ancient pagan practice. The Teutonic goddess of fertility, Berchta or Perchta, was worshiped by the women with rites which included offering their hair to her. In time this ceremony became obsolete and was replaced by a symbolic offering of the hair in the shape of a loaf representing the intertwined braids, the *Perchis-* or *Berchisbrod*. This is the word, and the practice, which Jewish ceremonial, curiously, has preserved in the loaf prepared especially for the Sabbath, say these scholars. Both the name and the shape are distinctive of German-Jewish usage. Yet even if this theory should be correct (other scholars have vigorously denied that there is any relationship with the goddess, and the issue is still —and will probably remain—moot) we should not be justified in concluding that the Perchta cult had found a place in Jewish ritual and belief. At most, all we can read into the *Berches* is an odd assimilation and survival of a long meaningless word.[48]

A chance remark in a thirteenth-century code leads us to perhaps the most interesting item in this catalogue. Jewish practice required that before entering the ritual bath all obstructions on the body, such as jewelry, which might prevent contact of the water with the skin, must be removed. The question arose whether a man or woman whose hair is badly matted must cut off this impediment to complete contact before bathing. "My opinion," our source states, "is that we should not require people to cut their hair when it is tangled and matted like felt, a condition called in German יילק"ש, and in French פלטרי"ד, for this disarray is caused by a demon, and we consider it to be courting mortal danger to shear such hair." The terms are obscure. A later authority, quoting this first one, comments, "ולקר"ט [probably another transliteration of the word represented by פלטרי"ד] is what we call הול"א לוק"א." The riddle is solved! These last words are the German *Holle-locke,* of which יילק"ש (spelled also in the first work היילק"ש) is no doubt a variant; פלטרי"ד must be the French *feltre, feutre,* our "felt." [49] The belief that in the night demons entangle the manes of beasts and the hair of humans is very widespread; we may recall Shakespeare's lines:

This is that very Mab
That plats the manes of horses in the night;
And bakes the elf-locks in foul sluttish hairs,
Which once untangled much misfortune bodes.

Who was this Holle after whom the elf-lock was named? Among the ancient Teutons Holle, or Holda, or Hulda, appeared as an ugly old witch, with long, matted hair and protruding teeth. In medieval Germany she had developed into the demon-witch who gobbles up children. She was held responsible for entangling hair at night; "er ist mit der Holle gefahren" was said of one whose hair was disheveled and knotted. Corresponding with *Holle-locke* is the term *Hollenzopf.*[50]

The lady made her way into Jewish life in her other rôle as well. It is reported that as early as the fourteenth century the ceremony called Hollekreisch was widely observed in Jewish circles in Germany. The Jewish boy receives his Hebrew name on the occasion of his circumcision; the girl child usually upon the first Sabbath after birth. Since the earliest days of the dispersion, however, Jews have also borne names drawn from the nomenclature of the people in whose midst they reside—names we may term secular or vulgar as distinguished from the Hebrew, the classical name. These secular cognomens usually correspond in one way or another to the Hebrew, whether as colloquial forms or translations, or related only by sound or appearance. The ceremony of the Hollekreisch, which marked the bestowal of its secular name upon the child, comprised these features: the baby (or the cradle containing the baby) was lifted into the air three times, usually by the children especially invited for the occasion, and each time the name was shouted out by the guests in unison. Often this shouting followed a formula. In modern times such formulas as "Hollekreisch! What shall this child's name be?" with the appropriate response, or "Holle! Holle! This child's name shall be . . . ," have been employed. In the seventeenth century the custom of Hollekreisch was observed in naming boys and girls only in South Germany, while in Austria, Bohemia, Moravia and Poland it was not used for boys at all, and only rarely for girls.

The earliest writer to speak of this custom, Moses Minz (fifteenth century), explained the term as a combination of a Hebrew and a German word—*ḥol,* "profane, secular," and *kreischen,* "to shout, call out"—which would render it "the ceremony of calling out the secular name." This explanation was accepted and repeated in the later references to the practice. A modern writer has derived the first part of the term from the call "Holla!" But it is unlikely that these explanations even approach the truth. As we have seen, Holle was the demon-witch who attacked infants; in this respect she provided a close parallel to the familiar Lilit. The further correspondences between the two: their connection with the night; the distinguishing physical feature, long hair, which they had in common; their propensity to attack prior to the naming of the child; all of these made the identification of the two a natural one. Shouting the child's name, which is mentioned in all the references to the ceremony, and tossing the infant in the air three times, were devices intended to drive off the demon Holle, and her fellows, just as in the *Wachnacht* ceremony on the night before the circumcision measures were taken to ward off attacks by Lilit. So close a parallel to Jewish belief and practice as that embodied in the Hollekreisch could have found no difficulty in winning a wide popularity among Jews.[51]

We are not yet ready to dismiss our unsavory friend Holle-Hulda. We must follow her devious course in Jewish folklore one step farther, though here we shall leave her playing a more attractive rôle. In a thirteenth-century manuscript there appears an invocation, in Middle High German written in Hebrew characters, to this self-same lady, Hulda, this time the goddess of love. In this passage there is a reference to Hulda's *hof,* which is nothing else than the famous Venusberg of the *Tannhäusersage.* "Der Venusberg ist Frau Hollen Hofhaltung, erst im 15. 16. Jahrhundert scheint man aus ihr Frau Venus zu machen," wrote Grimm. Ugly, cruel Holle becomes the lover's goddess, Venus! And thus she appears in a fifteenth-century Hebrew-Yiddish love-receipt: "Secure an egg laid on a Thursday by a jet-black hen which has never laid an egg before, and on the same day, after sunset, bury it at a crossroads. Leave it there three days; then dig it up after sunset, sell it and purchase with the proceeds a mirror, which you must bury in the same spot in the evening 'in Frau Venus namen,' and say 'allhie begrab ich diesen spiegel in der Libe, die Frau Venus zu dem Dannhäuser hat.' Sleep on that spot three nights, then remove the mirror, and whoever looks into it will love you!"[52]

4

MAN AND THE DEMONS

ATTACK

We may well believe, as we go through this material, that people pay dearly for their superstitions. It is difficult, of course, to judge the emotional tone, the intensity of the terror which the medieval Jew experienced in braving such a demon-ridden world. Our sources are wholly impersonal; writing of an introspective nature was altogether unknown. We can only conjecture on the basis of the chance personal comments that wormed their way quite incidentally into a literature which was primarily legalistic and exegetical. It is significant, for instance, that a homely little book like the Yiddish *Brantspiegel*,[1] intended for the intimate instruction of womenfolk, a book which certainly came closer to the folk psyche than did the more formal writing of the period, singled out as the foremost dangers to life and limb demons, evil spirits, wild animals and evil men. "All the while," ran the pious injunction, "that her husband is away from home the good wife should pray to God that He guard and protect him from all untoward events and dangers, whether they be from demons or evil spirits, wild animals or evil men." From such remarks in works of this type or in a book like *Sefer Ḥasidim,* in which a homely folk quality prevails, and from the anecdotes which frequently accompany them, it is apparent that no place, no time, and no man was exempt from the fear and the danger of spirit attack. The most compelling evidence lies, however, in the countless devices that were employed to ward off this danger, measures that entered intimately and often unconsciously into the least aspect of Jewish life during the Middle Ages.

Yet we must not imagine that this dread was so overwhelmingly oppressive as to paralyze man, whose adaptability has been his mightiest weapon in the struggle for survival. The invisibility of the demons was their most terrible attribute, but yet, as the Talmud sagely observed, it is fortunate that we are blind to their presence, for if we should see them swarming about us, we must collapse from sheer terror.[2] Like all the other dangers attending life, always implicit in the play of nature's forces, but fully realized only at rare and fragmentary intervals, man learned to take this one too in his stride, to accept it into his consciousness of the world, build his frail breastworks against it, and proceed about his affairs. Demons, in the practical business of living, were just one more uncomfortable feature of a far from easy life.

Occasional remarks seem to minimize the danger. Thus one writer informs us, "They are more God-fearing than men are . . . and should you ask why they do so much harm, they harm no one without good cause; if a man does not provoke them . . . he need have no fear." Prime provocation consisted in forcing them to do one's will, by means of conjurations, amulets, and the like. This was the strongest practical argument against demon-magic, and we hear it reiterated time and again—the man who enters into dealings with evil spirits will not escape them unscathed. Again there is the ingenious polemic according to which the non-monotheistic faith of "two certain peoples" lays them peculiarly open to demonic attack, "but unlike theirs is the portion of Jacob, who believe in the one God." But the implacable enmity of the spirits toward all mankind was an axiom of demon lore.[3] Superstition supported this belief with a wealth of instance. Many anecdotes tell of unprovoked physical attacks by the spirits; the man who is dogged by ill-luck is the special prey of demons; the etiology of folk-medicine was primarily demonic. The harm done by ill-chosen words and curses was traced ultimately to the demons, as was the working of the evil eye. Demons were believed to be the active agents in malevolent sorcery. In these ways did folk-belief express its conviction that most of the evil that man suffered was the work of his mortal enemies.

Man was in constant peril. If he dared to promenade alone he took his life in his hands. But the risk was greater outside the bounds of a settled community, and the requirement to accompany a traveller part of the way on his journey was explained on this score. "One should not turn back until the wayfarer can no longer be seen," read the injunction; the act of escorting him and keeping one's gaze fixed on his retreating figure as long as possible represented a sort of symbolic extension of civilization to keep him company and protect him from "the beings that rule uninhabited places." Of similar import was the charm recorded by Joseph Hahn; his father, it seems, would stick a splinter from the city gate into his hatband whenever he left on a journey. "No doubt it was a charm for protection," the son correctly surmised. The community accompanied him on his travels by proxy. The superstitious fear of interrupting a journey and returning home was no doubt based on an analogous line of reason: the forces of the outside world might thus be introduced into the home, and with them, ill-luck. Therefore, "once a man has set out, if he has forgotten something, he must not re-enter his house, but should stand outside and ask to have it handed out to him." [4]

Night time in particular is spirit time. When the mysterious dim of the night settles over the earth the demons, dwellers in darkness, bestir themselves. *Mazzikim* and *lilin, lutins* and *faes,* all flutter out of their hiding places. Therefore, liquids left standing overnight must not be drunk, nor should one drink from a well at night, for the demons may have imbibed of them. Foods placed under a bed for safekeeping during the night are undoubtedly contaminated by evil spirits; to partake of them is to court trouble. Even a covering of iron (a potent anti-demonic agent) is no security against nocturnal invasion. Similarly garlic, or onions, or eggs which have been peeled and left overnight are no longer fit for consumption.

In the natural order of things man should be tightly wrapped in his bedclothes at night, or else engrossed in his studies. God's protection, which rests over all creatures during the day, is man's safeguard when the sun shines. But the man who reverses the natural regimen and devotes his nights to some unsanctified labor, from him is God's protection properly withdrawn. For night has been given to the spirits, but the day is man's and God's. So we read, "If anyone goes out alone before cock-crow his blood is on his own head." Even in the privacy of his own home a man was hardly safe. "R. Jacob Mölln said that a man should beware not to spend the night alone even in his bed-chamber; he himself used to keep a boy beside him at night. One shouldn't walk through his yard without a light, or, God forbid! the evil spirits will pounce upon him. Human alertness avails nothing against them." A popular writer on folk morality, attesting to the strength of this belief, essayed a word of comfort: "When a man arises during the night to study, let him not fear the demons; let him rather consider how many there are who travel alone at night and suffer no harm. If he trust in God he may arise and have no cause for fear." Enhancing the fear of demons at night was the realization that man's vigilance is relaxed while he sleeps; even more, the soul having left the body, that both body and soul are peculiarly open to attack: "The body is like a house, the soul, its inhabitant; when the tenant leaves his home there is no one to look after it." Therefore most people fall sick at night, while they are asleep. Indeed, R. Jacob Weil confessed, "When I prepare for my afternoon nap I recite first the 'anti-demonic psalm' " for "all sleep is dangerous because of the demons." [5]

Great as the danger was every night of the week, on two nights especially was it heightened—the eves of Wednesday and Saturday. At these times hordes of peculiarly devastating spirits were let loose upon the world. During the Talmudic period Friday night in particular was considered an unhealthy time to be abroad alone, and the rabbis required that no man be left behind in the synagogue to finish his prayers alone after the congregation had concluded the service and gone home. For then he must negotiate the distance to his home without a companion. Special prayers were instituted for the *Ḥazan* to recite, so that the congregation might be detained until its slowest member had caught up with it. In the Middle Ages this fear of being left behind on Friday night was not so pronounced. The commentators explained that the Talmudic synagogues were situated in the fields, where the spirits congregate, whereas medieval houses of worship were located in town, and the late homegoer was not in pressing danger. Nevertheless some medieval rabbis made it a practice to linger until the last man was through with his prayers, in order to accompany him home, even pretending to be engrossed in a book so that the laggard might not be embarrassed.[6]

CRISES

Eternal vigilance was the watchword; the evil spirits were everywhere, impatiently awaiting the unguarded moment when they might seize one. But at certain critical stages of life, when man's resistance was undermined, or his attention was likely to have been distracted, or when his extraordinary joy unduly excited the envy and animus of the spirit world, the danger was heightened and the safeguards were correspondingly strengthened. These were the moments in the life cycle "when man's star is low": birth, illness, death, while marriage, man's happiest moment, was an especially perilous one.[7] These were the moments of man's greatest vulnerability when the struggle with the spirits grew intense. And just these were the occasions selected by the sorcerer as most propitious for his sinister work, the junctures when the curse and the evil eye took their greatest toll.

The moment of birth was a crucial one for mother and infant; all the evil forces of the natural and supernatural realms were concentrated upon extinguishing the faint spark of life that hovered between the two. Nor did the danger pass when the child was born. In Jewish belief the eight days after birth were equally fraught with peril. (The period varies among different peoples; in Germany, for instance, it ranged from nine days to six weeks following delivery.) This period was usually terminated by the initiatory rite, such as baptism or in Judaism, the circumcision. Originally of a composite social and superstitious character, circumcision came in Biblical times to assume a specifically national, and in the view of the prophets, a spiritual significance. In the succeeding period, with the development of clearly defined views about heaven and hell, this rite acquired a new value, in addition to the older ones. "God said to Abraham," according to the *Midrash,* " 'because of the merit of circumcision your descendants will be saved from *Gehinnom,* for only the uncircumcised will descend thither.' " The corollary of this belief, that uncircumcised Jews would have no "share in the world to come" was exceedingly popular in the later periods, and was often voiced in medieval writings. So strong an impression did it make that in Geonic times there arose the custom of circumcising infants who died before their eighth day, at the grave, and there giving them a name. Because of the great importance attached to this rite it was feared that the forces of evil would exert their utmost powers to prevent its consummation. The night before the circumcision, therefore, was held to be the most dangerous for the male child.[8]

The dangers that beset the bridal pair were attributable to the savage envy and rage that man's joys aroused in the evil spirits, perhaps, too, to their desire to frustrate the act that is responsible for the propagation of human life. Gathering force throughout the period preparatory to the wedding, these dangers assumed their highest intensity on the bridal night and gradually tapered off afterwards.[9]

The especial susceptibility of the invalid—his ailment was probably itself merely a symptom of demonic attack—was self-evident. The dying man was pictured as surrounded by evil spirits waiting to pounce upon him; therefore his attendants were cautioned to see to it that his limbs did not project beyond his bed, or he would come under the power of the demons. He was believed, too, to behold all around him the spirits of the dead come to welcome him to their midst. Death itself was caused by a spirit, or destroying angel. The widespread belief in the Middle Ages that at the moment of death a struggle ensues between the angels and the devil over the soul of the deceased was paralleled in Jewish thought by the notion that the demons seek to gain possession of the corpse while it is yet unburied. The corpse itself was also an object of fear. The dead had entered the world of the spirits, the soul hovered over its vacated shell, potentially capable of harming those who came near. For this reason contact with the dead was to be avoided, and the clothing of the deceased was not to be used again, "because of the danger." Indeed, fear of the soul and the spirits, and apprehension that the demons might do harm to the deceased, was the explanation advanced for the prohibition to leave a corpse unburied overnight. The sooner the body was out of the way the better for the living and the dead. But the process of burial was not the least perilous—the corpse was closely accompanied by a spirit retinue during the procession to the grave, the cemetery was infested with spirits, the journey home was made hazardous by the possibility that the spirits had not been left behind, that the ghost itself was an unseen member of the company. And when finally the funeral was over and the period of mourning commenced the danger had not yet been entirely obviated, the spirit of the deceased might still linger for a while about familiar places. As Samter summed up this most fearful episode for the living and the dead, "The dying man must be protected against evil spirits and all sorts of magic, perhaps in the last analysis against death itself; the corpse, on the other hand, brings the living into mortal danger, partly through the enmity of the evil powers which cling to it yet a while, partly through the desire of the soul to draw others along with it to the beyond." [10] The measures adopted to counteract the dangers implicit in death and burial provided for every one of these apprehensions.

SPIRIT POSSESSION

So long as the perpetual warfare between mankind and the demon world remained in a sense objective, that is, man's problem was to fight off attack from without, man, as we shall see, did not necessarily occupy the losing side of the struggle. He had ready at hand a host of magical weapons which could effectively protect him; he might even acquire the mystical learning that would enable him to lord it over his mortal enemies, bending them to his will. But the demons, too, were not altogether resourceless, and when they had recourse to what we have come to know in a more vital contemporary sphere of human conflict as "boring from within," man's plight became desperate. Spirit possession rendered the poor victim the physical "vessel" through which the demon operated and only extreme measures could avail to free him from the fiend.

This terrifying belief was especially widespread in later Jewish life. Popularized by the Lurianic *Kabbalah* it became a characteristic superstition of East-European Jewry. But it is found full-blown among German Jews at a time when the Lurianic concept could not yet have gained any wide popular acceptance. The initial appearance of a *dibbuk* is in a story included in the *Ma'aseh Book,*[11] which was first published in 1602, and which contains material whose origin is considerably earlier than that date. In this story the spirit which took possession of a young man was the spirit of one who in this life had sinned egregiously, and which could therefore find no peace. It had entered the youth's body after having been forced to flee its previous abode, the body of a cow which was about to be slaughtered. It is this form of the belief, possession by the restless spirit of a deceased person, which gained such popularity in later times. In essence this represents a version of the doctrine of the transmigration of souls, *gilgul,* which the older Spanish *Kabbalah* developed.

In earlier times we find a purer form of the belief in the possibility of spirit possession—a form familiar in Christian legend [12]—that is, that the demons proper may make their homes in man's body. This view found its rationalization in the legend that the demons, created on the eve of the Sabbath, are bodiless. Since all creation is engaged in the quest for perfection, all things striving to attain the next higher degree of being, the demons, too, are perpetually seeking to acquire the body of man, their greatest desire being for that of the scholar, the highest type of human. This is why scholars in particular must be careful not to be out alone at night. But just as woman, in herself imperfect, seeks perfection through union with man, so the demons seek to unite themselves primarily with woman, who represents the next degree of creation above them. This is why women are more prone to sorcery than are men; the sorceress is a woman through whom the demon that has possessed her operates, or one who through close association with demons has acquired their malevolent attributes.[13]

Demons who have taken possession of a human body exercise such complete control over it that the personality and the will of the victim are extinguished. They can be expelled only by the most powerful exorcisms. This was the method of liberation employed in the story from the *Maʿaseh Book* mentioned above. We have a most circumstantial account of such a proceeding in Nikolsburg, in the year 1696,[14] a date beyond the close of the period we are studying, when the Lurianic ideas had already gained wide popularity, but shedding light none the less on the procedure which was universally employed. The spirit in this instance proved extremely recalcitrant and was finally dislodged only upon its own conditions and after repeated efforts by the rabbi and congregation.

INCUBUS AND SUCCUBUS

The need of the spirits to find completion in the body of man was also utilized to explain the curious belief in sexual relations between man and demon. That the demons propagate their own kind we have already seen. It is to be expected that man's fertile imagination should lead him to speculate on the possibility of an unnatural union between the human and the spirit worlds, and upon the condition of the offspring of such a union. Just as in antediluvian days "the sons of God saw the daughters of men that they were fair; and they took them wives, whomsoever they chose" (Gen. 6:2), so in the Middle Ages it was not unknown for a lesser order of spirit beings to choose for themselves earthly mates. The lore of the incubus and the succubus finds its counterpart in medieval Jewish folklore.

The Jewish belief took its cue from the Midrashic legend about Adam's siring a demonic brood, and the assertion of the *Zohar,* sourcebook for all the mystic science of medieval Jewry, that even now the propagation of the species continues by virtue of the union of men with spirits in their sleep.[15] As to the manner of such union, it was generally agreed that man's nocturnal emissions often result from the efforts of the demons to arouse his passions, and that these provide the seed from which the hybrid offspring are born.[16] This takes place, of course, without man's knowledge or volition; the spirits, lacking bodies, have no means of achieving physical union with man.[17] However, in the guise of man or woman a demon may successfully pass itself off upon an unsuspecting human as a being of his own kind, and thus achieve its purpose.[18]

As to the children of such a union, they retain an essentially demonic nature, but in the kingdom of the spirits they rank very high indeed, occupying the positions of rulership. This is one of the reasons why demons are so avid for union with human beings.[19]

This belief created some interesting moral and legal problems. Was a man or woman who had been seduced by a demon to be regarded as an adulterer? And if so, was such a woman to be "forbidden" to her husband? If, today, the issue strikes us as grotesque it is only because we have lost faith in the realities of the medieval world. Isaac b. Moses of Vienna, in the thirteenth century, considered this question at length and solemnly concluded that a person who had been seduced by a spirit was not to be held guilty of fornication. In substantiation of his decision he recalled a legend of a pious man who was sorely grieved because a demon in human shape had enticed him into an indiscretion. The prophet Elijah appeared to him and consoled him: since this was a demon he had committed no offense. "If he had been guilty," R. Isaac deduced, "Elijah would not have come to him, nor spoken with him, nor would he have acquitted him." Three centuries later a Polish rabbi was consulted in the case of a married woman who had had relations with a demon which appeared to her once in the shape of her husband, and again in the uniform of the local petty count. Was she to be considered an adulteress? this rabbi was asked, and was she therefore to be "forbidden" to her husband, since she might have had intercourse with this demon of her free will? The judge absolved her of all guilt and "permitted" her to her husband.[20]

Finally, as a fitting climax to the story, we have the most unusual spectacle of a lawsuit between the inhabitants of a house and the demonic offspring of a former owner, a lawsuit argued by the contestants in strictly legal fashion before a duly constituted court, called into special sitting to hear the case. This occurred in Posen at the end of the seventeenth century. The account bears extended retelling, both for its intrinsic interest and for the light it sheds upon the beliefs of that and the preceding centuries. In the main street of Posen there stood a stone dwelling whose cellar was securely locked. One day a young man forced his way into this cellar and was shortly after found dead upon the threshold. Emboldened by this act the "outsiders," who had killed the intruder in their subterranean haunt, entered the house itself and began to plague the inhabitants by casting ashes into the pots of food cooking on the hearth, throwing things off the walls and the furniture, breaking candlesticks, and similar pranks. Though they did no harm to the persons of the inhabitants, these were so distressed and frightened that they deserted the house. A great outcry arose in Posen, but the measures taken by the local savants (including the Jesuits) were not sufficiently potent to oust the interlopers, and the foremost wonder-worker of the time, R. Joel *Baal Shem* of Zamosz, was sent for. His powerful incantations succeeded in forcing the demons to disclose their identity. They contended, however, that this house was their property and demanded an opportunity to substantiate their case before a court of law. R. Joel agreed, the court was convoked, and before it a demon advocate, who could be heard but not seen, presented his argument. We may still sense in this graphic account of the trial the dramatic tenseness of the scene, the earnestness of the advocate's plea, the solemn attentiveness of the three bowed gray heads on the bench, the open-eyed wonder, spiced with a dash of terror, of the audience. The argument ran in this wise: The former owner of the house had had illicit relations with a female demon who, appearing to him as a beautiful woman, had borne him children. In time his lawful wife discovered his infidelity and consulted the great rabbi Sheftel, who forced a confession from the guilty man, and obliged him, by means of an amulet containing fearful holy names, to break off this union. Before his death, however, the demon returned and prevailed upon him to leave her and her offspring the cellar of his house for an inheritance. Now that this man and his human heirs are all dead, contended the advocate, we, his spirit children, remain his sole heirs and lay claim to this house. The inhabitants of the house then presented their case: we purchased this house at full value from its owner; you "outsiders" are not called "seed of men" and therefore have no rights appertaining to humans; besides, your mother forced this man to cohabit with her against his will. Both sides here rested, the court retired for a consultation, and returned to announce that its decision was against the "outsiders." Their proper habitat is in waste places and deserts and not among men; they can therefore have no share in this house. To make certain that the decision was carried out R. Joel proceeded to deliver himself of his most terrifying exorcisms, and succeeded in banishing the intruders from cellar as well as house, to the forests and deserts where they belonged.[21]

THE EVIL EYE

The "evil eye," one of the most widely feared manifestations of demonic animus, is not always what the term implies; it comprehends two distinct types of supernatural phenomena, only the first of which should properly be so denoted.[22] This superstition affirms that certain baneful potencies are inherent in the "evil" eye itself, that they are natural properties of such eyes. Not a few unfortunate men are born *jettatori,* shedding rays of destruction about them with every glance, frequently themselves unaware of their dread influence. Some *jettatori* may be recognized by the peculiar and striking cast of their eyes; others pass unnoticed until sad experience unmasks them. They are to be found in all stations of life. Pope Pius IX, for one, was reputed to be possessed of the evil eye, and the women, while kneeling for his blessing as he passed, would make a counteracting sign under their skirts. This belief arises from the natural reaction of simple people to the arrestingly piercing and vital qualities that often illumine the eyes of men of strong personality, and is a response just as much to the personality as to the eye itself. There *are* baleful glances, just as there are malevolent men, and the superstitious imagination tends to run away with itself.

The second is the type the Germans denote with the words *berufen* or *beschreien.* Its root is the pagan conviction that the gods and the spirits are essentially man's adversaries, that they envy him his joys and his triumphs, and spitefully harry him for the felicities they do not share. "Just as hope never forsakes man in adversity, so fear is his constant companion in good fortune, fear that it may desert him; he apprehends equally the envy of the gods, and the envy of his fellow-men—the evil eye." The attention of the spirit-world is cocked to detect the least word or gesture of commendation. Demons are like men, Menasseh b. Israel wrote; "when a man receives praise in the presence of his enemy, the latter is filled with anger and reveals his discomfiture, for envy consumes his heart like a raging fire, and he cannot contain himself." [23] A glance that expresses approbation is as eloquent as a speech, and just as likely to arouse their malice. Such words and glances, in themselves perhaps innocent, constitute the evil eye, which brings swift persecution in its wake. We may say that this belief is a hypostatization of the evil which man discerns in invidiousness, a translation of a profound poetic truth into the language of superstition.

Rabbinic Judaism was acquainted with both aspects of the evil eye.[24] Several rabbis of the Talmud were accredited with the power to turn men into "a heap of bones" with a glance, or to cause whatever their gaze fell upon to burst into flames. But the second aspect was predominant. As has been pointed out by several scholars, the *jettatura* proper seems to have been introduced into Jewish thought by those Talmudic authorities who came under the influence of the Babylonian environment. The Palestinian sources, and in particular the *Mishna,* know the evil eye only as an expression of the moral powers of envy and hatred. The Palestinian view prevailed in later Jewish life, though the other was not unknown.[25]

In order to counteract the "moral" version of the evil eye it has become customary over a very wide area to append a prophylactic phrase, such as "May the Lord protect thee," "no evil eye," *"Unbeschrieen,"* to every laudatory remark. Medieval Jewry pursued not only this practice, but also the equally well-known device of expressing its approbation in highly unflattering terms: "A man will call his handsome son 'Ethiop,' to avoid casting the evil eye upon him," said Rashi. Any act or condition that in itself may excite the envy of the spirits is subject to the evil eye; taking a census or even estimating the size of a crowd, possession of wealth, performing an act which is normally a source of pride or joy—all evoke its pernicious effects. A father leading his child to school for the first time took the precaution to screen him with his cloak. Members of a family were reluctant to follow each other in reciting the blessings over the *Torah* before a congregation. A double wedding in one household, or indeed, any two simultaneous marriages were avoided for this reason. Even animals and plants were subject to the evil eye; a man who admired his neighbor's crop was suspected of casting the evil eye upon it.[26]

The early Jewish literature was little concerned with the explanation or the theoretical basis of this phenomenon. Even in the Middle Ages speculation on the subject was very much circumscribed, despite the example set by classical and Christian students who devoted much thought to the question whether fascination operates naturally or with the aid of demons. Thomas Aquinas, for example, accepted the explanation that "the eye is affected by the strong imagination of the soul and then corrupts and poisons the atmosphere so that tender bodies coming within its range may be injuriously affected." Of a similar nature is the opinion of R. Judah Löw, who attained a great reputation as the alleged creator of the *Golem* of Prague: "Know and understand that the evil eye concentrates within itself the element of fire," and so flashes forth destruction. On the other hand there is the view of Menasseh b. Israel, previously cited, which reflects Christian opinion, and is matched by the statement in *Sefer Ḥasidim,* "The angry glance of a man's eye calls into being an evil angel who speedily takes vengeance on the cause of his wrath." The same work rings in an interesting innovation on this belief. There are glances that heal, as others harm: "When a wicked man casts the evil eye upon someone, to do him damage . . . a pious man must immediately counteract it by bestowing upon the victim a glance that sheds beneficence. . . . Even if the first man has not expressly uttered a curse, but has merely said, 'How nice and plump that child is!' or has regarded him without saying anything, the pious one should bless the child with a glance." [27] Protection against the evil eye was essentially a matter of repelling the demons and evil spirits and practically all the anti-demonic measures were effective safeguards.

WORDS AND CURSES

Gregory the Great, in his *Dialogues,* relates that a priest once jocosely called out to his servant, "Come, devil, take off my shoes!" whereupon his shoes were whisked off by an invisible force, and the poor fellow was almost frightened out of his wits. Luckily he had the presence of mind to shriek, "Hence! vile one, hence!" and saved himself from further diabolic accommodation.[28]

The Talmud put the matter succinctly: "One should never open his mouth to Satan," that is, evil talk is nothing less than an invitation to the demons. But this was a counsel of perfection, which men could do little more than aspire to. Our speech is richly peppered with words whose connotation is unpleasant; how open our mouths at all without letting slip out such invitations to Satan? The danger is ever-present, but human ingenuity has devised several means of getting around it. One of these is the euphemism. One says "the enemies of Israel" instead of "Israel," "my enemies" instead of "myself," and people are not addressed directly, but in the third person, when some unpleasant eventuality is mentioned. To lead the demons astray, the true nature of a disease is hidden, as when the ailment "mal malant" is known as "bon malant." The one subject of conversation that is most ardently to be shunned, naturally, is death, and so when Joseph, in Egypt, asked his brothers concerning the welfare of their father and grandfather, they replied, "Thy servant, our father, is well, he is yet alive," and Joseph understood at once that his grandfather, Isaac, was dead. During the Middle Ages fear of publicly proclaiming the news of a death was pronounced, and the custom of pouring out the water in a home where a death had occurred was explained and accepted as a mute announcement. To this day in Eastern European villages, where the sexton calls worshipers to the morning service with three knocks upon the door, he omits the last rap when a member of the congregation has passed away overnight, the missing knock telling its own somber story. Instead of saying "so and so is dead," one says "so and so lives," and the cemetery is called "the house of life." Similarly, references to mourning must be avoided. The "Great" treatise on "Mourning" (*Ebel Rabatti*) has become the tractate "Rejoicing" (*Semaḥot*), mourning formularies are entitled "The Book of Life," and the concluding words of a rite connected with dreams, "Eat thy bread with joy" (Eccl. 9:7), are transposed because the initials of the Hebrew words spell "mourner." Again, news of a serious illness is withheld for three days lest the spirits make a premature end of the invalid when they hear people talking about his infirmity; the secret is not guarded any longer, if the illness continues, for fear that the patient may be deprived of the benefit of public prayer. When a person is sick one must not gossip about his sins.[29]

There is also a second method of cozening the spirits, namely, to nullify the possible effect of a remark with such formal comments as "God forbid," "may it not occur to you," "may God protect you," etc. Similar phrases are in use all over the world.[30]

If such simple devices impute to the spirits a degree of naïveté which does little credit to their vaunted cunning as man's antagonists, the explanation must be sought in man's unshakable belief in his own superior intelligence. When he sets himself to the task none of God's creatures is his peer in wisdom and shrewdness!

The medieval literature is full of warnings against "opening one's mouth to Satan," but warnings do not suffice and the lesson is driven home by frequent tales of the grievous consequences of such incaution. When women gossip about an invalid in the presence of children, the ailment is promptly visited upon the young ones; to scold a boy with the word *meshummad* (apostate) is to foredoom him; a man who said of his books "they are fit only to be burned" was privileged to witness that fate befall them; another man who misrepresented the state of his health was speedily stricken with disease. A scribe must not end a page with an ominous phrase, nor a scholar his studies, nor should a book be left open at such a place; one man who was so unwary as to neglect this admonition and left his studies at the words "And satyrs shall dance there" (Is. 13:21) awoke to find a demon disporting himself in his chair. There are dozens of such anecdotes. And sometimes the spirits performed holy labors too, as when they impressed upon R. Israel Isserlein a due respect for the words of the Talmud. While conducting a class he came across the plaint of a long-departed sufferer that "Podagra is as painful as the thrust of a needle in live flesh" (*San.* 48b); himself afflicted with gout, and therefore an authority in his own right, he took issue with this dictum. "We had not yet completed that tractate," writes his Boswell, "when he let out a series of groans such as I had never before heard from his lips, and neither before nor since have I seen him in such excruciating pain. 'In the future,' said the teacher, 'I'll put a bridle on my tongue.' "[31]

Vows and curses were especially singled out in this connection. A vow, let us say, sworn by the life of a child, is a serious matter, for at the least sign of backsliding the spirits are delighted to exact the penalty. And a curse is even more fraught with danger; it is a direct invitation, nay, a command to the spirits to do their worst. According to Jewish tradition, "the curse of a sage, even when undeserved, comes to pass"; in fact, "even the curse of an ordinary person should not be treated lightly." Demons are not the ones to draw invidious distinctions between persons or motives. Among Christians, as among Jews, an execration, whether seriously meant or not, was believed to bring dire consequences in its wake. "Sprenger [a German writer of the fifteenth century] tells us that if an impatient husband says to a pregnant wife, 'Devil take you!' the child will be subject to Satan; such children, he says, are often seen; five nurses will not satisfy the appetite of one, and yet they are miserably emaciated, while their weight is great." Parallels are to be found aplenty in the Jewish sources. Malisons take effect indiscriminately, sometimes on the curser, sometimes on the cursed, or even on their children—and in at least one instance we are informed that an innocent bystander paid the price. This is why, *Sefer Ḥasidim* counsels, one should not live among people given to cursing. "We know of many such cases," wrote one man, "but we do not wish to burden the reader with them." Well he might not, for his readers could have matched case for case. The power of the curse extended even beyond the grave—the soul of the deceased was made to suffer if his memory was reviled. It is on this basis that we can comprehend the peculiar dread that attached to the formal rite of excommunication which called down upon the head of the guilty one a most terrifying catalogue of maledictions.[32]

So strong was this fear that it was forbidden to repeat in direct discourse an overheard conversation which had included a curse, for however innocently spoken it might still take effect on the company present. Even the imprecations in Holy Writ evoked dread; *Sefer Ḥasidim* tells of a student who fell suddenly ill and died while studying a portion of Jeremiah calling down bitter maledictions upon Israel, and in the synagogue this superstition created a peculiar problem. The weekly reading of the *Torah* involved from time to time public recitation of such ominous selections, and the congregation feared the spirits might interpret them as directed against its members. For this reason communities were warned to make sure that the precentor was universally acceptable and befriended, or these curses might descend upon the heads of his enemies. Even so, individuals were hesitant about ascending the pulpit to recite the blessings over these portions, especially when Deut. 28 was read, for its malisons are penned in the singular person and present tense. In one synagogue, it is reported, "on a Sabbath on which the 'chapter of maledictions' was to be read, the Scroll of the *Torah* was shamefully permitted to lie open for several hours, because no member of the congregation was willing to come up to the pulpit." [33]

Some writers attributed the random effectiveness of curses to astrological factors—"not all times are equal," they explained; at intervals a man's star relaxes its vigilance, and a curse that is uttered in his presence at that moment will find in him its victim. But the pious *Brantspiegel* warned the irascible wife against scolding her husband because "die *mazzikim* stehen un' sehen das sie zornig is' un' shelt ihren mann un' freuen sich un' nehmen die *kelalot* [execrations] un' heben sie auf bis zu der zeit das Gott auf den menschen zirnt. da brengen sie die *kelalot* auch un' sie gehen selten lehr aus.

un' es wird ihr selbert der nach leid." According to either view, whether man's defenses be weakened by the defection of his star or the anger of God, the executers of the curse are the demons.[34]

Since the consummation of a curse may remain temporarily in abeyance, the threat hung over one's head like a poised sword. Some way out of this dilemma was ardently desired, and a formula was devised to meet this need:[35] "With the consent of the heavenly and earthly courts, of our sacred *Torah,* of the great and small Sanhedrins, and of this holy congregation, we release N son of N from all the curses, maledictions, oaths, vows . . . uttered in his home, or directed against him or any member of his household, be they his own curses or the curses of others against his person, or curses that he uttered against others, unwarrantedly or deservedly, in a moment of wrath or with malice prepense, intentionally or unintentionally, whatever their occasion or character. With the consent of God and of His celestial and terrestrial ménage, let them all be null and void, like unto a clay vessel that has been shattered. . . ." Solemnly pronounced by the religious authorities before the congregation, this formula provided the necessary psychological relief—now that God Himself had taken a hand in the matter the demons need no longer be feared.

5

THE SPIRITS OF THE DEAD

THE ties that bind man to his home and his associates are insoluble—even death cannot part them. Long after the body has departed this life, the spirit still frequents its ancient haunts, maintaining a shadowy connection with the world it knew and loved. This is the conception of death that has prevailed since man first had ideas on the subject, and it persists to this day more or less overtly. Among Jews it was never completely ousted by the doctrine of the immortality of the soul. After all, according to the prevailing polypsychism of the Middle Ages, man is possessed of several spirits: the soul, or *neshamah,* ascending to its Maker, leaves behind the *nefesh* and the *ruaḥ,* which are quite capable of performing the semi-terrestrial functions which tradition assigned to them. The *neshamah* departs for heaven as soon as the body is interred; the *nefesh* wanders forlornly back and forth between its former home and the grave during the week after burial and then also departs, but not for good—its longing for the body that formerly housed it brings it back to the grave many times, until after a year or so it is completely weaned away; the *ruaḥ* never forsakes its corporeal shell, even in death, but forever remains with the body. This scheme often broke down because the three terms were used interchangeably, so that it is uncertain whether the reference is to the "soul" in heaven, or the "spirit" on earth, but this much is abundantly clear: a spirit continues to inhabit the earth long after the body has moldered in the grave, and comes into frequent contact with the living.[1]

Countless anecdotes and traditions bear testimony to the belief in the continuance of some form of spirit life on earth. Medieval Jewish literature does not lack its share of ghost stories. From them we may deduce that the spirits foregather nightly by the light of the moon—according to Eleazar of Worms, the spirit is like a flame, and "this is why flickering lights are to be seen in a cemetery at night"—they converse with one another, or pursue their studies, very much as they did in this life. Occasionally a spirit council is called to adjudge disputes between the latest arrivals and older members of the company. On New Moon and *Hoshanah Rabbah* (the seventh day of the festival of Tabernacles), and probably on other nights as well, they congregate in prayer meetings, when they bespeak the well-being of the living. Some nights they gather in the synagogue, where, clothed in ghostly prayer-shawls, they conduct their own weird service. Once a man who fell asleep in a synagogue and was locked in by the sexton awoke to find himself in the midst of such a spirit congregation; to his amazement he discerned the forms of two men who were still among the living. Sure enough, within a few days these two passed away. Just prior to the attack on the community of Mainz during the First Crusade two men testified that they had listened in on such a ghostly service; their experience was interpreted by the congregation as a token of impending doom. The custom of knocking on the synagogue door before entering in the morning was probably intended to warn the spirit worshipers that it was time to leave.

Occasionally there are reports of encounters with less fortunate spirits—those who had been doomed to expiate worldly sins by various forms of penance. One such relates that a man who was traveling alone on a moon-lit night espied a long column of carts, drawn by men, while others sat in them. When they drew near he questioned them and learned that they were spirits of the dead, and that this was their punishment; when the cart-drawers grew tired, they got in and the others took hold of the shafts. *Sefer Ḥasidim* contains a score of such weird tales. Nor was it unknown for spirits to put in an appearance among the living during the daytime. An undertaker in Worms, coming to the synagogue one morning, recognized on the steps of the building a man whom he had recently buried. To his astonished queries the ghost replied that he had been transported to Paradise in reward for his pious life on earth; his visit home was merely to apprise his friends of his good fortune. The wreath of leaves that he wore, he explained, was made of herbs from the Garden of Eden, and was intended "to neutralize the foul odor of this world." He could afford to be disdainful of the world he had left behind! [2]

A frequent source of spirit intrusion upon the living is to be discerned in the notion that "the spirits retain their bodily forms," and apparently they retain too their former ideas of propriety and modesty. At any rate, they confront the living, usually in dreams, with complaints about their mistreatment by living beings, especially when the grave has been tampered with. More commonly, however, the plaint concerns, of all things, dress! A girl whose father had been too poor to provide her with a shroud could not come out into the open to foregather with the other spirits, and begged that her nakedness be clothed; another spirit, who had been buried with the sleeve of his shroud torn, said "he was ashamed before the others, who had whole garments, while his were torn." Visits of this nature were repeated until the grave was opened and the defect remedied.[3]

Similarly, the associations made in life are continued beyond the grave. The spirit likes to find itself among friends, or at least among others of its own station and character. The desire of Jacob to be buried with his ancestors (Gen. 47:30) was explained in this way, and so was the common injunction not to inter a wicked man among the righteous, nor even a "confirmed sinner" alongside a "moderate sinner," "for undoubtedly the righteous derive pleasure from a good neighbor even after death." Nor are quarrels extinguished by death: "two enemies should not be buried near one another, for they enjoy no rest together." Spirits who find themselves in uncongenial company may be counted on to plague the living in retaliation for this bad turn. In the event that one enemy precedes the other to the grave, the one left behind is in for an uncomfortable time, for spirits have long memories. "One should be very careful," counseled *Sefer Ḥasidim,* "that a dying man have no ground to distrust him, for the deceased will certainly seek revenge." It was already the custom in Talmudic times to beg pardon of the dead, in the presence of ten men at the grave, for any wrong done him, and this practice persisted throughout the Middle Ages. Better far to confess and be absolved than to face the wrath of his spirit.[4]

The Talmud discussed at length the question whether the dead are conscious of events that transpire among the living, and in raising the issue indicated that there was a strong positive sentiment on this point. In the Middle Ages it was no longer an issue. Nothing is hidden from the spirits, though naturally they are most interested in matters that affect themselves. When a man decided to make a musical instrument out of the remainder of some wood that had been used for a coffin, the spirit of the deceased warned him in a dream to refrain, and when he persisted caused him to fall seriously ill, until his son smashed the offending instrument at the grave of the perturbed spirit and left the pieces there; only then was his father's health restored. The dead are quite aware of everything that is said here on earth; laudatory or derogatory remarks concerning them are promptly rewarded or punished. Because of the alertness of the spirits to human actions, pious deeds performed on their behalf, such as prayer, charity, ascetic practices, lighting candles, have a double utility besides their purely ritual significance—they serve to improve the lot of the soul in the realm to which it has been transported, and they give "pleasure" to the spirit. Nor do they go unrewarded. The spirit, in its turn, "prays for the well-being of the living." Even activities not directly intended for the benefit of the dead, but reflecting credit upon them, delight their spirits, as when a son "pursues the way of the *Torah* and the commandments and does what is right and good." [5]

Obviously the spirits can help as well as harm the living. They have more or less direct access to the heavenly fount of justice, and by their intercession can avert an evil decree or produce a beneficial one. Here apparently it is the "soul" that is operative rather than the more terrestrial "spirit." Tradition has it that the righteous are granted one request when they reach heaven, but popular practice accorded them much more influence than that. In early times, and indeed until this very day in the Orient, a common method of winning favor in heaven was to make a pilgrimage to the grave of a saint or a sage, and to transmit one's request through him. An observant visitor to the tomb of Simon bar Yoḥai, for instance, at Meron, Palestine, will discern a host of written entreaties for the saint's aid heaped about his sepulchre. However, saint worship was never a part of Judaism and in medieval Europe even this custom fell altogether into desuetude.

None the less the ancient practice of visiting the cemetery to entreat the good offices of deceased relatives or scholars persisted. According to Judah the Pious, "one should not visit a grave twice in one day, but should unburden himself in a single session, and not return until the morrow." In addition to such individual visits, there grew up the custom of the entire congregation repairing to the cemetery annually on several occasions, such as the seven "rain-fasts," and on *Tisha' B'ab*, the anniversary of the destruction of the temple, and on the eves of New Year and the Day of Atonement, "that the dead may beseech mercy on our behalf." At least one of the reports displays a liberalism which echoes the catholicity of the custom, for "when there is no Jewish cemetery at hand," we are informed, "we go to a Christian cemetery." Many rabbis were disturbed by such goings-on. Unable to halt so deeply entrenched a usage, they tried at least to refine the spirit of the act. "One should not concentrate his attention on the dead who lie there," they wrote, "but should direct his prayer for mercy to God Himself, because of the merit of the righteous dwellers in the dust." The implied criticism is ample testimony concerning the popular interpretation of these rites.[6]

The spirits of the dead can be useful to the living in other ways, too. The future is an open book to the denizens of the supernatural realm, and like the demons and the angels, the deceased can by eavesdropping pick up the latest decisions of the court on high; "they flit through the universe to hear what has been decreed." Then they report back to intimates on earth, in dreams or in personal appearances. Sometimes this is in fulfillment of a compact entered into while still among the living. But in general the spirit-world is chary of its secrets and can be induced to reveal them only by magical means. As with demons and angels, mystical invocations and occult rites are effective in forcing the dead to obey the magician's will. The art of necromancy is a specialized function of sorcery.[7]

But the deceased were also inevitably regarded with a sense of dread. For all their usually beneficent attitude toward the living, they were still members of the unknown and uncanny spirit world, possessed of illimitable power—power for ill as well as for good. Witness the spirits of evil men which are assimilated to the demonic ranks, and become implacable enemies of humankind! It was best, at any rate, to keep on their good side, to seek their forgiveness, to obey their commands, to pray for their repose. Quite a few instances were related of the punishment visited upon foolhardy people; because of disobedience some fell ill and even died. One who neglected the precaution of expiating his sin toward a dead enemy saw him in a dream and heard the rhetorical question, "Do you imagine that the dead have no power to do harm?" Before he could gather his wits for a reply the spirit itself supplied the answer: it seized him by the "sinew of the thigh-vein" and wrenched it sharply. Nor was it only a dream. Forever after he suffered intense pain in that spot. Thus it would seem that dream contacts with the dead are quite real. Therefore one must beware not to accept anything from a spirit in a dream, or to kiss him; even more one should not kiss a corpse, or in a paroxysm of grief grasp the hand of the deceased and wildly pray that one may accompany him to the grave. This would be virtually "to bring death on oneself."

Sometimes the spirits invite the living to come along with them; to consent is tantamount to sealing one's death warrant. A person who has received such a grim invitation must repair to the grave of his would-be host and, having shed his shoes, must lie down on the mound and cry out three times, "By the will of God, and by my own will, I do not intend to go along with you or with any other deceased. Do not come after me, or after any of my beloved, you or your emissary, for my desire is to live in this world and not in the other." In the event that a spirit has threatened a living man, it is advisable to exorcise the dead in this manner: "With the consent of the celestial and earthly tribunals I conjure you in the name of the God of heaven and of earth, and by all the holy Names, that you desist from pursuing any human, whether man or woman, adult or child, near or far, and that you do them no harm with your body or your spirit or your soul. Your body must lie in its grave until resurrection, your soul must rest in that place where it belongs. I command this upon you with a curse and with an oath, now and forever." Any sensible spirit who understands the force of such a spell will thenceforth leave the living in peace.[8]

A curious conceit which was barely mentioned in the Talmudic literature came to have considerable significance in later times. In order to emphasize the sanctity and the importance of the Sabbath the early rabbis had pictured the day of rest as invading even *Gehinnom,* the realm in which the wicked expiate their sins. On the Sabbath its fires are banked, its tortures suspended, the spirits who are serving time there released to roam the earth. Even the souls of the wicked enjoy a weekly day of peace and respite! But when at eventide the angel Dumah, who has charge over them, herds them back to another week of torment they must obey his summons, however reluctantly.

Out of this fable succeeding ages erected an imposing structure of superstition. During the Middle Ages the belief that the spirits of the wicked are at large on the Sabbath played a most important part in the popular apprehension of the dead. While a degree of compassion was evidenced in the frequent admonitions (first uttered in Geonic times) to draw out the final Sabbath prayers so that the sinners might gain a few more moments of freedom, for they do not return to *Gehinnom* until the service is concluded, the prevailing note was one of dread. More than once the opinion was expressed that the evil spirits who, according to the Talmud, people the shadows on Friday nights, are none other than these souls of the wicked. They were known even to invade the synagogue. The *Maḥzor Vitry* offered a unique explanation of the special prayers introduced on Friday nights to prolong the service so that tardy worshipers might catch up with the congregation; the usual excuse was that it might be dangerous for them to go home alone, but according to this work, the danger lay instead in their being left alone in the synagogue at a time when, on this one night of freedom, the spirits might decide to visit the house of worship. But the greatest fear centered about those moments at the end of the day when the spirits were being driven back to their penance. There was the ever-present possibility that some might evade the angel's vigilance—if only for a short while—and vent their spleen upon innocent, unsuspecting humans. The Talmud had specified Tuesday and Friday nights as the occasions on which the demons were most to be feared; a later addendum included "the expiration of the Sabbath." [9]

The consequences of this belief and the dread it aroused were various. Several protective selections were inserted in the concluding service of the Sabbath, most prominent among them being Ps. 91, "the anti-demonic psalm." The *Habdalah* ritual, which marked the beginning of the new week, had long included as one of its features the smelling of pungent spices. It became customary to offer as an explanation of this rite the above legend; "when the Sabbath is over the fires of *Gehinnom* are rekindled and emit a fearful stench; we therefore smell these spices so that they may protect us from the foul odor of Hell." (Another common explanation was that the spices strengthened the body against the departure of the "additional soul" which inhabited it on the Sabbath.) The widely observed abstention from any form of labor on Saturday evening was due to the fear of these spirits. Israel Isserlein told a gruesome story to excuse his own meticulous care to refrain from activity. A scribe once got busy with his work as soon as the Sabbath was out; after he had stopped for the night "there came one who completed the book for him," but when the stranger ran out of parchment he stripped the skin off the poor scribe's back and continued his scribbling on it. The implication of the story is obvious.[10]

Another curious offshoot of this belief, the history of which is too tortuous to go into here in detail, was the notion that one who drank water or ate any food toward twilight on the Sabbath was "robbing his dead." Briefly, the original source of this idea was traced to a late Midrashic statement that each day at eventide Dumah releases the spirits in his charge—and now it is not only the spirits of the wicked, but all the dead during their first year after decease, before they have been assigned to permanent abodes—to gambol in the fields, to eat the fruit hanging on the trees and drink the water in the streams. "Therefore, whoever drinks water at twilight robs his dead." During the Middle Ages, in Germany and Northern France (in Provence, Spain, Italy and England the practice was unknown), this statement was associated with the idea of the Sabbath-rest of the spirits, and it became obligatory to refrain from consuming water or foodstuffs only on the Sabbath toward evening. In some places this prohibition was observed by everyone, but in most it was limited to those who had lost a near relative within the year. Still a further variation upon this motif transferred the prohibition to Friday evening, the explanation given being that the souls of the wicked, immediately on their release, plunge into the streams to cool off.

It seems more than probable that this last version contains the clew to the whole business. The story about "robbing the dead" is certainly too strained to account for the entire complex. Evidently two distinct elements are fused here; the one, fear of swallowing anything that might have been contaminated by spirits at the two critical moments, the beginning and the conclusion of the day of rest; the other, the Midrashic fable, which was so twisted as to fit the superstition. The only feature of the custom that derives from the second element is the provision that it is limited to mourners, but it is significant that the earlier sources speak of it as being observed by everyone, and that water from streams and wells in particular was avoided. Dread of the spirits, rather than compassion for the deceased, undeniably informs this usage.[11]

6

THE POWERS OF GOOD

DEPUTY ANGELS

THE characteristic and distinguishing feature of medieval Jewish magic was the function which it assigned to the angels, the agents of God. The magical use of angels was of course predicated upon the assumption that the world is very thickly populated with them, and that they play a unique rôle in nature. The figures vary from a mere few hundred thousand all the way up to 496,000 myriads—and these are only partial estimates.[1] We may readily believe this when we learn that every single thing on earth, animate or inanimate, from man through all of creation, birds and beasts, trees and brooks, even to the last blade of grass, owns its angelic representative above. This is the heart of the angel-lore. Houses and cities, winds and seasons, months and hours and days, each star above, each speck of dust underfoot, no thing in nature or in fancy exists independently of its *memuneh,* its heavenly "deputy" (literally, "appointed one").[2] These "deputies" are the agents through whom the universe operates [3]—in fact, the activities that go on in the world are nothing more than reflections of their acts. "It is a well-known 'mystery' that no nation is destroyed until its celestial 'prince' has first fallen." This belief was coupled with the conception of astrology that each man is accompanied by a star which governs his existence, so that we have sometimes the cumbersome duplication, the angel, or "deputy" of a man's star, both charged with guiding and guarding him, the ultimate responsibility residing with the angel. "Every affair in which a man is engaged here on earth is first indicated up above by the angel of his star." [4]

These angels are both representatives and defenders of their earthly charges in the heavenly courts, as well as motivators of action below. The "deputy angels" of birds or animals or men who have been wrongly dealt with plead their cause before God and see just punishment meted out to the malefactors. Similarly, the angels who preside over "places, stones and wood" are held responsible if a man stumbles and falls because of them. "When the time comes for a righteous man to die, the deputy of the star which is ruling at the moment begs that he may not die just then, for that deputy will be held accountable for his death." If a man's prayers are to be answered, the angel of his star must have first offered them directly before the Throne of Glory. In like manner, good fortune in business results from the intervention of a man's deputy angel, who "enters men's hearts" and induces them to deal with him to his advantage. One must consider the habits of the "deputies" as well as of the demons in rebuilding a house, and be careful not to alter the position of doors and windows, else the wrath of both will descend upon his head. "This is one of those things which, though very similar to the forbidden 'ways of the Amorite,' is nevertheless permitted," we are assured by a thirteenth-century source. A later writer used this warning to account for the fear of inhabiting new homes.[5]

This idea constitutes the main theoretical basis of medieval Jewish magic. Ubiquitous and all-powerful, the "deputy angels" were the perfect medium through which the sorcerer, when he had acquired the requisite secret knowledge and skill, could influence man and nature to obey him. His charms and operations were intended to bring under his sway the particular "deputies" who could effect his will at the moment. "There are incantations which work on water but not on land, and others, intended for the deputies who preside over the land which have no effect on water." The long lists in such a work as *Sefer Raziel* are proof of the arduous training that the novice in magic must undergo if he would learn how to direct all the *memunim* of air, wind, date, time, place, etc., which control a situation at a given moment. Further, since a deputy's province is prescribed by his very nature, the sorcerer must know how to substitute another, better suited to his designs, and thus effect a change in nature itself.[6]

We have some detailed, if sometimes not too clear, explanations of just how this "deputy" magic worked. In the case of a man who by an incantation had succeeded in discovering the identity and whereabouts of a thief, we are informed, the *memuneh* who had been invoked disclosed them not by appearing in person to convey the information, but by concentrating on the facts and "mingling" his thought with the thought of the magician. If the identity of the thief was known, but the hiding-place of the booty was not, then it might be discovered more directly by invoking the thief's "deputy." The familiar device of fashioning an image of one's enemy out of wax, or of drawing his portrait on a wall, and by piercing it with pins or nails causing him to suffer in a corresponding part of his body, operated along similar lines. The magician's "deputy" transmitted the blow to the victim's angel, who in turn inflicted it upon his human charge; sometimes a third intermediary was introduced into the process, the "deputy" of the image or picture. Desired dreams were induced by the angel in charge of such dreams who had been invoked for this purpose. And so on through the entire repertoire of magic devices, all were consummated through the intermediacy of the angels, or "deputies," who were subjected to the sorcerer's will by his magic art.[7]

This system was a singular translation of Platonic idealism into the theosophical lingo of the early *Kabbalah,* though to call it a "system" is to dignify it with an order and logic it made no claim to possess. It took shape through incidental attempts to rationalize on a single plane the effects of nature and magic, on the basis of those philosophical and mystical concepts which were current in medieval Jewish thought; one might say in thirteenth-century German-Jewish thought, for it was during this century and in this locale that the conception was elaborated and attained its greatest popularity. *Sefer Ḥasidim* and the works of Eleazar of Worms display the influence of this doctrine on almost every page. The unparalleled luxuriousness of invention that characterized thirteenth-century Jewish angelology, sired by this theory, seems at first glance to have been a striking departure from traditional Jewish belief. But a brief review of the development of Jewish angel-lore discloses its thoroughly orthodox mystical antecedents.

Scripture knew the angels as ministers in the celestial court, serving and glorifying God, occasionally acting as messengers and agents to perform His will on earth. The writer of the late book of Daniel was the first to individualize angels and to endow them with names and titles. In the Talmudic period the Biblical angelology was elaborated and enriched in three directions: angelic ministration was frequently inferred in Biblical narratives which made no mention of it, thus broadening the concept of angels as intermediaries between man and God; the personality of the angels was more clearly delineated through an effort to describe them, to name the more important ones, and to accord them peculiar spheres of influence, so that we have "princes" of fire, of hail, of rain, of night, of the sea, of healing, and so on; and finally they were appointed man's guardians to accompany him through his daily routine. The Essenes were said to have possessed an especially well-developed angel-lore, and the Enoch literature, reflecting Gnostic sources, had much to say concerning them, and implied their control of nature, man, and the future.[8] These two founts of mystical doctrine, while never formally admitted into Jewish thought and in fact frowned upon by rabbinic authorities, exercised a profound influence upon the extramural activities of the mystics. Their expanding doctrine was in no sense systematically organized during this period, and it remained in a fluid, uncoordinated state throughout its succeeding development. But the early literature contained ample seed for a rich later growth, which it experienced in the Geonic period, when a highly esoteric doctrine grew up, portions of which found literary expression in such works as the *Hechalot, Otiot de R. Akiba,* parts of *Sefer Raziel,* etc.

Along with this elaboration of angelology went its practical corollary, the utilization of angels in magic. The Talmud, though speaking often of angelic apparitions, knew nothing of the conjuration of angels as distinguished from the conjuration of demons. At most, there appears to have existed during the Talmudic period the practice of calling upon, or praying to the angels, as intermediaries before God, to intercede in a crisis.[9] Even Geonic mysticism was reserved on this point, but evidently during this later period, which saw so marked a development of angelology, the Talmudic prayer had been transformed into a magical invocation, as the *Aramaic Incantation Texts,* published by Montgomery, and such a work as the *Sword of Moses,* edited by Gaster, indicate. This was the foundation upon which thirteenth-century German-Jewish mysticism built an imposing structure of angel-magic. The earliest reference to angelic "deputies" that I have encountered in rabbinic sources occurs in the late *Midrash* to Psalms,[10] composed probably during the tenth century in Southern Italy. This work undoubtedly embodied much older material, but the absence of this concept in the Talmudic literature, and the fact that eastern Jewish mysticism entered Europe through the south of Italy at about this time, stamp it as a product of Geonic mystical speculation. The expansion of the *memuneh* doctrine in Germany, where it was introduced by the Kalonymides, into a veritable theosophy, embracing and crowning all the elements of earlier Jewish angelology, was the historically logical consequence of the Geonic development. But its emergence and popularization during the thirteenth century must be seen as one phase of the generally heightened superstitious atmosphere of contemporary Europe. The Gnostic-Manichæan heresies that had plagued the Church since the tenth century had sown widely and deeply in Christian circles the seed of ancient mystical lore. Jewish thought could not have been unaffected by such a heightening of mystical sensitiveness in such close proximity; the more so because it was already acquainted with a closely related doctrine. The wave that broke over Christian society inundated the Jewish community as well.

ATTRIBUTES AND FUNCTIONS

Despite this rich angelology northern Jewry raised few questions as to the origin of the angels, the elements of which they are constituted, their outward appearance—they were simply there, in the heaven above, clustered about the throne of glory, or all about one on earth, performing their heaven-ordained tasks, and no questions asked. The furthest that Eleazar of Worms would go in describing them was to say that they are "tenuous substance, as unsubstantial as the wind, which cannot be seen." [11]

This conception, however, created certain difficulties of a metaphysical and practical nature. If the angels are pure spirit, how can they be said to achieve the material effects which tradition ascribed to them, and magic demanded of them? Maimonides, the consistent and indomitable rationalist, denied altogether the possibility of the physical apparition of angels as well as the objective reality of the effects attributed to angel-magic, and dismissed them as self-delusion or optical illusions. So uncompromising a view, however, found few adherents. The Spanish philosophers Naḥmanides and Judah Halevi acknowledged the reality of angelic apparitions, but stipulated that they required a special perspicuity of vision on the part of the beholders. In the north of Europe even this last condition was excluded: angels possess the power to assume human (and animal) forms, and to appear in the society of man as completely physical beings, on a par with himself. In fact such transformations were common occurrences, the "prince of a man's star" frequently adopting the shape of his human charge and descending from on high to tread the earth. And if one demands an explanation of the process by which the transmutation of spirit into matter occurs, the answer is quite simple: "This is the great 'mystery' by which the holy angels appear on earth as men, or as other creatures, in accordance with God's will or by their own desire: they take some earth from beneath the heavenly pile, clothe themselves in a clod of this earth, and descend to eat and drink with men." [12]

One characteristic of the angels, in particular, merits attention both because of the frequency with which it was mentioned, and because of its practical consequences for religious and magical rites. Petitions were often addressed to heaven by way of the intervening angels. God, omniscient, comprehends all tongues, but the official language of the celestial court is Hebrew, and unfortunately the angels are monolingual (or, it may be, if they do have knowledge of foreign languages they choose to ignore communications addressed in them.) This principle was advanced in the Talmud, and since Aramaic was the spoken language of the people, the warning against praying in Aramaic was made especially emphatic. Only in the sickroom might one employ other tongues than Hebrew, for there the *Shechina,* the Presence of God, was believed to hover over the head of the invalid, and received the prayer directly.

This belief persisted in the Middle Ages and was utilized to explain, if weakly, the Aramaic prayers that are to be found in the ritual, and in particular, certain Aramaic lines in the *Kaddish:* they were couched in this language so that they might be unintelligible to the angels, for their contents were such as might annoy them, or arouse their envy of the superlative piety of the Jews. It was this belief too that made necessary the bestowal of a Hebrew name upon every Jew, in addition to his secular name, and the use exclusively of the Hebrew name in the course of a religious rite, for the angels certainly could not be expected to recognize an individual by any other. Even in the grave this principle still obtained. The Kabbalistic doctrine of *Ḥibbut ha-Kever,* which was familiar in Northern Europe, envisaged a three-day period, immediately succeeding burial, of interrogations and beatings by the angel of death, during which the deceased must identify himself by his Hebrew name. Woe betide him if it had slipped his memory! [13]

Of course, this idea met with frequent objections, and the retort of certain medieval commentators to the original statement in the Talmud should have permanently demolished it: "You say that even the thought hidden in a man's heart they know, and yet the Aramaic language is beyond their comprehension!" [14] But the sarcasm made hardly a dent in the popularity of the notion, and the angels as linguists remained in bad repute. This conception was not limited, however, to the sphere of ritual. In the practice of medieval Jewish magic it assumed more than academic importance. The literature was sometimes written in the vernacular, the directions being given in Aramaic or in Yiddish, but the charm itself, the magical command, when intended for angelic ears, appeared usually in Hebrew. However unorthodox in principle, magic is perhaps the most tradition-bound of cultural forms. The Jewish sorcerer, no matter how far he may have wandered at times from the spirit of official Judaism, could not free himself from those orthodox traditions that bore directly on his technique. If in fifteenth- and sixteenth-century manuscripts the order appears occasionally reversed, the incantations proper being couched in Yiddish, these usually bear the earmarks of direct transference from the German.

Individual angels with peculiarly angelic functions and forms, of a sort, entered intimately into the life of the medieval Jew. The ancient norms remained fixed, except that angels appeared much more frequently in the pages of medieval authors. Their prime function was still the adoration and service of God, but that service brought them into more frequent contact with men.[15] "The angels are the messengers of God; He impresses His will upon them and sends them forth to do His bidding," wrote Eleazar of Worms, and he explained that this work keeps them constantly occupied, for so many new tasks continually await them that they must rush to complete the present one. They can do nothing of their own will, he said, but act only upon God's command—a view which, while true to the traditional belief, cannot be reconciled with the part the angels were forced to play in medieval magic, for this implied a considerable degree of independence of God's will. Much closer to the prevailing opinion was the statement found in a Geonic responsum: "There are many acts which angels can perform of their own accord, without a special order from above. Therefore amulets are written and names spoken, to aid the angels in these matters." But when they are acting as messengers of the Lord, they carry out only one mandate at a time. Many of them have specific functions or fields of activity, and the orders which fall within their scope are of course assigned to them.[16]

God's will opens up to them His entire domain. Medieval Jews believed in an especially vigilant Providence which presided over the most intimate and minute details of human life, and which operated through the angels. They carried out the celestial orders and often appeared in human or animal form to exact the required punishment for transgressions of God's law, or, by "mingling" their thought with his, led man to make decisions which might run counter to his previously expressed intentions, and to perform acts out of keeping with his character and will.[17]

Viewed in this light the angels were the mechanism through which God maintained a close contact with His universe. But these angelic intermediaries could carry messages both ways, and the ancient practice of calling upon the angels rather than God directly in prayer became very widespread during this period. Indeed, the whole force of the mystical movement which stressed the secret values hidden in the letters and the words of the liturgy was directed toward bringing into rapport the angels who could most effectively reach the ear of the heavenly court. Finally, the position of the angels in heaven made accessible to them the founts of mystic lore; they were the source of that secret wisdom to which the mystic aspired. To them he turned for inspiration, and if his piety and learning—and sometimes his skill in magic—warranted it, his quest was not unrewarded. The book *Raziel* is supposed to have been transmitted to Adam by the angel of that name; Eleazar of Worms, who, incidentally, had a hand in the concoction of that work, boasted of his intimacy with various angels; a few centuries later we learn of a Kabbalist, Samson of Ostropol by name, who "was visited daily by an angel who taught him the mysteries of the *Torah*." Many a great mystic was reputed to have sat at the feet of such celestial mentors.[18]

Yet we learn little more concerning individual angels than their names and their functions; our authors were not interested in the angel but in his availability for magical ends. Occasionally some information culled from the mystical tradition is passed on, but with an air of pedantic scholarship. Metatron, the demiurge of classical Jewish mysticism, was important only because his name is the mathematical equivalent of *Shaddai,* one of God's names. Sandalfon is "taller than his comrades by a distance of five hundred years," it is true, but his significance lay in his intimate attendance upon the person of God Himself.[19] Dumah, who presides over the realm of the dead, the angels of destruction, others familiar from Talmudic times make their appearance. The Angel of Death retains his especial rôle in human affairs. The archangels still people the pages of medieval mystical lore, but their association with the planets obscures whatever individual characters they may have formerly possessed. The Name has swallowed up the Angel.

The position which the angel-deputy occupied in mystical speculation and magical practice made of medieval Jewish angelology so ambiguous and uncertain a field as to present peculiar problems of definition. In theory, of course, the *memunim* were angels, and as such inherited all the angelic attributes of form and character and function which had been delineated in the ancient literature. In fact, however, it may be questioned whether they were anything more to the medieval Jew than the mere names which served to identify them.

To set them to work the magician must know just which angels were involved in a specific set of conditions—which meant, in effect, that he must know the *names* of these angels, for the name was the controlling factor. The proliferation of angelic *names,* which accompanied the practice of medieval Jewish magic, tended to obscure the angelic personality, so that in the end the name itself became the prime consideration. Already during the Geonic period, writes Montgomery, "The angels came to be but plays on roots, invocations of the attributes or activities of deity, so that finally angel was merely synonymous with charm." [20] The angel was the theory which explained the practice. The practice itself raises the question: when is an angel more than a mere name? It would be extravagant to assert that the endless procession of angelic names with which *Sefer Raziel,* for example, regales us had any real relation to the angels themselves, or that it evoked in its medieval readers visions of definite creatures. So far as these unnumbered hosts, often so fantastically denominated, were concerned, the impression gained from a study of the literature is that we are really dealing here with a dual category. The one comprised the true angels as tradition painted them, the other, a vast multitude of mystical names, designated as angels and in theory accepted as such—an angelic host in suspension, so to speak, capable of being precipitated into its individual angelic components—but actually significant only for the mystical powers inherent in the name itself.

7

"IN THE NAME OF . . ."

THE POTENCY OF THE NAME

OUTSTANDING among those beliefs that are universally characteristic of the religion of superstition is the conviction that "a man's name is the essence of his being" (one Hebrew text says "a man's name is his person" and another, "his name is his soul"). This doctrine elevated the process of naming a child into one of major importance. The name carried with it all the associations it had accumulated in history, and stamped the character of its earlier owners upon its new bearer, so that the choice of a name was fraught with grave responsibility. But the desire to bless a child with a richly endowed name was balanced by the fear that the soul of its previous owner would be transported into the body of the infant—a fear which stood in the way of naming children after living parents or after any living persons, and thus robbing them of their soul and their life. This dread led indeed in some cases to a superstitious refusal to adopt the name even of a dead ancestor, since this would oblige the soul to forsake its heavenly abode and re-enter the realm of the living. It must have been this line of reasoning—if reason it is—that prompted Judah the Pious to provide in his testament that "none of his descendants shall be called by his name, Judah, or by his father's name, Samuel." Such a far-fetched extension of the superstition, however, was rare; the usual procedure was to name children after ancestors.

It was often observed that his name is the mainspring not only of a person's character, but also of his fate. Certain names bring good fortune, others, bad; the "heavenly decrees" that are associated with them determine which. One can discover the latent import of a name only by a close study of the lives of individuals who have borne it. It would be the height of rashness to saddle a youngster with a name whose owners have been unfortunate, or have died young, or have been murdered. The name that caused the misfortune would bring bad luck with it. For the same reason a widow or widower should not marry a person with the same name as the deceased mate. "Nor is all this to be regarded as silly superstition," we are solemnly assured; the writer testified to its truth from his own wide experience.

Confronted with two individuals of the same name, the spirits were as likely as not to choose the wrong one upon whom to lavish their unwelcome attentions. An angel executing a decree of sickness or death might visit it upon the first who answered to the designated name. Such things happened, as several anecdotes attest. The superstition against naming a child after a living person was consequently strengthened, and with it an avoidance of duplicating names in one family. A marriage in which the bride or groom bore the name of one of the in-laws, or which united two families owning a name in common, was discountenanced as imprudent indeed. Nor should several families with a common name reside in one dwelling. In such cases the spirits would be absolutely at a loss to distinguish the one from the other. People went so far as to avoid entering the home of a sick person who bore their name; should it be the moment assigned for the death stroke the hale might be assaulted in place of the ill. Yet, however solicitously these precautions were observed, it was not without some misgivings about their respectability. The same writer who protested that they were by no means "superstitions" offered a half-apology for advancing them: "Although one should not believe in superstitions," he wrote, to recall a previously quoted remark, "yet it is best to be heedful of them." Well, "heedful" his readers were, whether they believed or not.[1]

The essential character of things and of men resides in their names. Therefore to know a name is to be privy to the secret of its owner's being, and master of his fate. The members of many primitive tribes have two names, one for public use, the other jealously concealed, known only to the man who bears it. Even the immediate members of the family never learn what it is; if an enemy should discover it, its bearer's life is forfeit. In highest antiquity and in our own day, among the most primitive and the most civilized peoples, the occult power that inheres in the name is recognized, and the name itself is known to be a mighty and awesome force in the hands of the magician.[2]

To know the name of a man is to exercise power over him alone; to know the name of a higher, supernatural being is to dominate the entire province over which that being presides. The more such names a magician has garnered, the greater the number of spirits that are subject to his call and command. This simple theory is at the bottom of the magic which operates through the mystical names and words that are believed to control the forces which in turn control our world. The spirits guarded their names as jealously as ever did a primitive tribe. "Tell me, I pray thee, thy name," Jacob demanded of the angel with whom he had wrestled, but the angel parried the question and his name remained his secret, lest Jacob invoke him in a magical incantation and he be obliged to obey.[3] But a vast mystic lore of angel-names was inherited by medieval Jews, and expanded by them, so that many were initiated into these mysteries, and possessed the power to invoke the spirits. Higher than all, however, stands God—and the names of God which Jewish ingenuity invented (or discovered?) placed in the hands of the Jewish magician unlimited powers to manipulate God's world.

This belief was the source of considerable theological uneasiness, as we may well imagine. Its foremost adherents, namely Germanic Jewry, pious and God-fearing, found it difficult to square the undoubted powers which the Name accorded with the omnipotence of God, who Himself appeared to be subordinated to His name by this doctrine. All that they could do, in the effort to reconcile theology with superstition, was to evade the problem by asserting at the same time the power of the Name and the power of God. "One may not say that the invocation of God's Name obliges Him to do the will of the invoker, that God Himself is coerced by the recital of His Name; but the Name itself is invested with the power to fulfill the desire of the man who utters it." [4] The Name possesses an autonomous potency. And with this the theologians were obliged to content themselves.

ABRACADABRA

A characteristic feature of the evolution of magic has been its easy passage from the invocation of celestial beings to the manipulation of mere names, or words. Even though medieval Jewry insisted that it called upon the names of definite supernatural beings, it is obvious that this was nothing more than a polite bow in the direction of theological scruple. And just as in the magic that flourished on the periphery of other religions, so in Jewish magic, nominalism of this sort made room for the magic word, as well as the name.

Certain words come to assume occult virtues by reason of the tradition that has developed about them, or because of their fancied descent from the potent charms of ancient times or foreign peoples. As we have had occasion to note, magic is the most conservative of disciplines—like the law it clings to archaic forms long after they have lost currency. But its conservatism is not inspired by intellectual inertia. The very nature of magic demands a strict adherence to the original form of the magical name or word, for its potency lies hidden within its syllables, within its very consonants and vowels—the slightest alteration may empty the word of all its magic content. Inevitably, however, in the process of oral transmission of so secret a lore, and in its later literary transmission by all too fallible scribes, the word undergoes changes. In fact, since in time these words become unintelligible to the heirs of the tradition, often ignorant of their original sense and tongue, a process of mutilation sets in, which makes them altogether exotic and meaningless. Besides, we must give due weight to "the mystery which is thrown about magic rites; 'the wizards that squeak and gibber' (Is. 8:19) are universal; the Babylonian priest generally whispered his formulas; the solemn parts of Christian rites have likewise tended to inaudible pronunciation. There exists a tendency toward intentional obscuration of the formulas, which by psychological necessity would tend to even greater corruption." [5] The peculiar logic of magic makes a virtue of this process: the more barbaric the word the more potent it is likely to be. "So little is it necessary that the magic word possess any intelligible sense that most often it is considered efficacious in the degree that it *is* strange and meaningless, and words from foreign, incomprehensible tongues, in particular, are preferred."[6] Rashi, in the eleventh century, proved his familiarity with this phenomenon when he wrote: "The sorcerer whispers his charms, and doesn't understand what they are or what they mean, but . . . the desired effect is produced only by such incantations." [7] The repertoire of the Cherokee medicine man comprises mostly archaic expressions that have conveyed no meaning for centuries; many aborigines in India, as do Tibetan and Chinese Buddhists, regard the ancient Sanskrit prayers, which are wholly unintelligible to them, as much more potent than their own. The "abracadabra" [7a] of the modern stage magician reflects a phenomenon familiar to us all.

This same process occurred in Jewish magic, and the incantations of the Middle Ages are replete with startlingly outlandish words that look and sound as though they had been filched from the vocabulary of a stuttering visitor from some distant planet. "But magic is in its purpose a scientific exercise, and we must suppose that in general something intelligible was once expressed by the now unintelligible term. Much of the later nonsense was the survival of phrases of the lost tongue in which the charms had their rise." Sometimes, underneath the accretions and mutilations of centuries, the original Latin or Greek word may peer dimly forth; sometimes by dint of a vast erudition and a vaster ingenuity, the scholar can chisel off a letter here and there, hammer on new ones, and with an inflection all his own, announce to a breathless world the etymology of such a term. To tell the truth, the game is a hazardous one, for scholars rarely agree, and the result is hardly worth the labor—except to a scholar. These words are important to the magician just because they are what they are and as they are. Restore their original form, so that the meaning is plain, and even the boldest magician would be ashamed to conjure with them.

In Jewish magic the natural infiltration of strange words and names was furthered by a significant element in the mystical tradition. The Pythagorean concept of the creative power of numbers and letters was known in *Tannaitic* times; the famous *Amora* Rab (about 200 C.E.) said of Bezalel that "he knew how to combine the letters by which heaven and earth were created." [8] The Geonic mystic lore made much of this doctrine, and in the *Sefer Yeẓirah* it was elevated into one of the pillars of the *Kabbalah*. It was especially popular in the German *Kabbalah* of the thirteenth century which above all insisted upon the mysterious powers inherent in the letters of the Hebrew alphabet and developed a fine art of combining and recombining these letters to evoke from them their highest potency. Itself the source of many new magical words and names, this exercise made it all the easier for foreign words to find a place in the magical vocabulary.

The distinction between the word and the name, however, is academic so far as Jewish magic was concerned. Among most peoples it is real enough—the name belongs to some supernatural personage, the word is significant in and for itself. If a process of assimilation occurs at all, it is the name that is swallowed up by the word. Jewish magic was too sophisticated (I think we may consider this a mark of sophistication, for belief in the efficacy of a word *per se* seems to be the more primitive and naïve attitude) to accord any weight to words—*all had become names* by the Middle Ages, and earlier. Behind each word—though in our wisdom we may be able to discern its humble origin—a celestial power was posited. Sometimes the apotheosis of the word achieved the height of extravagance, as we shall have occasion to see later; *Hocus Pocus,* for example, was a Prince on high—or two Princes, to be exact. The literature of Jewish magic was predominantly an anthology of magical names. In practice the point was of no importance, word or name, the magician's taste was catholic; in theory Jewish magic insisted on excluding the word as such from its purview.

The invocation of these names was the commonest feature of medieval Jewish magic. Incantations most often consisted of a name, or a series of names, with or without an accompanying action. An element of danger was recognized in the indiscriminate handling of such powerful forces—like charges of dynamite, they could destroy the unwary magician. "Wherever God's name is uttered improperly there death stalks." The practitioner was repeatedly warned to prepare himself conscientiously for his rites: to purify himself in body and soul with ritual cleansings, by abstention from women and from unclean things, by following a restricted diet, and even fasting, over a period of days. "If a man who is about to utter holy names does not properly sanctify himself beforehand, not only will he fail in his efforts, but he must expect to suffer for his presumption." "Names may be taught only to pious scholars and sages, who will not misuse them." One must not even dare utter holy names aloud; it sufficed to "meditate on them in one's heart." [9] But fear of the names, however marked, did not prevent their frequent use, as our literature amply demonstrates.

The powers that were ascribed to the names were limitless. Nothing in nature or in man's fancy lay beyond their reach. To select only a few of the feats attributed to them: Judah the Pious was said to have caused a window to close about the neck of a malefactor, imprisoning him in a magic vise; the same Judah imparted all his mystical learning to a pupil by having him lick up certain names that the teacher had outlined in the sand; names were used to kill and to resurrect; and most wonderful of all, by means of a name "the heart of man may be turned to fear the Lord, so that even the most wicked may become righteous"! [10]

THE GOLEM

The greatest feat to which the magician aspired was that of creation. Discussing this subject in the pages of the Talmud, R. Papa observed that the creative power of magic covered only gross and massive objects and creatures, such as the camel, but not fine and delicate things, and R. Eliezer maintained that the demons, to whom the magician owes this power, can create nothing smaller than a barley-corn. This was the standard limitation imposed on sorcerers by medieval writers, though, as the *Gemara* explained: "The demons cannot actually create even large beings, but merely assemble already created but unused primeval matter." [11] Thus the ultimate act of genesis was reserved for God alone. It was nowhere suggested that human life could be created by ordinary magical means.

But the Talmud recognized also a second method of creation, which required the application of the "Laws of Creation," probably an oral collection of mystical traditions relating to the original creation of the universe. The kind of magic comprised in these "Laws of Creation" was the only one that was "permitted *ab initio.*" By means of it, "if the righteous so desired they could create a universe. Raba created a man and sent him to R. Zeira, who conversed with him but he could not answer; so he exclaimed, 'You are created by magic, return to your dust!' Rabbis Ḥanina and Oshaya used to sit every Friday and occupy themselves with the *Book* [read: *Laws*] *of Creation* and create a three-year-old calf which they ate." For a description of this method we must rely on the tradition preserved by the commentators; Rashi wrote, "They used to combine the letters of the Name by which the universe was created; this is not to be considered forbidden magic, for the works of God were brought into being through His holy Name." The Talmudic *Laws of Creation* (unrelated to the later mystical *Book of Creation*) appear, then, to have been an exposition of the familiar name-magic, the foremost constituent of medieval Jewish practice, but in consonance with the difficulty and the prodigiousness of its object, a very exalted and esoteric department. Medieval Jews, like their Christian contemporaries, were avid of the power to create human life, and believed implicitly in man's ability to do so. William of Auvergne (thirteenth century) wrote, "Men have tried to produce, and thought that they succeeded in producing human life in other ways than by the usual generative process," but the methods pursued by non-Jews were less subtle than the one proposed by the Talmud. For example, a fourteenth-century Christian writer cited the Arab Rasis (tenth century) on generating a human being by putting an unnamed substance in a vase filled with horse manure, for three days.[12]

The thirteenth-century German *Ḥasidim* (Pietists and Mystics) were especially intrigued by this problem. From them comes the use of the word *golem* (literally, shapeless or lifeless matter) to designate a homunculus created by the magical invocation of names, and the entire cycle of *golem* legends may be traced back to their interest. The earliest individual about whom such a fable was woven appears to have been R. Samuel, father of Judah the Pious, who was said to have constructed such a homunculus which accompanied him on his travels and served him, but which could not speak. Joseph Delmedigo informs us, in 1625, that "many legends of this sort are current, particularly in Germany," and we may well believe him. Among the better-known of these legends is the one connected with the name of Elijah of Chelm (middle sixteenth century) which developed during the seventeenth century. He was reputed to have created a *golem* from clay by means of the *Sefer Yeẓirah,* inscribing the name of God upon its forehead, and thus giving it life, but withholding the power of speech. When the creature attained giant size and strength, the Rabbi, appalled by its destructive potentialities, tore the life-giving name from its forehead and it crumbled into dust. These legends of the *golem* were transferred, not before the eighteenth century, to R. Judah Löw b. Bezalel, without any historical basis. The remains of the Frankenstein monster which he is supposed to have brought into being are said still to be among the debris in the attic of Prague's *Altneuschule.*[13]

At least one mystic, the greatest of them all in Germany, Eleazar of Worms, had the daring to record the formula, which occurs again later in several versions. The formidable nature of the project is apparent from the merest glance at the twenty-three folio columns which the very involved combinations of letters occupy. The image was to be made of "virgin soil, from a mountainous place where no man has ever dug before," and the incantation, which comprised "the alphabets of the 221 gates," must be recited over every single organ individually. A further detail, often noted, was the incision upon the forehead of the name of God, or of the word *emet* ("truth"). The destruction of this creature was effected by removing that name, by erasing the initial letter of *emet,* leaving *met* ("dead"), or by reversing the creative combinations, for, as R. Jacob b. Shalom, who came to Barcelona from Germany in 1325, remarked, the law of destruction is nothing more than a reversal of the law of creation.[14]

Yet, while not doubting its possibility, medieval Jews were in general skeptical of their own ability to imbue dead matter with life, and modestly confessed that manipulation of names of such a high order was beyond them. A thirteenth-century writer scornfully castigated those who proposed to duplicate the feat of Ḥanina and Oshaya with the taunt that "they themselves are dumb calves." In 1615 Zalman Ẓevi of Aufenhausen published his reply (*Jüdischer Theriak*) to the animadversions of the apostate Samuel Friedrich Brenz (in his book *Schlangenbalg*) against the Jews on this score. Zalman Ẓevi wrote wittily, "The renegade said that there are those among the Jews who take a lump of clay, fashion it into the figure of a man, and whisper incantations and spells, whereupon the figure lives and moves. In the reply which I wrote for the Christians I made the turncoat look ridiculous, for I said there that he himself must be fashioned from just such kneaded lumps of clay and loam, without any sense or intelligence, and that his father must have been just such a wonder worker, for as he writes, we call such an image a *ḥomer golem* [an unshaped, raw mass of material], which may be rendered 'a monstrous ass' [a really good pun], which I say is a perfect description of him. I myself have never seen such a performance, but some of the Talmudic sages possessed the power to do this, by means of the *Book of Creation*. . . . We German Jews have lost this mystical tradition, but in Palestine there are still to be found some men who can perform great wonders through the *Kabbalah*. Our fools [another pun on the word *golem*] are not created out of clay, but come from their mothers' wombs."[15] His heavy sarcasm, though prompted by apologetic motives, expressed the general Jewish attitude on the subject—it can be done, but no longer by us.

THE EVOLUTION OF NAME-MAGIC

"The invocation of angelic names in Jewish magic may be regarded as in part the parallel to the pagan invocation of many deities, and in part as invocation of the infinite (personified) phases and energies of the one God. Both Jewish and pagan magic agreed in requiring the accumulation of as many names of the deity or demon as possible, for fear lest no one name exhaust the potentiality of the spiritual being conjured." Here we have a natural development in magic fostered by religious belief and by logical necessity. But it is possible to trace with some degree of certainty various extraneous influences which also contributed to such a development within Judaism.

The culture of ancient Israel reflected preponderantly the influence of the two civilizations that dominated the ancient world: Babylonia-Assyria and Egypt. In both the invocation of names of gods, and the multiplication of these names to ensure greater magical efficacy was well known and widely practiced. In the multiplicity of the gods of these lands (in Egypt "there were gods for every month, every day of the month, and every hour of the day"), and in such a phenomenon as the fifty names of Marduk, we must seek the source of the ever-expanding Jewish angelology and the aggregation of divine epithets to be found already in the Old Testament.

The use of barbarous syllables and words, however, was rare in Babylonian magic, and its entrance into the Jewish magical science must be traced to Egypt. "In Egyptian magic, even if the exorcisers did not understand the language from which the Name was borrowed, they considered it necessary to retain it in its primitive form, as another word would not have the same virtue. The author of the treatise on the Egyptian mysteries attributed to Jamblichus maintains that the barbarous names taken from the dialects of Egypt and Assyria have a mysterious and ineffable virtue on account of the great antiquity of these languages. The use of such unintelligible words can be traced in Egypt to a very great antiquity." Hellenistic magic, the lineal descendant of the sorcery of ancient Egypt, displayed this phenomenon prominently, and thence it was reflected to Jewish sorcery. This accounts for the comparatively late emergence of such word-magic in Judaism. It is the Talmud which first "illustrates the use of these *barbarica onomata*." [16]

We have then, a fusion of these various streams at about the beginning of our era, the ancient Babylonian and Egyptian coming together in early Talmudic times, with the accumulated deposits washed down from their passage through Hellenism and the Jewish past. This is reflected not within Judaism alone, but in the more or less common culture of the entire Eastern Mediterranean basin. Gnosticism, the Greek magical papyri, early Christian mysticism, all display a striking efflorescence of this eclectic magic at the same time: a vast expansion of mystic nomenclature, and the prominence of bizarre terms. Origen believed that there is power in the words themselves, "as is to be seen from the fact that when translated into another language they lose their operative force." [17]

The magic of the Talmud depended largely upon the potency inherent in the form of the incantation, that is, in the word, and upon the magical action, for its most striking effects, and in consequence we find the barbaric word coming to occupy an important place. The invocation of names,[18] and in particular of angelic names, came distinctly and prominently to the fore only in the post-Talmudic period. The Aramaic texts published by Montgomery and others represent an intermediary stage in the process; while incomparably richer than in the Talmudic literature, the angelic nomenclature of these inscriptions was not yet so elaborate as we find it in later Geonic and medieval works. By the eleventh century the practice of invoking names had become so widespread that the good people of Kairowan (North Africa) felt impelled to write to Hai Gaon, head of the academy at Pumbedita, Babylonia, to ask his opinion on the momentous question, "whether it is true that there are countless names by means of which the adept can perform miraculous deeds, such as making himself invisible to highwaymen, or taking them captive?" His reply proved unsatisfactory, and again they wrote, telling him they had heard from Palestinian and Italian Jews, "learned and trustworthy men, that they had themselves seen magicians write names upon reeds and olive-leaves, which they cast before robbers and thus prevented their passage, or, having written such names upon new sherds, threw them into a raging sea and mollified it, or threw them before a man to bring about his sudden death." This time Hai Gaon replied at length; the upshot of his responsum was that the natural order of the universe cannot be altered by any such means. "A fool believes everything!" he warned his interrogators. But his skepticism did not win many converts. He himself mentioned a series of works in his letter, which marked the highest development of this doctrine during the Geonic period, and proved the futility of his strictures against it. One of these works, the *Hechalot,* devotes considerable space to expounding these names, while another, *The Sword of Moses,* discovered and published by

Gaster, consists almost entirely of mystical and barbarous names and prescriptions for their application. The Geonic period shows clearly, also, signs of that eclecticism which characterized Hellenistic sorcery; Montgomery remarks of his early post-Talmudic incantations that "what appears like a good Jewish text at times admits a pagan deity into its celestial hierarchy—somewhat as the medieval Church came to canonize the Buddha." [19]

This was the background of thirteenth-century Jewish name-magic, which improved upon its antecedents by multiplying the number of names, both of God and of the angels, available to the enterprising sorcerer, and succeeded in introducing into Judaism a host of pagan and Christian deities and terms, often in most confused and unrecognizable forms, and therefore all the more serviceable to the magician. Medieval Christendom, under the influence of the same Gnostic and Hellenistic tendencies, was equally well acquainted with the virtues and effects of name-invocation. The Hebrew names of God and of the angels, employed in the Greek papyri, proved especially popular, undoubtedly because of their strangeness. "Then there was the Notory Art," wrote Lea, describing the types of magic that came under the ban of the Inquisition, "communicated by God to Solomon, and transmitted through Apollonius of Tyana, which taught the power of the Names and Words of God, and operated through prayers and formulas consisting of unknown polysyllables, by which all knowledge, memory, eloquence, and virtue can be obtained in the space of a month . . . which Roger Bacon pronounces to be one of the figments of the magicians, but Thomas Aquinas and Ciruelo prove that it operates solely through the devil." During the early years of the Carlovingian dynasty the Church succeeded in suppressing a Bishop Adalbert "who taught the invocation of the angels Uriel, Raguel, Tubuel, Inias, Tubuas, Sabaoc, and Simiel." By the twelfth century manuscript works were in circulation in Northern Europe which "abound in characters and in incantations which consist either of seemingly meaningless vowels or of Biblical phrases and allusions," and in 1323 a monk was seized in Paris for possessing such a book. Despite the hostility of the Church the so-called Notory Art grew steadily in popularity during the later Middle Ages. It never achieved, however, the independent exuberance and creativeness of its Jewish counterpart, though it came in time to reflect it as a result of the introduction of the *Kabbalah* into Christian circles.[20]

THE NAMES OF GOD

Of all the names employed in magic, those associated directly with the person of the deity were accorded first place in the hierarchy of magical terms. Instinct with the very essence of omnipotence, they were surrounded from early times with an aura of superlative sanctity and awe. Already before the beginning of our era the Tetragrammaton had become the "Ineffable Name," too sacred for expression, uttered only once a year by the High Priest; a substitute took its place in popular usage.[21] During Talmudic times the number of "Ineffable" names grew; we hear of 12- and 42- and 72-letter names, which might be taught only to a select company of ultra-worthies.[22] Succeeding centuries witnessed the discovery of names of 8, 10, 14, 16, 18, 21, 22, 32, and 60 letters or syllables,[23] hedged around with a vast, well-nigh impenetrable mystic rigmarole which purported to unfold the esoteric significance and power of these names, all of which were supposed to derive, by a more or less devious route, from the original 4-letter name.[24]

Important as this secret lore was to the mystic, the pragmatic interest of the magician focused his attention upon the names themselves; though the Kabbalist insisted that a thorough grounding in theory was a prerequisite to the utilization of these names,[25] the magician was prepared to take the names and leave the theory to the scholars. For he knew that "the name of God creates and destroys worlds," [26] and his preoccupation was to acquire knowledge of *all* the names, and to set them to work for wholly practical, if more human, ends. Nor was he deterred by bitter diatribes against "those ignorant and impious ones" who dabble in *Kabbalah* with no firm comprehension of its deeper significance.

There was another category of names of God in use at an early time—the names and the attributes of God which appear in the Bible. Their virtues were known during the Talmudic period to Jew and Gentile, and we find them employed in Jewish, Gnostic and Hellenistic incantations; in the Middle Ages they remained favorites of Jewish and Christian adepts in the mystic lore. The list of ten such names drawn up by Isidore of Seville (seventh century), which was in general agreement with Jewish tradition, was frequently copied and commented on by later Christian writers; despite the hazards of transliteration and transmission they remain recognizable: El, Eloe, Sabbaoth, Zelioz or Ramathel, Eyel, Adonay, Ya,

Tetragrammaton, Saday, and Eloym.[27] Another name in common usage was the *Ehyeh Asher Ehyeh* ("I Am That I Am") which was revealed to Moses at the burning bush. These appellations were often employed in the charms, but they did not rank so high in mystical potency as the others.

First among the names, both in time and in occult power, was the four-lettered YHVH, the original name of God. Its powers were ascribed also to a wide range of variations upon it, from the particles YAH, YAHU, HU,[28] etc., to the twelve forms which it could assume by the transposition of its letters: YHHV, YVHH, HVHY, etc. The particle YAH in particular occurs constantly in the magical texts. The mystics went to great pains to prove that these surrogates for the Tetragrammaton were its exact equivalents in every respect, though their evidence is mainly of a formal nature. As we have seen, even the term Tetragrammaton assumed the power of the name itself. Not satisfied with the possibilities thus provided, the vowel points, too, were altered and transposed in order to create new variations of the Great Name, and such forms as YAHAVAHA, YEHAVHA, YAHVAH, YEHEVEH, etc., were added to the magician's portfolio. This practice was adopted in connection with all the names, for, as it is explained, "The consonants are the 'body' of the name, the vowels its 'garments,' and the body takes the form of the garments which clothe it . . . therefore the vowel is really the more important element, and the vocalization, which marks the transition from potentiality to actuality, determines the specific virtues of the holy names," i.e., their powers and even the times when they are especially potent.[29] The uncertainty that prevailed concerning the vocalization of these names, and the varying traditions concerning their pronunciation, made for a certain freedom in their use, and opened the way to an expansion of the possibilities afforded by any one name. But the powers of all the variations derived directly from the original name which constituted their base.

Of the multi-lettered names I shall discuss here only those of 22, 42, and 72 elements, which are the only ones that possess any constancy of form and content in our literature.[30] The others were the product of individual ingenuity, and made no lasting impression upon the practice of Jewish magic. All men felt free, granted the requisite skill and training, to extend the traditional magical nomenclature for private use by the application of the approved methods.[31] But these three names (in addition to the Tetragrammaton) were the foundation-stones of the magical structure; no self-respecting magician could afford to disregard them.

The name of 12 letters, mentioned in the Talmud, was a dead-letter in post-Talmudic times. It was unknown to the mystics, and although a tradition appears to have persisted relating it to the Priestly Benediction (Nu. 6:24–26), and some efforts were made to reconstruct it,[32] it played no part in Jewish magic. Its place, however, was taken by two new names, of 14 and 22 letters, the first of which was comparatively little used. It consisted of the words יהוה אלהינו יהוה, from the *Shema'*, and by means of *Temurah* (described in Appendix I), it appeared as כוזו במוכסז כוזו. Though recognized as a legitimate name of God,[33] and occasionally employed in incantations and amulets, its primary use was as an inscription on the back of the *mezuzah*.

The name of 22, however, is another matter, more interesting and puzzling—and much more important for the magician. Its debut was made in *Sefer Raziel*,[34] which, while largely ascribed to Eleazar of Worms, drew extensively upon Geonic mystic sources. It is therefore likely that the name is older than the book which introduced it to a larger Jewish public. More than this we cannot say concerning its age. It achieved a wide popularity very rapidly, was employed in many invocations and charms as an especially potent name, and in the seventeenth century it was introduced into the ritual of the synagogue, in a prayer which was attached to the reading of the Priestly Benediction.

The respect with which it was regarded was undoubtedly merited by its bizarre composition:

אנקתם פסתם פספסים דיונסים,

Anaktam Pastam Paspasim Dionsim (the vocalization is doubtful, but it was probably read something like this) and by the fact that the Hebrew alphabet, itself invested with mysterious potencies, likewise contains 22 letters. *Sefer Raziel* offers no interpretation of this name. It bears no discernible relation to anything in the Hebrew or Aramaic tongues. Despite the hazardousness of seeking to trace such terms back to foreign origins, efforts along this line have been made, with the usual success and unanimity. By dint of emendations and distortions such classical deities as the Greek Anaxos and the Zoroastrian Anahita, Hephaestos, Pistus, Poseidon, Priapus, and Dionysos have been variously discerned hidden behind these disguises.[35] The Greek gods masquerading in pious Jewish garb!

These scholars have gone too far afield in their zeal to discover the progenitors of this strange name. Its source may be sooner sought right at home, in Jewish tradition, which offers a clew that they have overlooked. Some scholars [36] have, indeed, derived this name from Jewish origins, pointing in particular to the acrostic of the initial letters of certain prayers in the liturgy, which spell it out. These prayers, however, were composed *post eventum* and display the inventiveness of late writers rather than the original source of the name. The seventeenth-century compiler of a Kabbalistic prayer-book, Nathan Hanover, who first introduced this name into the liturgy, was the author of a series of such acrostic prayers (based not only on the 22-letter name, but also on those of 42 and 72 letters), and also engaged upon a scholarly venture of his own in breaking down these terms into Hebrew words which he more or less obscurely related to Biblical passages. But these exercises are even less rewarding than those of the classicists; a cursory inspection shears them of any degree of plausibility.

Nathan Hanover, however, in inserting this name into the prayers in conjunction with the Priestly Benediction showed himself responsive to the most persistent tradition relating to it. The Blessing had long occupied an important place in mystical speculation, primarily because it was believed that during the existence of the temple the priests, while uttering it, had "swallowed" a secret divine name. The first appearance of the 22-letter name was made in association with that Benediction; two of the four instances of its occurrence in *Sefer Raziel* place them both together. Their relationship is rendered much more intimate by illuminating comments in two works which are especially close to the mystical tradition. One [37] informs us that "the name of 22, which is *Anaktam,* etc., is derived from five words which comprise 22 letters, namely, יברכך יהוה וישמרך יאר יהוה"; and the other is equally specific: "The name of 22 comes from the Priestly Blessing, according to the Kabbalistic tradition, by means of many 'alphabets.'" Knowing as we do the infinite possibilities opened up by the methods of transposition and substitution of letters in transforming divine names, and the popularity of such methods in Jewish mysticism, there is no reason to doubt the veracity of these writers. Not only do the total number of letters in the five words of the Blessing, and in the name, correspond, but there is an exact correspondence between the words and the component parts of the name. Both *Sefer Raziel* and Nathan of Hanover insist on reading the last term of the name as two words. We have then this parallel:

יברכך יהוה וישמרך יאר יהוה

אנקתם פסתם פספסים דיו נסים.

The famous Safed Kabbalist, Moses Cordovero (sixteenth century), has indeed left us a table of alphabetical permutations explaining in detail the derivation of this name from the Benediction.[38]

The name of 42 letters was known to Hai Gaon, who did not hesitate to indicate clearly just what it was, though he did not give it in full. He wrote, "Although the consonants of this name are well known, its proper vocalization is not rendered by tradition. Some pronounce its first part *Abgitaz,* and others *Abigtaz,* and the last part is sometimes read *Shakvazit,* and sometimes *Shekuzit,* but there is no definite proof." [39] His doubt concerning its proper reading is, to my mind, an indication of its antiquity; in a language such as Hebrew, written without vowel signs, the consonants are the constant element, while the vowels would tend to shift and change in the course of centuries of transmission, especially when, as in this case, the secrecy that surrounded the process and its oral nature tended to perpetuate individual variations. If it had been a comparatively recent creation such confusion would not yet have arisen, for the prime consideration in handing on such terms was to safeguard their form and pronunciation, and thus to conserve their potency. The medieval texts which give this name in full omit the vowel signs, and we can no longer reconstruct it as spoken; the variations in vocalization, which continued to be handed down by word of mouth, must have increased as time went on, so that in fact the name was employed in many versions. Limiting ourselves, then, to the consonants, the name of 42 was composed as follows:

אבגיתץ קרעשטן נגדיכש בטרצתג חקדטנע יגלפזק שקוצית.

Great virtues were attributed not only to the name in full, but also to its constituent parts, by the application of the allegorical or mystical rules of interpretation. For example, the fifth term "equals, by *Gematria,* the angel *Gzrel* [both add up to 241]; by uttering the name one invokes this angel to countermand any evil decree [*gezerah*] that has been issued against one in heaven"; the second, which may be read as two Hebrew words signifying "rend Satan," "is good for one who has gone mad or has been attacked by an evil spirit or demon; this name is to be written upon an amulet and hung around the neck of the victim, who will be cured by it." The parts of the name assumed the dignity and power of names in their own right. Some went even further and employed each letter as the basis of a separate name so that this one name became forty-two.[40]

It has been generally assumed that this name was derived from the acrostic of a prayer beginning *Ana Bekoaḥ,* ascribed to a rabbi of the second century, Neḥunya ben HaKana.[41] While it is highly improbable that this prayer was the source of the name, or that it dates back to the second century, this theory constitutes a recognition of the antiquity of the name. It no doubt represented the same sort of enterprise as was exemplified by Nathan of Hanover's efforts with the 22-letter name. The medieval mystics, however, possessed a tradition according to which this name is derived from the first forty-two letters in the Bible. This statement occurs several times and was accepted even by the famous Talmudist of the twelfth century, Rabbenu Jacob Tam.[42] There is no reason to doubt the truth of this report.

The "holy and awesome" name of 72—this time it is not letters, but syllables or triads—is the most powerful (*Raziel*[43] goes so far as to suggest that no magic can be effectively consummated without its aid) and at the same time the least mysterious of these artificially created names. Its composition was well-known in Geonic times, though the pronunciation of its elements was in doubt, and the renowned exegete, Rashi, felt no hesitation in disclosing its make-up.[44] The method adopted to construct this name was simplicity itself; perhaps the theory was that after a series of thoroughly mystifying terms, the analytical powers of the student would be too numb to penetrate this one. At any rate it is based on the three verses of Exodus, 14:19–21, each of which contains 72 letters, and was made up by joining the first letter of verse 19, the last letter of 20, and the first of 21, to form its first triad; the second letter of 19, the penultimate of 20, and the second of 21, to make the second triad, and so on until we have 72 three-letter terms comprising all the letters of these verses.

At first glance one might be tempted to pooh-pooh so obvious a performance, and the power attributed to its product—it seems to lack the most elementary attribute of a wonder-working name—mystery, strangeness. But we must remember that, leaving aside the mechanics of its construction, the name as employed was strange enough to satisfy even the most exacting:

והו ילי סיט עלם מהש ללה אכא כהת הזי אלד לאו ההע יזל מבה הרי הקם
לאו כלי לוו פהל נלך ייי מלא חהו נתה האא ירת שאה ריי אום לכב ושר
יהו להח בוק מנד אני חעם רהע ייז ההה מיך וול ילה סאל ערי עשל מיה
והו דני החש עמם ננא נית מבה פוי נמם ייל הרח מצר ומב יהה ענו מחי דמב
מנק איע חבו ראה יבם היי מום.

And, in the end, belief in the occult forces that resided in these names was the consequence of a hoary mystical tradition, which, in this case, encrusted the name so thickly that none but the most skeptical could have had the temerity to laugh it off. Rashi traced the tradition concerning this name, and its mystical employment, back to Talmudic times, and the tradition itself had it that this was the name which Moses learned at the burning bush and which he utilized to split the Red Sea before the fleeing children of Israel, and that at a later time the High Priest uttered it in the temple when he blessed the people. Granting the effect of such a teaching upon the receptive mind of the mystic, it is not difficult to understand how it could be believed that "whoever pronounces this name against a demon, it will vanish; at a conflagration, it will be quenched; over an invalid, he will be healed; against impure thoughts, they will be expelled; if it is directed against an enemy, he will die, and if it is uttered before a ruler, his favor will be won," and so on and on, realizing all those dreams of omnipotence that have tantalized men from the beginning of days. "But whoever pronounces this name while he is in a state of uncleanness and impurity will surely be struck dead." [45]

The printed text of *Sefer Raziel,* which gives this name of 72 in full, omits the vowels; a manuscript version of this work which I have examined, in including the vowels, proves that the same confusion existed concerning the pronunciation of this name as of the others.[46] After concluding the text of the name, the scribe appended a note to the effect that "there is another tradition of vocalization of the particles of this name, and I studied it carefully in connection with the text of the Biblical verses, but I found the one I give the better." A later student of this manuscript did not agree with him, however, and jotted down in the margins many variant vocalizations which he considered preferable.

The component parts of this name, too, were accorded special powers, and here also there seems to have been a considerable difference of opinion. The printed *Sefer Raziel,* for instance, divided the name into ten parts, nine containing seven triads each, the tenth comprising the last nine. The first part "has the power to conquer evil and to drive off evil spirits" and is therefore a prime remedy for serious ailments; the second is good for acquiring wisdom, and for protection against demons and the evil eye; the fourth will protect travellers; the fifth sharpens the mind and makes one a good student; the sixth is good for divination; the eighth ensures a favorable response to one's prayers, etc. The manuscript version, on the other hand, broke up the name arbitrarily into fourteen sections, ranging from three to nine triads, and distributed individual powers as follows: the first "causes love to enter one's heart and anger and hatred to depart," the second is "for enmity," the third is "for intelligence," the fourth can "silence those who speak evil," the fifth is "to find favor before a king or ruler," the seventh is "to make peace between disputants," the tenth "eliminates distance so that one may be miraculously transferred from one place to another," the eleventh is "to kill one's enemies," the fourteenth is to be used "against a demon, or to uproot a man from his city, or for any difficult enterprise." [47] Evidently this name was so powerful that any combination of its parts might be utilized to achieve a given purpose; the magicians apparently adjusted these combinations to suit their ends.

This observation applies to all the magical names of God; though in particular cases they were prescribed or employed for specific effects, in general we cannot assign a definite sphere to any of them. The magicians exercised great freedom of choice, selecting in a given case the name or names which they believed to possess the greater power, and determining their use by the specific request or magical act which accompanied the utterance of the names.

ANGEL NAMES

While the names of God in themselves were effective for the prescribed ends, often it was through specific angels that the given task was carried out. In employing the great name of 72, says *Sefer Raziel,*[48] the incantation must run in this wise: "I command you, Ḥaniel and Ḥasdiel and Ẓadkiel, by this name, to do thus and thus"; in other words, the name of God places within the magician's hands the power which God Himself exercises over His servitors. To know the names of the angels who are immediately concerned expedites matters. In fact, the intermediate powers represented by the angels are most often sufficient for the magician's purpose.

The angels, of course, are legion, and, in the practice of magic, the more that are set to work, the merrier. There are "seventy names of angels which are good for protection against all sorts of dangers" (the figure seventy occurs often, as for instance, the seventy attributes of God, the seventy names of Metatron, etc.); a typical incantation opens with fifty-six angelic names, and contains twenty-one more besides. Often, names of angels and of God are lumped together in one charm in grand profusion. An incantation which includes eighty-three angel names employs also, for good measure, the name YHVH, repeated three times unaltered, and again in eight of its twelve possible transposed forms, and the names of 42, of 72, and of 22. This prodigality of names to effect a single end owns a hoary precedent in the Geonic and Hellenistic magical literatures. At times, the magician's confidence was centered upon a single name, but one name alone seemed hardly potent enough, so he repeated that name: reciting "Uriel" 242 times is guaranteed to improve the memory!—that word at least will probably never after be forgotten. Most often, however, the magician's patience was not so long, and he contented himself with a mere mouthful of names, a good-sized one, that is.[49]

The names that appear most frequently are those of the three archangels, Michael, Gabriel and Raphael, often mentioned in Talmudic literature. They were called upon to perform every sort of function imaginable, usually in conjunction with lesser assistants. An old tradition, dating back at least to Geonic times, had it that there are seven archangels, each of whom is associated with a planet: those already mentioned, and Aniel, Kafẓiel, Ẓadkiel, Samael (occasionally Ḥasdiel and Barkiel are substituted for two of the others). The archangels are also brought into connection with the signs of the Zodiac.[50]

These angels were inherited, by and large, from preceding centuries. A much larger group was called into being to perform specific functions. Their names were usually concocted of a root indicating the function, and a theophorous suffix, usually "el." So we meet Shamriel, a guardian angel; Mefatḥiel, the "opener" of doors (the thieves' favorite); Ḥasdiel, Ḥaniel, Raḥmiel, angels of "benevolence," "grace" and "mercy"; Zachriel, who rules over "memory"; Morael, the angel of "awe" or "fear" who rules the month of Elul, preceding the New Year and the Day of Atonement; Paḥadron, the angel of "terror" who governs the month Tishri, in which these holidays fall; Naḥaliel, who presides over "streams," etc. Frequently the root term seems to have been chosen at random, having no apparent relation to the function of the angel as given, though it is likely that at the time of the creation of such names the word employed was intended to indicate the angelic character. Such are some of the names of angels assigned to the months: Ẓafniel, Amriel, Pniel, Bezachriel, Romiel, Barkiel, etc. Again we have angelic names composed in this manner whose first parts are hardly distinguishable as Hebrew roots at all: Daghiel, Duhael, Puel, Simusiel. The possibilities of this method were limited only by the resources of the Hebrew language, and if they were not exhausted it was only because so many other means of creating names were open to the mystic.

The products of these methods (*Gematria, Notarikon,* and *Temurah*) are only rarely recognizable as such. Sometimes, as with a name like *Ẓmrchd,* which is made up of the final letters of the first five verses of Genesis, we may hear the machinery creaking; usually one cannot tell whether they have been "legitimately" arrived at, or whether they are nothing more than random jumbles of letters which serve the purpose equally well. We must take them "as is," no questions asked; the attempt to discover some meaning in them, interesting as it may prove, is essentially beside the point—these terms possessed significance because they were "names" and not because they "meant something." Schwab's work, *Vocabulaire de l'Angélologie,* which dissects some thousands, often fails to be convincing when it attacks such bizarre names, and in the end adds little to our understanding of the psychology of magic by its rationalistic approach. What sense, for instance, can possibly be made of the names whose bearers are assigned by *Sefer Raziel* to supervise the months: *Arinaor, T'azbun, Lrbg, Arbgdor, Tḥrgar, Tshndrnis?* The ease with which they become something else a few pages further on shows that they cannot have meant much, if anything, to the compiler of that work. And then, which version shall we accept for analysis, the first, or the second: *Didnaor, T'achnu, Ylrng, Ant-*

gnod, Tuḥrgr? The effort to decipher them is pointless. "Names" are "names," and that is their sole explanation, so far as their rôle in magic is concerned. And since each of these month-angels is accompanied by his special retinue of 36, or 43, or 65 angels, as the case may be (*Sefer Raziel* is not chary with the figures), and there are countless angels presiding over every feature of our natural universe, and there are seven heavens, each with its "chief" and his "host," all bearing magical names, where is the end of such an etymological enterprise? [51]

BORROWED NAMES

Some of the names in use clearly betray a non-Jewish origin, but in their Hebraized form they were unrecognizable to the medieval Jews who were altogether unacquainted with the mythology and the languages of the Græco-Roman and Christian worlds from which they came. In the opinion of one scholar, "It is possible to construct, out of the names that appear in *Sefer Raziel* alone—allowing for the processes of reconstruction that were applied in this field—an entire pantheon of gods of the most diverse peoples." As we have seen, the names of various Greek gods have been suggested as the sources of the 22-letter name. While this interpretation appears doubtful, other names are clearly identifiable. Aphrodite put in an appearance as one of the angels of the planet Venus, appropriately enough, and Hermes was one of the guardians of the sun.[52] Despite the view of Blau that there is not "a single reliable instance" of the occurrence in Hebrew of the name Abraxas (the original form was Abrasax), famous in the annals of magic, it does make its appearance quite unmistakably in Jewish documents in both forms. Montgomery and Myrhman have discovered it in post-Talmudic incantation texts, Gaster has found it in the Geonic *Sword of Moses,* it occurs at least once in *Raziel,* and I have come across it again in a sixteenth-century text of an amulet published by Grunwald.[33]

We have noted the appearance of "Tetragrammaton" as one of the names of God; it occurred fairly frequently in the Hebrew charms. Similarly, other Christian forms made their way into Jewish exorcisms unrecognized: אלואי שבאוט, a literal transliteration of Eloë Sabaot, masqueraded as two legitimate names of God alongside the Hebrew originals, though occasionally a keen-eyed reader had the wit to see through the deception, and jotted down on the margin of a manuscript the caution, "this should read אלהי צבאות." "Alpha" is another word which assumed godlike proportions in the charms.[54]

One prescription suggests that when a man feels that he is being overcome by the powers of evil, they may be dispelled by the utterance of the name Pipi; again, written on a shelled hard-boiled egg and consumed, it is warranted to "open the heart" to wisdom and learning. Pipi—the name itself is intriguing, but even more so is its tortuous etymological career. Before the beginning of our era Hellenistic Jews had adopted the custom of substituting a *yod* for the *vav* in the Tetragrammaton, making it יהיה. "In the older manuscripts of the Septuagint the Tetragrammaton was retained in Hebrew letters. In Greek circles these Hebrew letters, *yod he yod he,* were not recognized as such, but read as the Greek letters, πιπι." [55] Thus Pipi became a magic name, and is to be found in Greek incantations. Jewish tradition, having borrowed this name from the Greeks, rendered it back into Hebrew—the Ineffable Name restored to its original tongue, but in how altered a form!

Three widely used angel-names, first prescribed by *The Alphabet of Ben Sira* [56] as a potent prophylactic against the depredations of the demon Lilit, and since accepted as a specific, have aroused much interest and speculation. They are spelled *Snvi, Snsnvi, Smnglf* (sometimes *Snmglf*), and were probably read Sanvi, Sansanvi, Semangelaf. Schwab illustrates the inadequacy of his approach by describing the first two as onomatopœic simulations of the twittering of birds (because these names are often accompanied by crude bird-like figures in amulets); the third he reads lamely as "poison découvert" (*sam niglaf*). Gaster, on the other hand, regards them as Hebraizations of three names of saints which played a similar rôle in Slavic legends of the child-snatching witch. The first was originally Anos, or according to Gaster's later revision of his opinion, Syno-doros or Sisyno-doros; the second, Saint Sisynie; the third, Satanael. To reach this conclusion the famous folklorist was obliged not only to emend the Hebrew forms of these names, but also to derive their originals from several versions of the legend belonging to different East-European peoples and languages, and from a figure who played a prime rôle in third-century Manichæism (which Gaster considered to be the ultimate source of the legend). The Jews, then, are to have drawn these three names from diverse sources, any one of which could have provided them with three effective terms, combined them for this special use, and so altered them as to require a feat of the imagination and of scholarship to discern their origins. Here we have the two extremes of etymological enterprise; the result of neither can be said to inspire much confidence. Gaster himself was quite well aware of the ultimate folly of such efforts; "nothing is more fallacious than to try etymologies of proper names," he wrote in another connection.

Another illustration of the difficulties encountered in determining the origins of mystical names is provided by the discussion that has centered about a well-known charm against forgetfulness, which is recited at the close of the Sabbath and on other occasions, with appropriate magical rites. It runs in this wise: "I conjure you, Poteh (or Purah), prince of forgetting, to remove my stupidity from me and to throw it onto the hills and the high places, by the holy names, by the name of Armas, Arimas, Armimimas, Ansis, Yaël, Petaḥel." (Another version gives these names as: Arimas, Abrimas, Armimas, Asiel, Ansiel, Ansipiel, Pathiel, Patha.) Certain scholars have distinguished here the corrupted forms of three names: Pathiel, the "opener," Ansiel, the "constrainer," names fashioned along orthodox lines, and a certain Armimas, who may be Hermes or Ormuzd, according to one view, or Arminius or Remus, following another. Greek, Zoroastrian, Teuton, or Latin—the range of possibilities is certainly wide enough! As to Poteh, or Purah, the dispute is just as lively, the suggestions even more ingenious, and the results even less convincing. I may add that this incantation was also recited by a child when it first entered school, with the additional tenfold repetition of: Negef, Segef, Agaf, names which were ascribed to the "angels of destruction." [57]

There are instances of entire phrases and sentences from the Latin and the Greek, transposed into Hebrew and employed as a series of names. Most often, of course, it is no longer possible to recompose the original passage, though its origin may be fairly obvious; occasionally one may reread the words as they were once pronounced. A charm guaranteed to heal a split tree contains two sets of "names" which Grunwald has read, quite plausibly, as "patriæ pax corona evocatur Dei" and "ut arcus offensionum submotus est, ita cave emovere." [58] Indeed, Güdemann has very ingeniously and convincingly reconstructed an entire paragraph in Latin out of a fifteenth-century German-Jewish manuscript. He surmises—and this is the only possible explanation—that this magical formula, composed by

Christians, was transposed into Hebrew characters, probably by Italian Jews, and was then adopted by German Jews, who, not understanding the language, took it to be a collection of mystical names and so employed it. This manuscript is particularly rich in such transliterations. One of the incantations in it, incidentally, contains the names "Akos Pakos," the earliest literary occurrence of the terms which, with slight orthographic variations, have become the hallmark of pseudo-magic in a dozen European tongues—our Hocus Pocus. It is known in European literatures only since the beginning of the seventeenth century. The origin of the term is uncertain—it has been claimed as of both Jewish and Christian derivation—but whatever its origin there is no doubt that it has been preserved for us by German Jews.[59]

A love charm has it that if three names, which have been read as the Greek words *ieros laos filos,* are written with ink on one's left hand "when you see the one you desire he will love you."[60] And, to cap the story, a "name of interpretation," employed by a preacher to gain special inspiration for his homily, is made up of terms which are probably Greek in origin, and among them may be recognized, of all things, the names of "Maria" and the "Parakletos," Jesus of Nazareth himself![61]

8

THE BIBLE IN MAGIC

THE WORD OF GOD

THE line that separates magic from religion is exceedingly tenuous, and the magician is never loath to step across it to appropriate for his own purposes purely religious objects and beliefs. Or perhaps I should put it the other way 'round—certain religious elements acquire in time an aura of sacredness and power which clothes them, in the eyes of superstitious people, with magical properties, and they thus offer themselves spontaneously to the sorcerer. In practice, the process involves not so much a deliberate act of appropriation on the part of the magician, who is himself a member of the religious group, as it does a utilization of those tools that lie at hand. The superstitious belief must exist in the mind of the people before it can be put to magical use. We have seen how the spirits, and even God, came to serve the magician. But the best illustration of this process is the rôle which sacred Scriptures play in magic the world over.

Today we may treasure Bibles for the profound religious and moral truths they reveal; historically, however, their virtue has consisted primarily in their divine origin. Scripture is sacred not only for the wisdom it teaches, but even more for its close association with the person of the deity who revealed it. It speaks in the voice of God, and therefore says more than one who runs may read. It possesses something of the personality and attributes of deity. And so there grow up schools of mystical and esoteric exegesis which profess to discover the hidden inner significance of the Word. And it *is* more than it appears to be: not only is it the word of the Lord, it is the Lord himself, an emanation from His being, a particle of His essence. God has revealed Himself to man, and by so doing has in a measure placed Himself within man's reach, to be aspired to as Ideal, to be prostituted as Power. Many men have searched earnestly and devoutly in Scripture for a vision of eternal truth. But many, many more have been content to capitalize Scripture for professional ends. Priest and magician, and the credulous masses upon whom they imposed, have been equally guilty of using the word of God for personal profit and power.

The Vedas among the Hindus, the Avesta and the Tao-Teh-King, Homer at the hand of the Greeks, the Old and New Testaments in Christian lands, the Koran in Mohammedan—for some men they have been storehouses of wisdom—for the masses, to whom through many centuries their contents were directly unknowable, they have been rather sacred works regarded as much with superstitious awe as with reverence, used as often for magical as for religious ends. Illiteracy, an obscurantist clergy which sought to make these books its private property, the position of the books in the ritual, often itself semi-magical, the mystical haze thrown around them, and, most of all, the superstitious credulity of the people—these factors combined to make of such scriptures tools in the hand of the magician as well as of the priest. The Bible, though perhaps better known to the Jewish masses in post-Biblical times than these other works have been to their own peoples, was similarly impressed into magical service. The very intensity of Jewish study of the Bible, and the centrality in Judaism of the doctrine of direct revelation, facilitated the subjection of this book to the fate of the others. It was drawn upon extensively for the formation of the cryptic names which constituted the heart of magical activity. In its totality, as well as in its major and minor divisions, its books and chapters and verses, it was directly employed in the magical science.

The *Sefer Torah,* the Scroll of the *Torah,* was a holy object, which must be treated with respect and veneration. A body of rules was developed regulating one's conduct in its presence: one must not lean on it, place anything upon it, touch it with unclean hands, kiss it immediately after kissing wife or child, have intercourse in its presence—admonitions which perhaps indicate also a measure of fear of the power of the book to retaliate and punish disrespect, a vestige of ancient taboo. But when an infant was ill and could not sleep, or a woman was convulsed in labor pains, the Scroll was brought in and laid upon the sufferer to alleviate the pain. Of course the religionists clamored against such impiety; some were willing to permit such practices only in case a life was in danger; others permitted the Scroll to be brought only to the entrance of the chamber in which a parturient woman lay "that the merit of the *Torah* may protect her," but not as a magical healing-device—and by such concessions acquiesced in popular superstition. Some there were who forbade these practices altogether: "It is not enough to brand people who do this as sorcerers and conjurers; they pervert the fundamental principle of *Torah* in making it a healing for the body when it is intended only for a healing of the soul." But such voices did not carry far. The curious womb-exhortation illustrates the popular attitude toward the Bible: "*Baermutter* [womb] lie down! With these words I adjure thee, with nine *Torahs,* with nine pure *Sefer Torahs!*" [1]

The report that the book of Leviticus was placed under the head of an infant in its cradle is too reminiscent of the above-mentioned use of the *Torah,* and of the prescription of a Latin physician of the third century that the fourth book of Homer's *Iliad* be placed under a patient's head to cure him of the quartan ague, to credit the explanation that this was done solely because the child's education would commence with a study of Leviticus. The Kabbalists made quite a to-do over certain portions of the Pentateuch to which they attributed a very deep mystical significance. Whoever reads the chapter about the manna (Ex. 16) daily will be insured against lack of food; a daily perusal of the verses which describe the composition of the incense (Ex. 30:34–38), with proper concentration on their esoteric meaning—"if people knew how important these verses are they would cherish each letter as though it were a crown of gold upon their head"—protects man against magic and evil spirits and plagues, even postpones death by warding off the attack of the Angel of Death. Most efficacious of all, in this respect, were the portions of the *Torah* which describe the sacrificial offerings; regular study of them in their mystical sense, which constitutes an effective substitute for the actual sacrifices, produces wondrous rewards.[2]

The words of holy writ were the most potent charms against the forces of evil. Upon all critical occasions, when spirit attacks were feared, such as prior to a funeral, or the night before circumcision (the *Wachnacht*), or indeed all the eight nights after birth, or the nights of holydays which are momentous for the fate of the individual, such as *Yom Kippur* and *Hoshana Rabbah,* studying the Bible and other holy writings was a common prophylactic. "As soon as a man has ceased his preoccupation with the words of *Torah* Satan has permission to attack"; this was the general principle.[3]

The use of "words of *Torah*" for specific magical purposes goes back to a hoary antiquity. The injunction of Deut. 6:9, "And thou shalt write them upon the doorposts of thy house and upon thy gates," whether originally meant altogether literally or not, was so understood, and the *mezuzah* from earliest times until today has been looked upon as an amulet to protect the home against demons. The utility of Biblical verses as charms was not unknown in the Talmudic period. If one dreamt of a stream, he was advised to recite Is. 66:12, "I will extend peace to her like a river" immediately upon waking, lest the words "distress will come in like a flood" (Is. 59:19) occur to him first; Ps. 29:3–10, containing seven references to "the voice of God," was suggested to protect one who must drink water on a night when the evil spirits are particularly active; the words of Nu. 23:22–23, beginning with "El" (God) and ending with "El," ward off the ill effect that results from a dog or a woman passing between two men. A sixteenth-century authority, R. Ḥayim b. Beẓalel, attempted to negate the obvious sense of such devices: "The Talmud advises us," he wrote, "that when a man recites the sentences beginning and ending with 'El' he cannot be harmed by any enchantment or sorcery; the point of this is that the man who believes wholeheartedly that God is first and last and besides Him there is no other god is certainly impervious to such harm." With due deference to the worthy and pious intention of this writer, the point is that the mere recital of these words has the indicated effect.[4]

In Talmudic times Biblical verses were often employed to heal wounds and diseases, despite rabbinic opposition to this practice. Even stronger was the prohibition against expectorating in the course of such a charm—spitting is a universally recognized magical act, and the authorities sought at least to eliminate this most objectionable feature; it was an act of irreverence unworthy of the Jew, they explained, avoiding the true reason. In later centuries this prohibition was drawn to a fine point, to get around its common transgression. It was limited to those verses in which the name of God occurs, and further "this is forbidden only when the verse is recited *after* expectorating, for it makes it appear that the name of God has been coupled with that act, and only when the charm is couched in Hebrew. If the name of God is uttered in another tongue, this prohibition does not apply at all." Even the effort to prevent such practices on the Sabbath was unsuccessful. Human need overrode the law, and in cases of serious illness the rabbis consented to be deaf and blind. In such matters law beats futilely against the iron wall of mass will; official Judaism was obliged to bow to popular superstition and accept practices which it would gladly have seen destroyed. These concessions are a tribute to the deep-rooted persistence of superstitious ways of thought and action.

One rabbi of the Talmud had gone so far as expressly to forbid all such medicinal use of the Bible; "It is forbidden to heal by words of *Torah,*" he insisted, "though it is permitted to use them for protection." His prohibition was disregarded, as we have seen; his permission recognized an ineluctable state of affairs which persisted throughout the centuries. Biblical verses were recited to ward off all sorts of dangers, imagined or real, danger from demons or snakes, from robbers and from "acts of God." Sabbath or week-day, the Bible performed functions for which its inspired creators had never intended it.[5]

One other purpose for which Biblical texts were employed was that of divination, which again is paralleled by similar usages among other peoples. I shall have more to say on this subject in a later chapter devoted to the divinatory arts.

THE USE OF THE WORD

The verses chosen for magical use were of two sorts: those which because they contained the name of God or spoke of His power and His mighty deeds, had come to be regarded as themselves possessed of power; and those which seemed to have a more or less direct bearing (allowing for mystical interpretations) upon the immediate situation in which they were to be employed. Examples of both these may be discerned in the instances cited above from the Talmud. In ancient times these verses were used directly and simply, as themselves imbued with occult force, to effect the desired result. But the Middle Ages departed from traditional usage; now the *names* that were hidden in each sentence of the Bible were responsible for the magic powers. Here again we find the effect of that sophistication which we noted in connection with the merging of the magic word into the magic name. We have seen how these names were pried out of the text and used independently. The texts were also employed, but rarely without the instruction, "Recite this verse with its name . . ." or the note, "the name that comes from these words is . . ." and the implication that were it not for this name the utterance of the verse would have no effect.[6]

The book *Shimmush Tehillim,* "The (Magical) Use of the Psalms," the most popular work on this subject, opens with the words, "The entire *Torah* is composed of the names of God, and in consequence it has the property of saving and protecting man." This little work—frequently reprinted in pocket size, and translated into several European languages—achieved the distinction of being placed on the *Index Librorum Prohibitorum* of the Catholic Church. The Psalms, in general, were very highly regarded for their potency, as well as for their beauty and religious fervor. *Tehillim* were read upon all critical occasions in the life of the people or of the individual; the entire book of Psalms was read through each week as a part of the ritual. In fact, a late work has it that this weekly recital constitutes the most effective protection of a community against harm. This same work reports a tradition that when a city is endangered it may be saved by reciting in order all those Psalms whose initial letters spell out the name of the city. *Shimmush Tehillim* is a medieval compilation of the uses to which individual psalms and verses may be effectively put; it promises the satisfaction of an extended miscellany of physical and psychic desires and needs, and sheds an interesting sidelight upon the life of the medieval Jew, and the hazards to which he was exposed. Grunwald has listed these "uses of the Psalms" in the *Jewish Encyclopedia* (III, pp. 203–4); I may mention a few of them here: prevention and cure of all sorts of ailments, protection against dangers, especially attack by evil spirits, highwaymen, and wild animals, to find favor with the authorities, against imprisonment, against compulsory baptism, and to escape arrest by the night watchman! [7]

Other portions of the Bible were also extensively drawn upon for similar purposes. The magical literature is replete with directions for the use of such quotations. Grunwald has published selections from manuscripts in German-Jewish folklore periodicals, and utilized some in his above-mentioned compilation for the *Jewish Encyclopedia.* As an illustration of this type of material I shall list here the prescriptions found in a fourteenth-century manuscript work, *Sefer Gematriaot,*[8] which, true to its title, consists of mathematical speculations and permutations on the text of the Bible, but is yet strikingly similar to *Shimmush Tehillim* in its listing of the magical uses of Biblical verses and the stress it lays upon the name which gives each verse or group of verses its peculiar virtue.

For a newly circumcised infant: Gen. 48:20
For protection at night: Gen. 49:18
To drive off demons and evil spirits (should be recited immediately before retiring, or over an infant's cradle): Nu. 6:24–27; Deut. 32:10–12
To counteract magic: Ex. 22:17 and Is. 41:24; Lev. 1:1; Nu. 23:21–23; ten verses which begin and end with the letter *nun,* in the following order: Lev. 13:9, Nu. 32:32, Deut. 18:15, Cant. 4:11, Prov. 7:17, Prov. 20:27, I Chr. 12:2, Jer. 50:8, Ps. 78:12, Ps. 77:21
To win favor: Gen. 46:17 and Nu. 26:46; Cant. 6:4–9
To gain a "good name": Cant. 1:15–16
To win credence in a dispute: Deut. 32:1–2
To have one's prayer answered: Ex. 34:6–7; Ex. 15:2
For a sweet voice: Ex. 15:1; Cant. 1:1
To strengthen the voice: Gen. 44:18
For the leader of prayer: Cant. 6:10–7:11
To arouse love: Cant. 1:3
At a betrothal: Cant. 4:1–5:2
For a newly married couple: Gen. 27:28; Nu. 24:5–7; Cant. 3:9–11
To maintain peace between man and wife: Cant. 8:5
To cure sterility: Deut. 7:12
To halt menstrual flow: Lev. 15:28
For a fever; Nu. 12:13; Deut. 7:15
For consumption: Lev. 5:19
For success: Gen. 39:2; Ex. 15:11
For profitable trade: Gen. 31:42; 44:12
To fatten fowl: Deut. 22:6 and Is. 10:14
To make flocks thrive: Gen. 32:15 and Prov. 27:26–27
On beginning a piece of work: Ex. 36:8
On entering a new home: Gen. 37:1; 47:27; Ex. 40:2
For safety on a journey: Ex. 15:13; Nu. 10:35–36; Cant. 7:12
To be saved from an impending danger: Ex. 6:6–7
In a time of trouble: Cant. 2:14; 5:2
Against an enemy: Ex. 15:5; 15:6; 15:9; 15:19; Deut. 22:6, Is. 10:14 and Prov. 1:17
To cause an enemy to die: Nu. 14–37
To be invisible: Gen. 19:11
To cause an enemy to drown: Ex. 15:10

To be victorious in war: Ex. 15:3; Deut. 21:10
To cause the strength of an opposing army to wither away: Deut. 4:24
Against pursuers: Ex. 15:4
Against wild beasts: Deut. 18:13
Against a highwayman: Ex. 15:14
Against robbers: Ex. 15:15; Deut. 11:25; Cant. 2:15; Gen. 32:2–3
Against slander: Ex. 15:7
To cause a man who has sworn falsely to die within a year: Ex. 15:12
To calm a raging river: Ex. 15:8
To dissipate a mirage or a hallucination: Ex. 15:16
For intelligence: Deut. 33:3–4
For good health after a fast: Lev. 26:42
To cause a curse to take effect: Lev. 27:29
For dream divination: Deut. 29:28; Cant. 1:7
Against the evil eye: Nu. 21:17–20

It will be instructive to examine some of these citations and see why they were chosen for their appointed tasks. The first and second, "And he blessed them that day" (Gen. 48:20) and "I wait for Thy salvation, O Lord" (Gen. 49:18) were obviously selected for the pious sentiment they express, and for their appropriateness. "Thou shalt not suffer a sorceress to live" (Ex. 22:17) suggested itself immediately as powerful counter-magic; reciting the three Hebrew words which comprise this verse in their six possible permutations, as the author proposes, and adding the words of Is. 41:24, "Behold, ye are nothing, and your work a thing of nought; an abomination is he that chooseth you," makes this a potent prophylactic against sorcery. The next verse suggested as counter-magical, Lev. 1:1, "And the Lord called unto Moses and spoke unto him out of the tent of meeting, saying," seems in itself to be altogether inappropriate for this purpose. But it is the opening verse of the Levitical code, the book devoted to rules of ritual cleanliness and sacrifice, and as such possesses the character of the entire book. In addition, it was to be read in its usual order, then each word was to be read backwards, and finally the entire verse was to be read backwards, these last two versions constituting mystical names. To cite another example, Ex. 6:6–7, which was to be recited in moments of danger, contains four "names," which are the Hebrew words translated "I will bring you out," "I will redeem you," "I will deliver you," "I will take you to Me"—what better choice could be made for such a purpose? Most of the verses are similarly suggestive of their possible uses. The "Song at the Sea" (Ex. 15) and the "Song of Songs" were especially favored in the above list, and for good reasons as the reader will see if he checks up some of the citations. "YHVH is a man of war, YHVH is His name" (Ex. 15:3), prescribed for victory in war, does not in itself promise such a result, but its emphasis on the name of the Lord and His warlike character rendered it a means of aligning God on the side of the reciter. Not all, however, are so obvious. Lev. 26:42, to be recited after a fast, was chosen because it contains sixty letters—but the manuscript does not tell us what the connection is (perhaps the "threescore mighty men" of Cant. 3:7). Why verses which begin and end with *nun* are counter-magical (these verses in themselves have no connection with the subject) is also not clear. Lev. 5:19, for consumption, was selected for the obscure names that were derived from it, rather than for any direct connection between the text and its use. Deut. 7:12, for sterility, again is more important for its name 'Akriel, angel of "barrenness," than for its simple sense, though the word *berit,* which occurs in this verse, is often understood to refer to the genitalia. And so it goes.

The manner of employing these quotations varied. Most often they were recited as they are to be found in the Bible, *with the addition of the mystical names.* Sometimes, as we have observed, the recital was complicated by reversing the usual order, or transposing words, or repeating them a given number of times. The words might be "whispered" over a cup of water, or written down and dissolved in a liquid, which was then drunk, or worn on the person in the form of an amulet, or traced on the skin of an apple and then eaten, etc. In other words, every device known to magic which was calculated to cause a certain effect to occur upon or within an individual, was called into play to bring out the occult forces inherent in the verses of the Bible.[9]

The most popular selection from the Bible thus used was the so-called *Shir shel Pega'im,* commonly interpreted the "anti-demonic psalm." The Talmud, in which this title was first employed, records variant opinions as to just which Psalm it designated, with the honors divided between Ps. 3 and Ps. 91. The latter was preferred by the weight of tradition, and during the Middle Ages Ps. 91 was employed at every opportunity, as well as at certain stated times, to obviate the ever-present danger from the evil spirits. Possibly as a result of a statement by Rashi the *Shir shel Pega'im* came to be denoted by the opening words of the final verse of Ps. 90 (*Vayehi No'am*), whether because Ps. 91 began with this sentence at that time, as indeed it does in several old manuscripts, or because the two were read in conjunction. This selection was officially accepted by Jewish authorities as the charm *par excellence* "to protect man against demons; nor is this usage to be included in the forbidden category of magical cures"; and it was inserted in the liturgy to serve this purpose. The traditional explanation of its effectiveness was twofold: it contains mystical names of God; it comprises 130 words (the final verse was repeated to make up the total), corresponding with the 130 years during which Adam had relations with demons while he was separated from Eve. We need not seek so far for an explanation, however; the plain sense of the psalm indicates such an obvious employment. It was recited nightly before retiring, to keep the demons from disturbing one's rest, and such famous rabbinic authorities as Meir of Rothenburg and Jacob Weil made it a point to speak these lines even before taking a nap during the day. It appeared frequently in magical formulas intended to drive off demons and to counteract magic, and was recited at funerals, when the spirits were unusually active, and upon all other such critical occasions.[10]

Such employment did not exhaust the potentialities of the psalm. Because the letter *zayin* is not to be found in it, it was believed to serve as a protection against all weapons (also *zayin* in Hebrew—puns were often turned to magical use), and itself to serve in place of a weapon when one was needed. A magical recipe to gain release from prison prescribed its daily recitation 72 times, along with other Scriptural selections. When one is riding across a bridge it is well to repeat these verses to forestall any accident (for Satan is always on the alert to take advantage of an opportunity to do harm). We have a report that during a *Rosh Hashanah* service in the city of Frankfort the *shofar* refused to function; the remedy employed was to breathe the words of the *Shir shel Pega'im* three times into the wide opening of the ram's horn, whereupon its hoarse notes were restored. Satan had seated himself inside the horn and had impeded its call until dislodged by the charm![11]

9

THE MAGICAL PROCEDURE

A MAGICAL performance was rarely a simple act, such as the recital of a Biblical verse or of a series of names. It was usually determined by such considerations as the qualifications of the magician and the attendant auspices, called into play the magic potencies of numbers, and comprised a variety of actions, such as the recitation of an incantation composed after certain rules, the performance of one or several of a number of traditionally accredited acts, and the application of sympathetic devices. An examination of these elements, which were variously combined in practice, is essential to an understanding of the operation of the craft.

The magical action was not one to be entered upon lightly. It was a dangerous adventure which might recoil disastrously upon the unwary practitioner. He was about to establish relations with the powers of the supernatural realm and the least breach in his physical and psychic adjustment to the task could cost him his life. The magician therefore often observed an arduous preparatory rite, lasting three days or longer, during which he purified himself by fasting, or abstaining from certain foods, by chastity, by ritual cleansings, by devoting himself exclusively to prayer and study. Coupled with his reputation for piety and learning he trusted that this would see him through.

The element of time was also very vital to the success of his enterprise. The formulas usually specify just when they are to be carried out. Astrological considerations loomed large in determining this factor, and new and full moon appear frequently as the most appropriate occasions. Often, however, the expiration of the Sabbath and the beginning of the new week was favored as most propitious, and it was suggested, indeed, that magical charms were best recited during or immediately following the *Habdalah* ceremony. The commonest specification was that the magical act be performed before sunrise, for the rising sun vitiates magic and drives the spirits into their hiding-places. Another frequent injunction was that one must be silent while performing the act; incantations were not to be uttered above a whisper.[1]

INCANTATIONS

The incantation was the most prominent element in Jewish magic. Sometimes it was accompanied by a varied "business," but most often it was considered all-sufficient in itself to produce the desired effect. Many of the formulas were captioned *baduk umenuseh,* "tested and proved," an appeal to experience rather than tradition; this phrase is reminiscent of the non-Jewish usage, which, following the example of Galen, attached to magical and medical prescriptions such expressions as "this has been experienced; it works unceasingly," or "a remedy tested in many cases." The incantation comprised several ingredients, all more or less constant: an appeal to ancient masters of magic, such as the statement that a certain charm for intelligence was "performed by our teacher Moses on behalf of Joshua"; citations from or allusions to Biblical passages; the invocation of angels; the enunciation of holy names; and finally the specific request or command. Sometimes this last was put in the form of a prayer, beseeching that it be God's will that such and such an act be done by His angels, by virtue of certain mystical names, etc.; or again the spirits were baldly and unceremoniously ordered to obey the will of their master, who had just uttered their names. The body of the formula, the command, often reads very much like a legal document in its solicitude to include every least aspect of the function it wishes performed, to leave nothing to the imagination or the initiative of the spirit addressed.[2]

A curious feature of the spell was its manner of identifying the individual in whose behalf it was voiced. In the Talmud we read that "all incantations are in the name of the mother," and Talmudic incantations followed this rule, despite the general principle that people are to be identified as children of the father rather than the mother. Apparently the spirit world recognized a different principle than did the human. This conception was not peculiar to Jews; among the Mandæans the "sacred" name of a person included his mother's name, and the same rule appears in Greek and Arab magic. In post-Talmudic Aramaic incantations, and in the medieval texts, it was quite consistently adhered to, the father's name occurring only rarely. This practice has been excused on the ground that *pater incertus, mater certa;* the *Zohar* (*Lech Lecha*) adopted this view when it counselled that certainty of identification in all appeals to supernatural beings, whether in prayer or in charms, is a prime requisite, and that the mother's name must therefore be specified. But it is very unlikely that a conscious aspersion on the character of the mother lies at its root. It is much more probable that we have here an illustration of the exceeding tenacity of magical tradition, and of the hoary antiquity in which this tradition had its beginnings. The practice seems to reflect the original matriarchal condition of society, when relationship was traced through the mother and not through the father. Of course medieval Jews had no thought of such an origin, but based it on the *Zohar's* theory, or on Menaḥem Recanati's explanation that "all magic comes from woman," or on the precedent voiced in Ps. 116:16, "I am thy servant, the son of thy handmaid." [3]

A familiar characteristic of magic is the injunction to do things in reverse, to walk backward, to put one's clothing on backward, to throw things behind one's back. The same principle applies in incantations, and Talmudic and medieval Jewish charms amply illustrate its operation. Biblical quotations were often recited both forward and backward, mystical names were reversed; sometimes the words were actually written backward as they were to be uttered, so that it requires considerable mental agility not to be taken in by the unnatural rendering. Phrases that are capable of being read alike in either direction were especially highly prized. The purpose was to capitalize the mystery of the bizarre and unfamiliar, and the power that is associated with the ability to reverse the natural order of things.[4]

One type of incantation whose power derived from its form rather than its content was especially suited to dispel demons. Its Jewish archetype is found in the Talmudic spell against the demon Shabriri, which runs:

Shabriri
briri
riri
iri
ri.

As Rashi explained its effect, "The demon shrinks and finally vanishes as he hears his name decreasing letter by letter." This theory is based upon the primitive identification of the individual with his name. A charm directed against a fever demon, quoted from Eleazar of Worms, runs: Ochnotinos, chnotinos, notinos, otinos, tinos, inos, nos, os. According to Perles, the incantation against the demon of forgetfulness, Poteh or Purah, which was recited at the expiration of the Sabbath and on the occasion of a child's admission to school, was also originally built on this model, reading: Armimas, rmimas, mimas, imas, mas, as. *Sefer Raziel* contains two examples of this formula, one involving the gradual diminution of the nine words of Cant. 7:6, probably intended as a general protective charm against demons, as the choice of a verse containing nine words would indicate, the other, for a "dream question," requiring the same operation on the name M'abrit. The latter recipe, which ordinarily requires the invocation of a spirit and not its exorcism, and the corruption of the Poteh formula, suggest that the specific use of this kind of incantation had been forgotten in the Middle Ages and it had come to be employed for general purposes. On the other hand, the reverse of this method was occasionally employed to enhance the potency of an invocation, by building up a name. One such charm, from the Hebrew version of the famous *Clavicula Salomonis,* employing the word Tetragrammaton as a mystical name, reads: ton, ramaton, gramaton, ragramaton, tragramaton, and concludes triumphantly, tetragrammaton.[5]

NUMBERS

The mystical virtues and powers of numbers were a favorite subject of speculation in the ancient world, and in the *Sefer Yeẓirah* and the later medieval *Kabbalah* this theme came in for a great deal of elaboration. But long before Pythagorean philosophy and Kabbalistic theosophy exalted the conception into systems of thought the common man had recognized the occult potency of numbers by according them an honored place in his superstitions. Medieval charms and magical recipes reflect this universal attitude. Just as the recurrent blows of a sledge-hammer drive a wedge inexorably into a recalcitrant block of wood, so repetition of an incantation enhances its force, by making it so much more difficult for the spirits to escape its compulsion. Directions must be meticulously observed; "incantations which are not repeated the prescribed number of times must be said forty-one times," we read in the Talmud.[6] Yet repetition may destroy the power of the spell if the *number* associated with the repetition has been improperly selected. For there are numbers whose effect in magic is negative, and others that possess a positive value. Similarly the number of objects used, the number of verses recited, etc., are a matter for careful consideration and choice, lest the effect of the magic be the reverse of that desired.

The common superstition that there is "luck in odd numbers" found its Jewish version in the Talmudic belief that even numbers are not merely unlucky, but actually dangerous. (This belief was more prevalent among Babylonian Jews than among Palestinian.) According to this idea even numbers, "pairs," invite demonic attack. Though this superstition was said by R. Samuel b. Meir to have lost its hold in post-Talmudic times, the thirteenth-century author, Jacob b. Judah Ḥazan of London, still reports a reminiscence of the Talmudic dispute over the number of cups of wine to be drunk at the Passover *Seder,* in which it was decided that four cups would do because Passover night was a "night of protection" against the demons. According to him, however, "a sick or weak man" had best imbibe a fifth cup, for his condition rendered him peculiarly susceptible to demonic attack, and the "night of protection" might not prove an adequate shield.[7]

The medieval writings contain many warnings against doing two things at one time, or repeating an action, such as "taking fire twice from the hearth when there is an invalid in the house, or a woman who has not yet passed the ninth day since her confinement." An unhappy fate was foreseen for any two couples who were married on the same day (in one community, of course). The rationalization that this would be a heaven-sent consequence of their disregard of the prohibition against "commingling two occasions of joy" was effectively blasted by those impertinent commentators who insisted that the proof match the proposition; how did this apply, they inquired, when the weddings occurred in unrelated households? To marry off two children at one time, or two sisters or brothers in one week, or indeed, to celebrate any two weddings within a week was to invite trouble. One of the couples would inevitably experience poverty, or exile, or untimely death. We can piece together a schedule of unlucky marriages involving "pairs": two stepchildren in one family; two brothers who marry sisters; a man who marries two sisters (the second after the death of the first); two brothers who marry a mother and daughter, or two sisters who marry a father and son; in short, any dual unions within two families. Nor should a man be permitted to serve as godfather for two brothers, else one of them must die.[8]

Three is the favored mystical number of all times—the first odd numeral after the unit. Religion, no less than superstition and magic, has done it obeisance; we need recall only the popularity of trinities of gods, or the three Biblical festivals and cities of refuge. The number three occurs more often in magical texts than any other. Actions and incantations were to be performed three hours before sunrise, or three days before the new moon, or three days in succession; preparatory rites were to last three days; the magical act comprised three stages, or required three objects; diviners could obtain answers to only three questions at any one time; the great Ineffable Name consists of 72 triads of letters; any experience that was repeated thrice was regarded as a portent; incantations were most often to be recited three times. The number three came to be recognized as a mark of magic, so that "anything that is repeated three times is magical" was a frequently quoted rule.[9]

"All sevens are beloved," says the *Midrash,* and we may well accept its verdict when we recall the manifold sacred associations of that numeral in Judaism. In magic the seven was second only to the three in popularity. Time and time again the instructions run: repeat seven times, draw seven circles on the ground, do this daily for seven days, etc. But what I imagine may be accepted as the classic illustration of the number seven in magic is this Talmudic prescription to cure a tertian fever: "Take seven prickles from seven palm-trees, seven chips from seven beams, seven nails from seven bridges, seven ashes from seven ovens, seven scoops of earth from seven door-sockets, seven pieces of pitch from seven ships, seven handfuls of cumin, and seven hairs from the beard of an old dog, and tie them to the neck-hole of the shirt with a white twisted cord." Extravagant as medieval magic often was, it cannot duplicate such an outbreak of sevens in one recipe.[10]

The number nine also has a long mystical history, resting upon its peculiar virtue as the square of three, but it appeared hardly at all in Jewish thought until the *Kabbalah* shed its fantastic light upon it. In the Jewish magic and superstition of Northern Europe, however, nine achieved a sudden importance for which there was no warrant in Jewish tradition. Demons have an especial affinity for this numeral: they congregate in groups of nine, and in nut trees which have nine leaves to the branch; incantations must be repeated nine times; if one has seen a demon he must not mention it to anyone for nine days; cures are effected with nine kinds of herbs, and are successful in nine days; "whoever wishes to heal a demoniac must recite the exorcism nine times, as they do in Germany, where they count nine knots, or they heal him with nine bits of wood called 'stilleti' which are obtained from nine bridges at the gates of nine cities." "As they do in Germany" is the key to this novel Jewish enthusiasm for nine, for native Teutonic magic was characterized by the doctrine of the nines, and in medieval German magic nine occurs very frequently. Along with other German folk-beliefs the potent nine wormed its way into Jewish superstition.[11]

These three numerals, of course, are not the only ones we meet in Jewish magic. Multiples of them occurred occasionally, and sometimes even numbers were inadvertently permitted to slip through the censorship exercised by superstition.[12] But these other numbers do not appear often or consistently enough to warrant the supposition that they were accredited with any special occult powers. Three, seven and nine were the potent numbers *par excellence* of medieval Jewish magic.

THE MAGIC ACT

The common idea that the essence of magic lies in a mysterious and mystifying activity is a product more of our theatrical pseudo-magic with its waving of hands and hocus-pocus, than of a knowledge of the facts. Medieval Jewish magic depended for its effects mainly upon the spoken word. But incantations were frequently accompanied by incidental actions whose significance lay in their symbolic or connotative values, some of which, in the course of millennia, have come to be recognized as of distinctively magical import.

Expectorating before or after the recital of the spell is one such universally known act, the mere performance of which was taken to indicate the intent of the recital, even though the words may have been altogether innocent of magical significance. Human saliva, especially that of a fasting man, was believed to possess anti-demonic and anti-magical, that is, generally protective, powers. Galen tells of a man who undertook to kill a scorpion by means of an incantation which he repeated thrice. But at each repetition he spat on the scorpion. Galen claimed afterwards to have killed one by the same procedure without any incantation, and more quickly with the spittle of a fasting than of a full man. Maimonides wrote, in his capacity of physician, that the spittle of a fasting person is hostile to poisons. In consequence of this belief charms to heal an ailment or to drive off demons or to counteract magic were usually prefaced by a threefold expectoration.[13]

The circle is another ancient and universal magical symbol. The invocation of demons is a dangerous business, and the magician must take steps to protect himself in the event that his spirit adjutants get out of hand. What simpler or more obvious device than to exclude them from his immediate environment? "Those who invoke demons draw circles around themselves because the spirits have not the power to trespass from the public to a private area," explained Menaḥem Ẓiyuni. By this magic act the ground and atmosphere surrounding the magician become a private, forbidden precinct. One of the most picturesque of ancient Jewish miracle-workers was Ḥoni *HaMe'agel* (first century B.C.E.), whose penchant for standing within a circle while he called down rain from heaven won him his title, "the circle-drawer." During the Middle Ages diviners who operated through the demons began their rites by inscribing the protective circle upon the ground. People who were believed to be peculiarly susceptible to demonic attack were defended by a similar invisible rampart; a widespread custom among German Jews was to draw a circle around the bed of a woman who had just been delivered of a child. In speaking of the dangers that beset a dying man several writers pointed out that his bed serves the same purpose as the magic circle, and that if a limb should project beyond it the demons will immediately seize him. In this connection it is interesting that in the Orient the general practice at a funeral is for the mourners actually to encircle the coffin seven times, reciting the "anti-demonic psalm." Similarly the late custom among East-European Jews (which also prevails in the Orient) for the bride to walk around her groom under the wedding canopy three, or seven times, was probably originally intended to keep off the demons who were waiting to pounce upon them. The magician's circle was usually inscribed with a sword or knife, and sometimes the directions require three, or seven concentric circles, the metal and the number adding to the protective virtues of this device.[14]

Of similar magical import was the insistence upon the use of new things, which is universally encountered. When the prophet

Elisha was asked by the people of Jericho to purify their water, which had been polluted, he said to them, "Bring me a new cruse and put salt therein" (II Kg. 2:20). Many of our medieval charms have the same provision. The apprentice sorcerer was instructed to place his decoction in a new cup or bowl; spells were to be engraved upon metal plates with a new knife; the circle was to be inscribed with a new sword; virgin earth was to be used to mold an image; water was to be drawn from a swift-flowing stream or a spring which continually renews itself; amulets were to be written on virgin parchment; the "first-born of a first-born" made a highly potent magical offering; one was to purchase the first object prescribed which he encountered, and at the first price demanded for it; the first person met in the morning, the first action performed at the beginning of a week, or month, or year, were portentous for the ensuing period. Such instances can easily be multiplied many times. New things, first actions, are innocent and virginal, like the boy or girl who were the best mediums in divination, uncontaminated by use or repetition or by years and experience. Therefore they serve the magician's purpose best, for they can exert their greatest inner potency on his behalf. An interesting variation on this theme, however, is the frequency with which "old wine" occurs in these charms, perhaps because of its natural superiority over the new, which men expected the spirits to appreciate as much as they did, or perhaps because it, too, was a "first." [15]

Despite the universal respect and fear which primitive peoples display toward magic, there is discernible in magic itself a paradoxical under-current of skepticism which expresses itself in various efforts to strengthen the omnipotent word. The many methods of transferring the word to the body, of bringing it into physical union with the person in whose behalf it is to operate, reveal the very human propensity to assist the supernatural with material reinforcements. This means of applying magic is best exemplified in the field of medicine, where the spells or the mystical names were frequently consumed just as though they were so many cathartics to expel the disease-demons. The same procedure was favored in charms to obtain understanding and wisdom, and to sharpen the memory. The injunction is frequently encountered to write the names, or the Biblical verses, or the spell upon a cake (the preparation of which was often quite elaborate), or upon a hard-boiled egg that had been shelled, and to devour it. According to a Geonic account, "all the scholars of Israel and their pupils" used to eat cakes and eggs so inscribed, "and therefore they are successful"; it has been suggested that the name of the famous poet Eleazar Kalir was derived from the *collyrum,* or cake, which his father fed him as a boy, and to which he owed his accomplishments. During the Middle Ages such delicacies were proffered to school children when they began their studies, "to open their minds." Magic cakes were also prepared for a bride, to ensure fecundity, and were administered on various occasions for good luck.

Incantations were also written upon apples and citrons and other foods, and thus consumed, or they were imbibed with liquids. To gain understanding it was enough to recite a group of seven names seven times over a cup of old wine and drink it, though usually the procedure was more naïve. Some prescriptions required that the spell be written on leaves or bits of paper and then soaked in wine or water, or that it be written with honey on the inside of a cup and then dissolved in water, and the resulting decoction swallowed. This was the essential character of the love-potions that were so popular during the Middle Ages; however fantastic their ingredients, their purpose was to transmit the charm in physical form to the body of the desired one.

Liquids that had been magically charged were also applied externally. To gain favor the suggestion was to recite various Psalms over oil and to anoint the face and hands with it. An undoubtedly effective restorative for an inebriate was to recite a charm over a bowl of cold water and to douse him with it. "To behold great wonders" one must bathe in scented water over which a spell has been uttered. And finally, material objects might be invested with the potency of the charm and become the agents of the magic so far as the world beyond one's person was concerned. To destroy an enemy's power one should recite given charms over wine or water and pour the liquid in front of his door, "but be careful not to spill a single drop on yourself"; or if one found his road blocked by highwaymen he should hurriedly grasp a handful of salt or earth, whisper the incantation over it, and fling it in the direction of his attackers, and they would be powerless to harm him. Again, if one's enemy was on a sea-voyage and one would rather he didn't return, it was a simple matter to inscribe a spell upon a sherd and cast it into the deep to seek out its victim. To calm a storm at sea, a similar clay-charm, or a mixture of rose-oil, water and salt over which the charm had been whispered, were recommended. Such prescriptions are legion, the purpose of all being to provide a physical agent to transmit the magic of the name to its destination.[16]

SYMPATHETIC MAGIC

Besides such magical procedures, which were incidental to the incantation, there was a host of operations in which the activity really took precedence. Not many required such heroic feats as the recipe for a spring which prescribed that one "dig his thumbs into virgin soil to the depth of a mile"! Most, a good deal easier of performance, were of the type that Frazer has characterized as sympathetic magic (comprising the two divisions, homeopathic or imitative, and contagious), in which the magician's acts were supposed to be duplicated on the person of his subject or in nature. The outstanding instance of this type of magic is the world-wide practice of attempting to injure or destroy an enemy by injuring or destroying a representation of him. Its survival may be observed even today in the more innocuous custom of burning or hanging a hated political figure in effigy. Behind the demonstration there lurks, we may be sure, the wish, if not the expectation, that the person of the victim might experience the fate thus visited upon his double.

During the Middle Ages this death-spell, the most terrible of all, was widely employed and universally feared; serf and king were overwhelmed with dread at the thought of the terrible fate that might at any moment be in the making for them through such machinations. There are many accounts of image-magic directed against the persons of high-placed people. In 1574 a Florentine, Cosmo Ruggieri, was arrested for having made a waxen image with hostile intent against Charles IX; the king died a month later of a mysterious consumption. In 1560 a waxen image of Queen Elizabeth, with a large pin stuck in the breast, was found in Lincoln's Inn Fields, and aroused consternation in the English court. *The Sword of Moses,* written during the Geonic period, contains one such prescription: "If you wish to kill a man, take mud from the two sides of the river and form it into the shape of a figure, and write upon it the name of the person, and take seven branches from seven strong palm-trees, and make a bow from reed with the string of horse-sinew, and place the image in a hollow, and stretch the bow and shoot with it, and with each shot say . . . [a series of names] and may —— be destroyed."[17]

Medieval Jewry was acquainted with this technique, as several references to "witches who prepare images of wax" indicate, but, apart from the two instances cited below, I have found no suggestion that it be employed either to harm or to kill an enemy. Its only common use seems to have been in forcing thieves to return stolen objects. This magic used against thieves differed somewhat from the more usual procedure in that it comprised drawing an image of the suspected thief on a wall, and striking or driving nails into some portion of that image, usually the eye, causing the original such severe pain that to gain surcease he would deliver himself up.

The frequent accusations that Jews had made attempts, sometimes successfully, upon the lives of Christians by this means, find absolutely no confirmation in Jewish literature. Jewish works on magic were by no means reticent or squeamish in such matters, and were subjected to no censorship, self-imposed or enforced from without, for they were intended solely for Jews, and were circulated among small, select bands of initiates. Had such a method ever been more generally employed, these works would bear testimony to that fact.

The two instances noted above are found in a fourteenth-century manuscript; though the technique differs they belong in the same category. To cause the death of an enemy "write his name upon leaves and let them shrivel up over a fire"; or "boil them in milk and say 'may the heart of —— boil in like manner' and your enemy's heart will boil and he will die." The same work suggests that this device may be employed to arouse love: burning a name causes that person's heart to burn with passion. A fifteenth-century work in mixed Hebrew and Yiddish, which shows unmistakable German influence throughout in its language and prescriptions, makes a similar suggestion concerning the more orthodox image-magic. This recipe is worthy of full quotation because it illustrates the "business" that often accompanied the charm. "Take virgin wax and make a female figure, with the sex organs clearly delineated, and with the features of the person you have in mind. Write on the breast, ——, daughter of —— [father's name] and ——, daughter of —— [mother's name], and on the back between the shoulders write the same, and say over it, 'May it be Thy will, O Lord, that N daughter of N burn with a mighty passion for me.' Then bury the figure, and cover it carefully so that its limbs are not broken, and leave it thus for twenty-four hours. Then bury it under the eaves, being careful that no one witnesses your acts, and cover it with a stone so that it doesn't break. When you disinter it, dip it carefully in water three times, so that it is washed clean, once in the name of Michael, again in the name of Gabriel, and the third time in the name of Raphael, and immerse it in some urine. Then dry it, and when you wish to arouse passion in her, pierce the heart of the image with a new needle, in that spot where it will cause most pain. So will she daily experience now this pain, now that." [18] Apparently the poor girl is to suffer doubly, from the pain of her love and her wound. Incidentally, this entire prescription is written backward.

There is one point that should be stressed in connection with this image-magic, which is true of all medieval Jewish magic. Among primitive peoples homeopathic and contagious devices, accompanied though they often are by spells, are believed to operate automatically; nowhere, in the many examples cited by Frazer and others, is there any intimation of the intervention of spirits. The simple act, by the rule of sympathy, produces its parallel effect. Jewish practice, on the other hand, while it utilized the general principle, as here, in theory at any rate, relied primarily upon the spirits for its results. The incantations that accompanied these acts contained all the customary elements which were intended to bring the spirits under the magician's sway, and several writers explicitly account for the transformation of cause into effect on the ground that the deputy angels of the images or figures transmit the blows to the deputies of their originals, who in turn produce the hurt in the intended victims. This spirit mediation, which distinguished the later from the more primitive magic, was also recognized by some Christians. William of Auvergne, for instance, wrote that "the only way in which the occasional seemingly successful employment of such images can be accounted for is that when the magician does anything to the image, demons inflict the same sufferings upon the person against whom the image is used, and thus deceive men into thinking that the virtue of the image accomplishes this result." [19] The point is important because it marks the distinction between the legally forbidden type of magic, which operated exclusively through "the performance of an action," namely, the sympathetic principle, and the more acceptable spirit-magic which the medieval rabbis hesitatingly tolerated.

The belief that anything that binds or in any way implies a binding may have a restrictive or harmful effect is widespread in ancient and modern superstition. It has found its way into Jewish folklore in such precautions as to loosen the bride's hair before the marriage, to untie all the knots in the clothing of bride and groom, and to be careful that no knots are found in a shroud. These precautions were based not only on the general superstitious dread of knots, but equally on the fear that such knots might have been the subject of a sorcerer's interest. For binding knots was a common homeopathic device, and even served as a description of magic, which, in the Talmud, was said to consist of "binding and loosing." In the book of Daniel (5:12,16) the ability "to loose knots" is listed as one of the magician's accomplishments. Talmudic literature contains several examples of this knot-magic, and the commentaries on the well-known reference in the Koran (Sura 113) to the magical use of knots relate that a Jewish magician bewitched Mohammed by tying knots, so that he became weak, refused food and neglected his wives. Nor was the physical act of tying a knot required; the magician could produce the same effect by word of mouth. The idea of binding is the constantly recurring refrain of a post-Talmudic Aramaic incantation: "bound, bound, bound" may be all the spirits and the demons and the magicians; and another Geonic spell summons the "evil spirit who sits in the cemetery and takes away healing from man" to "go and place a knot in N N's head, in his eyes, in his mouth, in his tongue, in his throat, in his windpipe. . . ."

The prophet's neglect of his wives is reminiscent of the most usual effect of knot-magic which, it was commonly believed, could prevent the performance of the marriage act. In medieval Germany this practice was known as *Nestelknüpfen.* There is at least one reference in Talmudic literature to "binding" a bride and groom on the *prima nox,* but the general credence placed in the power of this device by medieval Jewry was due more to the example of their German neighbors than to this remark. We hear much complaint in medieval Hebrew literature about the bewitching of man and wife so that they cannot cohabit, and the word *asar,* "to bind," occurs more than once with the meaning "to tie somebody by a knot-charm so that he cannot enjoy relations with his wife." [20]

There were many other magical acts which utilized the sympathetic principle, though its presence is sometimes obscured by the incidental details of the sorcery. A few illustrations may suffice to indicate the countless possibilities of this type. "To root a thief to his spot: gather some dust from the house in which the theft occurred [the dust on which he trod, like his clothes, or his nails and hair, is endued with the essence of his personality; such objects find an important place in contagious magic everywhere], bind it in a linen cloth and bury it in a grave, whether of a Jew or a non-Jew, and say, 'Just as this cloth, which contains the dust, cannot leave this spot without my consent and aid, so shall the thief be unable to stir from the spot where he now stands or sits without my leave.' " The operation of this principle is not so clear or direct in the following charms, but it is none the less present. To arouse passion, one must purchase a small hand-mirror at the first price demanded, scrape some of the pitch from the back of the glass, and write the name of his beloved in this space three times. He should then hold this glass in front of two dogs that are copulating, so that their image is reflected in it, and should also induce the girl to glance into it; then he must hide it for nine days in a spot which she passes frequently, and when that period has expired he must always carry it on his person. The intention is to excite the girl when she is in his company through the magic power of the sexual act, fixed in the mirror that has been associated with her name and person. Or again, to behold one's future wife: take salt from one house, flour from a second, and an egg from a third, knead them together secretly and eat the mixture at night before retiring; or, take salt, bread, and a knife which have been left behind on a table, and place them under your head at night. Here the intention, though admittedly far-fetched, is no doubt to create the illusion of a household by assembling household articles, and thus to induce the apparition of the woman who will preside over one's home.[21]

The use of parts of the human body and of animals in sympathetic magic was very common in medieval Europe, but exceedingly rare in Jewish practice. Although Jews were aware that the body suffers from misuse of any cast-off part of it, such as burning hair or finger-nails, or covering excrement with hot ashes,[22] this knowledge entered hardly at all into their magic. Christian sorcery prescribed the most various and obscene ingredients, such as human and animal blood, fat, hearts, sex organs, brains, excrement, etc., for internal and external application, largely because of their homeopathic virtues. Parts abstracted from corpses were highly valued, and were especially in demand for thieves' magic; scattered around a house they had the power of fastening a deep sleep upon its inmates; candles made from the fat or the finger of a dead person, particularly of a new-born or unborn babe, enabled the robber to see in the dark while himself remaining invisible. That medieval Jews forbore to employ these objects is perhaps not so much to their credit, as it is incidental to the force of certain stringent prohibitions in ancient Jewish law. The command against tasting any blood at all, or consuming flesh from an animal not slaughtered according to ritual prescription, or making any use whatsoever of a corpse, had become so deeply ingrained in the Jewish consciousness that the employment of such objects was abhorrent to them. A few of these practices found their way into Jewish magic, as was inevitable, but they are more illustrative of contemporaneous German usage than of Jewish. Of the small number that I have found, which I cite below, all but three are from late manuscript works which owe a great deal to German superstition, and can easily be matched in non-Jewish writings. Most of them are love-charms and prescriptions for love-philtres.

Thus, to arouse love: 1. Place a small copper plate upon which a spell has been incised in a new glass goblet filled with your sweat, and hide it in a place which the woman must pass. 2. (for a woman) Take a hot bath, cover the entire body with flour, and perspire profusely; wipe the sweat off with a clean white linen cloth, and wring it into a dish; mix in an egg; cut the nails from hands and feet and the hair from the entire body and burn these to a powder; bake them all together and serve. 3. Cut the finger- and toe-nails and the pubic hair, burn to a powder, leave standing in water for nine days and nights, and serve as a drink. 4. (written backward) Blow out the contents of an egg that was laid on a Thursday, and fill the shell with blood drawn from the left arm; place it under a setting hen, and as soon as its chicks are hatched, burn the contents of the egg-shell, together with some human excrement, to a powder; then buy the hen at the first price asked, tear it open and place its heart under your tongue "until it dies"; then burn the heart, too, to ash and mix the various powders together and serve; 5. or, more simply, buy a hen, tear its heart open, and place its tongue under your tongue. 6. Take some blood from the heart of a guinea-pig, leave it in a dish until it dries up, inject the dried blood into the quill of a feather, and place this surreptitiously between the two people when they are together. 7. Take a live mole, a male for a man, a female for a woman, and strike it on its right foot, "and it will bring you true love." This last is touted as "unequalled"! And finally, 8. "If a man will hang the tongue of the hoopoe at the right of his heart, he will vanquish every opponent, even the king himself; and if a woman will hang its left eye on her neck, her husband will love her, no matter how ugly she may be, and will never love another. Many Greek sages have tested this, and we also, and it is true." [23]

These few charms are altogether insignificant compared with the infinite variety current in Christian circles. One may marvel that such fantastic and often revolting concoctions and measures were expected to awaken the sweet sentiment of love, but to the medieval mind the connection was quite simple and logical. The man who has made his way into the body of his beloved through the medium of sweat, nails, hair, or blood, must surely find a place in her heart as well, while animals like the hen, the guinea-pig, and the mole, which were notorious for their ardent sex life and fertility, must move the most frigid individual to emulate them.

Animal parts, and articles associated with humans, were also employed magically for different ends, though on the same principle. For example, to cause a man who is far off to appear, one should take a piece of his clothing and spit on it (or cut it up), burn incense beneath the cloth in a new clay vessel, and while striking the vessel with a white stick, invoke certain names to produce the owner of the clothing. Or, to open a lock, smear the right foot of a male raven with the fat of a snake, and stroke the lock with it. And again, to torment an enemy with insomnia, take the head of a new-born dog, which has not yet seen the light of day, insert a metal plate inscribed with a spell in its mouth, seal it with wax, and stamp the wax with a seal bearing the impression of a lion; then hide it behind his house or in a place which he passes often. The incantation reads in part: "Bind him as with iron chains, tie him with bonds of brass and iron, and let him bark like this dog, and whine like its mother, and let no man loose him but I." The symbolism of the poor dog's struggles, and its mother's sleepless search for it, sealed, and stamped with the figure of the mighty lion, coupled with the magical binding, is calculated to rob the victim of his rest.[24]

Still another type of magical action comprised in essence an offering to the spirits, to gain their good-will and their aid, though its character was not perceived, or at least admitted, despite the recognition that "it is the custom of magicians to offer sacrifices and to burn incense to the spirits." One such prescription required that two white doves be slaughtered in a special manner, and their entrails mixed with old wine, pure incense, and clear honey, and the whole burned on the hearth; the smoke rising from this would induce a divinatory dream. Again, to produce rain, one must kill a white cock, tear it apart and extract its entrails, fill them with myrrh, frankincense, crocus, fine white pepper, "White Blossom," honey, milk, and old wine, and hold them up to the sun while reciting an incantation; if this doesn't work one must scatter milk, honey, and wine upon the earth seven times and utter the "mighty, fearful and sacred name," and "rain will descend immediately and the earth will be renewed." The first part is an offering pure and simple, the second combines this with the homeopathic device of imitating rain with the traditionally richest fruits of nature. A necromantic formula prescribes that one offer to the spirit of the grave a mixture of honey and oil in a new glass bowl, with the words, "I conjure you, spirit of the grave . . . to accept this offering from my hand and do my bidding." Such a frank confession of the purpose of a food offering was unusual indeed. These examples will suffice to illustrate a feature of magic that occurs frequently.[25]

10

AMULETS

MATERIAL OBJECTS

ONE of the most popular of magical devices was the amulet, worn upon the person or attached to objects and animals (the Hebrew word for amulet, *kame'a,* has the root meaning "to bind"). Even in our supposedly non-superstitious age the good-luck charm is still quite familiar, apologetically displayed on watch-chain, or carried furtively in the recesses of pockets and purses —the rabbit's foot, the horseshoe, lucky coins, rings engraved with Chinese or Hebrew letters, animal molars. How much more common, then, are such objects in societies which unashamedly and openly accept them for what they are, whether in the less sophisticated regions of our contemporary world, or in the medieval and ancient worlds, which did not for a moment doubt their efficacy! As a matter of fact, it has been suggested that all ornaments worn on the person were originally amulets.

Primitive religions make much of these peculiarly potent objects, and the Biblical Hebrews were well acquainted with their merits. Their use was very extensive in the Talmudic period, and, accepted by the rabbinic authorities, impressed itself strongly upon the habits of later times. Jewish amulets were of two sorts: written, and objects such as herbs, foxes' tails, stones, etc. They were employed to heal or to protect men, animals, and even inanimate things. We find the same types in use during the period of the Talmud and in the Middle Ages, though, of course, the intervening centuries and cultural contacts made for a greater variety. There was no legal prohibition against the use of such charms. In fact, the rules which were set up to distinguish proper from improper amulets lent them a definite degree of acceptance; though some rabbis frowned upon them, or urged the danger of preparing them, others actually suggested their use on certain occasions, and the common folk was very much addicted to this particular form of magic. Amulets were the favored Jewish magical device during the Middle Ages, and the fact that they were predominantly of the written type, prepared especially for specific emergencies and particular individuals, enhanced their magical character.[1]

The material objects that were employed as amulets because of their fancied occult power, were no doubt many more in number and variety than the literature discloses. The Talmud mentions several, and references to these are frequent in our sources, but it is difficult to determine whether these remarks reflect a contemporaneous use of the same charms. In this category were the fox's tail, and the crimson thread which was hung on the forehead of a horse to protect him against the evil eye. But a current fable of a too wily fox indicates that the virtues of the fox's tail, as well as other parts of his body, were known and probably utilized by medieval Jews. It seems that the fox had invaded a walled town, and when he was ready to depart found the gates closed. He decided to play dead in the hope that his carcass would be carted away to the garbage dump outside the walls. Along came a man who mused, "This fox's tail will do as a broom for my house, for it will sweep away demons and evil spirits," and off came the tail. Another man stopped and decided, "Here! This fox's teeth are just the thing to hang around my baby's neck," and out came the teeth. When a third passer-by made ready to skin the poor creature, the game got too strenuous and master Reynard came to life in a wild dash. The tale has more than one moral, for our purpose. As to the thread, red is a color regarded everywhere as anti-demonic and anti-evil eye, and in the Middle Ages we find Jewish children wearing coral necklaces, just as Christian children did, to protect them against the malevolent *jettatura.* Herbs and aromatic roots were also mentioned often as potent amulets. Fennel, for instance, was pressed into service against hurt of any nature, as this Judeo-German invocation indicates: "Un' wer dich treit [trägt] unter seinem gewande, der muss sein behüt', sein leib un' sein gemüt, von eisen un' von stahel, un' von stock un' von stein, un' vor feuer un' vor wasser, un' vor aller schlimme übel, das da ê [ehe] geschaffen wart, sint Adam gemacht wart. Das sei wahr in Godes namen. Amen." [2]

A Talmudic amulet which was widely employed in medieval times—it was well known to non-Jews also—was the so-called *even tekumah,* the "preserving stone," which was believed to prevent miscarriage. The Talmud does not tell us just what sort of stone this was. Several medieval writers were more informative, but unfortunately they employed one or perhaps several French equivalents whose meanings in Hebrew transliteration are not altogether clear, but which show that these were in common use. One writer went into some detail: "This stone is pierced through the middle, and is round, about as large and heavy as a medium sized egg, glassy in appearance, and is to be found in the fields," he explained. The French terms seem to indicate a hollow stone within which is a smaller one, a sort of rattle (perhaps the eaglestone or ætites); a later commentator calls it a *Sternschoss* (meteoroid).[3]

A man born with a caul was counselled to keep it on his person throughout his life as a protection against the demons who battle during a storm. A phallus-shaped stone inscribed with the Hebrew words "accident of sleep" and the words of Gen. 49:24, "But his bow abode firm" is to be seen in the Musée Raymond in Toulouse. Its intention is unmistakable; similar amulets must have been in use in Germany. Toward the end of the Middle Ages, if not earlier, there arose the custom of employing a piece of the *Afikomen,* a specially designated cake of unleavened bread at the Passover *Seder,* as an amulet, hanging it in the house, or carrying it in a pouch, to protect one against evil spirits and against evil men. A metal plate inscribed with the letter *heh* (a sign for the Tetragrammaton), worn about the neck, was no doubt another such amulet, despite the ritualistic explanation it received; similar charms are still in use today. In the fifteenth and sixteenth centuries we find references to charms which, by their nature, and by virtue of the prominence of German words in the text, seem to have been borrowed from non-Jews. Among these I may mention the following: To find favor in people's eyes, carry the right eye or ear of an animal on your person. To obtain a favorable hearing from a judge, get a straw in which there are three nodes, and place the middle node under your tongue in the morning; or else, place henbane (hyoscyamus) seeds, still in their husks, in your hair above the forehead. A charm that will put an insomniac to sleep is prepared thus: one must secure a louse from the head of the patient and induce it to crawl into a bone which has a hole in it, seal the hole, and hang the imprisoned insect on the patient's neck. An amulet that gives protection consists of a sprig of fennel over which an incantation has been recited and which has then been wrapped in silk, together with some wheat and coins, and then encased in wax. Other amulets, such as rings and medallions of various sorts, were no doubt similarly employed, for Jews had a reputation as metal-workers and engravers.[4]

Objects of this sort were used for more or less esoteric reasons. Sometimes the reputation for occult virtue outlived the original reason. Often what was involved was a sympathetic transference of the qualities and characteristics of the object to the wearer. In the case of the color red, for instance, it has been suggested that its magical power derives from its association with the blood of sacrifice, for which it is a substitute, and therefore it appeases the powers of evil. On the other hand, parts of an animal convey the special qualities of strength, or cunning, or courage which distinguish it. The stone within a stone represents the embryo in the womb; just as the one is securely imprisoned, so may the other be. This type of sympathetic amulet is well known and universally employed. Despite the paucity of evidence in our sources, medieval Jewry must have drawn extensively upon Jewish tradition and its non-Jewish neighbors for a multitude of such charms.[5]

An interesting instance of confidence placed in a non-Jewish talisman is afforded by a statement in a fifteenth-century work, *Leket Yosher:* "I recall that when my son Seligmann was born I had my wife make him a linen shirt, called a *Nothemd* in German, which everybody says protects the wearer against assault on the highway (but I myself was once attacked while I was wearing one, though, truth to tell, I'm not certain that another shirt wasn't substituted for it)." The writer's description of the *Nothemd* (also called *Sieghemd,* St. George's Shirt) is hardly satisfying: "It is square, with a hole in the center," is all he says; but contemporaneous Christian sources fill out his account. It seems that this type of shirt possessed a host of magical properties—it served as protection against weapons and accidents and attack, it procured easy and quick delivery of children, victory in warfare and in courts of law, immunity from sorcery, etc. One version of its manufacture required that it be made by girls of undoubted chastity, who must spin the thread from flax, weave it and sew it in the name of the devil on Christmas night. Two heads were embroidered on the front, the right with a long beard and a helmet, the left bristly and crowned with a devil's head-dress. On either side of the figures was a cross. In length the shirt extended from the head to the waist. According to other accounts (which omit the diabolic features) it was woven and sewn by a pure girl on Sundays (or on Christmas nights) over a period of seven years, during which she remained mute all the time. This was the nature (substituting Jewish forms for the Christian) of the *Nothemd* which our authority hoped would shield his first-born from the hazards of life.[5a]

GEMS

Precious and semi-precious stones, in particular, have been credited with superior occult powers by many peoples. In medieval Europe this was an unquestioned dogma of the religion of superstition, as well as a subject of theological speculation; a heated debate centered about the question whether their peculiar virtues were divinely implanted, or simply part of the nature of gems. Jews were the leading importers of and dealers in gems during the early Middle Ages, and Christian Europe attributed to them a certain specialization in the magic properties of precious stones: *Christianos fidem in verbis, Judæos in lapidibus pretiosis, et Paganos in herbis ponere,* ran the adage.

Indeed, there was good warrant in the Jewish background for such a specialty. The Bible (Ex. 28:17-20) speaks of the twelve gems, engraved with the tribal names, which were set into the High Priest's breastplate, leaving room for much mystical speculation in the later literature on the various aspects of these gems. But strangely enough the discussion limited itself to the mystical significance of the twelve gems, and touched hardly at all upon their magical properties. This subject seems to have been altogether out of the line of Jewish tradition and interest—though Jews were acquainted with it. The Talmud, for instance, remarks that Abraham possessed a gem which could heal all those who looked upon it. Such comments, however, are comparatively rare in Jewish literature. Like many other Christian ideas about the Jews, their reputation as experts in the magic virtues of gems was far wide of the mark. As Steinschneider remarks, "Hardly a single dissertation on this subject is to be found in Hebrew literature . . . and the little that does exist is very insignificant and recent, derived mainly from non-Jewish sources."[6] In the Hebrew literature of Northern Europe I have found only one discussion of the properties of precious stones, and that in the unpublished fourteenth-century manuscript, *Sefer Gematriaot.* While it unquestionably drew upon non-Jewish material, it acquired a definitely Jewish coloration in its cross-cultural journey, and is built upon the scheme of the twelve tribal gems. I give here a partial translation of the passage, the complete text of which may be found in Appendix II.[7]

"*Odem* [commonly translated carnelian, ruby] appertains to Reuben. . . . This is the stone called *rubino*. Its use is to prevent the woman who wears it from suffering a miscarriage. It is also good for women who suffer excessively in child-birth, and, consumed with food and drink, it is good for fertility. . . . Sometimes the stone *rubino* is combined with another stone and is called *rubin felsht*. . . .

"*Pitdah* [commonly, topaz] the stone of Simeon. This is the *prasinum* (?) but it seems to me it is the *smeralda* (?); it is greenish because of Zimri, the son of Salu (Nu. 25:14) who made the Simeonites green in the face . . . and it is dull in appearance because their faces paled. Its use is to chill the body. . . . Ethiopia and Egypt are steeped in sensuality, and therefore it is to be found there, to cool the body. It is also useful in affairs of the heart. . . .

"*Bareket* [emerald or smaragd] This is the carbuncle, which flashes like lightning [*barak*] and gleams like a flame. . . . This is the stone of Levi. . . . It is beneficial to those who wear it; it makes man wise, and lights up his eyes, and opens his heart. Taken as a food in the form of powder with other drugs it rejuvenates the old. . . .

"*Nofech* [carbuncle] This is the smaragd. . . . It is green, for Judah's face was of a greenish hue when he mastered his passion and acknowledged his relations with Tamar (Gen. 38). . . . This stone is clear, and not cloudy like Simeon's, for when he was cleared of the suspicion of Joseph's death his face grew bright with joy. The function of this stone is to add strength, for one who wears it will be victorious in battle; that is why the tribe of Judah were mighty heroes. It is called *nofech* because the enemy turns (*hofech*) his back to the one who wears it, as it is written, 'Thy hand shall be on the neck of thine enemies' (Gen. 49:8).

"*Sapir* [sapphire] the stone of Issachar, who 'had understanding of the times' (I Chr. 12:32) and of the *Torah*. It is purple-blue in color, and is excellent to cure ailments, and especially to pass across the eyes, as it is said, 'It shall be health to thy navel, and marrow to thy bones' (Prov. 3:8).

"*Yahalom* [emerald] This is the stone of Zebulun; it is the jewel called *perla*. It brings success in trade, and is good to carry along on a journey, because it preserves peace and increases good-will. And it brings sleep, for it is written, 'Now will my husband sleep with me (*yizbeleni*)' (Gen. 30:20).

"*Leshem* [jacinth] This is the stone of Dan, which is the *topaziah*. The face of a man may be seen in it, in reverse, because they overturned the graven image of the idol (Jud. 18).

"*Shebo* [agate] This is the stone of Naphtali, which is the *turkiska*. It establishes man firmly in his place, and prevents him from stumbling and falling; it is especially coveted by knights and horsemen, it makes a man secure on his mount. . . .

"*Aḥlamah* [amethyst] . . . This is the stone called *cristalo;* it is very common and well known. It is the stone of Gad, because the tribe of Gad are very numerous and renowned. . . . There is another gem called *diamanti* which is like the *cristalo,* except that it has a faintly reddish hue; the tribe of Gad used to carry this with them. It is useful in war, for it buoys up the heart so that it doesn't grow faint, for Gad used to move into battle ahead of their brothers. . . . This stone is good even against demons and spirits, so that one who wears it is not seized by that faintness of heart which they call *glolir* (?).

"*Tarshish* [beryl] This is the *yakint* [jacinth]; the *Targum* calls it the 'sea-green,' which is its color. It is the stone of Asher. Its utility is to burn up food. No bad food will remain in the bowels of one who consumes it, but will be transformed into a thick oil. For it is written, 'As for Asher, his bread shall be fat' (Gen. 49:20). . . . Sometimes the sapphire is found in combination with the *yakint,* because the tribes of Asher and Issachar intermarried. . . . Because the bread of Asher is fat for all creatures, and the faces of stout people are ruddy, the *yakint* is sometimes of a reddish hue.

"*Shoham* [onyx] This is the stone called *nikli* [*nichilus,* an agate]. It is Joseph's stone and it bestows grace. . . . One who wears it at a gathering of people will find it useful to make them hearken to his words, and to win success. . . .

"*Yashfeh* [jasper] This is Benjamin's; it is called *diaspi,* and is found in a variety of colors: green, black, and red, because Benjamin knew that Joseph had been sold, and often considered revealing this to Jacob, and his face would turn all colors as he debated whether to disclose his secret or to keep it hidden; but he restrained himself and kept the matter concealed. This stone *yashfeh,* because it was a bridle on his tongue, has also the power to restrain the blood. . . ."

WRITTEN AMULETS

These charms did not at all contest the far greater popularity of the written amulets, which contained the most powerful elements of Jewish magic—the names. Prepared by experts to meet particular needs, those of which we have a record differed widely in detail, but in general conformed to the underlying scheme of the incantation. There were some which consisted exclusively of Biblical quotations with or without the names that were read into them. Copies of Ps. 126, for instance, with the addition of the anti-Lilitian names, Sanvi, Sansanvi, Semangelaf, placed in the four corners of a house, protect children against the hazards of infancy; Ps. 127, hung about a boy's neck from the moment of birth, guards him throughout life. Or the inscription might consist exclusively of angel-names.[8] But these were comparatively rare. Most of the written amulets contained the combination of elements which centuries of usage had impressed upon this magical form.

The following text of a typical amulet, guaranteed to perform a very wide range of functions, will serve to illustrate the species: [9]

"An effective amulet, tested and tried, against the evil eye and evil spirits, for grace, against imprisonment and the sword, for intelligence, to be able to instruct people in *Torah,* against all sorts of disease and reverses, and against loss of property: 'In the name of Shaddai, who created heaven and earth, and in the name of the angel Raphael, the *memuneh* in charge of this month, and by you, *Smmel, Hngel, Vngsursh, Kndors, Ndmh, Kmiel, S'ariel, Abrid, Gurid, memunim* of the summer equinox, and by your Prince, *Or-'anir,* by the angel of the hour and the star, in the name of the Lord, God of Israel, who rests upon the Cherubs, the great, mighty, and awesome God, YHVH Ẓebaot is His name, and in Thy name, God of mercy, and by thy name, Adiriron, trustworthy healing-God, in whose hand are the heavenly and earthly households, and by the name YHVH, save me by this writing and by this amulet, written in the name of N son of N [mother's name]. Protect him in all his two hundred and forty-eight organs against imprisonment and against the two-edged sword. Help him, deliver him, save him, rescue him from evil men and evil speech, and from a harsh litigant, whether he be Jew or Gentile. Humble and bring low those who rise against him to do him evil by deed or by speech, by counsel or by thought. May all who seek his harm be overthrown, destroyed, humbled, afflicted, broken so that not a limb remains whole; may those who wish him ill be put to shame. Save him, deliver him from all sorcery, from all reverses, from poverty, from wicked men, from sudden death, from the evil effects of passion, from every sort of tribulation and disease. Grant him grace, and love, and mercy before the throne of God, and before all beings who behold him. Let the fear of him rest upon all creatures, as the mighty lion dreads the mightier *mafgi'a* [cf. *Shab.* 77b]. I conjure N, son of N, in the name of Uriron and Adriron (sic). Praised be the Lord forever. Amen and Amen.' "

The elements that stand out in this text are: 1. most important, the names of God and of angels; 2. the Biblical expressions or phrases, descriptive of God's attributes, or bespeaking His protection and healing power, such as "YHVH Ẓebaot is His name," "who rests upon the Cherubs," etc.—these are more manifest in other amulet texts than in this one, but in less elaborate texts they are dropped altogether; 3. the meticulousness with which the various functions of the amulet are detailed; 4. the name of the person the amulet is meant to serve, and his mother's name.[10]

Not all amulets were so long, or so complicated, or so inclusive as this one, but almost all included these four elements. Where the charm was to perform a single function, it was, of course, much simpler, but did not differ essentially from the sample given. As *Sefer Raziel* stressed, one must be careful to include the names of the angels that are in control of the immediate situation, and which have the specialized powers it is desired to call into operation. A charm intended to heal or ward off a particular ailment should specify the name of the demon that is responsible, if it is known. As an instance of a much simpler amulet, which, while omitting the Biblical phrases, fulfills the other requirements, I may cite the following formula:

"To win favor, write on parchment and carry on your person: 'Ḥasdiel at my right, Ḥaniel at my left, Raḥmiel at my head, angels, let me find favor and grace before all men, great and small, and before all of whom I have need, in the name of Yah Yah Yah Yau Yau Yau Yah Ẓebaot. Amen Amen Amen Selah.' "[11]

In addition to the written inscription amulets were also often adorned with magical figures. Among these may be singled out the pentagram (popularly identified as the "Seal of Solomon") and the hexagram. The hexagram in particular has acquired a special

ספר רזיאל
קמיע
אחרת לחן ולחסד כתוב על קלף צבי כשר בשמן דחנינה וח סר יהוה בעולם יהי חסרן יהוה על
פב"פ לכשם שהיה עם יוסף הצדיק שנאמר ויהי ה' את יוסף ויט אליו חסד ויתן ארת חנו בעיני כל רואיו
בשם מיכא"ל גבריא"ל רפא"ל אוריא"ל כבשיא"ל יה יה יה יה יה יה יה יה אהיה אהה ארה
אהה אהה ידו ידו ידו ידו ידו ידו ידו ידו יה
קמיע
אחרת שלא ישלוט באדם שום כלי זין כתוב בקלף של צבי כשר ותלי בצוארך שמות הקדושים האלו
עתריאל וריאל הורדיאל המדריאל שובריאל שובראל עורדיאל שוריאל
מיכאל גבריאל הגריאל הגדה אל שובריאל צבחר אתניק צורטק אנקתם פסתם
פספסים דיונסים לייש ועת כקו יתי יהוה אבג יתץ קרע שטן נגד יכש בטר צתג חקב
טנע יגל פזק שקוצית קבצקאל אהמנוניאל ומסתיה הירשתיאל עאנה פיה אלעה
אבג יתץ אלעה עה עה
עזר לפלוני בן פלונית
מצמצית
כתז
שדי
ה
י
ו
ה
יהוה

Courtesy of the Jewish Theological Seminary Library, New York

TWO MEDIEVAL AMULET TEXTS: *Upper Portion*, "FOR GRACE AND FAVOR"; *Lower Portion*, "TO SAFEGUARD A MAN AGAINST ALL WEAPONS."—FROM *Sefer Raziel*, AMSTERDAM, 1701.

place in Jewish affections, and is regarded as the symbol of Judaism, under the name "Shield of David." So strong has the connection between this seal and the Jewish people become that it seems today to have behind it centuries of traditional usage. It may surprise some readers, then, to learn that only in the past hundred years or so has the *Magen David* been widely accepted and used by Jews as symbolic of their faith, in the sense that the cross and crescent are of Christianity and Mohammedanism. The hexagram, in fact, has no direct connection with Judaism. Both these figures are the common property of humankind. The Pythagoreans attributed great mystical significance to them; they played a mystical and magical rôle in Peru, Egypt, China, and Japan; they are to be found in Hellenistic magical papyri; the Hindus used the hexagram and pentagram as potent talismans; they occur often in Arabic amulets, and in medieval Christian magical texts; in Germany, where it is called the *Drudenfuss,* the pentagram may still be seen inscribed on stable-doors and on beds and cradles as a protection against enchantments. Their magical virtues were known in Jewish circles at an early time; they are to be found often in early post-Talmudic incantations, and occur fairly often in medieval amulets and *mezuzot.* Names of God and Biblical texts were frequently inscribed within the triangles of the magical hexagram.[12]

Of another sort, but equally widely employed in Jewish amulets, was a series of figures constructed by joining straight and curved lines tipped with circles, in this manner:

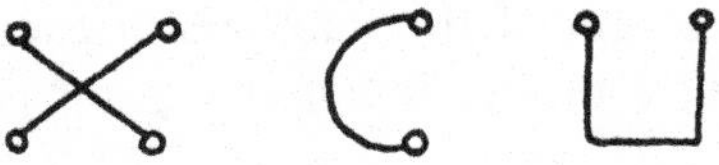

Interspersed among these are to be found circles, spirals, squares and other geometric forms. Figures of this order appear in early Aramaic amulets. What their original purpose or nature was it is difficult at present to determine. Were they merely intended to mystify, or did they possess some meaning? Several medieval writers constructed magical alphabets by allotting a sign to each of the Hebrew letters, but unfortunately no two of these alphabets correspond, nor are they of any help in deciphering amulet inscriptions. One must conclude that these alphabets were individual creations which, instead of being the source of these signs, were inspired by them. These figures appear in small groups, or in wild profusion, at the end of amulet texts, depending upon the ingenuity of the magician. Some amulets consist entirely of such signs, with no written text at all. The following charm illustrates all the elements:[13]

"An amulet for grace and favor; write upon deer-skin: 'By Thy universal name of grace and favor YHVH, set Thy grace YHVH upon N, son of N, as it rested upon Joseph, the righteous one, as it is said, "And the Lord was with Joseph, and showed kindness unto him, and gave him favor" in the sight of all those who beheld him [Gen. 39:21]. In the name of Michael, Gabriel, Raphael, Uriel, Kabshiel, Yah (repeated eight times), Ehyeh, Ahah (four times), Yehu (nine times)'

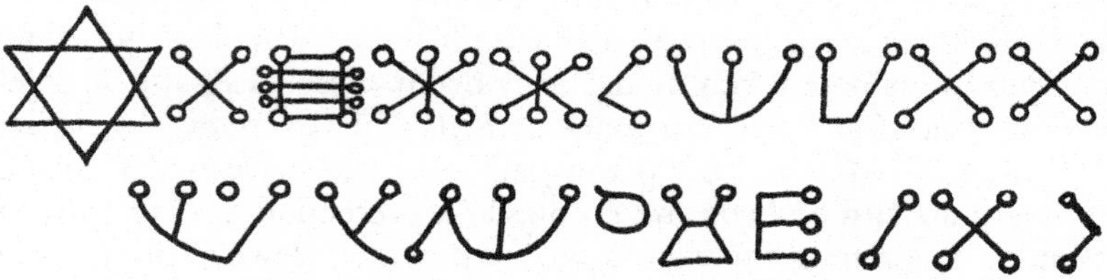

Concerning still another amulet type it is difficult to speak with assurance. The earliest northern Jewish record of it seems to have come to us from the sixteenth or seventeenth century, though it was mentioned by Abraham ibn Ezra in the twelfth. Yet there is little doubt that it must have been known in the North quite as early. This is the *Zahlenquadrat*, or "magic square," a square figure formed by a series of numbers in arithmetic progression, so disposed in parallel and equal rows that the sum of the numbers in each row or line taken perpendicularly, horizontally, or diagonally, is equal. It looks simpler than it sounds:

4	9	2
3	5	7
8	1	6

This is the simplest of these figures; others comprise sixteen boxes, 25, 36, etc. Agrippa von Nettesheim (1486–1535) in his *De Occulta Philosophia* gave these number-squares a special astrological significance, associating each with a planetary deity, in which form they became very popular among Christian Kabbalists and magicians. The numerals in these Christian amulets, of which quite a few are in existence, are frequently in Hebrew, and as a result there has been a tendency to regard them as Jewish. There can be no question, however, despite the Hebrew (Christian magic often employed Hebrew characters) that these astrological amulets, if employed by Jews at all, were so used only after Agrippa had developed his system, and reflected Christian practice.[14]

Leaving aside, then, the late astrological aspect of these number-squares, we find that the simple figure of nine fields, given above, has had a long and varied career in the history of magic. It was highly regarded by the ancient Chinese and Hindus, and is frequently encountered in Arabian magic. For Jews it must have possessed an especially potent character, for apart from its background in Oriental magic, and the mystical light which the Pythagorean theories cast upon its combination of numerals, the Hebrew letters which Jews employed as numerals had particular magical importance: the heart of the figure, the number five, is the Hebrew letter *heh,* which also serves as a symbol of the Tetragrammaton, while the sum, fifteen, is in Hebrew *Yah,* a particle of that name, and independently important as a powerful name of God. An examination of the manuscript material in European collections should disclose some examples of it.

PREPARATION OF AMULETS

Judaism officially countenanced the use of amulets to heal and to prevent disease, as well as to protect the individual. The presence in them of mystical names and quotations from the Bible even raised the difficult issue of their "sacred" character. They were regarded as sufficiently "sacred" not to be worn in a privy, unless encased in a leather pouch, and yet not "sacred" enough to warrant being saved from a fire on the Sabbath. The question arose, furthermore, whether they might be carried on the Sabbath, when it was forbidden to have on one's person anything that could be technically included in the category of burdens, and when it was also forbidden to apply remedies except in cases of serious illness.

The popular addiction to this form of magic was so strong that it was futile to prohibit altogether the use of amulets on the Sabbath, and instead a set of rules was created which distinguished between effective and "approved" (literally, "expert, experienced") amulets, which might be worn on that day, and those technically classed as unapproved. According to these rules, an amulet prepared for a specific function, which had been successfully employed by three different persons, was "approved" as equally effective for all, and an expert who had written three different amulets which had been tested by three individuals was himself "approved," and the products of his skill were permitted to all. Such amulets might be worn on the Sabbath, others not. These principles were established in the Talmud, and were frequently reiterated in the medieval literature. Medieval authorities were willing to forego a test in the case of recognized physicians: amulets written by a "rechter doktor, der gewiss is', un' gedoktrirt is' " were automatically "approved" as coming within these provisions. Their necessity was explained in this wise: were the effectiveness of the amulet, or the writer, to rest solely upon a test made in a single case, the cure might be attributable to the "star" of the patient or physician, rather than to the amulet itself. None the less, however insistently these rules were repeated by the rabbis, popular observance was lax. Even the authorities did not forbid the wearing of "unapproved" amulets on weekdays, though this was the subtle purpose of the legislation, and the rabbinic responsa indicate that they were freely worn on the Sabbath as well. The lust for miracles was more compelling than religious scruple, and rabbinic regulation of the amulet industry was as often honored in the breach as in the observance.[15]

Besides these official regulations there grew up certain generally accepted rules affecting the writing of amulets. While various materials are mentioned, such as several types of parchment, metals, clay, etc., the one most commonly used and expressly preferred was a parchment made from deer-skin. The prescription of ritual and physical cleanliness and purity applied to writers of amulets as well as to other practitioners of Jewish magic, and the formulas frequently specify that the parchment must be *kosher,* that is, ritually acceptable. Emphasizing the religious character of amulets was the benediction, on the order of those prescribed in the liturgy, to be recited before writing one: "Praised be Thou, Lord, our God, King of the universe, who hast sanctified Thy great and revered name, and revealed it to the pious ones, to invoke Thy power and Thy might by means of Thy name and Thy word and the words of Thy mouth, oral and written. Praised be Thou, Lord, King, Holy One; may Thy name be ever extolled."[16]

Lest the writing of amulets be mistaken for a wholly religious act, however, a further element interposed to reveal its fundamentally superstitious character. Not all times were fitting for the task, if success was to be assured. *Sefer Raziel*[17] provides us with a table of hours and days which are most propitious for this exercise—a table which evidence from other sources proves was generally accepted: Sunday, the seventh hour (the day began at about six the preceding evening), Monday, the fifth, Tuesday, the first, Wednesday, the second, Thursday, the fourth, Friday, the fifth and tenth hours. As to the days of the month, to give all the information for those who may have occasion to use it: amulets may be written at any time during the day on the 1st, 4th, 12th, 20th, 22nd, 25th, 28th; in the evening only on the 17th; in the morning only on the 2nd, 5th, 7th, 8th, 11th, 14th, 16th, 21st, 24th, 27th, 30th; and not at all on the remaining days. These times were selected as especially propitious, or the reverse, because of the astrological and angelic forces which were then operative.

"TEFILLIN" AND "MEZUZOT"

Two ritual objects of ambiguous character, the phylacteries and the *mezuzah,* played a part in superstitious usage as well as in religious. The phylacteries undoubtedly developed from some form of amulet or charm, and while their religious nature was already firmly impressed upon them, the Talmud still retained reminiscences of their magical utility in several statements which indicate that they were popularly believed to drive off demons. A prominent rabbi braved the displeasure of his colleagues and wore them in the privy, which was believed to be demon-infested; and in the Middle Ages as well as in Talmudic times they were placed upon a baby who had been frightened out of his sleep by demons. But the effect of religious teaching and custom, and perhaps also the fact that until the thirteenth century the manner of performing the rite and the composition of the phylacteries were far from standardized, so that the entire matter was a moot theological issue, in this case made for a triumph of religion over superstition. During the medieval period there is hardly a sign that they were still regarded as anti-demonic (their use to calm restless infants was unquestionably a reflex of the Talmudic practice). True, we read at times that the *tefillin* ward off the unwelcome ministrations of Satan—but the sense is figurative: the pious man who fulfills the minutiæ of ritual need not fear the powers of evil.[18]

The *mezuzah,* on the contrary, retained its original significance as an amulet despite rabbinic efforts to make it an exclusively religious symbol. Descended from a primitive charm, affixed to the door-post to keep demons out of the house, the rabbinic leaders gave it literally a religious content in the shape of a strip of parchment inscribed with the Biblical verses, Deut. 6:4–19, 11:13–20, in the hope that it might develop into a constant reminder of the principle of monotheism—a wise attempt to re-interpret instead of an unavailing prohibition. But the whitewash never adhered so thickly as to hide the true nature of the device. In the Middle Ages it is a question whether its anti-demonic virtues did not far outweigh its religious value in the public mind. Even as outstanding an authority as Meir of Rothenburg was unwary enough to make this damaging admission: "If Jews knew how serviceable the *mezuzah* is, they would not lightly disregard it. They may be assured that no demon can have power over a house upon which the *mezuzah* is properly affixed. In our house I believe we have close to twenty-four *mezuzot.*" Solomon Luria reports that after R. Meir had attached a *mezuzah* to the door of his study, he explained that "previously an evil spirit used to torment him whenever he took a nap at noon, but not any longer, now that the *mezuzah* was up." With such weighty support it cannot be wondered at that the masses followed R. Meir's way of thinking. Isaiah Horowitz further dignified the proceeding by making it emanate from God Himself. "I have set a guardian outside the door of My sanctuary [the Jewish home]," the deity proclaims, "to establish a decree for My heavenly and earthly households; while it is upon the door every destroyer and demon must flee from it." [19]

So potent did the *mezuzah* become in the popular imagination that its powers were extended to cover even life and death. A Talmudic statement, expounding the Biblical promise, "that your days may be multiplied," has it that premature death will visit the homes of those who fail to observe the law of the *mezuzah* meticulously; in the Middle Ages the literal-minded took the Talmud at its word, and seized upon the pun in the *Zohar* which split *mezuzot* into two words, *zaz mavet,* "death departs," as ample authority for their view that every room in a house should be guarded by a *mezuzah.*

In more recent times, when a community was wasted by plague, its leaders inspected the *mezuzot* on the doorposts to discover which was improperly written and therefore responsible for the visitation. The *mezuzah* has even come off the doorposts; during the World War many of the Jewish soldiers carried *mezuzot* in their pockets to deflect enemy bullets; it has today become a popular watch-charm among Jews.[20] I have even been told of a nun who dropped her purse one day, and among its contents, scattered on the ground, was—a *mezuzah!*

Non-Jewish recognition of the magic powers of the *mezuzah* is not, however, a modern phenomenon. According to Rashi, pagan rulers long ago suspected Jews of working magic against them when they affixed the little capsules to their doors. And, as we have seen, some Christian prelates in the Middle Ages were eager to place their castles, too, under the protection of the humble *mezuzah*.[21]

If we turn now to the *mezuzah* itself,[22] the rules relating to its preparation, and its contents, we are confronted with striking evidence of the extent to which it had become an amulet, pure and simple, in the Middle Ages. The prescription of a high degree of cleanliness and ritual purity preparatory to writing it, while pertinent to its sacred character as an extract from Holy Writ, was none the less of the same nature as that which appertained to the amulet. It was to be transcribed preferably on deer parchment, and the hours which were best suited for its successful preparation correspond with the amulet table given in *Sefer Raziel,* as well as the astrological and angelic influences which were called into play at these times. According to a frequently quoted passage attributed to the Gaon Sherira (tenth century): "It is to be written only on Monday, in the fifth hour, over which the Sun and the angel Raphael preside, or on Thursday, in the fourth hour, presided over by Venus and the angel Anael." This passage, and many others, lumped together *mezuzot, tefillin,* and amulets—indicating that the three were generally regarded as possessing the same essential character.

Rashi stated that both *mezuzot* and amulets contained in common a special type of "large letters," which were peculiar to them. A later commentator suggested that these were in the ancient Hebrew script, but we have no text of an amulet or *mezuzah* containing such letters. Rashi may have meant that certain important elements of the *mezuzah* were written in larger characters than the rest, which indeed we find to be the case with the magical names in many amulets, or he may have referred to the mystical figures, favored in both amulets and *mezuzot*.[23] What is more, we find included in the *mezuzah* verses which speak of God's protection, names of God and of angels (usually written in large letters), and various magical figures of the type mentioned. In brief—the *mezuzah* was actually transformed into an amulet, by embodying in it the features which we discovered to be characteristic of these charms.

We may discern a gradual process at work here. Originally, according to Jewish law, the *mezuzah* was to contain only the prescribed verses; the slightest change, whether of addition or omission, even of a single letter, invalidated the whole. Then, toward the end of the Geonic period the first move to introduce amulet features into the *mezuzah* was made. The face of the *mezuzah* was not invaded, but innovations were introduced upon the back of the parchment, concerning which there was no prohibition. The name Shaddai was inscribed there and a tiny window opened in the case so that the name was visible. This name was considered especially powerful to drive off demons, and by the method of *notarikon* it was read as "guardian of the habitations of Israel." The custom spread rapidly throughout the Jewish world and was adopted everywhere, without a word of censure from the authorities, even the mighty Maimonides agreeing that there was no harm in it, since the name was written on the outside of the parchment.[24]

At the same time, or perhaps subsequent to this first act of daring, another name was added to the *mezuzah,* still on its reverse: the 14-letter name of God, *Kozu Bemochsaz Kozu,* a surrogate for the words *Yhvh Elohenu Yhvh* of the *Shema',* with which the text of the *mezuzah* opens. The earliest reference to this practice was attributed in a fourteenth-century manuscript, *Sefer Asufot,* to the Gaon Sherira; the earliest literary occurrence of this name is in *Eshkol HaKofer,* by the Karaite, Judah Hadassi (middle of the twelfth century). Maimonides (in the same century) fails to speak of it, though he refers in detail to other features of the *mezuzah.* It is likely that he was not acquainted with the practice, or at least that it was not followed by southern Jewry, for Asher b. Yeḥiel (1250–1327), an eminent German scholar who spent the latter part of his life in Spain, stated specifically that it was observed in France and Germany, but not in Spain.[25] From this we may judge that there grew up in the Orient two distinct traditions; one, which prescribed the addition of the name Shaddai alone, made its way to Southern Europe, where it was adopted; the second, adding both names, was introduced in the North (the northern codes all mention both names). This is not unlikely, for we know that the Kalonymides brought with them to the Rhineland a private fund of mystical tradition of Oriental origin, of which this may well have been a constituent. In time the northern practice invaded the South as well. The 14-letter name also possessed highly protective virtues; before leaving on a journey one would place his hand on the *mezuzah* and say, "In Thy name do I go forth," thus invoking its guardianship, for the Aramaic word employed equalled numerically the name *Kozu*.[26]

The next step marked a decided advance. Despite the stringent prohibition against altering in any way the face of the *mezuzah*, and the active and justified opposition of most of the authorities, names, verses, and figures were added. The original impetus here too seems to have been Geonic, though the earliest reference to the change was again in Judah Hadassi's work. During the succeeding two centuries *mezuzah*-amulets achieved a wide popularity; several examples of them have been published by Aptowitzer. Some authorities deviated from the conventional opposition. R. Eliezer b. Samuel of Metz (after 1150 C.E.) voiced only half-hearted disapproval; the *Maḥzor Vitry* regarded the innovations not merely as private usage, or even customary (as distinguished from the legally required form), but as an integral part of the *mezuzah;* while the *Sefer HaPardes* made the additions obligatory, as important, even, as the *halachic* prescriptions.[27] But most of the rabbinic authors unanimously seconded Maimonides' vigorous and uncompromising condemnation of such tampering with the words of Scripture. By the fifteenth century this attitude had triumphed, and even the mystics and Kabbalists of first rank omitted all reference to the magical *mezuzah,* or expressly rejected it. From then on we hear no more of it.

Aptowitzer distinguishes three main types of *mezuzah*-amulets, Palestinian, French and German; the last two are so closely alike that we may regard them as essentially one, but the first is altogether distinct and different. It is interesting that though such *mezuzot* were known in Southern Europe and Northern Africa, we have no extant examples from these regions. Instead of describing these *mezuzot* in detail I give here the text of two of them from the manuscript work *Sefer Gematriaot*,[28] which were unknown to Aptowitzer, and which differ somewhat from those he published. They illustrate clearly the distinctive features of these charms.

I

אנקתם   פסתם

1. יברכך יהוה   שמע ....לבניך   מיכאל
2. וישמרך יאר   ודברת......ובשעריך   כוזו אל אלהים   גבריאל
3. יהוה פניו   והיה ....ומלקוש   עזריאל
4. אליך ויחנך   ואספת........להם   במוכסז יהוה שדי   צדקיאל
5. ישא יהוה פניו   וחרה ....אלה   שרפיאל
6. אליך וישם   על לבבכם......ובקומך   כוזו יה אהיה   רפאל
7. לך שלום   וכתבתם ....הארץ   ענאל

פספסים   ודיוסנים (sic)

On the back of this *mezuzah*, behind the word והיה of line 3, appears the name שדי.

II

1. שמע ישראל יהוה אלהינו יהוה אחד: ואהבת את   יה
2. יהוה אלהיך בכל לבבך ובכל נפשך ובכל מאדך והיו   יה
3. הדברים האלה אשר אנכי מצוך היום על לבבך: ושננתם   מיכאל
4. לבניך ודברת בם בשבתך בביתך ובלכתך בדרך   יהוה
5. ובשכבך ובקומך וקשרתם לאות על ידך והיו לטטפת   גבריאל
6. בין עיניך וכתבתם על מזוזת ביתך ובשעריך: שמרך
7. והיה אם שמע תשמעו אל מצותי אשר אנכי
8. מצוה אתכם היום לאהבה את יהוה אלהיכם ולעבדו   עזריאל
9. בכל לבבכם ובכל נפשכם ונתתי מטר ארצכם בעתו   יהוה
10. יורה ומלקוש ואספת דגנך ותירשך ויצהרך ונתתי
11. עשב בשדך לבהמתך ואכלת ושבעת השמרו לכם   צדקיאל
12. פן יפתה לבבכם וסרתם ועבדתם אלהים אחרים
13. והשתחויתם להם: וחרה אף יהוה בכם ועצר את   צלך
14. השמים ולא יהיה מטר והאדמה לא תתן את יבולה

15. ואבדתם° מהרה מעל הארץ הטובה אשר יהוה נתן לכם — שרפיאל
16. ושמתם את דברי אלה על לבבכם ועל נפשכם וקשרתם — על
17. אתם לאות על ידכם והיו לטטפת בין עיניכם: ולמדתם — רפאל
18. אתם את בניכם לדבר בם בשבתך בביתך ובלכתך ø — יד
19. בדרך ובשכבך ובקומך: וכתבתם על מזוזות ביתך — 
20. ובשעריך: למען ירבו ימיכם וימי בניכם על האדמה — ענאל
21. אשר נשבע יהוה לאבותיכם לתת להם כימי השמים °° — ימינך
22. על הארץ °°°  אוריאל יופיאל חסדיאל — 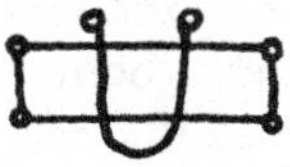

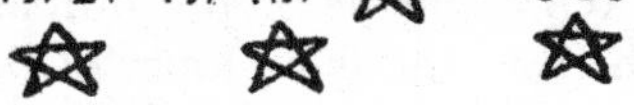

These names and figures are to be inscribed on the back of the *mezuzah*: שדי behind והיה of line 7,  behind כימי השמים of line 21, כוזו במוכסז כוזו at the bottom, and  and  in positions which the text does not clearly identify.

The first, a "Palestinian" *mezuzah,* contains the names of 14 and 22 letters (the former on the face instead of the back of the parchment), as well as six other names of God (El, Elohim, YHVH, Shaddai, Yah, Ehyeh), seven names of angels (Michael, Gabriel, 'Azriel, Zadkiel, Sarfiel, Raphael, 'Anael), and the Priestly Benediction. The second, of the "German" type, contains the same seven angel names and three more at the end (Uriel, Yofiel, Ḥasdiel), the name Yah, twice, the words of Ps. 121:5, the pentagram and other mystical signs, with Shaddai and the 14-letter Kozu, and more figures on the back.

It would take us too far afield to discuss in detail the minor differences between these versions and those of Aptowitzer, which similarly vary from one another. These variations are apparently idiosyncratic, involving the choice and position of the angel-names and of the names of God, the particular magical figures used, the choice of pentagram or hexagram, etc. The general outline was fixed, the details were apparently subject to the whim and esthetic taste of the scribe. While these two *mezuzot* are less elaborate than some of the others, they do possess one striking distinction, namely the insertion of circles and once of a ø in the body of the text. The others were careful at least not to corrupt the Scriptural citation, in which respect they were more closely observant of the prohibition against tampering with the *mezuzah*.

Sefer Gematriaot[29] offers also a detailed mystical apologia for the various unauthorized features, of this nature: the 22 lines correspond to the 22 letters of the alphabet, the ten pentagrams to the ten commandments, and their fifty points to the fifty "gates of understanding" and also to the fifty days between Passover and Pentecost (the "days of the giving of the Law"), the seven angel-names to the seven planets and the seven days of the week, the ten circles to the ten elements of the human body, blood, flesh, bones, etc., five of them to the five names of the soul, the three at the end to the three faculties, hearing, sight and speech, or to heaven, earth and atmosphere, etc. But this rigmarole didn't obscure the true significance of the innovations.

These features make it sufficiently evident that during the Middle Ages the *mezuzah* acquired all the trappings of the legitimate amulet, becoming one in actuality as well as by reputation. No wonder that Jews regarded it with such respect. No wonder that Gentiles envied them its possession.

11

THE WAR WITH THE SPIRITS

It is erroneous to assume that magic is practiced exclusively by professionals, or that it represents always a conscious, deliberate act. As Karl Goldmark once said, "Civilized people lose their religion easily, but rarely their superstitions." There is an anecdote of a well-known actress who, when asked by a zetetic reporter what was her favorite superstition, replied, "Thank Heaven, I have none!"—and unconsciously "knocked wood" as she spoke. How many of us still "knock wood" when we hear or utter a word of praise, without in the least being aware that we are repeating an age-old magical act whose purpose is to distract or frighten away the jealous spirits? Fear of the supernatural has been productive of the greatest number and variety of magical protective devices; and just as the fear has vividly colored man's consciousness of the universe, so these devices have become automatic responses to it. In this sense magic was, and still is, an integral pattern in the fabric of social usage, having influenced profoundly not alone folk-habits, but equally as much religious ceremonial and rite.

RELIGIOUS DEFENSES

The methods of warding off the spirits fell into three general categories: 1. to drive them away, or at least to render them powerless by the application of certain approved means; 2. to buy them off with gifts, to bribe them and thus conciliate them; 3. to deceive them by disguising their intended victims, or by pretending that the situation was other than it actually was. Each of these methods, and often two or all three of them combined, was known and employed by Jews and even found expression in special ceremonies which have become part and parcel of Jewish ritual.

The first category comprised by far the greatest number and variety of procedures. Foremost among these is the power of the religious life to protect the individual. Piety and personal purity constitute a coat of armor which no demon or magic can pierce. The merit of one's ancestors also serves as a protection. From among the multitude of anecdotes that point this moral, the following perhaps best illustrates the apotropaic and remedial virtues of piety: A certain righteous and pious Jew was about to die when a man came to him with a story that his wife had been rendered barren by sorcery, and requested that so soon as the righteous one enter heaven he repair to the throne of God and beg Him to release her from the spell. The sage promised to do so. Within the year the spell was removed and she bore a child. Not only is the truly religious man himself secure, but his merit carries sufficient weight up above to shed security upon his descendants and friends. The man whose life had been devoted to a holy occupation sometimes bore with him to the grave testimony of that fact, instanced in the custom of burying with the performer of circumcisions the foreskins which he had severed, "to drive away from him every demon and destroyer." The practice of fashioning the coffin of a scholar out of the table at which he had pursued his studies probably had a similar purpose.[1]

Various religious acts and occasions were believed to bring immunity against the powers of evil. "Satan is powerless" on *Yom Kippur;* the blowing of the *shofar* at the conclusion of the day "drives off evil spirits" and confuses and confounds the devil. Indeed, the later Kabbalists surrounded the ritual of *shofar* blowing on the High Holydays with a series of Biblical readings whose inner mystical significance and whose "names" furthered this end. Some held that on the Sabbath "we need no other protection" than the merit of the day itself, for "we are all engaged in fulfilling religious duties." On the basis of the interpretation of a Biblical verse (Ex. 12:42) Passover, too, was regarded as "a night of protection" from the demons. This belief aroused an unwonted sense of security, and led to the suspension of certain customary protective measures. It was permissible to employ even numbers, such as the four cups of wine; the prayers recited before retiring were very much abbreviated, passages intended to protect the sleeper being omitted; the doors of houses and rooms were left unlocked overnight as a mark of confidence; when the holiday fell on a Sabbath, the evening prayers inserted in the service to enable late-comers to catch up with the congregation were omitted; if a death occurred immediately before

Passover, when water had already been drawn for the preparation of *Mazzot,* there were some who held it unnecessary to pour this water out, for "it is a night of protection" and the spirits can do no harm.[2]

Study is a uniquely Jewish form of worship; one of the chief features of the religious life is a scholarly regimen. Study therefore was another form of protection. The Bible in itself possesses anti-demonic virtues, as we have seen. The regular reading of the Bible in the synagogue service was believed to protect Israel from the wiles of the devil. "So long as Israel studies the *Torah* Satan has no power over them," and therefore, it was explained, immediately upon the reading of the last verse of Deuteronomy the first verse of Genesis is read, on the holiday of "Rejoicing over the *Torah,*" so that the rehearsal of God's law may not be interrupted even for a moment, and Satan get his chance. It was believed that a man should expire with "words of *Torah*" on his lips, obviously not only as a passport to the heavenly regions, but also as a safeguard on the road. The protective power of study was not limited to the Bible, but extended to all works of Jewish religious import, particularly the Talmud. There is a legend of two demons who were frustrated in their attempts to attack a certain R. Benjamin because his perpetual immersion in his studies rendered him immune. It was this belief in the security of the scholar which gave rise to the notion that the demons accept the challenge and are ever on the alert to distract his attention from his studies and thus pierce his guard.[3]

As the most important single feature of worship we may expect to find prayer singled out as especially powerful in this respect. The destroying angels, among whom is included the angel of death, have no power over those who have participated in the three daily prayer services, or who have recited the prayer *Yozer Or,* the "Eighteen Benedictions," or the grace after meals. As evidence of this fact attention was called to the absence of the letter *peh* in the titles of the services, and in the prayers mentioned, for this letter distinguishes the names of the destroying angels; its absence implies their absence, too.[4]

When a man believes himself to be threatened by demons, or by magic of one sort or another, an appeal to God should win him safety. In an extremity he can resort to extemporaneous prayer. The most direct method is recommended in dealing with a demon who unexpectedly confronts one: "Don't run, but drop to the ground before him; so long as you are prostrate he will not harm you; and pray in the name of God that he do you no hurt." However, the provident man fortified himself with one or another of the many petitions especially composed for such needs—prayers which besought protection against demons, illness, magic, the evil eye, the whole catalogue of perils that beset the superstitious—prayers that concentrated on only one of these dangers, or, more often, lashed out against all of them together, in long-winded, iterative supplication. The Kabbalists, toward the close of the period, were especially prolific of such prayers. Already in the pages of the Talmud we read that "the demons keep away from everyone who recites the *Shema'* before retiring." There grew up an increasingly elaborate scheme of prayer around this nocturnal recitation of the *Shema'*, to reinforce its protective powers, and coupled with straightforward pleas for deliverance from "the terrors that threaten by night" were potent Biblical verses and Psalms, magic names, appeals to the angels, three- and sevenfold repetitions, prayers with obscure mystical connotations, etc. There was no attempt to disguise the purpose of this prayer-service; it was frankly admitted time and again that "it exists only because of the demons."

This night-prayer offers an interesting illustration of the tenacity of magical and superstitious forms. One of its constituents invokes the protection of the angels: "at my right Michael, at my left Gabriel, before me Uriel, behind me Raphael." This is nothing more than a Jewish version of the ancient Babylonian incantation, "Shamash before me, behind me Sin, Nergal at my right, Ninib at my left," or, "May the good Shedu go at my right, the good Lamaššu at my left," etc.[5] And across millennia and continents Ireland provides us with a doggerel Catholic version:

O! Holy Mary, mother mild,
Look down on me, a little child,
And when I sleep put near my bed
The good Saint Joseph at my head,
My guardian angel at my right
To keep me good through all the night;
Saint Brigid give me blessings sweet;
Saint Patrick watch beside my feet.
Be good to me O! mother mild,
Because I am a little child.

While it is difficult to dissociate the religious from the superstitious in such pious practices as fasting and charity, which as expiatory measures served to avert the evil consequences of sin, there can be no doubt that they were believed to exert a certain degree of compulsion upon the supernatural powers. The words of Prov. 10:2, "Charity delivereth from death," were reiterated with enough insistence to lead one to believe that some degree of literalness attached to them. We read that "God forgives all the sins of everyone who fasts on three consecutive days and nights, four times a year, namely, before the tenth of Tebet, before the seventeenth of Tamuz, before *Rosh Hashanah,* and during the ten succeeding days of Penitence." In an unavailing effort to avert assault during the First Crusade, the Jews of Trier, we are informed, distributed almost all their possessions to the poor. This was a fairly common practice in the Middle Ages, individuals sometimes stripping themselves even of their clothes and giving them away, to gain relief from serious illness and other afflictions. Private fasts and almsgiving were recommended in a host of situations: before undertaking a journey, to cure an ailment, to change one's luck, to remedy barrenness, to counteract an omen of death, or an ominous dream, and so on. Communal fasts were also decreed on occasion: for rain, when a pogrom impended, when an unduly heavy tax burden had been laid upon the community, etc.[6]

MAGICAL DEFENSES

Of course, the most obvious means of protection was to post a guard over the threatened individual. This was the purport of the warning against going out at night unaccompanied. The well-known German-Jewish institution of the *Wachnacht,* celebrated with feasting and prayer and study all the night preceding a circumcision, constituted a close watch against demonic attacks. Speaking of people whose condition renders them an easy prey to the spirits, one writer says, "I have known many to observe a meticulous watch over them, in particular over a pregnant woman and a mourner, who are not left alone for a moment, and who are not permitted to go out of doors unless accompanied by an adult or at least by a child." [7]

But a physical guard was not of itself warranted to relieve all fear, and most often supernatural forces were set into operation. The demons must be met on their own ground. Prominent among the anti-demonic measures was the method of magic, the exorcism. All the familiar devices were resorted to—invoking the angels and the holy names, reciting Biblical verses, magical numbers, etc. Most potent among the protective names was *Shaddai*, "Almighty." It was inscribed on the outside of the *mezuzah;* the phylactery straps were so knotted that in combination with the letter *shin* on the head-box they spelled it out; it was uttered prior to departure on a journey; *Kohanim* (descendants of the priestly caste), while offering the Priestly Benediction, spelled it out with their fingers; one did the same to fend off an anticipated assault by a thug; even the dead were afforded its protection, for in some places the fingers of a corpse were bound in such a way as to form the three letters of this name.[8]

The following spell was prescribed to expel demons from a place which they were believed to infest: "Measure off the spot in the four cardinal directions, and mark its borders with strings. Stretch another string the length of the area, alongside one of the borders, and have ten men carrying a Scroll of the *Torah* walk along this string to its end; then move the string a trifle, so that their footprints will touch the impressions made on the first line, and have them follow this second line; repeat this until the entire area has been covered. On each line, the *Torah* preceding them, they should recite the following: the Priestly Benediction (Nu. 6: 24–26), the 'anti-demonic psalm' (Ps. 91), Lev. 26:42, Ezek. 45:12, Deut. 11:12, Is. 62:4, Is. 45:18, Ps. 85:2, Ps. 67:2, Deut. 28:8. They must recite these on each line, and they must tread the entire plot of ground thoroughly. When this has been done they should say, 'With the consent of God, and with the consent of the *Torah,* and of Israel, who guard it, may it be forbidden to any demon, male or female, to invade this place from this time forth and forever.' " Incantations and charms of this sort are to be found aplenty. Before setting out on a journey it was a common practice to invoke the protection of angels. To free a demoniac of his unwelcome visitant one should "fill a new pot with freshly drawn water, pour in some olive oil, and whisper Psalm 10 over it nine times, with the mystical names that appertain to that Psalm, and then bathe the patient with the liquid." Scriptural verses, universally employed against the evil eye, were frequently recommended in Jewish literature for this purpose. Outstanding among these verses were the Priestly Benediction and Gen. 49:22.[9]

Furthermore, Jewish superstition was conversant with the fairly large class of things and actions which have been universally credited with anti-demonic virtues. Here a brief summary of the extensive material may suffice.

Light was one of these protective agents, due, no doubt, to the circumstance that demons shun the light, and also because of the purificatory and expiatory virtues of fire, the source of light. In the Talmud we read that "carrying a torch at night is as good as having a companion (to keep the demons away), while walking by moonlight is equivalent to having two companions." *Sefer Ḥasidim* advises that "anyone who is threatened by demons and approaches fire before uttering a word about it, will not be harmed nor die." This belief partly explains the ubiquity of lights at religious and semi-religious exercises, especially those associated with moments of crisis, although it would be absurd to deny that lights were used also, and perhaps more frequently, because of other significances, symbolic, ritual, superstitious, attached to them.[10]

Water is as potent a cleansing and piacular medium as fire, and consequently it possesses similar protective virtues. If a man who has been bitten by a snake reaches a stream first, the snake dies, but if the snake gets there first, the man dies. Running water neutralizes a magic act, and destroys the magical properties of things; it dispels mirages created by demons, and drives off the spirits themselves. To bar the demons from entering one's home, one must pour water, prepared according to a magic recipe, over the threshold. Many prescriptions for expelling a demon from a possessed person require bathing in water. It was also a common ingredient of superstitious medicaments.[11]

The most powerful liquid, as we have seen, was supposed to be spittle, especially the sputum of a fasting man. Therefore it was suggested that one may protect himself in unclean places, which the spirits haunt, by spitting three times, and even evil thoughts, which are the work of demons, may be dispelled in the same way.[12]

A form of frontal attack upon the spirits is practiced by some peoples, who resort to throwing things or shooting into the air to drive them off. While such practices were not altogether unknown among Jews, the noise that usually accompanies warfare was substituted for the physical encounter. In Talmudic times it was customary to rattle nuts in a jar to scare away the demons that frequent privies, and a precautionary measure against swallowing evil spirits along with some water was to strike the vessel sharply before drinking. Medieval Germans believed that the crack of a whip and the ringing of church bells have the same effect; on the *Polterabend,* preceding a wedding, the demons that threatened bride and groom were driven off by setting up a great clamor and breaking pottery; the same custom is preserved in the "bellin' " that still accompanies a wedding in the Kentucky mountains. Noise-making also figured at Jewish weddings as a measure of protection, as we shall see.[13]

As among other peoples, metals, and iron, in particular, were the most frequently used anti-demonic objects. Eleazar of Worms suggests an explanation which has been favored by modern students of superstition; for protection against demons and witches one should strike a tool made of "acier," he wrote, "for metals are the products of civilization," and thus evidently antipathetic to the spirit masters of primitive pre-metal society. However, this is only one of the explanations advanced nowadays. The magic circle was to be drawn with a knife or sword; a piece of iron suspended in water protects it against demonic contamination during the *Tekufah;* iron was put into a hen's nest to guard the chicks against suffocation and fright during a thunderstorm; pregnant women kept a knife with them when alone; the key to the synagogue was placed under the pillow of the dying man.[14]

Salt was another such substance which figured prominently in the folklore of European peoples. Thus it was believed that salt is never found at the witches' Sabbat feast, and the Inquisitor and his assistants at a witch-trial were warned to wear bags containing consecrated salt for protection against the accused. Jewish folklore credited salt with an equally high potency. In Ezek. 16:4 we learn that new-born babes were rubbed with salt, a practice still current in the Orient. According to medieval authorities, salt must be set on a table before a meal is begun "because it protects one against Satan's denunciations." The Kabbalists were more outspoken: "It drives off the spirits," they wrote, "because it is the mathematical equivalent of three YHVH's; therefore one should dip the piece of bread over which the benediction is recited, three times into salt." "After each meal eat some salt and you will not be harmed." For this reason salt was used in many rites connected with birth, marriage and death, and in medicine.[15]

Very often salt and bread were jointly prescribed to defeat the stratagems of spirits and magicians. When a witch assaults a man, he can bring about her death by forcing her to give him some of her bread and salt. Murderers ate bread and salt immediately after their crime to prevent the return of their victim's spirit to wreak vengeance upon them. Schudt reports that a Jewish woman advised him to hang bread and salt on his daughter's neck to protect her from harm; "she had done this to all her children and in consequence they had all prospered." The common practice of bringing salt and bread into a new home before moving in, usually explained as symbolic of the hope that food may never be lacking there, was probably also in origin a means of securing the house against the spirits.[16]

Along with salt, sharp herbs and condiments in general have been widely regarded as anti-demonic, and have had an important place in religious rites of purification. This is not true, however, of Jewish practice to any appreciable extent, though such ingredients were occasionally prescribed in medicaments, where their power to expel spirits may have been their recommendation, along with their more natural medicinal properties.[17]

Among the most widely used anti-demonic devices in Europe is the gesture called "to fig" (in German, *die Feige weisen,* in French, *faire la figue,* in Italian, *far la fica,* in Spanish, *hacer el higo*), recognized as a sign of defiance and insult in ancient and modern times. It is made by closing the fist and inserting the thumb between two fingers. Its peculiarly obnoxious character, to men and spirits alike, derives from the fact that it is meant as an obscene representation of the sexual act. Menasseh b. Israel was correct both in his explanation of the intent of this gesture, and his association of it with the Talmudic recommendation that to protect oneself against the evil eye one should place his right thumb in his left fist and his left thumb in his right fist. While this gesture differs in form, its significance is the same. In the Middle Ages, however, Jews were acquainted with the authentic "fig": "If a demon confronts a man he should bend his thumb between his fingers," or, more explicitly, "When a man encloses his thumb in his fist he simulates a pregnant woman, and they [the spirits] do not harm him." People who employed this gesture were warned that it infuriates the demons at the same time that it renders them harmless; therefore, a weak person, "especially one who is dangerously ill," should forbear to use it, for the spirits may subsequently take vengeance on him. Variations on this theme were also employed: For safety on a journey one should place the little finger of the right hand in the left fist and recite a charm formula. The fingers were used as phallic symbols to the same end, and we learn that a witch is transfixed when one raises his index finger and thumb and recites the name "Uriel" seven times, or that an "evil impulse" may be vanquished by pressing the thumbs on the ground, repeating "Pipi" nine times, and spitting.[18]

STRATAGEM

These methods constitute the arsenal employed in the war against the spirits—weapons of more or less direct attack. But strategy knows more devious means of disarming a foe. The gift—or bribe, depending upon the viewpoint—has been proven easily as effective in conciliating demons as men. "If a sorcerer or a witch demands anything of you," we read in *Sefer Ḥasidim,* "don't hesitate to give them a coin or two, so that they shall not bewitch you, just as you would make a present to the demons, or to a maniac, to forestall their doing you some harm." In magic, as we have observed, the offering played a conspicuous and often deliberate rôle. Countless customs among all peoples have cunningly preserved the good-will offering to the spirits, so that to this day Jews and non-Jews innocently continue to tender their gifts of peace to the unseen powers. The harsh building-sacrifice, once universally observed, which involved originally the immolation of a human being to secure the stability and safety of a structure, was in time mitigated into an animal sacrifice. Medieval Germans still felt the need of protecting their homes by burying a fowl or an animal in its walls; I know of no analogous Jewish practice during the Middle Ages.

Offerings to the spirits made their appearance in many guises. When a beast or fowl upset a dish or some other utensil this was taken to be an ill omen; one must kill the offending creature at once. The sacrifice of the animal may appease the spirits. In a sense the offering represents a substitute for the intended victim, which the spirits are ready to accept even when it is proffered accidentally and not by design. "When an angel is dispatched to take a man's life, if another born under the same planetary influences chances to die, the first is spared." When the angel of death comes to town the dogs are immediately aware of his presence and freeze in their tracks; if a dog's master should push him forward, the animal will drop dead; "the dog then serves as a substitute for the man whom the angel of death has been sent to kill." [19]

A superstitious dread of unnatural behavior manifested itself in a summary destruction of the offender. A cow which bore twins, or a hen that laid two eggs in one day, was executed; a tree which produced fruit twice in one year was cut down. In one instance, when a child was born with two sets of teeth and a rudimentary tail, its life was barely saved by the vigorous intercession of a "wise man." Although the Talmud condemned the practice of killing a crowing hen as "heathenish superstition," fear that this aberrant behavior betokened misfortune persisted, and the unlucky fowl met a speedy death. It has been argued that the references to this practice are merely a figurative expression of the male conviction that woman should keep her place—if she attempts to usurp her husband's authority she becomes dangerous. An Italian proverb employs the same figure: *In quella casa non è mai pace, dove la gallina canta ed il gallo tace.* But ingenious though this supposition is, it pays little regard to the plain sense of the texts. There can be no doubt that the practice was observed quite literally and that the execution was regarded as a means of appeasing the powers that had decreed the impending bad luck. The observation that "the hen's head is chopped off at the threshold of the house" can indicate nothing else than that it was an offering to the spirits.[20]

The *Kapparah* rite is an interesting version of the famous "scapegoat" offering, which occurs in various forms among many peoples. It was first mentioned in early Geonic times, and probably originated toward the end of the Talmudic period. The following account, quoted by Rashi from a Geonic source, describes a form of this rite which was no longer followed during the Middle Ages: two or three weeks before *Rosh Hashanah* the head of the family planted beans in little baskets, one for each member of the family; when these sprouted on the eve of the New Year he would circle the head of each individual with his basket seven times, saying, "This is in place of this person, this is his surrogate, this is a substitute for him," and throw it into the river.

The procedure that prevailed in the Middle Ages, also mentioned in Geonic writings, differed. It involved the slaughter of a cock for the male, a hen for the female, on the eve of *Yom Kippur* (in Geonic times a ram, or lamb, or goat might also be used), after the following ritual: the fowl was passed three times around the head of the subject, while various Biblical passages were recited; the announcement was then made, "This fowl is my substitute, this is my surrogate, this is my atonement." Some old texts significantly add, "May it be designated for death, and I for life." According to one account, after the fowl was slaughtered, "the entrails were thrown on the roof for the birds of heaven"; the usual procedure was to present the entire fowl to the poor "as an act of charity in accordance with the words 'Charity delivereth from death,'" but some of the rabbis frowned upon this method of disposal, favoring rather the distribution of the money value of the bird, "for when it is given to a poor man, he says to himself, that man has transferred his sins to the cock, and I seem to him of so little worth that he sends it to me." In Spain the rite did not meet with the approval of several of the leading authorities. R. Solomon b. Adret (thirteenth century), who stated specifically that it was observed without objection in Germany, was himself poorly acquainted with it and confused it with another local superstitious custom. The earliest editions of the *Shulḥan 'Aruch,* the authoritative law code of modern Jewry, contain the opinion of its Palestinian author, Joseph Caro, that this is "a silly custom" and its observance "should be checked"; under the influence of the sixteenth-century Polish annotator, Moses Isserles, the first words were eliminated from later editions. It is possible that the rite was not observed in Angevin England, for the author of the only code composed there introduced his description of it with the words, "I have found in the *Seder of R. Amram* that . . .," implying that he was not acquainted with it from his own experience.

The intent of the rite was to transfer the sins of the individual to the fowl, and by offering this substitute to the supernatural powers save oneself from the punishment decreed in heaven. The various features of the ceremony accentuate its superstitious and even magical character. Fowl are closely associated with the spirits in Jewish and non-Jewish lore, and are the commonest oblation to them. The Hebrew term for "rooster," *gever* (a word which, it should be noted, attained fairly wide currency only in post-Talmudic times), also means "man," making the one a palpable substitute for the other. The cock is employed to represent a man, the hen, a woman, in many magic rites. The circles which are described about the head of the individual, and the numbers three and seven, are well-known magical elements. The words which effectuate the substitution have all the earmarks of a typical incantation. In the earlier texts the words "this is my atonement" are not present; they were added later so that the initials of the Hebrew terms might form the word

Ḥatach, "which is the name of the angel appointed over this." The belief that evil spirits roost on roofs occurs often (the Talmud places them under the eaves), and many folk-customs, including the German, display instances of placing offerings to the spirits on a roof. In view of this the requirement that the entrails be thrown on a roof acquires special significance. Thus analyzed there can be little doubt of the true meaning of the rite, which is still observed today. It is probably the most blatantly superstitious practice to have entered Jewish religious usage, for where the significance of other such practices has long been lost sight of, the purpose of this one is too apparent to escape even the dullest wits. However little meaning the details of the rite may convey to the uninformed, the substitution of fowl for man is unescapable.[21]

Not unrelated is the rite of *Tashlich,* observed on the first day of *Rosh Hashanah,* which derived its name from the words of Micah 7:19, "Thou wilt cast (*tashlich*) all their sins into the depths of the sea." The first direct reference to it in its modern form is by R. Jacob Mölln (Maharil, d. 1425), and the general impression has therefore been that it originated not earlier than the fourteenth century, with the German Jews. Professor Lauterbach, however, has shown that this ceremony represents merely the latest version of a complex of superstitious practices centering about the belief in the existence of spirits in bodies of water, which reaches back to remote antiquity. Maharil's comment is suggestive of a connection with the first form of the *Kapparah* rite, for he speaks of people "throwing bread to the fish in a river." This apparently was the essential feature of the ceremony, for in later times *Tashlich* was postponed if the first day of the New Year fell on a Sabbath, on the ground that carrying bread was a violation of the Sabbath rules.

Whatever its origin, the explanations varied widely. Maharil viewed it as a symbolic affirmation of faith: according to a Midrashic legend, when Abraham was on his way to fulfill God's demand that he sacrifice Isaac, Satan flung a swift-flowing stream across his path, but the patriarch pressed forward, confident that God would respond to his plea for aid. Mölln, then, stressed the mere act of visiting a river as paramount, and in fact, opposed the practice of throwing crumbs into it. Others suggested that since the limitless deep saw the beginning of Creation, visiting a body of water on New Year was the most impressive reminder of the Creator's might; or that man should emulate the river, endlessly renewing itself, forswear his evil ways and return home a new man; or that the fish which devour the crumbs illustrate the plight of man, who is "as the fishes that are taken in an evil net" (Eccl. 9:12), and arouse him to repentance; or, again, that the fish, whose eyes never close, symbolize the Guardian of Israel who slumbereth not. These explanations only too patently evade the main issue, the bread offering to the spirits. Under Kabbalistic influence an attempt was made to limit the rite to shaking one's clothes at the river-side ("to dislodge the *kelippot*," the clinging demons of sin) and reciting various prayers and Biblical selections "whose secret significance is very profound." What the popular conception of the purpose of this rite was may be gleaned from the rabbinic animadversions against "those men, with as little sense as a woman, who say, 'I am going to the river to shake off my sins,' and grasping the edges of their garments shake them violently and imagine that in this way they can slough off a whole year's transgressions." However, it is with this meaning for the masses that the ceremony has survived.[22]

Less formal food offerings were also fairly common. The Talmud cites the opinion of R. Eleazar b. Pedat: "He who leaves crumbs on the table is to be regarded as a worshiper of heathen gods," and from the discussion it would appear that not only "crumbs" but sometimes whole loaves were set on the table at the conclusion of a meal. Other usages of the same nature were popular in Talmudic times; try as they might the rabbis could not root them out. They compromised by forbidding the leaving or scattering of food "that may spoil," thus accepting the practices but obscuring their purpose. In the Middle Ages the Talmudic custom was sedulously observed; crumbs, "but not morsels of bread," were left on the table, the explanation offered being that this was a symbolic expression of hospitality to the wayfarer and the needy. Still we find that on certain occasions, notably on the eve of a circumcision, a table was set especially for the delectation of the spirits.

On Friday nights, too, a loaf of bread and a cup of wine were set aside during the meal or left standing overnight. Some advanced the dubious rationalization that this was "in commemoration of the manna" which fell in double portion on the eve of the Sabbath, but there were rabbis who saw through the shallow evasion and did not hesitate to categorize it as "setting a table for the demons." Yet it continued to be done, sometimes with the frank admission that "it extends fullness of blessing over the entire week." During the Passover *Seder* a cup of wine is filled expressly for the Prophet Elijah, who is believed to visit every Jewish home on that occasion, and the door is opened for him to enter—this time the offering is to a good spirit, rather than an evil one. But during the same service there is a late custom, which arose in German-Jewish circles, to pour out a drop of wine at the mention of each of the ten plagues, possibly to placate the evil spirits, who may be impelled by the reference to so many disasters to visit some of them upon the celebrants. Israel Isserlein's biographer wrote of him, "He always spilled some of the water from his cup before drinking," thus observing a universal Jewish custom going back to Talmudic times. The explanation then given was that the water might have been contaminated by a demon —but obviously merely spilling some of it doesn't purify it all. The intention was to induce the demon to neutralize the possible ill effect of the water by making him a libation.

On Saturday evening, during the *Habdalah* ceremony which marks the beginning of the new week, another libation was offered to the spirits, as part of the ritual. Some of the wine was poured upon the ground "as a good omen for the entire week, to symbolize good fortune and blessing," for was it not written in the Talmud, "A man in whose home wine does not flow like water is not among the truly blessed"? This custom was not mentioned earlier than the Geonic period; the Talmudic support was wholly arbitrary, for the plain sense of the words is the reverse of the interpretation here given them. The Talmud speaks of overflowing wine not as a symbol of blessing to come, but as a token of blessings already enjoyed. The Geonim admitted that the custom was not altogether respectable when they included it among a list of superstitious practices. Centuries later we come across a recognition of its true significance which shows the retentiveness of the popular memory. Moses Mat in the sixteenth century wrote that this practice is intended to "give their portion to the company of Korah," namely, to the powers of evil. And that portion was not inconsiderable. As one rabbi in Silesia remarked, "If I had the wine that is poured upon the ground in Austria during *Habdalah* it would suffice to quench my thirst for a whole year!" This custom of pouring out some wine over which a blessing had been recited, which appears again in the wedding ceremony, may have been considered by some people not as an offering to the spirits, but as a means of driving them off. Christians in those days believed that consecrated water had such power, and Jews may also have believed that the wine of the "cup of blessing" would have the same effect.[23]

The final weapon in the anti-demonic strategy is that of deceit. It figures prominently in the initiation, marriage and burial rites of primitive peoples and not a few examples have been collected from European folk-customs. Medieval Jews, however, resorted to this device only rarely. Apart from several instances connected with birth and marriage, to be cited later, it was most commonly employed in changing an invalid's name so that the spirits who might be charged with effecting his death would be unable to locate him. This deception was also practiced by individuals who had suffered a run of bad luck; just as criminals adopt aliases to evade the police, so medieval Jews embraced new names to give their spirit harriers the slip. Changing one's residence, or moving out of a city altogether, was another way of confusing and eluding the demons; this remedy was suggested to people whose fortune had soured, to couples whose children died young, to men who had lost their peace of mind through the operation of love charms.[24]

BIRTH, MARRIAGE AND DEATH

Birth, marriage, illness, death—these were the moments when a pall descended upon man—not only upon the individuals directly involved, but upon all those who were in their vicinity. It was in such moments that the whole battery of anti-demonic weapons was trained upon man's mortal enemies, that we find a massing of all those superstitious devices which from time immemorial have been accredited with potency to counteract magic, curses, the evil eye, to cure disease, to shatter the onslaught of the evil spirits.

A brief enumeration of the customs associated in Jewish life with these critical moments, which display either singly or in combination the anti-demonic measures described, may astound many Jews familiar with some of them as a respectable part of Jewish ceremonial. The Jewish propensity for re-interpreting ineradicable primitive usages and endowing them with religious values has successfully masked their true significance, at least in the western world. In Eastern Europe and in the Orient, where more primitive attitudes still prevail among the masses, an awareness of the real import of such customs still persists, albeit along with a doctrinal acceptance of the rationalizations which the rabbinic purifiers of Judaism have promulgated. This was the case during the Middle Ages—most teachers struggled valiantly to uproot the superstitious ideas, if not the actual practices with which they were associated, but many comments reveal the ineffectuality of their efforts. Not all of these practices were employed collectively, nor were they of equal moment; the selection varied from place to place and from time to time, often according to individual predilection, and was frequently accompanied by the recital of Biblical verses, amulets, etc.

Birth

1. The woman in childbirth was closely guarded; men were stationed in the house who prayed for her and her child, and recited various Psalms that were believed to be effective against the spirits. They were warned, however, on no account "to gossip about any sins that she might have committed." After the birth of her child she was not permitted to stir out of the house alone until after the circumcision.[25]

2. The Scroll of the *Torah* and phylacteries were placed on her bed, or at least brought to the door of her room.[26]

3. Candles were lit in her behalf.[27]

4. During the last days prior to delivery she would keep a knife with her when she was alone. According to a late report, which probably reflects an earlier usage, the key to the synagogue was placed in her hand during labor; in isolated country places and villages where there was no synagogue the key to a church was borrowed for this purpose.[28]

5. A circle was drawn around the lying-in bed, and a magical inscription (reading "Sanvi, Sansanvi, Semangelaf, Adam and Eve, barring Lilit") was chalked upon the walls or door of the room.[29]

6. I know of no record of an actual offering to the spirits at this time, though it was customary among the Germans, and occurs in Oriental Jewries. However, a prime protective amulet bore the figures of fowl, which may be taken to have been a refinement of an earlier offering.[30]

7. It was suggested, to ease labor pains, that a woman should wear an article of her husband's clothing, such as his doublet, trousers, or belt.[31]

Circumcision

1. The rite itself must be considered as in some degree a measure of protection against the forces of evil. It is significant that the heightened danger which threatens both mother and infant during the eight days prior to the operation subsides immediately afterward. Circumcision ushers the child into the community of Israel and at the same time evokes the guardianship of the powers of good. Certain incidental usages illustrate the potency attributed to circumcision. A Geonic source is cited as authority for this practice: the bloody foreskin was placed in a bowl containing water and spices, and each member of the congregation, as he left the synagogue (where the rite used to be performed), would bathe his hands and face. A late work suggests, as a "wonderful charm," that during the days preceding the rite the foreskin of a child previously circumcised be put into the mouth of the infant who is about to undergo the operation. In a thirteenth-century manuscript we read: "Why was it ordained that the cloth [upon which the circumciser wipes his blood-stained hands and mouth] be hung at the door of the synagogue [during and after the operation]? My uncle, Ephraim of Bonn, said that the sages explained it thus: Israel was redeemed from Egypt because of a double blood merit, the blood of the Paschal lamb and the blood of circumcision; and Israel 'shall take of the blood and put it on the lintel' of their houses (cf. Ex. 12:7) as a token that the Destroyer shall not have power over their homes, to do them harm. . . ." [32]

2. The child was very carefully guarded during these eight critical days.[33]

3. "The essence of protection is to remain awake nights and study *Torah* until the circumcision." The writer might have added, and to recite mystical prayers and Psalms, for these were included in the vigils. This should be done "particularly on the night before the circumcision, because the spirits are most incensed then," or, as another writer put it, "because Satan strives to harm the child and to prevent it from experiencing the religious rite of circumcision, for he is very much provoked that Jews should keep the commandment by whose merit they are saved from *Gehinnom*." This is the *Wachnacht,* during which an unremitting watch was maintained over the child, eked out with prayers and study. The occasion of a circumcision was celebrated in ancient times with a feast on the night be-

fore, or on the day of the performance of the rite. In the Middle Ages both feasts were observed, or rather the one was begun in the evening and continued on the following day. The special *Wachnacht* custom developed out of this. How early this happened we cannot say; the references to it go back no further than the sixteenth century, and the name itself was not used until later. One sixteenth-century writer did record that in Elsass the name used was *Gitot Nacht* while in other parts of Germany and in Metz it was called *Wazinacht,* but these transliterations are not very helpful. They have been variously interpreted as *Gottesnacht* and *Weizennacht,* as French and German versions of *Wachnacht,* and as *Güets Nacht* and *Waizen-Nacht.* Whichever of these translations may be correct, the suggestion of Güdemann that the terms signify *Spuknacht* may be accepted as essentially faithful to the temper of the observance.[34]

4. It was customary, in some places, "to set a table with varieties of food on the night before the circumcision, with the explanation that they are doing this for the child's star" (or "to bring him good luck"). The rabbis pointed out that this was nothing else than an offering to the spirits.[35]

5. The custom of setting aside a chair for the Prophet Elijah during the circumcision goes back to early times, and was connected with a legend that God had rewarded the prophet for his zealous defense of this rite with the promise that he would be present at every circumcision. In origin, this custom was of a piece with the offering to the spirits, to bribe the evil ones, and to entertain the good ones, and is analogous to similar practices among the Romans. It was not merely a symbolic gesture; something of Elijah's presence was actually believed to inhabit his chair. During the Middle Ages it was customary for the assembled guests to rise before the ceremony, and to greet the unseen visitor with the words, "Blessed be he that cometh."[36]

6. "This also is a protective measure," we read: "the house should be full of light" on the days before the circumcision, and candles were lit in profusion, especially while the circumcision was being performed. The purpose was not to obtain light, for the rite was performed during the daytime. The variety of explanations indicates uncertainty about the real reason, or a desire to obscure it. "The commandment is a lamp and the *Torah* is light" (Prov. 6:23) was cited as Scriptural basis for the practice; or it was explained as "an expression of rejoicing and honor"; or again, as a notice to

Jewish passersby that the ceremony was in progress, originating in an ancient proscription against circumcisions which consequently had to be performed in secret. In more recent times it was customary to light thirteen candles, ostensibly to correspond with the thirteen occurrences of the word "covenant" (*berit*) in the Biblical chapter (Gen. 17) which speaks of circumcision, or with the thirteen tribes (including the half-tribes of Ephraim and Menasseh), or with the twelve tribes plus one for the child, this last candle being permitted to burn itself out.[37]

7. The *Hollekreisch,* which has already been described, was a measure to drive off evil spirits during the ceremony of naming the child, by shouting and tossing the infant in the air.[38]

Marriage

1. Both bride and groom (in some places only the groom) fasted on the wedding day. A variety of far-fetched explanations was offered for this custom; one, which attained the height of absurdity, was that the groom might not be suspected of inebriety during the ceremony! [39]

2. The groom was escorted from his home to the synagogue by attendants; "just as a king is surrounded by his guards, so the attendants surround the groom," was the significant parallel. Sometimes the entire congregation accompanied him. For a while before and after the wedding the groom was forbidden to venture out-of-doors alone.[40]

3. The wedding procession, in broad daylight, was preceded by young men bearing lighted torches or candles, which were sometimes thrown into the air. Loud and often discordant music characterized the procession.[41]

4. The custom of breaking a glass at the wedding, which, according to some, goes back to Talmudic times, was a regular feature of the medieval ceremony. The groom would step on the glass, or dash it on the ground, or shatter it against the north wall. The explanations generally account for this practice as a token of sadness which should leaven all rejoicings, or more commonly after the fourteenth century, as a sign of mourning for the destruction of Jerusalem; but some of the very rabbis who advanced these explanations were aware of their artificiality. There are indications that the real purpose of the custom had not been forgotten, as in the comment that it was

intended "to give the accuser [Satan] his due." The demons were believed to come from the north, and therefore the detail that the glass was thrown against the north wall has special significance in this connection. The custom combined an attempt to frighten off the demons with noise, and a direct attack upon them.[42]

5. The wedding ceremony contained several instances of presenting gift-offerings to the spirits. Some of the wine over which the marriage blessings had been recited was poured on the ground. A special feature of this practice, mentioned in one source, namely, to scatter the wine over the entire house, may perhaps be accounted for as due to the belief that the "wine of blessing" drives away the demons. In Talmudic times it was customary to strew food, such as wine and oil, parched corn and nuts, fish and meats, before the bridal pair; during the Middle Ages the practice usually was limited to scattering grains of wheat over and around them, just as we do today with rice. In some places gold coins were mingled with the wheat; in others, salt was scattered over the couple. The Talmudic custom of carrying a hen and rooster before the bride and groom was transmuted in the Middle Ages to flinging a pair of fowl over their heads. The commonest explanation of these practices was that they were symbols of fertility and prosperity. But as Samter has shown after a study of similar usages all over the world, such fertility symbols are at bottom offerings to the spirits to gain their good-will. The presence of the gold coins, which may be viewed either as bribes, or as an anti-demonic use of metal, and of salt, which certainly was intended to drive away the demons, emphasizes the general nature of these customs.[43]

6. An effort was made to introduce a note of mourning into the ceremony, ostensibly over the destruction of Jerusalem. Bride and groom wore white shoes, ashes or dust was strewn upon the heads of both, or of the groom alone, or a strip of black cloth was wound around their heads, they were clothed in funereal garb, the bride wearing a shroud called a *sarganes,* the groom, a hooded cloak, or *mitron,* "as mourners do in the Rhineland." The custom of crying and wailing at weddings has remained prevalent to this day, especially among the Jews of Eastern Europe and the Orient. The real purpose of all this doubtless was to delude the demons into imagining it was a sorrowful and not a joyous occasion, and thus to avoid arousing their envy and hatred.[44]

7. During the ceremony the groom's *mitron,* or his prayer-shawl,

was spread over the head of the bride, and immediately after the wedding he "placed in her bosom" his doublet, girdle and cap. These may have been vestiges of an ancient exchange of clothes between the two, a custom frequently encountered among other peoples. The widespread custom of covering the bride's face with a veil, which prevailed throughout the Middle Ages, was originally intended to hide her from the spirits.[45]

8. In some places the groom carried a piece of iron in his pocket during the ceremony. Toward the end of the Middle Ages it became customary to march the bride three times around her mate, apparently a version of the magic circle. And finally, to point the moral, no sooner was the ceremony over than "they would rush the groom off to the wedding chamber before the bride, by way of rejoicing." A strange "way of rejoicing" indeed! The mad dash was only to get him to the bridal chamber before the demons, recovering from the bombardment to which they had been subjected, prevented him from enjoying his newly won connubial happiness.[46]

Death

The same motifs are repeated in the customs connected with death. A dying man was on no account to be left alone. Mystical prayers were prescribed to be read in his presence, notably the prayer *Ana Bekoaḥ,* which contains an acrostic of the powerful 42-letter name of God. Candles were lit beside his bed, quite frankly, "to drive away the demons." It was suggested that a loaf of bread be placed beside him "to straighten his limbs," in other words, to ease his final moments. Chicken feathers, no doubt because of the relationship that existed between demons and this fowl, were believed to prolong the death-agony, and therefore bedding containing such feathers was removed from beneath the dying man. Such practices were intended to repel the demons, who, in their struggle for the body of the departing one, were held responsible for the anguish that he suffered. But death itself is the work of spirit forces, and the very measures that oblige the demons to keep their distance, and thus make death easier, have the same effect upon the angel of death, and upon the soul preparing timidly for its exit from the body, and therefore delay the end. This was undoubtedly in the mind of many folk who resorted to these measures. However, believing that death is an inherent phase of life, and that it is decreed by God, the rabbis strongly opposed such efforts to delay its coming. Thus, they forbade shouting at a dying man, or engaging in any noisy occupation, such as chopping wood, for noise prevents the soul from leaving the body. Similarly, salt delays death, and one should not put any upon the dying man's tongue for that purpose; but it was permissible to remove salt if it had coagulated upon his tongue. It was also customary to place the key to the synagogue under his head, though this too was forbidden by the authorities.[47]

THE CORPSE. The rules for preparing the corpse for burial were compiled in early post-Talmudic times, and comprise practices such as closing the eyes, placing metal or salt on the body, setting a light at its head, etc., which were undoubtedly originally intended to confound the spirits and the ghost of the deceased, both of which the survivors feared. While it was forbidden to place a Scroll of the *Torah* on the coffin, as seems to have been done at times, it could be set near the body. The Talmud lamely explained the watch over the corpse as intended to protect it from rodents and other such marauders, but later writers confessed that it was meant as a protection against attack from the spirit world. A ritual of study and prayer for this watch was developed during the Middle Ages. The Polish Kabbalist, Isaiah Horowitz, wrote, "I have received a tradition that those who watch the corpse from the moment of death until it is covered with earth should gather around it so closely that not a breath of 'outside' [a term often applied to demons] air can seep past their guard; they should constantly repeat this prayer without an instant's pause, even a thousand times"; the prayer is the acrostic of the 42-letter name of God. Another late medieval custom was to march seven times around the corpse and to recite "certain Biblical selections which drive away the spirits so that they may not seize the body." The belief that a clenched fist, the "fig," is anathema to demons, led to the practice of bending the fingers of a corpse so that even in the grave their depredations might be forestalled. The rabbis inveighed against this "heathenish" custom, and insisted that the fingers must be straightened out before burial, but the practice persisted. In later times it was modified and the fingers were bent in such a way as to form the name *Shaddai*, again arousing rabbinic displeasure. Finally, those who had prepared the corpse for burial were instructed to wash in salt and water, and to beware even of turning over the board upon which the body had lain lest they incite the ire of the deceased and "some one die within three days." [48]

BURIAL. Funeral rites reflect in a dozen ways the ever-present fear of the supernatural, temporarily heightened as the demons and the ghost of the deceased hover in uncomfortable proximity to the living. Several times the warning is repeated not to set a coffin containing a corpse on top of another, and not to leave a grave open overnight, "or someone will assuredly die in a few days"; one source has it "within nine days." The numeral is indicative of the cause of apprehension; the spirits are touchy about such things, and make speedy reprisal. This explanation is not given in the sources, but as an illustration of the tenacious popular awareness of the purposes of superstitious acts I may note that in recent times, among Russian Jews, when a grave had been dug and was not used promptly, it was filled in overnight and a rooster was buried in it![49]

1. The custom of pouring out all the water in and near a house in which a death has occurred is not mentioned in Jewish sources earlier than the thirteenth century, and is evidently a medieval innovation. It was observed by Christians in Germany and France at a still earlier date, and was no doubt borrowed from them. The Jewish practice, which does not follow the more usual and simpler procedure of pouring water across the threshold after the corpse has been removed, to bar the way to the homesick ghost, is susceptible of several explanations. In Christian France, where the same custom existed, these three explanations were offered in the fifteenth century: the soul of the deceased might drown if all the vessels were not emptied; the water reflects the struggle between the soul and the demons, which human eyes may not behold; the soul bathes in it thrice before leaving for the other world, and it may not therefore be used.

The contemporaneous Jewish explanations differed: spilling the water constitutes a silent annunciation of a death, which it is dangerous to mention aloud; the angel of death, who according to Talmudic legend fulfills his mission with a sword steeped in poison, might let a drop of the deadly fluid fall into the water, and thus render it unfit to drink. The fact that *all* the water in and near the house was spilled exposes the first explanation as an obvious rationalization; the second sounds more "realistic," according to medieval standards. In modern times Jews in Eastern Europe set a glass of water and a towel beside the bed of a dying man so that the angel of death may cleanse his sword and wipe it. But this same custom also prevails among non-Jews, their explanation being that the soul bathes and dries itself before departing on its long journey. This is the likeliest interpretation not only of this late custom, but of the earlier one also; it emerges quite explicitly from the many examples of this and related practices which scholars have collected from all over the world. Fear that the immersion of the soul would contaminate the water for the living was responsible for *all* of it being poured out, to make sure the danger was averted. Even food prepared with water was suspect. Interestingly, a sixteenth-century Inquisitorial "Edict of Faith" posited the following as an unmistakable mark of Marranism (adherence to Judaism while professing Christianity): "Pouring water from jars and pitchers when someone has died, believing that the soul of such persons will come and bathe in the water."

We must recognize, however, that such customs are rarely simple in their motivation and meaning, but rather come in time to represent a perplexing maze of folk-notions. This usage was observed for any or all of the reasons advanced—or for none at all, except the apprehension that something terrible would happen if it weren't. There is a possibility, even, that the water was also intended as a libation to the spirits or to the soul of the deceased, for "if one who is about to drink water and has already said the blessings, hears that someone has died in town, he should sip a little and pour out the balance." And yet this provision may merely be the result of a desire to maintain the custom, without understanding its meaning, under special circumstances, namely, when a blessing, which requires that some of the water be drunk, has been said. So complex do the motives behind these observances become that it is well-nigh impossible to single them out with any assurance. It may be of interest to recall that we have in English a colloquial expression which commemorates this widespread custom of pouring out liquids—when a person dies we say he has "kicked the bucket"![50]

2. There was considerable difference of opinion in Talmudic and medieval literature as to whether mourners should precede or follow the coffin out of the house. The view that "no man should go out first" was predicated on the belief that "the spirits roam the universe to learn what is decreed above concerning the living," and beholding a condemned sinner before their attention is absorbed by the coffin and its occupant, may pounce upon him. More simply,

the demons await the exit of the corpse, but are prepared to seize a living victim if he makes his appearance first. It was generally agreed, moreover, that women should walk apart from men in the procession, because the spirits display a marked partiality for womankind; "the angel of death and Satan dance before them," it was explained, or, again, "the spirits of uncleanness cling to them." This caution was observed especially on the return from the cemetery, and "in Worms the men turn their faces to the wall when the women walk by" on their way home.[51]

3. On the way to the cemetery, and after the body had been interred, it was customary, at least toward the end of our period, to recite the "anti-demonic psalm" a number of times, "to drive away the demons." Shabbetai, the son of Isaiah Horowitz, instructed his sons in his testament, "While my body is being lowered into the grave have seven pious and learned men repeat Psalm 91 seven times." [52]

4. The custom of tearing up some grass and earth, after the conclusion of the funeral rites, and tossing it behind one's back, cannot be traced earlier than the eleventh century. Eliezer b. Nathan, in the twelfth century, did not know, or pretended not to know, the origin of this usage; he introduced his explanation with the words "it seems to me," and went on to base it on three Biblical verses, Ps. 103:14, Ps. 72:16, and Job 2:12, which speak of earth, grass, and sprinkling dust upon one's head as a token of sorrow. Later writers, citing this explanation, describe the action as an expression of faith in the resurrection of the dead. Eleventh-century rabbis, quoted in later works, said it was done in order "to mark a separation between the mourners and death." But in the thirteenth century one writer, Samson b. Ẓadok, indicated that its real purpose was not altogether forgotten. "This is the reason why they throw it behind and not in front," he wrote: "I read in a *Midrash* that the soul accompanies the body of the deceased to the grave, and is unable to leave that spot until it receives permission from the congregation; throwing the earth and grass behind one is a sign that the permission is granted, meaning, in effect, 'Go in peace.'" We have here undoubtedly a borrowed custom. It is met with in medieval Germany and France, where along with the general belief that throwing things to the rear repulses the demons who lurk at one's back, there are specific instances of this device being used after a funeral to drive away the spirits, or the soul itself, which may follow the mourners home. The superstitious intent of this usage is enhanced by the fact that a manuscript source

dating from the thirteenth century mentions that the action is to be repeated three times. It was this custom that was responsible for a charge of magic levelled against the Jews of Paris in the twelfth century; luckily R. Moses b. Yeḥiel demonstrated to the satisfaction of the king that it was not intended "to cast a magic spell over the Gentiles, to kill them," but to signify the Jew's belief in the resurrection, and averted a disastrous outcome to this venture in Gentile superstition.[53]

5. In Talmudic and Geonic times, it was customary for the funeral procession, on its return from the cemetery, to stop and sit down seven times. Although several medieval authorities maintained that this practice had been dispensed with altogether, it persisted in some places, seven or three sittings being observed. Toward the end of our period these halts were coupled with the recitation of Ps. 91 to verse 11, which comprises seven words, one word of that verse being added at each stop. It was frankly admitted that this was intended to confuse and shake off "the evil spirits which follow them home." After the service the chief mourners passed between a double line of people and were then escorted home by the entire company.[54]

6. The custom of washing the hands after a funeral is very widespread; it seems to have made its way into Judaism in the early post-Talmudic period, and was generally observed during the Middle Ages. Before entering their homes all those who had visited the cemetery bathed their hands, and some, their eyes and face also. In certain mystical circles the lavation was performed three times. Efforts were made to find a Biblical precedent for this act, but along with such pious endeavors there was a general admission that it was done "to dispel the spirits of uncleanness" which cling to one's person, these being "the demons that follow them home." [55]

7. Mourning rites were most stringent during the seven days after interment, when the soul was believed to suffer intense agony on being parted from the body, and to wander disconsolately back and forth between its former home and the grave. (The earlier distinction between a three- and a seven-day stage of mourning found no practical expression in the Middle Ages.) The ensuing periods of a month and a year represented a gradual weaning away of the soul from the body, and a commensurate easing of the mourning rites. Many of the observances and customs which applied during the first period indicate a desire to protect the mourners against the

soul of the departed, and also a suspicion that the mourners themselves are or may be contaminated by contact with the spirit world. Thus, people forbore to drink out of a glass that had been used by a mourner, or to borrow anything from him during the seven-day period. The mourners were forbidden to leave their homes, except on the Sabbath and holidays, when, in some communities, they were escorted to the synagogue by the members of the congregation. Yet there are instances of refusal to permit mourners to join in the synagogal service, even on the High Holydays, and some would deny mourners the privilege of officiating at services throughout an entire year after their bereavement. It was customary to keep a candle burning in the death chamber during the week after burial; one report has it that each night of the week a small wax candle and a cup of water and salt were set on the spot where the head of the deceased lay when he died. "When I read my account of this custom to R. Israel Isserlein," wrote Joseph b. Moses, his disciple, "he shrugged his shoulders, but he didn't tell me to cross it out." The practice of "wrapping the head" in a mourning cloth was perhaps originally intended to disguise the mourners; if so, its significance was lost sight of in the Middle Ages, when we find that in some places it was dropped altogether "because the Gentiles laugh at us," while in the Rhineland it led to the adoption of a distinctive mourning costume with a cowl, the *mitron*. Of similar import were the customs of letting the hair and beard grow, of changing one's seat in the synagogue, and the like.[56]

12

NATURE AND MAN

UNDERLYING the popular approach to medicine, and indeed, the entire body of magical and semi-magical procedures, was an intriguing misconception of the nature of the world and its inhabitants. Along with the idea of spirit causation went a great number of odd and often grotesque notions. While the Jewish material does not offer a complete picture of the medieval view of nature, it provides us with enough individual superstitions and conceits to suggest the outlines of that picture, and to help us the better to appreciate some of the oddities of medical—and magical—practice.

THE WONDERS OF NATURE

Heir to all the fantastic notions concerning the universe that were current in the ancient world, with equal title to the wild and wonderful tales that swept medieval Europe, it is a source of surprise not that Jewish literature laid claim to these ideas and stories, but rather that it made so little of them. Compared with the intense popular interest that was focussed upon the curious and weird phenomena of nature in the Europe they inhabited, the Jews may be said almost to have neglected the subject altogether—allowing for the circumstance that Jewish writings, with their juridical and exegetical orientation, did not fully reflect the state of popular credulity. None the less the "facts" that may be culled from them make strange reading enough.

The familiar fables of mythical lands and creatures are duly represented. There are regions in which all of nature is masculine, and others where only females thrive—and the explanation is profoundly "scientific": matter is composed of the four elements, earth, fire, water and air, upon the harmonious combination of which sex depends; the unbalanced atmosphere of these lands is inimical to the subsistence of one or the other sex. On the peak of a certain mountain is a miraculous spring; whoever speaks after drinking its water instantly falls dead. Or again, there exists a marvellous herb which produces intense hunger; one who touches it must eat immediately or die. And as to the creatures, the whole menagerie of monstrosities is on view: men with dog-heads, horns or beaks, with the bodies or heads of lions, or serpents, or oxen; two- and three-headed men, four-armed men—one authority vouches for the fact that there are 365 varieties of human monsters, though he makes no attempt to enumerate them. And of course, there are the serpents that spit fire, the prodigiously hybrid animals, and the fabulous phoenix, whose body shrinks to the size of an egg on its thousandth birthday, and is then reborn for another millennial lease on life. (Incidentally, the phoenix was often cited by Church Fathers and rabbis as conclusive proof of the resurrection of the dead.) [1]

A legendary creature which stirred up quite a fuss in medieval literature, both Jewish and non-Jewish, was the man-plant, the mandragora root, often pictured in illuminations as a human form with leaves growing out of its head, to which Shakespeare referred in *Romeo and Juliet:*

> And shrieks like mandrakes' torn out of the earth,
> That living mortals, hearing them, run mad.

The Franco-German school of Talmud commentators adopted this prodigy to explain certain obscure terms in that work and in the Bible. R. Samson of Sens (second half of the twelfth century) cited R. Meir b. Kalonymos of Speyer as authority for this description: "A sort of long string grows out of a root in the ground, and to this string the animal called *yadu'a* is attached at its navel like a gourd or melon, but the *yadu'a* has the shape of a man in every particular, face, body, hands and feet. No one can approach closer than the radius of the string, for it uproots and destroys everything within its reach. One may capture it only by shooting at the string until it breaks, whereupon the animal dies." This account was followed by the later commentators.[2]

With regard to the more normal members of the animal kingdom we may glean a host of illuminating bits of information. The belief in spontaneous generation was as firmly rooted among Jews as among non-Jews. Mice, worms, insects are often the children of dust and mud and filth; gnats and flies are fathered by the atmosphere; man's sweat and body-heat produce some types of lice and worms, and a carefully differentiated species of louse springs full-blown from his head.

Most curious among the notions concerning spontaneous generation was the fable of the "barnacle-goose" (*Branta leucopsis*), which was universally accredited during the Middle Ages. It was believed that this bird was generated from the barnacle, a shell-fish growing on a flexible stem, and adhering to loose timber, bottoms of ships, etc., a metamorphosis to which many writers allude, and which is solemnly described in a good number of scientific works. This conception was accompanied, in Jewish literature, by other theories as to its place of origin: trees, from which the birds grow like fruit and hang by their beaks until they fall off, rotting wood, brine, etc. The determination of the true nature of this bird was of considerable ritual importance. Was it fowl, or fish, or fruit? Was it forbidden or permitted as a food? Did it require ritual slaughter or not? These questions were variously answered in accordance with the version of its origin which the authorities accepted. It is of interest that a similar problem agitated Christian ecclesiastics—was it permissible to eat these birds during Lent? Which again hinged on the issue as to whether they were fish or fowl.

The fable was turned to good account against the "obstinate" Jews by Church authorities. "Be wise at length, wretched Jew," wrote Gerald of Wales (twelfth century), "be wise even though late! The first generation of man from dust without male or female [Adam] and the second from the male without the female [Eve] thou darest not deny in veneration of thy law. The third alone from male and female, because it is usual, thou approvest and affirmest with thy hard heart. But the fourth, in which alone is salvation, from female without male—that, with obstinate malice, thou detestest to thy own destruction. Blush, wretch, blush, and at least turn to nature! She is an argument for the faith, and for our conviction procreates and produces every day animals without either male or female." Jews needed no coaxing to accept the fable, but the argument failed to move their "hard hearts" to confess the truth of the Immaculate Conception.[3]

Animals that copulate during the daytime never bear their young at night. Ritually unclean animals which see at night, such as dogs, cats and mice, have no vision at all until they are nine days old. On the other hand, *kosher* animals, that is those which may be eaten, may be recognized by the fact that they cringe when a hand is passed over them, while unclean animals do not. We read that "many times" fowl are born and live without hearts, and that food remains in a dog's stomach for three days, so that it can go that long unfed. In our ignorance we may believe that dogs follow the scent of an animal upon the ground, but a "true investigation" revealed that it is not the odor but the breath of the animal upon the ground that the dog picks up; some bright hares are aware of this and outwit the dogs by keeping their snouts in the air as they race to their hiding-places. Certain shell-fish, when cut into pieces and thrown back into the river, reunite the severed parts of their body and nonchalantly swim away. Cows whose udders are unprotected while they are at pasture are likely to be milked by a species of leach (the French word *sangsue* is used).[4]

In an age when poisoning was an obsession, the following precaution was in high repute: "When a man finds himself among suspected poisoners and he is afraid they will tamper with his food or drink, he should procure a knife with a handle of snake bone, and stick it into the table. If there is any poison present the handle will quiver, for the snake is full of venom, and like attracts like." Popes Clement V and John XXII owned such knives, the handles being made of serpents' horns.[5]

FOLK BIOLOGY—PROCREATION

A detailed discussion of the singular physiology that passed for science among the masses would make a full treatise. Here a brief presentation of the popular ideas concerning procreation, always a favorite field of speculation, will furnish a typical illustration of the sort of biological knowledge with which the folk medicine operated.

It was widely believed that comestibles play an important part in the procreative process, not alone by arousing passion, but also more directly by "multiplying" or "decreasing the seed," and determining the character of offspring. Spicy or heavy foods heat and thicken the blood, which manufactures the sperm, according to this view, and thus increase the flow of semen; they are thus conducive to a quick temper and wit in children. Light or unseasoned foods cause the children to be dull-witted and simple. In consequence foodstuffs were divided into two broad categories, those which "chill" the body and therefore have a deleterious effect upon the procreative powers, and those which "heat" the body and awaken sexual desire. In the first group are mentioned salt and salted fish, such as herring, legumes, melons, etc.; in the second, spices, strong wines, eggs, milk-foods, boiled lentils, roasted garlic, and a "five-finned fish." The references to the sexual properties of foods usually imply that most people are already sufficiently well-informed and need no further instruction.

On the other hand, various devices for quenching passion, in addition to the consumption of "chilling" foods, were known. The man who felt himself being overwhelmed by an impure desire could conquer it by "pressing his big toes firmly into the ground and resting the entire weight of his body upon them without leaning against a wall; this will banish all sensual thoughts." But "there is nothing that destroys passion so effectively as cold water; sit in it until you have subdued your desire," a sovereign and familiar remedy.[6]

The ancient taboo against a menstruous woman persisted undiminished throughout the Middle Ages. Great pains were taken to avoid the slightest contact, even between man and wife. This policy was carried to such extremes at times that the rabbis found it necessary to scold "those who throw the key or coins into their wives' hands." Yet, it is not to be wondered at that such inordinate measures were adopted, for the whole traditional lore of Judaism served to emphasize and enhance the taboo, threatening those who broke it with the direst consequences, here and in the hereafter, for themselves and their children. The Talmud contains a charm against snakebite which illustrates perfectly the abhorrence with which the woman in menses was regarded; when a woman meets a snake on the road, it is enough for her to announce "I am menstruating" for the reptile to glide hastily away! There is even a theory that the very atmosphere is polluted by the glance of a menstruating woman, a theory which may be tested by a "true experiment": "If a woman at the commencement of her period stares fixedly into a bright metal mirror she will behold in it a drop of blood, for the demon that is in her glance creates an evil influence in the air which adheres to the mirror; verily she is like the viper that kills with its glances." To have sexual relations with such a woman was not alone to commit a mortal sin, but to jeopardize one's very health and sanity.[7]

Not all times were equally favorable for coition. It was believed that children conceived during the first three days of the week would be born on the Sabbath; therefore the "pious ones" exercised restraint on these nights. But Friday night was the most propitious for conception because the sacred associations of the Sabbath would inevitably condition the child's character. The first half of the lunar month was preferred above the second because the waxing moon shed a beneficent influence upon offspring. A conception that occurs in the middle of the night is the most promising; here the explanations traverse a wide range from the purely mystical to the grossly material. One view has it that during this time of the night the "forces of uncleanness" are dormant; a second, that voices in the street are then least likely to distract a man's thoughts to another woman, which would have a very deleterious effect upon his child; still a third, that in the first part of the night a man's system is overheated by the food he has consumed, while toward morning it is too chilled. A reason to suit every taste! [8]

The prohibition against cohabitation during the day or in an illuminated place goes back to the Talmudic apprehension that the demons who are driven off by light may also perversely be attracted by it. Therefore the warning is advanced that one who stands naked before a burning lamp at night will become epileptic, and children conceived before a light will be similarly stricken, the Hebrew word for epileptic, *nichpeh,* having the sense of "forced, or seized" by a demon. In consequence of this dread elaborate precautions were taken to exclude all light from a bedchamber at night. But the fear of epilepsy in children was restricted to the influence of artificial lights; the light of the sun was believed to produce white eruptions, the moon, scurfiness which finally develops into leprosy, the stars, stammering. Undoubtedly such ideas were originally advanced to enhance the virtue of sexual modesty, but the threats they embodied were just as surely accepted as literally true.[9]

Of a similar nature were the fearful consequences believed to follow abnormal and perverted methods of coitus, and impure thoughts at the moment of conception. This last matter loomed especially large in all considerations of the subject, for it was universally believed that the parents' state of mind was directly transmitted through the seed to the infant, and intimately affected its character and its physique. Therefore parents were sternly warned not to have relations when they were on bad terms, and not to think of other individuals or of unpleasant and unworthy things, but to fix their attentions upon holy and pure thoughts which would have the best influence upon children. Some of the later mystics went to the absurd length of drawing up lists of appropriate subjects for concentration on such occasions: the great and pious figures of Jewish history. In short, "the embryo is formed in consonance with the thoughts and emotions of the parents," and "the greatest part of infant mortality is due to neglect of this principle." Indeed the delightful suggestion was offered in all seriousness that "most bastards are bright because the union of their parents is consummated in love and joy"![10]

There existed a strong conviction that things seen before and during conception make so powerful an impression on the mind that their characteristics are stamped upon the offspring. This is, of course, a universal superstition. If, on the way home from the ritual bath to which she repaired after her period (a procedure preliminary to intercourse), "a woman encounters a dog, her child will have an ugly dog-face, if she meets an ass, it will be stupid, if an ignorant lout, it will be an ignoramus." "Anything she meets makes a vivid impression on her and she thinks about it at the time of coition so that the child is affected thereby. . . . Therefore she should return to the bath. . . . But there are two exceptions to this rule. If she meets a horse, she need not return to the bath, for even if she should think of it there would be no harm, for a horse is of a happy disposition, and so she may have a son whose heart will rejoice in the study of *Torah*. And if she meets a scholar she need not go back and repeat her ablution. On the contrary she should think about him all the time." To avoid the possibility of inauspicious encounters many women chose to be led home from the bath blindfolded "imagining meanwhile that a pious man was coming to meet them."

Then, too, there was the well-worn fable of the white king and queen who bore a black child, or conversely, the black parents and the white infant, which cropped up frequently in classical and Talmudic literature, and went the rounds during the Middle Ages; the explanation, *bien entendu,* was that the mother's attention during intercourse was focussed on a picture hanging on the wall. Which brings us to a point that was often made: the mother's thoughts, and not the father's, exert the decisive influence upon the child. The classic instance of this superstition, of course, is the trick that Jacob played on his father-in-law, Laban, when he set peeled rods in the watering-troughs so that "the flocks conceived at the sight of the rods, and the flocks brought forth streaked, speckled and spotted" (Gen. 30:37-39).[11]

The Middle Ages were especially prolific of fertility potions, many of them concocted of parts of animals which were noted for their fecundity. Among these the hare and the fish were outstanding. Often, however, a wholly magical treatment, such as the recital of Biblical verses, was relied upon to cure barrenness. On the other hand, the Talmud mentions a "root-drink" which could produce sterility, and preparations to induce abortions were also known.

The problem of relieving the pains of childbirth found many solutions. Besides the purely magical treatments, already discussed, there were many folk remedies of a dubious character, e.g., the suggestion that the woman be fed mother's milk, the idea probably being that it may transmit to her another woman's success in surmounting the ordeal. Several prescriptions suggest primitive attempts at anesthesia; one such requires that a strong frankincense be burned before the parturient woman (but it must be in a "new clay bowl"); another, that she inhale the smoke of burning felt. The effect of this last, however, is thus naïvely described: "The woman will sneeze and expel her infant"! [12]

There were several interesting theories concerning the factors that determine the sex of the child. According to one, which owned Talmudic warrant, the sperm is male, the egg-cell female; whichever makes its entry second into the womb "subdues" the first and impresses its gender upon the offspring. Consequently the parent whose emission is delayed determines the child's sex. The same conclusion was also derived from a contrary premise, namely, that the will of the parent who first experiences an orgasm is paramount. This view, however, rather unreasonably insists that all men desire girl children, and all women, boys. Still a third opinion was based upon a remarkable anatomical fable. Within the womb there are seven sacs, three at each side and one in the center; if the spermatozoa enter those at the right, the child will be a boy, the left sacs produce girls, and the middle one, children who are sexless or hermaphroditic. Therefore the mother can control the sex of her child by lying either on her right or left side.[13]

There were manifold infallible ways of discovering the sex of the child prior to birth. The male lies face-down in the womb, the female face-up (the corpse of a drowned man or woman floats in the same manner). At the instant when the child pushes its way into this world one can tell its sex by noting the direction in which its head is turned. But most of the prognostics did not necessitate waiting until they were no longer needed. The desired information could be obtained long before. Thus, if a pregnant woman drips some milk from her breast upon a board or rock, if it spatters the child will be a boy, otherwise, a girl; or, if the milk sinks in water, she will bear a girl, and if it floats, a boy; if her loins ache, she is carrying a boy, but if her belly pains, it is a girl; if she is quick about her housework and her spinning, she will have a son, while if she is sluggish and can barely get around, a daughter. The right- and left-motif was also prominent. A right breast fuller than the left betokens a male heir; the same is indicated if, on rising from her seat, a woman leans on her right hand; but if she feels the fetus knocking against her left side, it is a girl, and so on.

These signs were evidently drawn from non-Jewish folklore, for the medieval literature abounds with parallels. It is noteworthy, though, that the Jewish sources retail these investigations and experiments to satisfy no mere curiosity, however justified the thirst for knowledge may be in this case, but rather to meet a pious need. They are meant for parents who reside a considerable distance from the nearest performer of circumcisions. Should they wait until the child is born to determine whether or not they require his services, it would be impossible to initiate their son into the covenant at the prescribed time; therefore science is pressed into the service of religion, and the summons can go out, if the prognostication so indicates, long before the boy has opened his eyes to the light of day.[14]

This account may close with two interesting legends. The first, voicing the prevalent belief in the possibility of impregnation without physical contact, relates that the daughter of the prophet Jeremiah entered a hot bath soon after her father had left it, and there received her father's seed. The son of this unusual conception was named *Ben Zera'*, "son of seed," but when he grew older and came to understand the significance of his name he was ashamed of it and changed it to Ben Sira, by which pseudonym we know him as the author of *Ecclesiasticus*.

The second tale is of a young scholar of the town of Enns, in Austria, who went off to a distant city to pursue his studies, leaving behind a young wife. Eleven months after his departure she bore a child and provided the good folk of the town with a tidy morsel of scandal. But the graybeards got together and agreed that in view of her unquestioned piety this event could not be regarded as suspicious, for a study of ancient literature revealed that such a delayed birth was not unheard of, though admittedly unusual. The arresting feature of this story is that the scholar's name was *Shlumiel,* which has become the colloquial epithet for all those bunglers whose enterprises invariably go awry.[15]

FORGETTING AND REMEMBERING

In a community in which learning was the most honored pursuit and a retentive memory the most prized attribute, we must expect to find superstition invading the precincts of scholarship itself. The Talmud contains a list of actions which induce forgetfulness: "eating what has been nibbled by a mouse or a cat, eating an animal's heart, eating olives, drinking water in which someone has washed, placing one foot over the other while washing them, and some add, using one's garments as a pillow." There follows then a series of ten things which are "bad for memorizing study."

There is ample evidence in the medieval writings that these admonitions were scrupulously observed, though the first group seems to have made the stronger impression. Thus we are informed that Meir of Rothenburg, Maharil and Israel Isserlein, leading lights in their generations, very carefully avoided sleeping on their clothes; Maharil, when on a journey, would prefer a hard saddle under his head to a soft bundle of garments. R. Meir went the Talmud one better and refrained from eating even the hearts of birds. To this day pious Jews avoid passing between two women, because the Talmudic passage warned that this is "bad for the memory." (Fear of brushing against a menstruating woman also enters here.) Another of these superstitions which is still widely observed is not to read an inscription on a tombstone. A commentator observes, "I have seen scrupulously pious men place a stone on the marker, with the explanation that this destroys the ill-effect of reading the inscription." Wiping one's hands on one's clothes, putting on two garments at a time, mending clothes while one is naked, these acts were believed to exert a similar debilitating effect upon the memory. An antidote for the last is to put a splinter of wood in the mouth. The modern version among East-European Jews, derived from German custom, is to keep a bit of thread in the mouth while mending garments that are on the body. A related idea was that drinking from narrow-necked flasks is bad for one's visual and aural faculties.[16]

The belief that there is an intimate connection between the

demons and the finger-nails has some obscure relation to another of these superstitions, namely, that cutting the nails in the order of the fingers causes loss of memory. The ancient Persians made much of the dangers associated with the finger-nails and prescribed a specific order of paring them; from them this belief came over to the Mohammedans and Jews, but it was the latter who brought it and the memory into conjunction. The proper manner of cutting the nails, as given by the medieval writers, varies somewhat; the Zoroastrian order was accepted for the left hand only. The commonest version is as follows: left hand, 4, 2, 5, 3, 1; right hand, 2, 4, 1, 3, 5. One of the earliest references reads: "Left hand, begin with 4 and end with 1, right hand begin with 1 and end with 4. Paring any two nails in sequence causes forgetfulness." But this source insists that the operation must begin with 1 or 4. "To begin with 3 causes the death of one's children, with 5, poverty, with 2, a bad reputation." This superstition, however, was not universally respected; Meir of Rothenburg, for one, had the temerity to disregard it, as did the sixteenth-century mystic, Isaac Luria.[17]

Accompanying these superstitions were a good number of a reverse order, to preserve and strengthen the memory. Prominent among them was the above-mentioned invocation of the "Prince of Forgetting," Poteh or Purah, uttered on Saturday evening after *Habdalah* and on other appropriate occasions, such as the initial enrolment of a child in school. Other incantations were also prescribed. Biblical verses relating to the prophet Elijah were recited at the close of the Sabbath for the same purpose; "mentioning his name at this time is good for the memory and brings good luck during the week."

An interesting group of recipes is comprised under the name "small Baladur" (also written "Balazur"). The plant Baladur (Anacardia) was considered by the Moslems a potent memory strengthener and in this rôle it appeared in Jewish medicinal literature also. In time, however, the meaning of the term was forgotten, and all sorts of prescriptions came to be denominated "the small Baladur." So widely accepted was this term that in the end it was taken to be distinctively Jewish, and there was even a current proverb, allegedly quoted from the Talmud: "Review, review [your studies] and you'll have no need of Baladur." The word seems to have penetrated German Jewry from the South fairly late, but the recipes were probably known long before they were dignified with this title. Among the simpler ones are the following: eat hazel nuts for nine days, beginning with six and adding six more each day; eat pepper seeds for nine days, beginning with one seed and doubling the dose until it reaches 256 seeds on the ninth day, and each time, before you consume them, recite Deut. 33:8-11 and Ps. 119:9-16; grind cloves, long peppers, dates, ginger, galanga-root and Muscat nuts in equal quantities, beat them with olive oil into a paste, and eat a little every morning before breakfast. One may judge from the progressive complexity of these three recipes the extent to which ingenuity multiplied ingredients and mystification in others. But all, whatever their composition, were equally touted as the original "Baladur." [18]

13

MEDICINE

MAGIC AND THE DOCTOR

MEDIEVAL medicine was a curiously indiscriminate compound of science and such superstition as we have been describing. The Greek-Arab-Jewish tradition, itself well freighted with a large residuum of early magic, provided none the less a fairly "scientific" foundation upon which the European peoples superimposed their own ancient folk notions and nostrums until the whole made a most imposing and fearsome structure. The medieval "theriac," a mélange of a thousand and one weird and exotic medicaments, is probably at once its aptest example and metaphor. So darkly obscured was his science that the physician was often a powerful exponent of magic and superstition. A fourteenth-century Frenchman, Jean Gerson, made the penetrating observation that "when one censures the pestiferous superstitions of magicians and the follies of old wives and sorceresses who promise to cure the sick by their accursed rites, people object that similar practices of ligatures, characters, figures and employment of outlandish words may be found on the part of grave and learned doctors of medicine and are inserted in their books. Therefore they must be efficacious, although no natural explanation is offered of them." One can sympathize with Sebastian Brant's (fifteenth century) pungent comment:

Des abergloub ist yetz so vil
Do mitt man gsuntheyt suchen will
Wann ich das als zu samen such
Ich maht wol drusz eyn ketzerbuch.

"Eyn ketzerbuch" is a pat characterization of the contents of this chapter.

Northern Europe, walled off from the enlightenment that radiated from the Arab lands, produced not a single Jewish physician of note. Jewish practitioners of medicine there were aplenty, but their science was little more than a faint reflection of the learning of their southern co-religionists. The sole original medical work from that region written by a Jew, who lived toward the end of the thirteenth century, probably in the Rhineland (he was in personal contact with the great doctor Heinrich of Erfurt, court physician to the Bishop of Cologne; and himself claimed to have cured the secretary of Pope Martin IV), discloses a considerable acquaintance with the more reputable phases of medieval medicine, but it displays too the contemporary addiction to magical and folk remedies, impossible of "natural explanation." "I have seen illnesses, upon which the greatest medicines had no effect, cured by spells and charms," he wrote. As may be expected these were the remedies that proved especially popular among the masses. It is unfair to suggest, as some have, that Jewish medical superstition is to be regarded mainly as an imitation of the Christian. The Talmud had established a discipline broad enough to serve as an adequate basis for any later accretions, and while many popular remedies were directly borrowed from non-Jews, the rationale of superstition and magic in medicine was part and parcel of the Jewish cultural heritage.[1]

We find, of course, among the popular prescriptions a goodly number of items that have no basis other than tradition and a naïve associationism, such as that washing is harmful to aching teeth, or that cutting the beard is a cure for sore eyes, or that lioness's milk is a specific for certain ailments. There are dozens upon dozens of receipts that belong in this category—the so-called folk medicine, those old wives' cures that have been handed down from grandmother to granddaughter through the ages. Often enough they make no sense at all, and when some dim glimmering of reason shines through, the explanation seems as little rational as the prescription. Consider the following: to remove warts, smear them with horse's blood; for a toothache, mix salt, oil, pepper and a little garlic, bind the mixture *on the pulse,* and leave it there overnight; as a remedy for insomnia, induce a louse captured on the patient's head to crawl into a hollow bone, seal the bone, and hang about the patient's neck.[2]

The German belief that water (called *heilawac* or *heilwag*) drawn at certain holy seasons possesses curative powers (a belief which can be traced back to early Teutonic and Christian ideas), is paralleled by the Jewish notion that at the termination of the Sabbath Miriam's well, to which a Midrashic legend ascribes miraculous medicinal virtues, moves about from river to river and from well to well. It was therefore recommended that water be drawn at this time, "and everyone who is ill, and is fortunate enough to get some of that healing water and drink it, even though his body be wholly broken out with sores, will be immediately cured." The admonition that one must be silent while fetching this water is found in both the Jewish and German sources.[3]

According to a statement in the Talmud, "a heavy step detracts one five-hundredth from the light of the eyes," so that if no preventive measure were adopted one should go blind in time. The Talmudic suggestion was that the recital of the *Kiddush* in the synagogue on Friday evenings serves such a purpose, but in Geonic times this was taken to mean either drinking the *Kiddush* wine (the opinion of Hai Gaon) or bathing the eyelids with this wine (Natronai Gaon's view). Medieval Jews accepted either or both interpretations, and the *Kiddush* wine came to be used in these ways as a remedy for weak eyes. It is interesting to compare with this practice the injunction found as early as the fourth century in the 23rd *Catechesis* of Cyrillus of Jerusalem: "If a drop (of the Communion wine) remains on your lips, smear your eyes and forehead with it."

Staring intently at the Sabbath lights was also considered by some medieval Jews to be a strengthener of weak eyes. A custom which probably had a similar purpose, though it was explained as an expression of "love of the commandments," was to dilute the wine remaining after the *Habdalah* ceremony, at the expiration of the Sabbath, and to bathe the eyes and face with the mixture. (A further medicinal use of sanctified wine is to be discerned in the custom of feeding some of the wine over which the blessing had been recited at a circumcision to the mother and the infant; while the usual explanation was that the people in whose behalf the benediction was said ought to taste the wine, it was also admitted that "both mother and child require medication, and the blessings promote health.") Still another remedy for weak eyes was to gaze fixedly into a mirror for a while; "some scribes set a mirror in front of them when they are writing, and occasionally stare into it, so that their sight may not be dimmed." [4]

A most popular medieval panacea, almost universally employed, was the abstraction of blood, to permit the bad to flow away while the good remains in the body. Even healthy people were advised to undergo this operation periodically, for as a twelfth-century German enumerated its advantages, "It contains the beginning of health, it makes the mind sincere, it aids the memory, it purges the brain, it reforms the bladder, it warms the marrow, it opens the hearing, it checks tears, it removes nausea, it benefits the stomach, it invites digestion, it evokes the voice, it builds up the sense, it moves the bowels, it enriches sleep, it removes anxiety. . . ." Cupping was also often prescribed, especially for abdominal ailments, for it "restores the bowels to their place." [5]

Psychic treatment was not unknown. "Music hath charms to soothe a savage breast"; well, medieval Jews applied this cure quite literally to heal people who had gone out of their minds, and it was believed that the *Alpdrücken,* who were especially susceptible to the charms of music, could be seduced by its sweet strains to vacate the body of a demoniac. Frightening a patient was another sovereign remedy. An invalid afflicted with chills was startled out of his ailment with the news that his friend had died suddenly, and in an even more wonderful cure, a man who had been eviscerated by a sword-thrust groaned so lustily when he beheld what purported to be the slaughter of his children, that his bowels were drawn back into his body, and it was possible to sew up the wound and save his life. In fact, magical cures and incantations were occasionally permitted by the rabbis not because of their direct effect upon the disease, but in order to set a superstitious patient's mind at ease.[6]

One of the most widespread medical superstitions is the homeopathic doctrine, *similia similibus curantur.* The English "hair of the dog that bit you" is matched by the Mishnaic "lobe of its liver" as a remedy for a bite. Maharil is credited with the view that "we may not employ any of the cures and charms given in the Talmud, for we no longer know how to apply them correctly . . . except the one found in *Shab.* 67a: 'When a bone sticks in one's throat he should place a similar bone on his head and say, One, one, gone down, swallowed, swallowed, gone down, one, one.' This cure is tested and proven, and is therefore the only one that may be used." Medieval Jewish literature contains many instances of the application of this principle, of which only one or two need be cited here. To stop bleeding, "take some of the blood which has been shed, parch it in a pan over the fire until it becomes dry and powdery, and place it on the wound." A poultice to halt excessive bleeding after a circumcision was made of flax that had been smeared with egg-yolk, the mother's pubic hairs, and the ashes of a feather and a bit of cloth that had been steeped in the blood. In the same category were the cures effected by abstaining from "likes." A man afflicted with a headache would eat no head of bird or animal; if his heart pained, or his stomach, hearts or entrails were excluded from his diet. And just as likes cure, so do contraries. "Every cure is the natural contrary of the ailment," we read; therefore cold cures fevers, and heat cures chills.[7]

THE CAUSES OF DISEASE

These, however, are the incidentals of the popular practice of medicine as it was known in the Middle Ages, and was and still is understood by primitive people. By far the larger part of this medicine fits into a definite ideological scheme. No matter how irrational many of the prescriptions may seem to us, we must recognize that "these modes of treatment follow directly from their ideas concerning etiology and pathology. From our modern standpoint we are able to see that these ideas are wrong. But the important point is that, however wrong may be their beliefs concerning the causation of disease, their practices are the logical consequences of those beliefs." W. H. R. Rivers, when he wrote these words, had in mind the natives of Melanesia, but they are equally applicable to the natives of medieval Europe. He grouped the causes of disease, as generally conceived by mankind, in three chief classes: "human agency, in which it is believed that disease is directly due to action on the part of some human being; the action of some spiritual or supernatural being, or, more exactly, the action of some agent who is not human, but is yet more or less definitely personified; and what we ordinarily call natural causes." All of these causes are clearly indicated in Jewish sources.[8]

The first cause, human agency, is to be met with in the machinations of the sorcerer. By his evil art he can visit all sorts of infirmities upon his enemies, or the enemies of his clients. An anecdote in *Sefer Ḥasidim*[9] reveals the presence of this belief among medieval Jews. The mother of a child who had been bewitched came to a sage and said to him, "My baby cries incessantly because a certain woman has cast a spell over him. I know a way to cure him, and at the same time to transfer the illness to this woman's own child." The sage reproved her, "If the mother has sinned, her child certainly has not!" His humaneness was as rare in those days as the belief in the magical causation of disease was common. We have seen, too, that some people are possessed of the power of the evil eye, by which, sometimes unwittingly, they can inflict disease upon one.

Supernatural agency is the most commonly designated cause of disease. The demons, in particular, are singled out as responsible agents, and medieval medical lore in this respect followed closely the teaching of the ancients. Egyptian and Greek magical papyri, the Talmud and the New Testament, all abound with such diagnoses, and often identify the ailment with the demon, indicating the belief that disease is caused by an actual penetration of the invalid's body by the evil spirit. Jesus gave his disciples power "over unclean spirits to cast them out and heal all manner of sickness and all manner of disease" (Mt. 10:1). There is a demon known to Jews as the "neck-twister," who attacks children; moonstruck youngsters suffer alternately from chills and fevers because the morbific demons who pervade the moon-shadows are constituted of fire and hail. The coma called *Hirnbrüte* is induced by demons. Even when a human being is the ultimate cause, the spirits are the direct sources of illness, for magic and the evil eye operate through them. It is interesting to note, in view of our modern ideas on hygiene, that these disease-breeding demons haunt marshy places, damp and deserted houses, latrines, squalid alleys, fetid atmospheres. This demon etiology is even susceptible of a theory of contagion: "One should not drink another's leavings," we are warned, "because if the first man has a disease a spirit goes out of his mouth into the liquid; it is mortal danger to drink it." It was thus possible to establish the general rule that "all maladies that come upon one suddenly are caused by the spirits." [10]

Sometimes the angels, as well as the demons, bear a share of the responsibility. The idea that sickness is a heaven-sent punishment for one's sins, frequently encountered, necessitates angelic intermediacy in executing the decree. Besides, certain epidemic diseases, such as measles, may be transmitted by angels who are especially appointed to this function.[11]

Apparently the most virulent type of malady is that produced by the spirits of deceased evil-doers, which join the demonic ranks. "When these spirits injure a man, there is no human remedy capable of healing him; it is more painful than any other ailment, and only his Creator can relieve his pain." [12]

As to the "natural" sources of illness, etiological diagnoses did not limit themselves to the more credible causes (according to our view) inherent in diet, or age, or accidents, or "atmospheric conditions" (a favorite), but went afield to hunt up some rather bizarre physiological phenomena, such as the *spiritus* that fills the body cavities, or the deterioration of the blood. There is an interesting account of an operation performed on Solomon b. Ḥananel of Mainz by the noted physician R. Sheshet, in Barcelona, which involved the removal of a tribe of worms that had caused the patient to suffer from a severely debilitating ailment.[13]

TREATMENT

This last category of disease responded to more or less "natural" treatment, which does not concern us here, except as it falls within the group of folk remedies already briefly mentioned. But no "natural" remedy, however we may strain the sense of that term, could possibly reach and destroy the supernatural causes of disease. Only a powerful counter-magic could root out the effects of magic and deflect the demonic onslaughts. However determined their formal resistance to the practice of magic may have been, the rabbis were obliged to recognize the logic of such a medicine. Two of the leading authorities of the *Gemara,* Abaye and Raba, who were so often in heated opposition, concurred in the rule that "nothing done for purposes of healing is to be forbidden as superstitious." During the Middle Ages the issue was placed squarely before at least one rabbi, Israel Isserlein, who wrote to his correspondent, "Regarding your question as to whether an invalid may consult a magician, know that we have found no explicit prohibition of such a course, for the Biblical strictures against sorcerers do not apply in this case." On the basis of this decision Solomon Luria vouchsafed a still broader license: "If a serious illness is caused by magic or evil spirits one may even resort to a non-Jewish magician for a cure." But it was not really necessary to obtain the magician's aid; the ordinary remedies applied by the doctor or the layman utilized the entire range of magical devices.[14]

The Talmudic literature contains scores of references to the use of charms in healing wounds and diseases, so that medieval Jews accepted their efficacy as a matter of course. Even religious leaders did not hesitate to employ them. "Once when R. Simḥah had a pain in his eyes, a woman taught R. Abigdor Cohen a certain spell which he recited twice daily, even on the Sabbath, to relieve R. Simḥah's suffering." Another report tells of a man who used to recite charms to heal the sick; if they were successful the cure was effected within nine days, if not, the patient died in that period. Here at least, was one honest physician, unafraid to disclose the alternatives inherent in his treatment. Many Christians had no scruples about using Jewish doctors; neither was there any Jewish prejudice against being cured by non-Jews, provided they did not insert the formulas of their own religion in their incantations. Yet even this minor restriction was not taken too seriously, for according to R. Menaḥem of Speyer, "The sounds effect the cure, and not the words of the incantation; therefore a Christian may be permitted to heal a Jew even if he invokes the aid of Jesus and the saints in his spell." The reputed medicinal virtue of Christian relics was a medieval dogma which Jews allegedly recognized in at least one instance, when they testified to a miraculous cure which they had witnessed in Aix-la-Chapelle, according to the report of Charlemagne's historian, Einhard, but to use them themselves was more than they could countenance. We have an account of a Jewish woman who, though she was seriously ill, refused to be healed by a stone which came from the grave of Jesus, which her Christian friend had offered to her.[15]

Medieval remedies, whatever their therapeutic value, were often accompanied by incantations, which were regarded as the effective agent in the cure. The operation of blood-letting, for example, or the concoction and administration of magic potions to heal disease, or to induce abortions, are cases in point. Frequently, as with R. Simḥah's affliction, the spell in itself sufficed. The variety of such charms is infinite, and follows the type of the magical incantation, with the specific request that the demon or the disease, or both under a common name, be expelled from the patient's body. Several ancient German magical cures of this order have been preserved in Hebrew manuscripts. One which has aroused considerable interest is the fourteenth-century rhymed *Bärmutter* charm against colic and labor pains, in which the bowels and the womb are directly apostrophized: "*Bärmutter* (womb), lie down, you are as old as I am. If you bring me to the grave, you will be buried with me. There is a book called the Bible; *Bärmutter,* lie down! Lie down in your proper place, in compliance with the will of God's holy power. . . ." Another Jewish version of this spell invokes angels, patriarchs, matriarchs, altars, heavens, *shofars,* etc. (seven of each), the sun, the moon, the name of God; still another calls upon nine angels and nine scrolls of the *Torah* to enforce its command; while a contemporaneous Christian version conjures the *bermuoter* by "the sacred blood, the sacred day, the very sacred grave, the five holy wounds, and the three holy nails which were driven through the hands and feet of our lord Jesus Christ." The details of invocation are adjusted to suit the religious sensibilities of the patient, but the purport and even a good part of the phraseology is the same in all. Another such spell runs: "I conjure you, wound, by our dear Lord, that you neither bleed nor swell, as the wound which our dear Lord produced when He extracted a rib from Adam's side to make him a wife did not bleed nor swell. . . ." Numbers played an important rôle in medical practice, as in magical, and the remedial measure often included this element, as above, or else was to be repeated a given number of times, or on several succeeding days, 3, 7, 9, as the case might be. *Sefer Ḥasidim* cites the German usage, "To cure a person who has been harmed by a demon, the charm must be repeated nine times, as they do in Germany." [16]

Sometimes the mere repetition of a magic name is sufficient to effect the cure, or the name is inscribed directly upon the person of the invalid, or is brought into action by means of a specially prepared amulet. Of three such magic names, which were to be written on the forehead to stop bleeding, our informant writes, "I myself have tried the last two, they have been repeatedly proven, and are unequalled in the whole world." To ease labor pains the prescription is to incise a name upon virgin clay and to fasten this on the navel of the parturient woman, "but remove it as soon as the child is delivered, or her viscera will also be extruded!" Or, "inscribe this name on the woman's wedding ring, and place it under her tongue, and say ten times, 'Go out, you and all the company of your followers, and then I will go out.' And then the child will be delivered." Still another device is to inject the name into the body, where its presence will assuredly dislodge the plaguing spirit. Thus, a name written on an apple and consumed on three consecutive days is guaranteed to heal fevers, and the inscription *satur arepo tenet opera rutas,* which possesses the highly potent magical virtue of reading the same backward as forward, eaten on an apple, or an egg, or cheese, is warranted to induce an abortion; or the name may be inscribed on a leaf and dissolved in water, which is to be drunk, or may simply be whispered over the liquid and thus imbibed.[17]

The importance of Scripture in magic made it a prominent adjunct of medicine also. The Talmudic prohibition against using "the words of *Torah* for healing" is sufficient evidence of the popularity of such a therapeutic at an early time. The *Torah* scroll was itself laid upon the body of a sufferer or brought into the sick-chamber, for its curative virtues, and many Biblical selections were singled out as specifics for various ailments, to be recited, or inscribed on amulets, or consumed. For example, to ease a confinement, "recite Ps. 20 nine times and each time concentrate on this name. . . . If this doesn't help repeat it another nine times. The lying-in woman must be able to hear the recital of these verses. If this still doesn't help her, say, 'I conjure you, Armisael, angel who governs the womb, that you help this woman and the child in her body to life and peace. Amen, Amen, Amen.' "[18]

SOME SOVEREIGN REMEDIES

These magical devices, intended to expel the demonic cause of disease, by no means exhausted medical ingenuity. Many of us have good reason to recall the old notion that the viler a medicine tasted the better it was. This idea is not altogether irrational—if nauseous drugs disgust humans, they are likely to have the same effect on demons; therefore the more obnoxious the dose the more likely it is to weary the demon of his human habitat. What is bad for the demon must be good for the patient. Some of the heroic remedies excused by this theory can have had little worse effect upon the invalid than upon the demon. The most disgusting filth has found a place in medical prescriptions. In 1699 there appeared in Frankfort a volume entitled, "Curieuse, Neue Hauss-Apothec, Wie man durch seine eigne bey sich habende Mittel, als dem Blut, dem Urin, Hinter- und Ohren-Dreck, Speichel und andren natürlichen geringen Mitteln seine Gesundheit erhalten, fast alle selbst vor incurabel gehaltene Kranckheiten . . . heilen . . . möge und könne," which, besides the items included in the title, describes the medicinal value of the bones, marrow, skull, flesh, fat, hair, brain, heart, nails, sweat, after-birth, semen, menses, etc. From earliest times such medicines have been favored by physicians. The Talmud knows of the use of human and animal urine and excrement as a medicament to be taken internally as well as applied externally, and in the Middle Ages fine distinctions were made regarding the specific medical utility of a child's urine, or a horse's, or a donkey's, of the excrement of men and women, or of she-asses, or of swine. Concerning Israel Isserlein it is reported that "the only remedy he used for his gout was occasionally to rub some warm urine over the aching area." Human spittle, especially from a person who had gone without food for some time, was considered a prime cure for ailments of the eye.

It must be said, however, that although all those bodily parts and products mentioned in the *Curieuse Hauss-Apothec* were very frequently prescribed in non-Jewish medicine, Jewish medicine religiously refrained from recommending their use, for the same reasons that precluded their magical employment. The consumption of blood, in particular, was abhorrent to Jews; there is not a single instance in all of Jewish literature of the prescription of blood for internal medicine, and the very rarity of the suggestions that horse's blood, or the menses, may be applied externally serves only to bring out in bold relief the sharp prejudice against these usages. Reptiles and vermin of all sorts were also highly regarded for medical purposes, and were often taken internally in the form of powders, or bound upon a wound, alive, to close the gash and to knit fractured bones, and poultices for open wounds were made of spiders' webs.[19]

A favorite antidote, usually practiced by old women, was to encircle the diseased part, an abscess or rash or a painful spot, such as the eye or the head, with the finger or with some object, such as a ring, while reciting a charm. Where the object was of metal its anti-demonic virtues were relied upon to dispel the pain, though the commentators rationalized a Talmudic reference to such a cure with the explanation that it was intended to cool a fevered area, or to prevent it from spreading; but the primary utility of the circle lay in its magical significance, to ban the evil spirits within its periphery. Eye ailments, particularly the carbuncle (anthrax), euphemistically called *bon malant,* were thus treated.

A popular medieval remedy of a similar nature, known to the Germans as *messen,* was applied by Jews even on the Sabbath, when all mensuration was forbidden. The Hebrew accounts of the procedure are not very clear—it was evidently so well known that it required little description—"one measures three times three ells with the patient's belt and recites the charm formula." From German sources we learn that it was used both as a cure and to prognosticate the future course of the ailment. According to these accounts, to cure a severe headache a thread was wound three times around the head and hung in a tree; when a bird flew through the loop it carried the pain off with it. Or, the invalid's belt was stretched three times over the length and breadth of his naked body, and then hung on a nail with an appropriate incantation; after a while the belt was measured, and if it was longer or shorter than before, this was interpreted as a portent of the progress of his illness. It is to such procedures that the Hebrew sources refer.[20]

The purpose of many remedies, such as the one just cited, was to transfer the disease to an animal, or to an inanimate object, or to another person. The Talmud describes various measures to shake off a fever by passing it on to an ant or to water and the like, measures which were duplicated in the Middle Ages. Or the ailment might exchange victims through a commercial transaction. "Once a man was mortally ill, and another jokingly said to him, 'I'll buy your illness from you for such and such a sum'; the invalid promptly responded, 'It's a bargain.' Immediately, he arose cured, and the purchaser sickened and died." [21] Jesting is a dangerous business when spirits have no sense of humor.

A quite extraordinary healing device was predicated on the belief that illness and death are often visited upon man for his sins, by the angels, at God's command. Jews visualized the celestial administration as conducted in much the same bureaucratic manner as a mundane government. The decrees issued from the seat of the Supreme Ruler were distributed among the various secretariats and in time assigned to angelic attendants for execution. Not unlike their earthly counterparts, the angels tended to go about their tasks methodically, but not over-intelligently, carrying out the letter of their orders without any great concern with or comprehension of the wider import of their errands.

The human analogy suggested the possibility of outwitting them by a crafty dodge. The Talmud knew of four courses that might be pursued to counteract an adverse decree from above, namely, almsgiving, prayer, change of conduct, and *change of name*. Lest there be any doubt of the intent of this last method, Moses of Coucy plainly explained that the one who changes his name as much as declares to the angel looking for him, "I am not the person you are seeking, I am not the one who committed the sins you charge me with." And, of course, the angel takes him at his word. During the Middle Ages the belief that changing the name of a sick person can save his life and effect his cure by hoodwinking the angel charged with bringing his ailment to a fatal conclusion was very pronounced and much more generally accepted than in earlier periods. It seems to have been acted upon almost universally among German Jews when an illness was prolonged and severe. Interestingly enough, the very same course is followed on the opposite side of the earth, in Borneo and the Kingsmill Islands. In modern times, when Jews effected such a change of name, they usually selected one which in itself suggests a long life, to make doubly sure that the angel of death will avoid the invalid, such as *Ḥayim* ("life"), *Alter* ("old man"), *Zeide* ("grandfather"), etc. During the Middle Ages the customary procedure was to find a new name "by lot," opening the Bible at random and choosing the first one that appeared. Israel Bruna, in his responsa, protested against the adoption of the name of a wicked person when such was the first found, and ordered it to be passed over for the first righteous one, citing "the memory of the just is blessed, but the name of the wicked shall perish" (Prov. 10:7) in extenuation. Israel Isserlein went further, and demanded that the new name contain not a single letter of the old and that it have a greater numerical value, although when he changed his own son's name during an illness he adhered to neither of his requirements.

This change of name was and still is solemnly effected before an assembly of ten persons by an expert reader who holds a scroll of the *Torah* in his hands while he repeats a prescribed formula whose institution is attributed to the Geonim. After announcing the new name, the ritual formally notifies the heavenly authorities of the change, and requests them to take cognizance of it and to consider this person as not identical with the one who bore his former name, "for he is another man, like unto a newborn creature, an infant who has just been born unto a long and good life." The new name then becomes the true name, even though the old remains in use, and in legal documents the individual is identified by it with the notation that he bears his former name as an alias.

However, since Jews were known by their parents' names as well as by their own, as Isaac son of Abraham and Sarah, there still remained some room for apprehension lest the angel's order identify the child by its parents (which is especially likely to happen when the child is being punished for its parents' sins); a change simply of its own name would then be ineffective to save its life. The way out was not hard to find—change his parents as well! Which is just what was done. The real parents would sell their invalid child to another couple who, because their children were alive and well, appeared to be in high favor with the heavenly powers. Thus the child acquired new parents, and the angel of death was twice confounded. If he tried to locate the child through the parents he could not trace it, and if he hunted up the parents to punish them by killing their child he found they had none.[22]

HERBS

Herbs are the prime constituents of most folk remedies, and medical science has been able to show in more than one instance that they possess true healing properties which take them out of the class of old-wives' simples. Undoubtedly such herbs were prescribed because they were known to be successful in treating various ailments, but their merit was usually ascribed not to any natural qualities inherent in the plant, but rather to the occult virtues they were believed to possess, or even to the magical spells and techniques with which they were applied. Only thus can we understand the common use of plants and grasses among Jews and Christians, as amulets against disease, to be worn on the person.

An interesting reference to the magical apparatus that accompanied the preparation of a herbal remedy, which has given rise to considerable confusion, is to be found in *Sefer Ḥasidim*. In the course of a paragraph on improper magical practices, such as the invocation of angels and demons, whispering charms, and divining by dreams, there is included "the *bukaiẓa,* called in German *biguraich* (and in French *plantaina*), which it is forbidden to invoke." The difficulty of deciphering these transliterations led Güdemann and Perles to suggest some ingenious etymologies; the first read the German word as *becherweihe,* which he interpreted as "divining with goblets," while the second, relying upon a misspelling of one word and an emendation of another, took this to refer to divination by the call of the cuckoo, both well known in medieval Germany. Alas for the scholarly toil and ingenuity that went into these efforts! The solution of the puzzle is much simpler and more obvious. A fourteenth-century writer, in *Sefer Asufot,* divulged its key in these words: "I have heard that the juice of the plant called *wagruch,* and in French, *plantain*, is equally good when there is no olive oil," in preparing an ointment to stop the flow of blood. The first word, *bukaiẓa*, is the French *boucage*, a medieval term for a medicinal plant related to the plantain. German sources indicate that this herb (*plantago*), variously called *wegarih, wegarich, wegawarte*, etc., was a very important item in medieval folk medicine, and that its potent virtues were accounted for on the basis of several legends. In conjunction with the German material *Sefer Ḥasidim* proves the essential rôle of the magical invocation in preparing this and other plants for medicinal use.[23]

For a pain in the neck it is recommended that one wind elder leaves (*Sambucus*) about the neck, and at the same time recite a given spell. Herbs gathered in a cemetery, and even soil from a grave, or earth or water gathered at a crossroads, were considered of high medicinal value, because of their association with the spirits and their consequent occult potency.[24]

It should be noted that most of the herbs are referred to by their German or French names; medieval Jewry, in other words, borrowed its herb-lore and the accompanying medico-magical techniques from its neighbors. *Fenouil* (fennel), whose healing properties were highly regarded by French and Germans, was recommended by a Jewish writer for abdominal disorders and apprehended miscarriage; *akeleia* seed (columbine, *Aquilegia vulgaris*), prescribed for many ailments in German sources, makes its appearance in a Hebrew work as a cure for bad eyes when taken internally—a use that may have been suggested by the shiny black appearance of the seed. The sap of a plant "which is called *Schelwurz* (celandine, *Chelidonium*) in Germany" is recommended for spots in the eye and cataracts. A decoction of "*salvia* or *sauge* in French" (sage) is suggested as a cure for paralysis, and to aid the digestion "take saltpeter and sage and bay and cinnamon, beat them thoroughly in honey, and pour the mixture often into your mouth; whatever has disturbed you will flee; drink some wine afterwards."[25] It is usually impossible to divorce the purely therapeutic from the superstitious and magical in such prescriptions; the three are as thoroughly intermingled as the ingredients of the above recipe should be. Which is, it must be confessed, quite unexceptionable. Ailments that are brought about by magic, or by demons, or by superstitious "natural" causes, are not to be cured with mere drugs and herbs, but only with the occult powers that are inherent in or conjured into these medicaments.

14

DIVINATION

DETERMINISM VS. FREE WILL

THE THORNY problem of free will, which has defeated greater philosophers than German Jewry produced, came no nearer a solution than where the rabbis of the Talmud had left it. The rabbinic authorities of Northern Europe were not distinguished for their concern with metaphysics; the problem interested them only in its more immediate and practical aspects. Is man's life foreordained? Is there any point in trying to live the good life? Do sincere repentance and piety affect the course of a man's career? Is it possible to discover future events? These were the questions that engaged their attention—and to all they resolutely answered "yes." For rabbinic Judaism straddled the issue of free will by positing a thoroughgoing determinism which, in some mysterious manner, still left men free to exercise discretion. While the general course of man's life is laid out for him at birth, the choice of good or evil rests with him—thus ran the unfathomable enigma. But "theirs not to reason why"; the solution had been advanced in Talmudic times and medieval Jewry didn't pry into its mechanism. As one man put it in astrological terms: the tenor of his life, which is conditioned by his "general" star (*mazal hakelali*), can hardly be influenced by a man's merit; his discrete acts, and the separate events of his life, which are imposed upon him by "particular" stars (*mazal perati*), only slightly more. Yet, "It lies within the power of each to do the good or the evil deed, and no external compulsion or restraint is exerted upon him. . . . To quote the rabbis, 'Everything is in the hand of God, except the fear of God' [*Ber.* 33b]. If the quality of good or of evil were implanted in his very nature, it would be as impossible to turn man from good to evil, or from evil to good, as it is to alter the natural tendency of matter to fall or of fire to rise." In other words, though a man's activities are predetermined, he alone is responsible for their moral complexion.

The theological issue does not concern us here. What does is the deterministic view of life which governed the masses. Granting the credit value of good deeds and repentance on the celestial balance sheet of a life, it was none the less the general view that "nothing ever happens to a man except at God's command"; "He decrees who shall be a scholar, and how much and for how long he shall study, and whether he will compose one, or two, or three books" and "just how many steps he will take in his lifetime, and how many men his eyes will behold." [1] Essentially this was a thorough fatalism, though the rabbis were careful not to permit it to dominate the religious view of life.

The corollary of this conception is obvious. What is already decreed in Heaven ought in some way be ascertainable by man. The universe is one close-meshed unit; heaven and earth, animals, plants, angels, demons, man, all are creatures of God, manifestations of His will, all so sensitively intertwined that each reacts immediately to the slightest alteration in the composition of the whole. (This doctrine is summed up in the elaborate comparisons between man and the world, between microcosmos and macroanthropos, which are to be found in Talmudic and medieval Jewish literature. Such treatises adduce parallels between the human body and the universe in the most minute detail.[2]) Events predetermined in the mind of God impinge upon one or another aspect of His universe long before they reach the final stage of occurrence on earth; the superior sensitivity of certain parts of the world, and even of parts of man's immediate environment and body, makes them responsive to what is yet to be long before it is. Upon this theory is reared the great science of divination—perhaps the most important single division, practically speaking, of the magical technique. Man's task is to discover means of recognizing and reading the signs which a generous nature spreads before his eyes. And to this task, however the theory may have been phrased, man has devoted himself from earliest days. One may venture to say that human curiosity about the world and study of natural phenomena in the long pre-scientific millennia were fostered as much by this one motive as by any other. Even the elementary search for food and shelter did not require and produce the detailed knowledge of our environment that the search for the future did. Paradoxically, seeking to learn what will be, man came to know what is. We need recall only the immense debt which our knowledge of the heavens owes to the astrological interests of our ancestors, or the anatomical studies pursued originally only for divinational ends.

OMENS

The simplest and most direct means of discerning the future is through the ability to interpret the natural omens which point it out. Most often such interpretation indicates merely the advisability or inadvisability of following a certain course; again, at times the world about us has a more elaborate story to tell. The ancient literature of the Jews shows their acquaintance with the art of reading omens—though they were amateurs at it compared with other peoples, the Babylonians, or the Romans, for example. The Talmud frowned upon the conscious and deliberate practice of this art, but acknowledged that one could not avoid heeding those signs that thrust their lessons under his nose. "Although one may not deliberately divine by them [that is, purpose in advance to employ them for such ends], a house, an infant and a woman may be regarded as prognostics." This cryptic remark is amplified by the commentators in the *Gemara:* if after one has erected a house, or married a wife, or fathered a child, his affairs are successful or the reverse on three separate occasions, he may consider these to be portents of good or bad fortune. This passage was construed in later times as granting *carte blanche* to pursue the art, and to expand it.[3]

During the Middle Ages, taking omens from bodily phenomena was a very popular pastime among Christians and Jews. The following passages, from thirteenth-century works, seem to have been lifted from non-Jewish sources. One opens, "Just as the astrologers foresee events from the stars, so there are some who can foretell the future from human signs. If the flesh under one's armpit quivers, they will be broaching a match to him soon, and if it is the flesh at his loins, his wife will be unclean, or he will sleep alone; if his eyelids quiver, he will be seeing corpses and graves, and if the skin of his neck, he will soon be involved in a quarrel. Similarly every part of his body can presage coming events." The department of "itches" was especially well developed. "If the sole of one's foot itches . . . he will be journeying soon to a strange place; . . . his ears, he will hear news; his eyelids, he will behold a novel sight or read an unfamiliar book; his tongue, he will speak of new things; his eyebrows, he will behold men or women whom he has not seen in a long while;

his forehead, people are looking for him and want to see him; his palm, he will hold in his hand gold or silver; his nose [he will be angry]; under his eyes and near his nose, he will weep. Itching in any part of the body is an omen. . . . God apprises man, through bodily phenomena, of what will transpire." [4]

Sneezes also were regarded as in some degree portentous. According to primitive views sneezing is the work of the spirits, and this is why, the world over, a sneeze is met with the customary pious response calling down the blessing of God on the sneezer. Jewish legend has it that before the time of Jacob people died suddenly without any warning, in the nature of illness, of their impending demise; they simply sneezed and fell dead. The sneeze, then, was an omen of death; hence the blessing which was intended tc negate its prophecy. Various responses have been used by Jews: "Health!" "God bless thee!" "God help thee!" etc., while the one who sneezed quoted Gen. 49:18, "For Thy salvation I wait, O Lord." The ominous nature of the sneeze is not mentioned in medieval Jewish literature, beyond the recital of this legend, but the masses were probably alive to it. Several writers repeated the contrary Talmudic statement to the effect that sneezing during prayers is a good, and letting wind, a bad sign.[5]

Animals, too, were closely watched for signs of the future. The disconsolate howling of a dog is a certain indication that the angel of death is strolling through town. If a dog drags his rump along the floor in the direction of the door, this too is a token of approaching death. The starling shrills when it observes in the stars that a guest is about to pay one a visit. Birds in general, ancient standby of the augur, presage the future by their cries and the manner of their flight. One of the medieval mystics has an interesting theory as to how they gain the information which they thus pass on. It seems that there is a type of spirit that flits about in the upper atmosphere listening in surreptitiously on the conversations of the "princes of the stars," who of course are aware of what is to transpire on earth, and indeed are responsible for earthly events. These spirits gossip about what they have overheard, and the birds, flying among them, pick up the bits of information which they unwittingly disclose to men. The snail, or the mole, which is noticed burrowing in a house and casting up the earth behind, is proclaiming that an adulterous act is soon to be committed there. The admonition that one should keep a rooster indoors to be warned when God is angry becomes clear when we connect it with the instruction to kill immediately any goose or cock which upsets a dish or any other vessel. This is a sign of bad luck which the death of the fowl may help to avert. One of our authors grudgingly apprises us that "there are wise men who can foretell the future by means of trees and herbs," and then drops the subject without going into detail.[6]

"No superstition," wrote Grimm, "struck deeper root throughout the entire Middle Ages than those omens comprised under the terms *aneganc, widerganc, widerlouf.* Every animal, human being or object which one unexpectedly encountered the first thing in the morning, indicated good or bad fortune, and admonished either the continuance or the abandonment of the day's enterprise." The Talmud knew of this type of augury, but its prohibition did not prevent the Jew from aping his neighbor. "If he meets an ugly person, or cattle, or a beast, or a bird," scolds the *Brantspiegel,* "or he hears a cross word, or a curse, he says, 'This is a bad omen.' " (In certain German districts it was believed that if one beholds a Jew in the morning it is a very unlucky sign, and if the Jew peers through the window, the entire week will be ruined.) In the same way, it was considered unlucky to begin a day, or a week, or a year with an act that involved some loss, for it was feared that the succeeding period would take its character from that act. If the tax-collector was making his rounds, or a friend was so thoughtless as to try to collect an old debt, they were put off until the next day. Why make bad enough worse?[7]

A bucolic environment and interest are displayed in the prediction of weather from the omens. For instance, one list cites the following phenomena as indications of protracted heavy rains: If the pigs or goats are in rut and are unsated, if after they have wallowed in mud they return for more, if the cattle in grazing bury their muzzles into the earth, or stretch their necks toward the north, if the dogs paw holes in the ground, if the cattle dip their lips into the water when they are not thirsty, if spiders' webs fall off of themselves when there is no wind to blow them down—all these are certain signs of the coming floods.[8]

Among other such superstitions I may mention the following: A seminal pollution on the Day of Atonement was generally believed to token death within the year, though the Talmudic authorities differed as to its interpretation. It was a widespread custom to enter upon a period of fasting when a Pentateuch fell to the ground, which was construed as an ill omen; as a sixteenth-century writer said, "I haven't seen any support for this custom in any book, but 'I haven't seen it' is no proof." If anyone who has performed a regular religious duty for years, such as leading the prayers on a holiday, is unable to do so one year, this may be taken as an indication that some disaster will visit his household. An error in prayer also betokened misfortune. An interesting belief in the Rhineland was to the effect that when the flames on the hearth leap unusually high, a guest is about to arrive. If one should douse the fire with water, the visitor will be drowned; "this is true and irrefutable, for many men have tested it"! German Christians also held this view, and the idea met with in medieval Lorraine, that by covering the fire a girl could rid herself of a persistent suitor, is explicable only on the basis of the same conception.[9]

Foodstuffs were on occasion regarded as tokens of good fortune. If eggs were not to be eaten on Saturday evening, the beginning of the week, because they were associated in folklore and custom with mourning, the New Year dinner included a variety of foods that were suggestive of prosperity and happiness: the head of a lamb, "that He may put us at the head and not at the tail-end" of things, fat meats, and sweets such as apples dipped in honey, "that the new year may be prosperous and happy," pomegranates, "that our merits may be as numerous as its seeds," fish, which are proverbially symbols of fruitfulness, and others. A fish called *Barben* (the barbel, *Barbus vulgaris*) was served "because its name suggests 'mercy'" (in *mhd.* the *Barbe* was called *barm,* which could be interpreted as a form of *erbarmen,* "to be merciful"). Still other suggestive foods were excluded from this meal; most notable, as an indication of the extreme tenuousness of some of these associations, was the avoidance of nuts, because *egoz* (nut) is arithmetically equivalent to *ḥet* (sin). In some communities it was customary to set the table for this meal completely with new linens and utensils, "as a good omen." [9a]

The portents which were read out of, or into, the accidents of life, were no doubt vastly more numerous than the literature discloses. Every individual could, and probably did, have his private stock of superstitions, in addition to those that were generally accepted. There were some who were better trained in this science than others, and these set up as experts. The degree of skill that was attainable is disclosed by the statement that "there is a science by which a man, by looking at a cut of meat, can tell whether the butcher had intercourse the night before"! [10] This may not be foretelling the future, which is, after all, not so difficult if the alibis are prepared in advance, but it does involve a much rarer skill, discovering what happened last night, which, as any historian can testify, is no easy job.

THE PROGNOSTIC ARTS

A passive interpretation of omens did not satisfy the lust for knowledge. The quest proceeded to an active creation of signs and portents. In common with the foremost non-Jewish thinkers, religious and lay, the rabbis were forced into the difficult position of forbidding on moral and religious grounds practices whose efficacy they could not deny. Try as the Church and Synagogue did to stamp out what they regarded as a vice, their more or less open admission that this "vice" could bring results served to advertise its usefulness to the masses. Whether deriving from the Jewish background, which had had occasion to assimilate much from the Oriental and the Græco-Roman cultures, or from its Christian contemporaries, medieval Jewry was acquainted with and employed a wide variety of the methods of divination commonly resorted to everywhere. The Germans, in particular, were devoted to this science—divination had been a prominent feature of the ancient Teutonic religion and maintained its popularity in Christian times—and the Jews who inhabited the Germanic lands were strongly subjected to this influence.[11]

Some of the forms of divination involved merely the application of a superstitious principle, with no additional magical apparatus. One such was to set a lighted candle in a place where there was no draught to extinguish it, during the ten days between *Rosh Hashanah* and *Yom Kippur*. If the light went out, it signified that the individual would not live through the year; if it burned down to the end, it meant he could count on one more year of life, at the least. These ten days are traditionally accepted as the period during which the fate of each man is determined in heaven. Light is universally regarded as a symbol of life. The association is logical and obvious, if we accept the premises.[12]

Even more intimately bound up with the human being than light is man's shadow, which among primitive peoples is regarded as a part of the body, or a projection from it. We are acquainted with the belief that one may harm an individual by treading on, or striking, or stabbing his shadow. On the night of *Hoshana Rabbah,* the seventh day of the Feast of Tabernacles, when it was believed that the decision concerning men's fate during the new year, which had been reached by *Yom Kippur,* was finally and irrevocably indited in the celestial book of records, the practice became widespread among medieval Jews to go out into the moonlight and observe whether the shadows they cast were by some ill chance devoid of heads. The lack of a head was an unmistakable sign that the decree which had already been executed upon the shadow would before long be visited on the body. The colophon of a sixteenth-century manuscript contains these words by the scribe: "On the night of *Hoshana Rabbah,* 5315 A.M. [1556 C.E.] I saw the shadow of my head in the moonlight; praised be God, for now I am assured that I shall not die this year." This belief was and is to be found throughout the Christian communities of Northern and Eastern Europe, the particular seasons at which it is observed being, of course, derived from the Christian calendar: Christmas eve, New Year's eve, Epiphany, etc. The earliest Jewish reference to it with which I am acquainted is by Eleazar of Worms; a short time later we find it mentioned by the famous Spanish commentator and philosopher, Naḥmanides. I should add that the Jewish basis for this custom was adduced from a rendering of Nu. 14:9 which gave the sense "their shadow is removed from them" to words which are usually otherwise translated. This custom was repeatedly mentioned by later German-Jewish writers.[13]

A related belief was that the reflection of a man who is doomed to die will show him with his eyes and mouth closed, even though he has them wide open. According to our sources (Eleazar of Worms, again, is the first to speak of it), on a certain night of the year the Gentiles would peer into a basin of water with eyes and mouth gaping wide, to discover their fate. In time, we learn, this practice (oil occasionally being used instead of water) was transferred by Jews to the night of *Hoshana Rabbah,* though some observed it on *Yom Kippur.*[14]

Of a similar nature was the belief that if one saw his image with a halo encircling his head, this too was a token of imminent death; when God has finished His daily stint of signing decrees, runs the explanation, He wipes His pen on the hair of a worthy man, whom He is about to take unto Himself, and thus is bestowed upon him the nimbus which his reflection boasts. This was the Midrashic explanation of the "beams of light" that emanated from Moses' head, and in the Middle Ages, it seems, God still clung to His ancient ways. It is, further, "well known in medicine" that when a man has been bitten by any virulent animal, such as a mad dog, "if he beholds the image of the dog when he looks into water, the bite will be fatal." [15]

The familiar use of Scripture in divining (Bibliomancy) was not unknown to Jews. The Romans had thus employed Vergil; the Bible was already put to this use by Christians before the eighth century; in medieval Germany hymn- and prayer-books served the same purpose. But Jews did not have to borrow this device from their neighbors. In Talmudic times it was a common practice to ask children what verses they had studied that day in school, and to accept them as good or bad omens, an expedient that persisted throughout the Middle Ages. The more usual procedure of opening the Bible at random and taking the first word or sentence that strikes the eye as a portent, was also followed. Similarly, "if, upon awakening, one recalls a Biblical verse, this is to be regarded as a 'minor prophecy,' and if it is an ominous passage, one should fast." [16]

These methods required no special skill and could be readily applied by anyone. Many of the more highly reputed techniques, however, were not available to the uninitiated. Among these were the rather technical skills of Anthroposcopy (divining by the features) and Chiromancy (by the hand), still as widely pursued today as ever. During the thirteenth and fourteenth centuries works on these subjects were very popular in Christian circles. I know of no extended discussion of them in Jewish literature, but they were undoubtedly familiar to Jews. The *Zohar* distinguished four primary facial types, corresponding to the creatures which appeared in Ezekiel's vision: the man, the lion, the ox, and the eagle. The formation of the head thus indicates the character and temper of the man, for "Physiognomy does not consist in the external lineaments, but in the features which are mysteriously drawn within us. The features of the face change according to the form which is peculiar to the inward face of the spirit." Physiognomy was employed not only to distinguish the true character of a man, but also to prognosticate his action in the future. The art of interpreting the lines which appear in the soles and palms, and on the forehead (Metoposcopy), more properly divinatory, is mentioned in Geonic literature and crops up occasionally in the medieval period. One writer went so far as to explain the rite of examining the finger-nails by the light of the *Habdalah* candle on this ground: "We are accustomed to study our hands in the light because the wise man can read in them our fate and the good fortune which is about to befall us." [17]

Casting lots (Sortilege) was a common divinatory practice during the Middle Ages. Though such simple devices as tossing a coin, throwing dice, etc., were employed, the procedure even in these cases was complicated by rules specifying when the operation might be performed, and just how the lot was to be held, and how to interpret the results, as well as by the recitation of prescribed prayers or charms. A form of lot which the Jews learned from "Esclavonia" utilized a piece of wood from which the bark had been peeled on one side; the smooth side was denominated the "woman," the rough, the "man." It was tossed into the air twice. If the "man" fell uppermost the first time, followed by the "woman," this was a good portent; the reverse betokened ill luck, and two of a kind was taken to be non-committal. There were also Hebrew "Books of Lots" which, like their Christian counterparts, were of Arabian origin; the Jewish versions appear to have been composed mainly in Southern Europe and in the Orient. They were probably used in the North as well, but there is no such work which can definitely be traced to Northern Europe. These works comprised sets of rules for finding answers to specified questions by means of the twelve signs of the Zodiac, the twenty-two letters of the alphabet, the names of the twelve tribes, animals, birds, cosmic phenomena, etc.[18]

A man's name, the matrix of his character and personality, was also useful in deciphering his fate (Onomancy). One method, employed to determine which of two competitors would triumph, was to calculate the numerical values of their names, and divide them by nine. If the two were of the same type, that is, both were Jews, followed the same trade or profession, possessed the same degree of learning, etc., the one whose name after the operation left the larger balance, was the superior. If they were dissimilar in type, then the smaller balance denoted the successful one.[19]

Geomancy, which, Thorndike says, "seems to have been nearly as popular in the medieval period as the ouija board is now" (or was in 1923, when he wrote these words), was well known to Jews as well as Christians. Thorndike describes it as "a method of divination in which, by marking down a number of points at random and then connecting or cancelling them by lines, a number or figure is obtained which is used as a key to sets of tables or to astrological constellations. The only reason for calling this geomancy, that is, divination by means of the element earth, would seem to be that at first the marks were made and figures drawn in the sand or dust. . . . But by the Middle Ages, at least, any kind of writing material would do as well." Our sources tell us of "diviners who use sand and stones," and one refers more specifically to those who "make dots on paper or in sand." The reference is unmistakably to practitioners of geomancy.[20]

These instances involved not merely the divinatory process itself, but also certain magical acts to which was attributed in the end the success of the venture. Tossing a coin or dice, after all, has significance only if some supernatural power who knows the future is directing their fall. The operation of the magic is manifest in these prescriptions: To discover the identity of a thief, one should knead little balls of clay, write the name of a suspect on each, and drop them into a pot of water. Then Psalm 16 is to be recited a number of times, along with its mystical names, and the command, "Disclose to me the man who stole these objects." We are solemnly assured that the ball bearing the right name will promptly rise to the surface. A variation is to write the names upon stones, heat them in a fire, and then drop them into a hole in the ground. This, of course, is to be accompanied by the appropriate charms. The stone that is marked with the thief's name will be the first to steam. The same device was employed to find the answers to other problems. A fifteenth-century manuscript gives this version: write "yes" on one leaf and "no" on another, roll two pills out of virgin earth and place the leaves in them (or the pills may contain several possible replies to a given question). Draw some water secretly from a spring, pour it into a bowl, slip the pills into it silently, and then say, "I conjure you by the Lord, who created heaven and earth, to reveal to me what is true, to conceal what is not true; I conjure you by the staff with which Moses divided the sea"; etc. Conclude with Ps. 4, 12, 15, 31, 55. The pill which first breaks open and permits its leaf to float to the top gives the answer to the question propounded. Still another, to discover the month in which one is destined to die, requires that the names of the angels who preside over the months be incised on twelve golden discs, which are to be dropped into oil, over which the charm is recited. The oil is then to be set out under the stars, in a new glass vessel, for seven nights, care being taken that at no time during this period is it exposed to the rays of the sun. On the seventh night, at midnight, the proper disc will rise to the surface. The oil and the discs are to be preserved, for the former now possesses miraculous healing powers, while the latter make potent amulets against evil spirits and the evil eye. These receipts indicate clearly the intimate connection between magic and divination.[21]

Other methods, equally well known in Christian Europe, were to interpret the shapes assumed by drops of oil or melted wax floating on the surface of a basin of water, and to suspend a ring of pure gold over a goblet of water and divine by the sounds it makes as it strikes against the sides of the goblet (departments of Hydromancy). Plants were also utilized (Botanomancy): "On Monday evening, after sunset, go into a field and find the yellow, broad-leaved mallow, face the east and dig a hole there, bow, encircle the spot once, bow again toward the east," and recite a charm which concludes, "If my venture is to prove successful, then you must remain in bloom; if not, then must you droop to the earth." Return in the morning and learn how your undertaking will turn out.[22]

THE DIVINING PRINCES

The most prevalent form of divination practiced by Jews, if we may judge from the frequency with which it is mentioned—it is often cited as the type of the magical act—was well known in oriental and classical antiquity, and was frequently resorted to by medieval Christians. It was carried out with the aid of a polished or reflective surface—crystal, finger-nail, wax, sword, arrow- or spear-head, mirror, water, the palm of the hand smeared with soot and oil, all of these, and more were used—into which an innocent child was made to gaze fixedly until he beheld the figures that disclosed the desired information. John of Salisbury, who died in 1181, writes of his own experience as a boy, when his instructor, a priest, after performing various adjurations and sorceries, had him and a companion look into polished basins or finger-nails smeared with holy oil or chrism and report what they saw. The other boy saw some ghostly shapes but John thanks God that he saw nothing and so was not employed henceforth in this manner. He adds that he has known many *specularii* and that they have all suffered loss of sight or some other evil. Even the holy patens "daruf man Got in der mess handelt und wandelt" were used by unscrupulous priests for this purpose.[23]

This technique was known to Jews in Talmudic times: "It is permitted to enquire of the 'princes of oil' and the 'princes of eggs,' but [one does not do so because] they lie." It may even be that Joseph's divining cup (Gen. 44:5) was similarly employed.[24] During the Middle Ages the Talmudic terminology was retained, and we read of "princes" of glass, the thumb-nail, etc. The "princes" were the figures that appeared upon the polished surfaces, and though "they lie" medieval Jews were nothing loath to take their chances on what they might reveal.

The procedure seems to have been fairly well fixed. Several medieval German accounts parallel closely the following instructions from a fifteenth-century manuscript:

"First take some flax and make a candle wick out of it; then roll the candle, a span or more in length, from virgin wax. With a finger-nail incise seven rings around the candle and set it on the ground. Draw seven circles around it with a sword, and seat yourself in the center, with the boy on your lap. The lad should not be older than nine years, and should be short. This operation should be performed on a Saturday or Monday or Thursday night. The boy grasps the candle in his hand, and you say into his right ear, 'Adam Ḥavah Abton Absalom Sarfiel Nuriel Daniel,' and say nine times, '*Gerte,* I conjure you with these seven names which I have mentioned, to appear in the wax of this candle, carefully prepared and designated for this purpose, and to answer me truthfully concerning that which I shall question you.' Then ask the boy, 'What do you see?' If he says, 'I see a woman' and if she is dressed in black, order the boy to command her, at his master's wish, to be clothed in white and to jump and dance. As soon as the boy sees her he is to say, 'Thy coming be in peace,' and after the jumping, '*Gerte,* I conjure you in the name of my master, that you show me the hiding-place of the property stolen from N son of N and where it may now be found, and that you show it to me in such a way that I may recognize it.' And if he doesn't recognize it, then the boy is to direct the woman, in his master's name, to write the location of this place clearly, in large letters and with the vowel points, so that the boy may be able to read it. Don't be dismayed and confused if you try this procedure two or three times and she doesn't appear; she may be asleep. When she departs the boy should say to her, 'Go in peace, and come again when my master wishes.' "[25]

The details differed for the various materials employed, but the general outline of the performance was in all cases as it is here given. So widespread was the use of this device that it was accepted as entirely proper by pious Jews, and was permitted even on the Sabbath. A case is recorded in which the plaintiff, evidently a professional diviner, sued his client, who had appealed to him to discover the whereabouts of some stolen property, for the stipulated fee, one mark, which had not been paid him. The defendant claimed that he owed this man only "his hire for his labor," but R. Isaac b. Samuel (twelfth century) decided for the diviner on the ground that "in such matters it is customary to pay more than merely enough to cover the labor involved"—that is, he recognized the professional status of the plaintiff. It is significant that not a word of condemnation or censure was expressed in this decision.[26]

While this means of divination seems to have been most often used in cases of theft, it was also employed to disclose events that were yet to occur. The "princes" whom the diviner conjured were bound to reply to any question put to them, provided, of course, that the sorcerer had the power to make them respond.

What was the nature of the "princes," and in what degree were the visions that the boys reported real? In the fourteenth century a French writer contemptuously dismissed these phenomena with a skepticism that rings quite modern: "Magicians are especially prone to employ as their mediums children who are credulous and impressible, and who, influenced by tales heard from old wives, are ready to see a demon in every shadow." There were others who accepted the occult significance, if not the objective reality of such visions, adopting Plato's explanation that "the soul of the gazer is thrown back upon itself by the luminosity of the object seen and then exercises its latent powers of natural divination," thus arguing that one may behold the future while in a hypnotic trance. But by far most of the medieval and ancient writers, and the masses too, did not for a moment doubt that these images were real enough, honest-to-goodness demons, though some few, like the priests who used their patens as crystals, "hetten glauben das allein die hailigen engel darin erscheinen möchten und chain tewfel." Dr. Hartlieb had no patience with such a notion; "dieselben haben gar vast geirret," he wrote.[27]

The same questions agitated Jewish minds. In general the

"princes" were held to be evil spirits, minions of the "power of uncleanness," and the technique was usually denominated "divining by the invocation of demons." This was the sole field in which the demons were privileged to function in behalf of the Jewish magician. Eleazar of Worms, however, insisted that they were angels, the *memunim* or celestial deputies, who could be compelled to appear in the shape of their earthly doubles by the proper invocations. The *memuneh* of a thief, summoned to show himself in a polished surface, thus gave away the identity of the malefactor, and re-enacted his actions at the time of the robbery. But R. Eleazar was not prepared to admit that the child actually beholds these "princes" in physical form, which was the view of one school of "philosophers." Other philosophers hold, he wrote, that these visions are hallucinations, with which demons and angels have the power to delude men. Still a third group maintains that the angels penetrate the minds of men and so shape their thoughts as to create a true picture, which, although it is not perceived through the senses, possesses nevertheless subjective reality. This last corresponds to his own view of the matter.[28]

NECROMANCY

The ancient art of calling up the spirits of the dead for divinatory purposes was well known in Biblical and Talmudic times. Though forbidden by the Law of Moses, Saul resorted to this means to consult with his deceased mentor, Samuel, through the medium of the famous witch of Endor. Talmudic strictures were hardly more effectual, for Rab, one of the leading authorities, among others, questioned the dead. Similarly in the Middle Ages, while the rabbis maintained the traditional doctrinal opposition (striking, besides, a note of compassion at times: "The dead speak only with great difficulty, therefore it is forbidden to force them by incantations and other means to reveal the future"), the sources disclose that various methods were known and employed. However, judging from the comparatively few references, this mode of divination played only a minor rôle in Jewish magic, due to the consistently condemnatory judgment of the leaders of Jewish thought, and the deeply ingrained sentiment of mingled fear and respect and affection for the dead.

Medieval writers repeated the meager traditional lore. We read that the deceased may be interrogated only during the first twelve months after death, when their bodies remain intact in the grave while their souls ascend and descend. The ghost, when called upon by name, rises feet first from the grave. On the Sabbath, however, when the spirits of dead and living celebrate the day of rest, the necromancer too must perforce call it a holiday. And finally, it is noted that "the questioner hears, but sees nothing, the questioned sees, but hears nothing, and others present neither see nor hear." [29]

The Talmud knew two kinds of necromancy, one in which the dead is raised by naming him, the other in which he is questioned by means of a skull. During the Middle Ages these two types were often mentioned, but it is questionable whether they were still employed. The references to them do not carry conviction. Other methods seem to have been more popular, such as the practice of two friends covenanting that the first to die will return to reveal the secrets of the celestial realm to the other. He might do so in a dream, but he could also appear during waking hours. "The deceased requests of his deputy angel that his intangible spirit be clothed in and united with matter so that he may carry out his part of the compact." In so far as the agreement contemplated such an apparition it may presumably be included among the necromantic arts.

There are several legends reporting such a transient visit from the grave; one tells of a R. Benjamin b. Zeraḥ who, on his deathbed, promised to warn the members of his congregation if any disaster impended. A short while after his demise he appeared in the synagogue and divulged that at the instant of death he had seen a heavenly decree inflicting a persecution upon them. Some writers, however, refused to consider this method necromantic. They made a distinction between "questioning the immortal spirit," which they claimed included such compacts as well as an appeal to the spirit of the dead, and is permitted, and "questioning the corpse" directly, which is forbidden. But such fine hair-splitting need not concern us, as it didn't medieval Jews in general. In common with their German neighbors, of whom Michael Behaim of Sulzbach (fifteenth century) wrote:

Auch wirt unglaub do mit bewert,
Das man eins toten sel beswert
Und zwingt das sie erwider vert
Und sagt wie ir beschichte,

they invoked the dead, spirit and body, to gain the information they sought. Indeed, not only the spirit, but actually the body was believed to rise from the grave, for we are told that "if one were to open the grave while the necromancer is conversing with the dead it would be found empty." [30]

Other methods described in the sources comprise: 1. "incantations" at the grave, which were apparently not favored, for the word *laḥash* usually denotes a forbidden type of magic; 2. spending the night on the grave, clothed in a distinctive garment and burning spices and incense while waving a myrtle wand, "until one hears an exceedingly faint voice from the grave responding to his questions, so faint that it seems hardly to be sensed by the ear, but rather to exist in his thoughts"; this method was also frowned upon for it was included in the forbidden category of magic which depends solely upon "the performance of an act" for its results; 3. "A man and a woman station themselves at the head and foot of a grave, and on the earth between them they set a rattle, which they strike while they recite a secret invocation; then while the woman looks on the man puts the questions, and the deceased reveals the future to them"; 4. a method which seems to have been acceptable, for it invoked the dead by means of angelic names: "Stand before the grave and recite the names of the angels of the fifth camp of the first firmament, and hold in your hand a mixture of oil and honey in a new glass bowl, and say, 'I conjure you, spirit of the grave, Neḥinah, who rests in the grave upon the bones of the dead, that you accept this offering from my hand and do my bidding; bring me N son of N who is dead, and make him stand erect and speak with me without fear, and have him tell me the truth without fear, and I shall not be afraid of him; let him answer the question which I shall put to him'; and the deceased will immediately appear. But if he doesn't, repeat this invocation a second time, and if necessary, a third. When he appears place the bowl before him, and converse with him. Hold a myrtle wand in your hand." [31]

BURIED TREASURE

One of the peculiar beliefs that were epidemic during the Middle Ages, especially in Germany, was in the presence of hidden treasure in the earth. The folk-tales of Northern Europe have familiarized every child with the ghostly blue flame that sometimes flickers on the ground above the hiding-place of a hoard. But only too rarely were such fitful markers to be encountered, and people were not content to await patiently the stroke of luck which would make them rich. The divining-rod (Rhabdomancy) provided a surer means of uncovering the riches of the earth. There are some today who still insist that the forked stick can disclose hidden springs—of water, not of wealth (I have myself seen the rod incline toward the earth in the hands of credulous country-folk, but it refused to work for me)—but just as the object of the search has become prosaic and trivial, so has the technique degenerated. A modern water-diviner could never hope to find any more solid treasure than he seeks; the magic has evaporated, the quest has literally lost its charm.

Several fifteenth-century Jewish formulas for making and using a divining-rod, which adhere closely to the texts of German recipes, have been printed. The Yiddish-Deutsch in which the spells are couched, the names employed in them, the very belief on which they are based, clearly indicate that they were borrowed from German originals. The following directions given in one text are characteristic of the entire genre: "On midsummer night, after sunset, go to a year-old hazel tree and select four rods which grew that year; bind them together and grasp them in your left hand, while you pass the right, in which you have placed gold and silver coins, three times around them, and recite this: 'May these rods be as successful as our father Jacob's were, for when the flock beheld them, they bore young in their likeness; may these rods as surely reveal to me hidden treasures, whether of coin, or valuable objects, or jewels. I conjure you by the name of El Shaddai, the rock of ages, by the name I Am That I Am, by the name of Him who knows the future, by the name of Michael, of Kutiel, of Luel, by the name of Luel, of Kutiel, of Michael.' Leave the silver and gold there, and in the morning, before sunrise, go to these rods and cut them, in the direction of the sun, and in the direction of the four cardinal points, east, west, north, south, and as you cut each rod, say, [the preceding is in Hebrew, what follows, in Yiddish-Deutsch]: 'Liber Gott, ich bitte dich, dass du gebst Macht zu diesen Ruthen, dass sie mich müssen weisen auf die Statt die Rechtfertigkeit, so da liegt verborgen Silber oder Gold, gemünzt oder ungemünzt, es sei verborgen oder es sei sonst dar kommen, es sei ober der Erden, es sei unter der Erden, in Gottes Namen Amen.' " There follows an adjuration of the rods by various names and natural phenomena. Then slits are cut and they are set into each other to make two forks, while another spell calling on El, Eli, Eloa, Agla, Adonai, Sabaot, Tetragrammaton, is recited. Two boys carry these forks into the open fields and the diviner follows them, muttering fearful spells which make no sense at all in Hebrew but are really transliterations from the Latin. The invocation ends finally, "I conjure you by the living God, I conjure you, rods, by the true God, by the holy God, that from this moment you bend toward the spot where this treasure is concealed," etc. When the rods have fulfilled their destiny (or should one say "if"?) and the digging begins, there is another hocus-pocus jumble of words, in which "hocus-pocus" makes its debut in literature. And then comes the grand climax, the glitter of gold and jewels through the broken earth. But at this juncture the treasure-hunter is apparently struck dumb—or else it is left for him to find the words which can adequately close his profitable adventure.[32]

The device was used not only to discover buried wealth, but also to obtain sought-after information. The rods were prepared in the same way, but the invocation was adjusted to suit one's needs. This one is typical: "I conjure you, hazel rods, by the Creator, and by the Patriarchs . . . that you reveal to me my request concerning my friend. If he has done it, then go upward; if he has not done it, then remain still. By the almighty God, Amen." There follows a series of other conjurations, by "the three who were ready to die for the truth" (Dan. 3:19ff.), by the *Torah,* by the Tetragrammaton, and by other, less comprehensible names, intended to impress upon the forked stick its owner's insistence upon a truthful reply.[33]

There were also other methods of tracing hidden treasure. One of them required that a certain "holy and pure" name be inscribed on a small gold plate "which has been refined seven times," and bound with a blue thread on the neck of a male white dove, which was then to be set loose. The spot on which it alights conceals the hoard. One must circumambulate the place seven times before beginning to dig, "and if it is in the daytime, speak the name of the sun in that season, and if at night, the name of the moon." Another instructed: "When something is concealed in a house or in a room, and you don't know where, dig a pit in the center of the place, a man's height deep and as wide as you please; dry the sides of the pit as well as you can, and kindle a fire in it. Then put dung or the like on the fire, cover it with a tub, and damp it well so that no smoke can come out. Then you will see the smoke issuing out of the ground in the spot where the hidden thing lies." [34] It must be a mighty precious "thing" to warrant such heroic measures to recover it!

TRIAL BY ORDEAL

The ordeal is not usually thought of as a divinatory device, but this is its essential character. It constituted an invocation of supernatural aid, an appeal to the immediate judgment of God, an elaborated mode of sortilege. During the Middle Ages various forms of the ordeal were popular, and were sanctioned by Church and State; indeed special liturgical formularies were drawn up for its application, and it was conducted directly under the ægis of the clergy. Jews also occasionally resorted to the ordeal. The best-known Biblical example is the procedure employed in the case of a woman suspected of adultery (Nu. 5:11–31), which was abolished before the year 70 C.E. A privilege issued by Henry IV. to the congregation of Speyer in 1091, providing that "Jews could not be compelled to undergo ordeals by fire and water," might be construed as a concession to an active Jewish aversion to ordeals. But medieval Jews were not opposed to ordeals *per se;* they merely refused to submit to tests which had been endued with a sectarian character. In fact they forbade bathing in "unclean water" upon which priests had invoked the name of their God preparatory to using it for the water-ordeal. This form was not employed by Jews because its popularity with Christians had stamped it as "heathenish," but other acceptable forms were recognized. When some hot-headed young men proposed the immediate execution of certain suspected sorceresses, "the sage" reproved them with the words, "Israel is not in his own land!" and suggested instead that an announcement be made in the synagogue, at a time when the suspects were present, that if any children were harmed "the teeth of these women would be ground with the stones that surround the well, and the guilty ones will die within the hour." [35]

A popular medieval belief which was accepted by Jews was that the wounds of a murdered person begin to bleed again in the presence of the murderer—the so-called "trial by blood" or "ordeal of touch." The Jewish sources note two curious variations on this theme, which are apparently unique: if a man who has just had some soup draws near, the corpse will spurt blood (therefore one should always consume a piece of bread after soup), and also if one approaches it with a knife to which particles of food adhere. A cognate belief, met with in the folklore of several peoples, is embraced in the "kinship ordeal," according to which the body of a father possesses an affinity for the blood of his son. A story is told of Saadia Gaon, and again, of Solomon, before whom two claimants to an estate appeared, each maintaining he was the true son and heir. The judge had a bone from the dead man's body placed successively into two bowls containing blood drawn from their veins; the bone absorbed the blood of the real son, but rejected the blood of the impostor.[36]

Israel Isserlein's biographer relates an incident which, while it did not constitute an actual ordeal by fire for judicial purposes, involved a challenge reminiscent of Elijah's contest with the priests of Baal. A preacher and miracle-worker (probably the well-known Franciscan, John Capistrano, the fifteenth-century scourge of heresy) came to Wiener-Neustadt, Isserlein's home, and launched a vitriolic attack upon Judaism. The rabbi publicly offered to follow the cleric through a bonfire, to test the relative merits of Judaism and Christianity, but "the priest went his way and nothing came of the matter." [37]

The trial by combat, or duel, was another form of the ordeal carried out under ecclesiastical auspices, with the aid of the prescribed ritual. In theory at least, it was not a test of strength and skill, but of righteousness, and its special character derives from the faith of the combatants that God would sustain the arm of the just man. Despite its superimposed Christian features, however, Jews are to be included among medieval duellists, though it is possible that the more objectionable parts of the rite were eliminated when the contestants were Jewish. Otherwise it is difficult to understand how pious Jews could have subjected themselves to a trial which involved the invocation of the Christian deity. At any rate, Frederick I of Austria, in 1244, issued a privilege to the Jews which provided that if the murderer of a Jew could not be convicted by direct proof of the commission of the crime, but strong circumstantial evidence fixed the deed on him, then the relatives or friends of the Jew could appoint a champion to meet the accused in a duel. This privilege, which was incorporated in statutes issued by various Central European rulers, contemplated the appearance of Christians in the lists in behalf of Jewish litigants. But Jews themselves also took up the sword or lance to settle a dispute with the aid of God. On

November 28, 1194, the royal court in London issued the following order: "A day is fixed for Chermin the Jew and Samson, brother of Brin, for the plea by duel on the octaves of St. Hilary. . . . Let them come prepared for that duel at Totelle." The English "Fine and Oblate Rolls" for the years 1204–1206 record that "Elyes Blund, Jew of Lincoln, gives 200 marks and 2 marks of gold that the duel pledged against him at Nottingham, in the sixth year, may remain." Nor was it unknown for Jews on the continent to fight duels, relying upon the supernatural to judge the merit of their cause.[38]

15

DREAMS

THE DREAM IN HUMAN AFFAIRS

IN THE long pre-Freudian centuries, before the mystery of the dream was reduced to all too human terms, when men still listened for the voice of God in the still of the night, dreams played a greater rôle in shaping ideas and actions and careers than it is easy for us today to believe. If we have come to look upon these nocturnal visions as the products of experience, we have simply reversed the older, though not yet altogether discarded, view which made of them initiators of experience. The supernatural world communicated with man through the dream, and spoke words of counsel and command which he felt impelled to heed. Galen, in 148 C.E., at the age of seventeen, turned to the study of medicine because of a dream; in 1244 Ludwig IX took up the cross for a like compelling reason. How many such instances might be adduced to indicate the vital decisions that turned upon such a motive!

The dream was not less potent an incentive in Jewish life; for instance, at about the time of Ludwig's venture, Moses of Coucy wrote, "At the beginning of the sixth millennium [1240 C.E.] there came to me the command in a dream vision, 'Arise, compose a book of religious instruction in two parts!' " which was the genesis of his *Semag*. Two centuries later, a certain Gershon b. Ḥiskiya, who was in prison in France, was led by a dream to write a book on medicine. Two centuries later again a dream prompted the composition of Menasseh b. Israel's *Nishmat Ḥayim*.[1]

Even legal and ritual problems of some moment were decided at the instance of "the master of dreams." The very day on which the Tosafist, Efraim b. Isaac of Regensburg, permitted the consumption of sturgeon as a *kosher* fish he was obliged to reverse himself because in a dream "they" had made clear to him that he was in error. R. Meir of Rothenburg admitted that a dream had caused him to change his opinion in a matter affecting wages, despite contrary precedents, the rulings of his French colleagues, and his own previous decisions. In fact, there lived in the thirteenth century a man, Jacob Halevi of Marvège, who gathered in a volume a series of responsa which had been handed down to him in dreams, relative to such ritual issues as shaving the beard and cutting the hair, how and when *tefillin* should be worn, when certain blessings should be recited, whether milk foods may be eaten after meat, ritual slaughter, etc.—matters that can seem trivial only to those who are insensitive to the demands which an ardent piety makes upon devout people. He did not limit himself to these questions; sometimes his queries were in a lighter vein. It is reported that he once asked "the master of dreams" whether Jesus and Mary are hinted at in the Bible, and received the reply that the words "the foreign gods of the land" (Deut. 31:16) are mathematically equivalent to those two names. It is a pity that he didn't convey to us the reply to his question as to how soon the Messianic era may be expected. Others, too, merited heavenly edification. In the same century an anonymous writer asserted that dreams had cleared up many difficulties in Maimonides' *Guide* for quite a few puzzled students, and Isaac b. Moses of Vienna, who was very much concerned about the correct spelling of the name "Akiba" had that too straightened out for him by the obliging "master of dreams." Heaven was more co-operative in those days than it is today.[2]

The dream thus constituted a very real factor in medieval life—even the line that separated physical reality from the more tenuous spirit world which was supposed to rule dreamland was not too precisely and permanently drawn. In Havre, in 1637, the city court declared a child legitimate when the mother swore that her husband, missing for four years, had embraced her in a dream. To such fantastic lengths Jewish belief did not go. Yet a vow or a decree of excommunication pronounced in a dream was held to be real and binding, even more so than one uttered during waking hours, for the latter could be voided before a court of three men, while the former required a full congregation of ten, the idea being that since the deity had somehow been involved in the dream action, only a *minyan,* over which the *Shechinah* presided, had the power to release the dreamer.[3]

But the greatest force that the dream exerted was as a prognostication of, and guide to, the future. In this conviction the leaders of Church and Synagogue were at one; Thomas Aquinas found himself in the company of the rabbis of the Talmud and the Middle Ages. "Dreams are a sixtieth part of prophecy" ran an old adage; the mathematics may have been correct once upon a time, but since the gift of prophecy had been withdrawn from the world, the proportion must be raised considerably to do justice to the medieval view. It was in dreams that the supernatural world communicated directly with the natural; its knowledge of the future could most readily be transmitted to men through this medium. "Not a thing transpires on earth," wrote one authority on the subject, "without having first been announced in a dream." Another wrote, "Nothing happens to a man, good or ill, before he has beheld some intimation of it in a dream." How seriously this dictum was taken we may judge from an anecdote: a man dreamed that he would marry a certain woman, but when he sought to fulfill his destiny, she refused him. Now he *was* in a dilemma; if he married someone else, which he was quite ready to do, it would be tantamount to dooming his wife to an untimely death, for his dream must undoubtedly come true. Though "the sage" whom he approached with his problem quoted Talmud to refute Talmud: "dreams neither raise nor lower," that is, "disregard them and follow your own inclination," it was no easy matter to convince him that he need not wait until his dream-mate changed her mind. Instances of this sort could be cited in great number. And the reports of dreams that came true are legion. After relating one such true dream which R. Israel Isserlein had, his biographer wrote, "And I know many more dreams of his that came to pass." There are still many people who can testify in a like vein concerning themselves or their friends. Solomon Almoli, in his *Pitron Ḥalomot* ("The Interpretation of Dreams"), proved logically that this was no superstition. Jews and Gentiles agree, he wrote, that portents occur during waking hours; there can be no doubting that they come from God, for they show themselves in time to be veracious intimations of the future. Nor can one for a moment question God's power to introduce them into our dreams. Indeed they can the more readily appear at night because "then our physical energies are weakened and the mental strengthened." After this compelling argument it was hardly necessary to adduce, as he did, "proofs" from Gentile literature and from Jewish, as well as on rational and sensational grounds.[4]

WHERE DREAMS COME FROM

Not all dreams were of supernatural origin nor possessed equal significance. Corresponding to a variety of causes, various types of dreams commanded respect in differing degrees.

It was recognized that many, if not most, dreams are produced by physical stimuli. Heavy, rich foods "cause a vapor to rise into the brain" which during the night disposes itself in fantastic images. Physical needs and desires, or sensations, such as heat and cold, experienced during sleep, similarly affect the mind, so that one's dreams bear a close relation to one's physical state. Menasseh b. Israel wrote, "When one is overheated at night he may dream that he is warming himself before a fire, or enjoying a hot bath; if he is cold, he dreams of ice and sleet and snow." Such dreams are unworthy of attention, they "speak folly" and are "vain and idle conceits." [5]

Another common source of dreams are man's thoughts during the day. "When a man concentrates on certain ideas for a long time, the power of thought to conjure up definite images remains active at night." Dreams that can be traced back to such a cause are no more credible than the first category. But another sort of dream, produced by "the vigor of the soul" (*ḥozek hanefesh*), merits consideration on the part of the dreamer, for it is a "prophecy in miniature." Menaḥem Ẓiyuni described the process thus: "The imaginative faculty refashions at night the perceptions which have been impressed upon one's fancy during the day; during sleep when the senses are idle, this faculty overpowers him so that the vision seems as real as though he were beholding it in actuality. Such a dream is reliable in proportion to the vividness of his powers of analogy; it comes to him without his having thought of its subject matter at all, which, in fact, is often quite unconventional. These dreams constitute the 'miniature prophecy' of which the rabbis said that it is bestowed particularly upon imbeciles and infants, because they are not graced with intelligence and their apperceptive powers are undeveloped. Therefore what the imagination makes of sense perceptions during waking hours is clearly visioned while asleep, for it conceives of things that are true and that come to pass." [6] The psychology of dreams as expounded by Ẓiyuni has a modern ring; it was not his own, however, for he confessed that he had cribbed it from non-Jewish "theologians." Apparently the unexpressed theory behind this dissertation is one we have met before, namely, that the soul, untrammelled by the physical universe and left to its own resources, possesses the power to apprehend the future.

What is probably the most primitive and universal theory is also met with in Jewish dream-lore. While the body is asleep, the spirit, or soul, leaves its corporeal prison and wanders over the face of the earth, reporting back its experiences to the sleepless mind. When one dreams of meeting a friend who is far distant, it is the souls of the two, annihilating space, which have made contact. Some men, of a higher spiritual capacity, behold these visions clearly and well defined; for most men they are confused and obscure. We dream of the dead because their immortal souls are still capable of haunting the earth and meeting ours. "But animals have no soul, therefore a man cannot dream of an animal that has died or has been slaughtered." Reports of the dead appearing in dreams are numerous. The teacher and father-in-law of Eliezer b. Nathan, R. Eliakim b. Joseph, visited him one night to correct a misconception which had led to an erroneous ritual decision; R. Meir of Rothenburg once helped an earnest student, who had never met him in life, to unravel a badly snarled Talmudic passage; Rashi disclosed to his grandson Samuel the correct pronunciation of the Tetragrammaton; according to the popular legend, on the third night after he had been tortured to death, R. Amnon of Mainz appeared in a dream to his teacher, R. Kalonymos b. Meshullam, and dictated the solemn *Unetanneh Tokef* hymn which he had composed while writhing in pain. These are a few of the more notable visitations. Visions of the lot that deceased ancestors are enjoying, whether in Paradise or *Gehinnom,* disclosures of hidden treasure, exhortations to repay debts contracted by the visitant, such is the burden of most dreams about the dead.[7]

Those dreams, then, that derive from natural causes, physical or mental, are not the stuff out of which the shape of time to come can be pre-constructed. Dreams that result from the peregrinations of the soul may or may not be thus useful, depending upon the presence of the one factor that stamps them as truly portentous, the supernatural. All really significant dreams come ultimately from God. (In practice, of course, the definition worked the other way around—those dreams which the expert branded as significant were *ipso facto* God-born.) A Talmudic sage quoted God's assurance, "Although I have hidden my face from Israel, I will communicate with him through dreams." Such direct communication was in effect during the Middle Ages, as well as in ancient times, according to some writers. Menasseh b. Israel distinguished two degrees of deistic dream inspiration: the first, vouchsafed to all men alike, he termed "providential," the product of God's solicitude for His creatures. Such dreams are devoted to the minor concerns of human existence; evil men are warned against the deeds they ponder during the day, good men receive mildly prophetic or admonitory visions. He testified that he himself had had such dreams foretelling the death of acquaintances, which came true. The imagery and symbolism of these dreams is usually beyond the comprehension of the ordinary man. The second degree is the "prophetic," in which direct communion with God is experienced only by rare, blessed spirits.[8]

Most of the medieval writers who discussed the subject, however, inclined toward the view that God-sent visions are transmitted through the intermediacy of angels. Sometimes we read of an angel especially appointed over this department, "the master" or "dispenser of dreams," sometimes it is the *memuneh,* man's deputy angel, who molds his sleeping thoughts to apprise him of the will of God. At times this angel does nothing more than direct the drama of man's waking thoughts on the stage of his dream, and "since not all thoughts are true, not all dreams are true." But when the angel introduces his own plot onto the stage, the vision assuredly has some peculiar and significant meaning.[9]

There is still a further possibility—the dream may be the work of a demon. As *Sefer Ḥasidim* says, "When a man suddenly beholds in his sleep a woman with whom he has never had relations, and whom he may not even have consciously desired, such a dream is caused by a demon or spirit. . . . The demon does not actually penetrate his thoughts but whispers into the depths of his aural cavity." The demons seem to be responsible mainly for dreams of passion, though there are cases in which it is impossible to determine whether an evil spirit or an angel is to be held accountable.[10]

"DREAMS FOLLOW THEIR INTERPRETATION"

The cardinal feature of portentous dreams, as we have observed, is obscurity. Graphically, "What is shown a man in a dream is as though he were to find himself in the midst of a strange people whose tongue he doesn't understand, so that they can only suggest things to each other in sign language, as one does with a deaf person." And just as today it requires a trained psychoanalyst to decode the dream cipher, so in the past the dream was taken to an expert to be read aright. The basic principle had been laid down in the Talmud: "All dreams follow their interpretation," that is, as the dream is interpreted, so will it come to pass. Indeed the Talmud went a step further to the logical corollary of this principle: "An uninterpreted dream is like an unread letter," having neither good nor evil implication, as though it had never been experienced. The rabbis sought to give recognition in these statements to the psychological impact of a favorable or unfavorable prediction, and were subtly implying that it might be best not to seek the meaning of a dream. But, in Talmudic times and later, these words were taken literally. The wise followed the better counsel, and refrained from courting trouble—"One should not relate his dream to any man, and especially not his wife," *Sefer Ḥasidim* advised, for so long as it was his own secret its effect upon his career remained nil. Those who could contain their curiosity, however, were few. The *Gemara* tells a tale of one man who got several different interpretations of his dream—and *all* came true. But *Maḥzor Vitry* specified that the first interpretation is binding on the dream, and this became the generally accepted rule.[11]

The author of a widely read dream book, Solomon Almoli, refused to accept the Talmudic view, for, he argued, it would destroy the whole science of dream interpretation. If it were so, one need either not bother about dreams altogether, or secure only favorable interpretations. It is impossible that God's will, disclosed in a dream, can be nullified by such naïve methods. We may ascribe this denial of the traditional view to professional jealousy, but in effect the tradition did no harm to the interpreter's business.

There was some difference of opinion as to the qualifications of the dream expert. Some maintained that his skill must be innate—his star must have determined at his birth that this should be his forte. This was the reply that Jacob Halevi of Marvège received when he put the question to "the dispenser of dreams." But Almoli would have none of this. If it were a matter of fate, he wrote, some people would be infallible interpreters, and there were none such. Skill in this field is the result only of intensive training. Some interpreters rely upon dream books and can decipher particular dreams, but the true expert is one who has high intelligence, and an understanding of the principles of the science. He must know how to evaluate the circumstances and environment of the dreamer, and to differentiate the fine shades of meaning of dream symbolism, to reject the inconsequential elements of the dream and to single out those that are significant. Amateurs can only blunder upon the true meanings. A typical professional point of view!

Along with their reputed skill as magicians, Jews owned a high reputation as dream interpreters and were sought out by Christians for this purpose. Because of the tradition that "dreams follow the interpretation" it was feared that the Jewish expert might be held responsible in heaven if he translated the dream of his Christian client in terms of Christian worship—he might be the cause of his client's "sin" in pursuing Christian practices. For instance, if he told a priest that his dream signified that he was destined to become a bishop, the priest would apply himself more assiduously than ever to his clerical duties. But the ready rejoinder was to the effect that the Christian would continue in his error regardless of the dream, so the interpreter was really not accountable. "Even though the expert refuses to interpret the dream," it will come true, it was admitted, with the reservation, however, that if a Jew's dream points to some evil act the interpreter should not disclose it, for "one who tells a Jew that his dream signifies that he will sin is to be regarded as causing him to sin." [12]

The general public was acquainted with the professional methods through a host of dream books, many of them attributed to Joseph or Daniel. These books, popular among Christians, Jews, and Mohammedans, had much in common, and were in essence versions in different tongues of a common fund of tradition. One such book, already mentioned, the *Pitron Ḥalomot* of Solomon b. Jacob Almoli, first published in Salonica about 1515 (under the title *Mefasher Ḥalmin*), republished in Constantinople in 1518 and 1551, in Cracow in 1576, and many times after, was the outstanding Jewish work on the subject. Almoli was a Turkish Jew, who flourished at the beginning of the sixteenth century; he collated all the older Jewish material, and made extensive use of the non-Jewish, admitting his indebtedness to the *Gemara,* to Hai Gaon, to works ascribed to Rashi, Joseph, Daniel, as well as to translations from non-Jewish sources. Among those he quoted were Ibn Sinna, Ibn Roshd, Aristotle and Plato. Though his book was written toward the end of the period it represents the information current throughout the earlier centuries. Some of the passages on dreams in the German-Jewish literature, in Eleazar of Worms's *Ḥochmat HaNefesh,* for example, or in the manuscript work *Eẓ Ḥayim,* by Jacob b. Judah Ḥazan of London, both thirteenth-century writers, display a close affinity with Almoli's later compilation. We have no such extended work from Northern Europe, but there can be no doubt that German Jews were acquainted with most of the subject matter which Almoli presented. His book became very popular and in 1694 was translated into Yiddish, in which form it still has a wide circulation among the Jewish masses.[13]

Since this work contains the only systematic organization of the material, it may not be amiss to summarize it here. It is divided into three parts, the first dealing with the classification of dreams and the general principles of interpretation, the second constituting a full glossary of dream symbols, the third devoted to an elucidation of the methods of counteracting the effects of ominous dreams. Part I comprises eight "gates": 1. defining the dream and its various types; 2. whether or not to rely on dreams; 3. distinguishing between reliable and unreliable dreams; 4. describing the customary and the extraordinary elements of dreams; 5. three basic principles which the interpreter must follow; 6. the interpretation must take into account the client's profession or trade, and his circumstances; 7. whether or not the interpretation is the determining factor in the effect of a dream, containing a "great investigation" into this subject; 8. the time when dreams may be expected to materialize. Part II contains five "gates": 1. divided into five sections, on the symbolism of inanimate matter; 2. five sections, on flora; 3. six sections, on fauna; 4. four sections, on humans; 5. three sections, on "higher beings," such as "the planets and stars, thunder, and books"! A perusal of Part II leaves one wondering what natural phenomena Almoli could possibly have neglected; he was careful to include all the derivatives, such as objects made of wood and metals, etc., wine and oil, eggs and honey and cheese and milk, cooked dishes, clothing. Part III, consisting of three "gates," discusses the "dream-fast" and the ritual devices of "turning a dream to good" and "releasing" one from the effects of a dream. Almoli covered the field thoroughly; his erudition explains his scorn of those who would rely on the stars, or on a hastily digested smattering of data to qualify as experts.[14]

THE TECHNIQUE OF INTERPRETATION

The Bible offers several classic examples of dream interpretation, symbolical in the case of Pharaoh's dreams, allegorical in that of Nebuchadnezzar. In Talmudic times puns often provided the key, e.g., dreaming that something will occur in the month of Nisan means one will suffer no temptation (*nissayon*). If the dream could be brought into connection with some Biblical verse, that verse indicated its significance, *e.g.,* to behold a camel (*gamal*) means that the dreamer's death has been decreed in heaven, but he will be delivered from his fate, because Gen. 46:4, in which the words *gam 'aloh* occur, contains the reassuring promise, "I will go down with thee into Egypt, and I will also surely bring thee up again." During the Middle Ages these methods remained in use, but the most favored was to interpret by analogies, or by antitheses. Very often the association is obscure, though it no doubt derives from one of these methods or from an ancient, well-authenticated tradition. It is interesting to notice how frequently the interpretations of dreams in Christian sources correspond with the Jewish.[15]

The following excerpts from thirteenth-century Jewish works [16] provide some idea of the manner of interpretation. From *Ez Ḥayim:* "All liquids are of good omen, except wine, if the dreamer is an uncultured person; all fruits are auspicious, except the date, and all vegetables, except turnip-heads, but the root indicates wealth; . . . wheat signifies peace; barley, atonement for sins; laden vines, his wife will not miscarry; white grapes are a good omen; black grapes in season are good, but out of season they indicate he will soon be praying for mercy; . . . a white horse is a good omen; a red horse is bad, he will be hounded and pursued; a donkey, he may be confident of salvation; . . . if he dreams he has lost his property, an inheritance will soon come his way; . . . if he is on a roof he will achieve greatness; if he is descending, he will be humbled"; etc. Eleazar of Worms offers these: if a man dreams he has a pain in one eye, a brother will fall ill; in both eyes, two brothers will be ill; if a tooth falls out, a son or some relative will die; if he sees a king, or a groom, or a wedding ceremony, or any celebration, he will soon be a mourner; dividing meat indicates a quarrel; fire in an oven signifies evil events; snow in summer, a fire; a vineyard, his wife is or will be pregnant; grapes, he will be blessed with a child; carrying a bird or a fish in his bosom means his wife will bear a child; if an unmarried person has this dream, he will soon be wedded; a group of people partaking of delicacies indicates they will all have cause to weep; an angel in the moon means war; a snake-bite indicates prosperity; and so on.

It will be more instructive, however, to examine the principles by which the interpreter made his decisions.[17] It was first necessary to evaluate the credibility of the dream, which required a study of the stars, of the dreamer's character, of the foods he had consumed before retiring, both in their planetary relationships and their potentiality for inducing *spiritus* in the body, and his thoughts on the preceding days. The day of the month and the week, the hour, the land in which the dream was beheld also help to determine the degree of reliance which is to be placed upon it. Similarly, if the dream images are clear and vivid and leave the dreamer moved or agitated, the dream is trustworthy. If the dream leaves little impression, it may be disregarded. One of the rules frequently advanced is that a dream which occurs in the early night, before the process of digestion has started, either has no significance or concerns the past; a dream which comes in the middle of the night, while the food is being digested, may or may not have importance; but most dreams that occur in the early morning, when the process of digestion has been completed, come true.

Similar criteria were employed to determine how long a period may elapse before the dream comes to pass. A man's character, for instance, helps decide this, for the righteous person is forewarned long before an event is to occur so that he may have ample time to prepare for it, while the wicked are not given much warning. The general rule is that most dreams are speedily realized, usually on the same or the next day; occasionally realization of a dream may be delayed, but never longer than twenty-two years (this is based on a Talmudic remark).

As to the actual process of interpretation, there is no substitute for a knowledge of the dream language, Almoli writes, but there is one rule that must constantly be kept in mind, namely, that the same symbol may have different connotations for different men. As an example he cites the case of a man who dreamed that his horse was able to negotiate a turbulent stream only with great effort. If the dreamer is a scholar, then the horse signifies wisdom, and the dream indicates that his learning will carry him successfully through some very difficult situations; if he is not a scholar, the horse means strength, and the dream implies that he will be engaged in a physical struggle from which he will emerge victorious. Quick-wittedness has always been the fortune-teller's most precious endowment.

DREAM DIVINATION

The gold that the fates pour into a man's lap serves only to whet his greed. The effort to induce divinatory dreams succeeded upon the realization that dreams could be put to such a use. Saul tried, and failed. If countless others failed too, inevitably there were some who could claim success, and "nothing succeeds like success," especially in the field of magic. In Talmudic and Geonic times the techniques of asking a "dream question" were familiar to everyone. During the Middle Ages this proved a popular form of divination, though it hardly met with the approval of the religious authorities. *Sefer Ḥasidim* contains the statement, "If a man decides, I will put a 'dream question' to find out which good wife I shall take, he will never be successful," yet the same work tells of a pious Jew who asked the prince of dreams "who will sit beside him in Paradise? And they showed him a young man in a distant land." An interesting anecdote concerns a man who inquired how long he would live and received the reply in French, *mil ans,* which he interpreted literally, but his life was ended at eighty, for *mil* in Hebrew transliteration equals eighty. One of the questions put by Jacob Halevi of Marvège was whether it is proper "to invoke, by means of the 42-letter name of God, the angels who are appointed over learning and wealth and victory and favor," and the reply came, "Holy, holy, holy is the Lord of Hosts, and He Himself will provide all your needs." As we have seen, Jacob Halevi solved many ritual and legal problems in this way, and the fourteenth-century R. Jacob b. Moses Mölln (Maharil), or his father, resorted to the same device to resolve at least one ritual question.[18]

In consonance with the prevailing conception of the origin of dreams, two agencies were mainly invoked to serve divinatory purposes: the dead, and the spirits generally or the genius of dreams in particular. As we have noted, one way of ensuring a nocturnal visit from the beyond was to make a dying man take an oath that after his death he would return and answer any questions put to him. Or two friends might make a mutual vow that the first to die would come back in a dream to paint for the other a picture of the next world. Such practices were common among Christians as well as among Jews, as this verse from Hans Vintler's *Blumen der Tugend* (1411) discloses: [19]

> *So send denn ettliche*
> *wenn sy sechend ain liche*
> *so raunent sy dem totten zu*
> *und sprechend 'kum morgen fru*
> *und sag mir, wie es dir dort gee.'*

Another course was to stretch oneself on the grave of a pious man and beseech him to answer one's questions in a dream. There is a story of a young student who adopted this procedure to learn whether certain ascetic practices he wished to adopt would be considered sinful or meritorious in heaven; that night the deceased came to him and carried him off to Paradise where he beheld the rewards that would be showered on him for his piety.[20]

The dead, however, were not always willing to obey the summons of the living, and in such a case force could be applied. This required the services of a professional sorcerer. A woman who was on bad terms with her son died without leaving a will disclosing the hiding place of her money. The son employed a sorceress to wring her secret from her. The woman "performed her sorceries with a knife" and then went to sleep, whereupon a demon appeared to her in a dream with the knife piercing his heart. She refused to be moved by his entreaties and extract the blade until he produced the information she sought. He returned with the mother and forced her to reveal her secret. The son got the money, but a few nights later his mother came to him in a dream and apprised him of the price he would have to pay: "In proportion to the suffering you brought upon me by your vile act will reverses and torments be heaped upon you." [21]

On the other hand, angels and spirits could be invoked to appear in dreams by the usual methods. Jacob Halevi who, it is reported, induced his divinatory dreams by putting himself in a trance, used a simple request: "Oh, supreme king, great, mighty and revered God, guardian of the covenant and fount of grace for Thy followers, preserve Thy covenant and Thy grace for us, and command Thy holy angels who are appointed over the replies to 'dream questions' to give a true and a proper answer, unqualified and specific, to the question which I shall ask before Thy glory," etc. It is interesting that sometimes the answer came that in heaven itself there was a division of opinion, which, by a strange coincidence, usually corresponded with a like division among the rabbis here on earth; and sometimes the first reply that Jacob received was unsatisfactory, so that he had to repeat his question two and three times, insisting upon a clearer response. Certain Biblical selections were also useful toward this end. Ps. 23 and 42, each recited seven times with its "names," were guaranteed to produce dream replies. If one writes Deut. 29:28 and its "names" on his hand and sleeps with that hand under his head the angel of dreams will favor him.[22]

Direct invocation of angels was also resorted to, with the usual preliminary rites of ritual cleansing and fasting. One simple invocation runs as follows: " 'I conjure you, Duma, prince of dreams, in the name of the Almighty God, that you come to me this night and answer my question. And when you wish to indicate good or evil, show me for evil: priests and churches, wells, cisterns, caves and graves; but for a favorable sign show me: schools, synagogues, open books and scholars studying them; and let me not forget the apparition.' Then go to sleep. But speak to no man concerning this. It should be done only on Sunday night, and only in urgent matters. Do not make sport of this!" *Sefer Raziel* has a much longer charm, heavily weighted with angel names, which concludes with a series of Biblical quotations. The same work contains other prescriptions for a "dream question"; one advises writing a name upon "ruled parchment" and placing it under one's head after reciting a spell; another, "tested and tried," suggests washing the hands thoroughly and anointing the left hand with "water of lilies," after which an invocation is to be written on it, then, "sleep on your right side, and you will see and be astounded!" Still another prescribes a more complicated procedure: secure two white doves and slaughter them with a two-edged copper knife, one edge for each dove, extract their viscera, knead them together with three shekels of wine, some fine frankincense and some pure honey into a thick paste, and cut it into small cakes; on the three days preceding the new moon, before sunrise, perform the prescribed purificatory rites, put on a white garment but no shoes, and burn some of these cakes on the hearth, while reciting the names of the angels who are in charge of the new month; on the third day let the house fill with smoke, lie down on the floor, recite the angel names and then sleep. "And the angels will appear and tell and reveal everything you may ask, in a clear vision, not in parables. You need have no fear." [23]

NEUTRALIZING OMINOUS DREAMS

Since unfavorable as well as favorable dreams come true, and the event therefore came to be regarded as the consequence of the dream, it was believed that if one could somehow nullify the dream itself in advance its effects would be obviated. Thus, in the prayers to be recited at night before retiring there is a specific request to "save us from evil dreams," while some writers make it a point to note that some of the Biblical verses included in these prayers, such as Cant. 3:7-8, and Nu. 6:24-26, "have the property of counteracting evil dreams" (the first because it speaks of "threescore mighty men" gathered about a bed, the second because it contains sixty letters—and a dream is "one sixtieth part of prophecy"), and that Ps. 128, also part of these prayers, contains references to vines and olives, which, according to the Talmud, are favorable dream symbols. Indeed there arose toward the end of the medieval period the custom of boldly announcing before going to bed, in the manner of "to whom it may concern," "I hereby proclaim that whatever unpropitious dream I may have this night, I shall not tomorrow observe the customary fast," which declaration, we are assured, "is a preventive of evil dreams, but, God forbid! should one nevertheless behold such a dream, he must on no account fast, or the angels of dreams will be very much provoked."[24]

Once the dream has been experienced, however, other means must be adopted to forestall its consequences. As in the case of an illness, a dream may be sold and its effect transferred to the purchaser. An instance of such a transaction is recounted in *Sefer Ḥasidim,* with perhaps a sly dig at the interpreter who had no faith in his own interpretation; a certain Gentile who had dreamt he was riding a red horse was overwhelmed with despair when the interpreter told him this presaged his imminent death. The interpreter offered to purchase the dream "for the price of a drink," a proposal which his client accepted with alacrity. The next day the interpreter was dead—though the narrator does not consider that the drink rather than the dream may have been responsible for his sudden demise. Again we learn that a literal acting out of the dream may destroy its symbolic significance. When a person who is married dreams he is carrying a bird in his bosom, this signifies the birth of a child, but if the bird flies away it portends disaster. To save himself he should fast and distribute charity among the poor, the customary procedure, but he should also place a fowl in his bosom, a cock if the dreamer is a man, a hen for a woman, and then permit it to fly off. Now that the dream has been scrupulously enacted, the apprehensive dreamer may breathe easily again. Still a third method is to recite, immediately upon waking, a Biblical verse suggested by the dream, which contains a promise of good. If one dreams of a well, he should say, "And there Isaac's servants digged a well" (Gen. 26:25); of a river, "Behold I will extend peace to her like a river" (Is. 66:12); of a bird, "As birds flying so will the Lord of hosts protect Jerusalem" (Is. 31:5); of a dog, "Against any of the children of Israel shall not a dog whet his tongue" (Ex. 11:7); of a mountain, "How beautiful upon the mountains are the feet of the messenger of good tidings" (Is. 52:7); of a *shofar,* "In that day a great *shofar* shall be blown" (Is. 27:13); of a bullock, "His firstling bullock, majesty is his" (Deut. 33:17); of a lion, "The lion hath roared, who will not fear?" (Amos 3:8); of shaving, "Joseph shaved himself and changed his raiment and came in unto Pharaoh" (Gen. 41:14); and so on.[25]

The most widely used methods of counteracting the effect of a bad dream, the "dream fast" and the rite of "turning a dream to good," were instituted in Talmudic times. These, coupled with the usual expiatory acts of prayer, charity and repentance, were held to be effective devices, and were observed not alone by the common people but also by some of the outstanding rabbis of the Middle Ages, such as Meir b. Baruch of Rothenburg and Israel Isserlein. Indeed they came to be regarded as the inevitable sequel of every bad dream, and of every dream whose significance was in doubt, so that their observance became almost automatic, though their true purpose was never lost sight of. They are observed by some pious Jews even in this day. A third device, the "release" from an obligation incurred in a dream, such as a vow or an excommunication, has already been described.

The Talmudic basis of the *Taʿanit Ḥalom,* the "dream fast," is the following passage: "Rab said, 'Fasting is as effective against evil dreams as fire against shavings;' R. Ḥisda added, 'One must fast on the same day on which the dream occurred;' and R. Joseph added, 'Even on the Sabbath.' " These dicta raised three issues, concerning the first and second of which there was fairly general agreement. Fasting, the accepted rite of penitence and expiation, was believed to carry great weight with the heavenly council. The dream constitutes not a final and irrevocable judgment, but rather a warning of impending doom, which may be postponed and perhaps altogether negated by pious deeds and a righteous life, of which the fast was the first instalment. "It seems to me," wrote Almoli, "that this fast is to be regarded practically as an obligation upon the dreamer, and not as a voluntary act which he need not observe if he so pleases." We may judge how important it was considered by the fact that even on those occasions when fasts were forbidden an exception was made in favor of the *Ta'anit Ḥalom*. During the month of Nisan, for instance, when even the *Jahrzeit* fast in commemoration of the death of a father or mother was not permitted, this "dream fast" was the only one allowed. And not only the dreamer felt bound to observe this fast, but if his dream seemed to carry an ominous message for a second party, that person too observed it.[26]

The requirement that the fast must follow the dream on the same day was explained on the ground that the adverse decree might be intended for immediate execution; or, as one writer put it, each day has its own angels who are charged with carrying out the heavenly decisions. A delay of even one day may make the fast ineffective. Any other voluntary fast but the *Ta'anit Ḥalom* may be postponed.[27]

The only difficulty was with regard to the observance of this fast on the Sabbath and on holidays. Some medieval rabbis felt that R. Joseph had gone too far in his endorsement of what was essentially a superstitious practice, though it had introduced a religious element into the belief concerning dreams. They did not state their objection, originally voiced by R. Kalonymos (in the twelfth century) and often repeated, in so many words, but got around the Talmudist's opinion with the qualification that "nowadays one should not observe the *Ta'anit Ḥalom* on the Sabbath, because we are no longer expert in the interpretation of dreams." The subterfuge was no more successful than if they had roundly denounced the institution or expressly forbidden it on the Sabbath without apologies. As it was they left a convenient breach through which the more superstitious could clamber. Obviously Jews were still dream experts, so far as the masses were concerned. Maharil wisely wrote, "It is better that a man fast on the Sabbath because of a dream, than that his heart be troubled; he'll derive more pleasure from the fast than from his food." Others tried to soften the objection to the Sabbath fast by offering minor concessions. R. Meir permitted it if the same dream had been repeated three nights in succession, while some harked back to a tradition associated with the name of Hai Gaon, who had allowed it after three particularly ominous dreams, namely, if one beheld a *Torah* scroll burning, or the conclusion of the *Yom Kippur* service, or his teeth or the beams of his house falling. The list was, as may be expected, extended; dreaming of any part of the *Yom Kippur* service, of reading in the *Torah,* of getting married, of being kissed by a deceased person, equally warranted a fast on any occasion. But Isaiah Horowitz, the sixteenth-century Polish mystic, who himself "usually advised people not to fast on the Sabbath," admitted, "I have known many people to make light of these restrictions, and fast on the Sabbath whenever their spirits were depressed by a dream." [28]

To appreciate the full moment of this dream fast we must further consider that it entailed a *second day's fast* immediately after, to atone for the desecration of the holyday—two days of fasting in succession! This duplicate fast was scrupulously kept. True, sometimes permission was granted to infirm or sick people to postpone it, if a double fast might prove too arduous for them. But otherwise there were no slackers. And to bring home more sharply the high regard in which this remedy for ill-omened dreams was held by the people, they did not refrain from observing it even on *Rosh Hashanah,* if necessary, when a *Ta'anit Ḥalom* on the first day of the holyday entailed not only fasting on the next day also, but on both days of *Rosh Hashanah* in every succeeding year! (If, however, occasion for fasting arose on the second day, then only that day's fast was repeated annually.) Nor did they hesitate to keep this fast on the eve of *Yom Kippur,* the most trying day in the Jewish calendar. It required great faith, indeed, to produce such stanch devotion! [29]

When the fast was completed, the final remedy was resorted to, the *Hatavat Ḥalom,* the rite of transforming an ominous dream into a favorable one. As recorded in the Talmud, it was performed as follows: The dreamer gathered three friends and said to them, "I have beheld a good dream!" and they responded, "Verily, it is good, and may it be good, and may God make it good." This was repeated seven times (but, following the precedent attributed to the twelfth-century rabbi Isaac b. Samuel the Elder, the number of repetitions was reduced to three, "the usual number of times an incantation is recited," as later writers explained). Then the dreamer recited three verses in which the word "to overturn" appears (Ps. 30:12, Jer. 31:12, Deut. 23:6), three verses containing the word "redeem" (Ps. 55:19, Is. 35:10, I Sam. 14:45), and three which speak of "peace" (Is. 57:19, I Chr. 12:18, I Sam. 25:6). This prescription was followed in the Middle Ages, and was extended to include Hab. 3:2,

Ps. 121, Nu. 6:22-27, Ps. 16:11, concluding with the words of Ecc. 9:7, "Go thy way, eat thy bread in peace." To avoid the slightest unlucky intimation, moreover, the order of these last words was altered, for their initials spell the word *avel*, "mourner." If the purport of the dream had been forgotten, the Talmud provided a prayer which was warranted to ensure that no harm would befall the dreamer.[30] Thus fortified he could throw off the oppressive weight of his dream and "eat his bread in peace"—until another night visited another evil vision upon him.

16

ASTROLOGY

WE POSSESS no one body of doctrine that describes so pervasive and dominant a pattern in the fabric of modern life as did the "science" of astrology in the medieval. According to one of the foremost students of the Middle Ages, Prof. Lynn Thorndike, "Astrology is the most widespread, as it is the most pseudo-scientific of any variety of the magic arts. Indeed, it has ceased to be merely one method of divination and claims to study and disclose the universal law of nature in the rule of the stars, by which every fact in nature and every occult influence in magic may be explained"; it is "the fundamental doctrine of the medieval *Weltanschauung*." Just as among Christians barely a murmur of opposition was heard, so Maimonides was the sole Jewish authority of prominence who dared raise his voice against this superstition. "Know ye, my masters," he wrote to the congregation in Marseilles, "that all those matters that appertain to astrology in no wise constitute a true science, but are wholly folly. . . ." His was "a voice crying in the wilderness." Menasseh b. Israel once more expressed the prevailing view when he scornfully waved aside the Maimonidean strictures with a series of citations from Jewish and non-Jewish literature. "And now, since the God-given *Torah* and the words of our rabbis prove the truth of this science, who can deny it?" he challenged. "In all periods there have been great astrologers among our people, and most notably in the land of Spain." It is true that astrology produced its foremost Jewish exponents and practitioners in the south of Europe—many a court, lay and ecclesiastical, in the Provence and Spain, boasted its Jewish astrologer; the northerners were amateurs by comparison. I have found not a single trustworthy reference to a recognized Jewish astrologer in Germany and France—an instance, perhaps, of typical northern parochialism which rigorously excluded the Jew from court attendance, or, again, a commentary on the inferior quality of his skill. But, however short he may have been on theory, the German Jew was by no means unacquainted with the practical utilities of the science.[1] Though the literature is not as informative as one might wish, we may derive from it those general rules which were the bases of the astrological science.

The debate over the determining rôle of the stars in the life of man, broached in the Bible and heatedly argued in the pages of the Talmud, continued unabated through the succeeding centuries. The issue was hardly at all whether the stars influence men but rather just how vital and irremediable their influence is. It was generally accepted that every man has his star in heaven (often regarded as complementary to his "deputy" angel), whose history is conterminous with his own, that the special character and position of that star at his birth determine the general outline of his career, that the heavenly constellations at any given moment control earthly events and human acts, and that therefore a study of the heavens can disclose the future. Both their tradition and the example of their neighbors inclined medieval Jews to acknowledge such doctrines as axiomatic. But the tenets of Judaism obliged them to subjoin an important qualification: the stars determine human actions, but they too are creatures of God, established by Him to perform this special function, and therefore the influence they exert is subject to His will. Repentance, prayer, piety, charity, good deeds—the religious virtues—are the instruments by means of which man can induce God to alter His decrees, and consequently to modify the fate that is "written in the stars" for him. This is the purport of a mass of medieval Jewish discussion of the subject; once granted, there was no check upon the utilization of astrology for divinatory ends. Several writers expressly excluded this science from the forbidden category of "magic," and practically all German-Jewish writers tacitly or openly admitted its aid in guiding man's footsteps.[2]

The close association that was posited between the angels and the heavenly bodies also served to foster this divinatory science. The seven archangels, in particular, were believed to play an important part in the universal order through their association with the planets and the constellations. There is some variation, in the different versions, in the angels assigned to the planets, and even the names of these angels are subject to sudden change on a single page. The five lists I have collated[3] (containing some variant readings and some omissions) give the following result. The numerals represent the number of times a name appears on these lists.

Sun	Raphael (4), Michael (2)
Moon	Gabriel (4), Aniel (or Anael) (1)
Venus	Aniel (4), Ḥasdiel (1)
Mercury	Michael (2), Ẓadkiel (1), Barkiel (1), Ḥasdiel (1), Raphael (1)
Saturn	Kafẓiel (3), Michael (1)
Jupiter	Ẓadkiel (4), Barkiel (1)
Mars	Samael (4), Gabriel (1)

I might have included additional lists, but they would only have raised the numerals without altering the preponderance of votes for the angels in the first column. It is interesting to compare with these results a set of these associations which entered medieval Christian thought by way of the Moslem philosopher Averroes: the Sun and Michael, the Moon and Gabriel, Venus and Anael, Mercury and Raphael, Saturn and Cassiel (Kafẓiel), Jupiter and Sachiel (Ẓadkiel), Mars and Samael. This conception probably derived from the Gnostic mysticism of the beginning of our era, which in its turn was unquestionably influenced by such ancient notions as the Babylonian seven planetary spirits, and the seven Amshaspands of Persia.

Some of the archangels also found themselves bound up with the twelve signs of the Zodiac and consequently with the months, with new ones invented or borrowed from ancient sources to make up the required number. Here, too, there is no permanency about the association; an angel may be divorced from his stellar charge without notice, and another substituted. The following is a fair sample of these alliances: Aries-Michael, Taurus-Gabriel, Gemini-Raphael, Cancer-Uriel, Leo-Guriel, Virgo-Nuriel, Libra-Yeshamiel, Sagittarius-Ayil, Capricornus-Ubaviel, etc.[4] It must be remembered, also, that these names change according to the season of the year, so that there are four shifts supervising the heavenly bodies.

The usual primitive interpretation of eclipses and comets as portents of disaster is encountered. Eclipses of the moon were taken to be especially ominous for the Jewish people. Eclipses of the sun which occurred on October 26, 1147, and September 4, 1187, threw German Jewry into consternation; later it was learned that on these days the

German Crusaders had suffered serious reverses in Palestine. In 1456 there occurred one of the periodical appearances of Halley's comet which was noticed by almost all the Christian chroniclers of the time, and was variously interpreted as an omen of great earthquakes, of pestilence (both of which visited Southern Italy in that year), etc. Not to be outdone, Israel Isserlein, in Wiener-Neustadt, mounted a tower which stood in "the street of the Jews" and examined the comet at close range, and then portentously announced, "Its tail points toward Vienna!" "In the same year," comments his biographer, "the 'King of Vienna' [Ladislaus VI Posthumous], whose father had initiated anti-Jewish persecutions, was poisoned in Prague [by George of Podiebrad], and the Hungarian king [Ladislaus Corvinus] was murdered in his capital." [5]

The idea that the planets and the fixed stars rule over the affairs of the material world was an ancient dogma which had received the sanction of the foremost astronomer recognized in the Middle Ages, Ptolemy. The influence of his exposition had made itself felt in Jewish thought even before his *Tetrabiblos* reached Western Europe in Latin translation during the twelfth century. Eleazar of Worms, who could not have been directly acquainted with the astronomer's work, advanced his explanation that the properties and powers of the heavenly bodies were consequent upon their composition out of one or more of the four elements, earth, air, fire, water, and their possession of one or more of the four elemental properties, hot, cold, dry and moist. But these theoretical considerations were of secondary import; the human utility of astrology occupied the major part of Jewish interest and attention. The planets and the stars were studied with an eye to their expediency in various divinatory exercises: genethlialogy, or the casting of nativities or horoscopes; elections, or the selection of favorable hours for beginning contemplated enterprises; and the so-called judicial astrology, obtaining answers to specific questions. To these ends tables were set up delineating the fields of influence of the heavenly bodies. Saturn governed poverty, wounds, illness, death; Jupiter, life, peace, joy, wealth, honor, sovereignty; Mars, blood, the sword, evil, war, enmity, envy, destruction; Venus, grace, beauty, passion, conception, fertility; Mercury, wisdom, intelligence, learning, trades and occupations; the sun, daily activities, and sovereignty; the moon, growth and decay, good and evil. Then there were more detailed tables, giving the planets and stars which rule each hour of the day and night and the nativities and elections of these hours, on this order:

Second [i.e., Sunday] night

1st	hour Jupiter	propitious for setting out on a journey or taking a bride; one born in this hour will be handsome and wise;
2nd	hour Mars	do not approach a woman, and do not engage in trade; nativity—one will be poor, or will die in infancy;
3rd	hour Sun	propitious for every enterprise; nativity—one will be poor, will suffer misfortunes, and will die by the sword;
4th	hour Venus	good for trade and marriage; nativity—one will be a conspirator and will be killed;

and so on through the week. Nativities were also taken according to the day of the week. While this was not strictly approved astrological method, the Latin names of the days, paronyms of the planets, led to the days being credited with the virtues of the stars. Jews never adopted the week-day names in use in Europe, but for astrological purposes they accepted the planetary associations. (One writer, for instance, suggested that Friday was the favorite wedding day because it was Venus's day.) The length of one's life could be similarly forecast. If birth occurs in the "house" of Saturn (the heaven was divided into twelve "houses," each presided over by a planet) the child will enjoy 57 years on earth; if in Jupiter's "house," 79; in Mars's, 66; Venus's 22; the sun's, 77; etc.[6]

There was also great interest in astrological weather prediction, and many treatises were written on the subject. We have no extended Jewish discussion, but ample evidence to indicate that Jews were familiar with the method and were not averse to utilizing it. Predictions were based on observations of the sun and its relation to the constellations, on the phases of the moon, and on the physical appearance of these two bodies, the color and shape of the clouds, unusual astronomical phenomena, etc.

Certain periods were also chosen as symptomatic of the weather for the entire year. Each of the four days between *Yom Kippur* and *Sukkot* was equated with three months, so that if it rained on the first of these days, one could anticipate heavy showers in the months of Tishri, Ḥeshvan and Kislev. The days near the summer and winter solstices were similarly regarded as portentous; the 13th of Tamuz indicates the weather that will prevail during Tamuz, Ab, Elul and Tishri, the 14th corresponds to Ḥeshvan, Kislev, Tebet, Shebat, etc. A late tradition ascribed to Judah the Pious, which is probably authentic since it tallies with a remark in a thirteenth-century work, displays a more direct economic concern with the weather: when it rains on the 19th of Tamuz and not on the 21st, the price of foodstuffs will be high until the spring, and then will fall; if it rains on the 21st and not on the 19th, prices will be low until spring and will then rise; if it rains on both days, prices will be high all year; but if it rains on neither day, food will be abundant and cheap throughout the year. A common method of predicting weather, among Christians, was on the basis of the twelve days following Christmas (the season of the winter solstice). Jews adopted this practice, eliminating, of course, the reference to Christmas; one month of the year was assigned to each day from the first to the twelfth of Tebet (corresponding to the "Twelve Nights") and the daily weather during this period was accepted as indicative of the weather during the correlated months.[7]

Lists of unlucky days, sometimes called "Egyptian Days," are of rather common occurrence in medieval Latin works. Undoubtedly a relic of the ill-omened days in the ancient Egyptian calendar, they were largely determined on astrological grounds. These were pre-eminently days on which patients should not be bled; in some cases the warning was extended to cover any work of importance. Such lists based on tradition and astrology are to be found in medieval Jewish literature as well. Phlebotomy was regarded as a very dangerous operation when performed on the eve of a holiday, or on *Hoshana Rabbah;* some included the entire months of Tamuz, Ab, Elul and Shebat in the list, others only the first day of Iyar, Elul and Tebet when these fall on a Monday or Wednesday, and still others included the first of every month, and the period between Passover and *Lag B'omer.*

Certain days of the week were also singled out as unfavorable: Monday, Tuesday and Thursday; Sunday, Wednesday and Friday were regarded as especially opportune for blood-letting. However, if Wednesday fell on a 4th, 14th, 24th, or during the last four days of the month, it was also included among the inauspicious days. Monday and Wednesday were regarded as unlucky for new undertakings, and it was an accepted rule that "one does not begin anything on Monday or Wednesday"; the explanation that "on these days the stars are unpropitious" is no doubt the correct one. As Mordecai Jaffe, who offered this reason, continued, "One should not inquire concerning the astrological portents before beginning an undertaking, but when he knows that the stars are unfavorable he should not act counter to them and rely on a miracle." Eleazar of Worms published a list of 59 days through the year when it was "good to set out on a journey." [8] The astrological factor was also of great importance in magical pursuits. As we have seen, special days were designated as particularly favorable for writing amulets and *mezuzot*. Besides, the association of the angels with the planets and stars made it necessary, before invoking angels, to determine just which astrological influences were dominant. Magic leaned heavily upon astrology.

According to some, the Roman superstition which forbade marriages in May was preserved in the Jewish custom not to celebrate a wedding between Passover and Pentecost, with an exception allowed on *Lag B'omer*. This prohibition was judaized into a mark of mourning, and was associated with the tradition that during this period, in the second century, a great many of Akiba's pupils were destroyed by a plague. A thirteenth-century manuscript, *Sefer Asufot,* explains it on the ground that during these months the Jewish communities of the Rhineland were decimated by marauding Crusaders, but the custom was introduced into Judaism long before; it is first mentioned in a Geonic responsum of the eighth or ninth century. As we noticed above, this period was also considered inopportune for blood-letting. The mourning motif was emphasized by further prohibitions against cutting the hair, paring finger-nails, wearing new clothes and working after sunset.[9]

The moon is universally believed to exert a most powerful influence upon terrestrial phenomena, and during the Middle Ages Christians and Jews rarely entered upon an important activity without having first observed the lunar auspices. The waxing moon advances growth and development, the waning moon promotes decay and death. Eleazar of Worms diagnosed a mental ailment as due to the contraction of the brain during the last quarters of the moon, and its expansion during the first. Again he warned that clothing soaked in water, trees that have been cut down, fruits and grains harvested while the moon is diminishing rot away very rapidly. Marriages were celebrated during a waxing moon, "not for any superstitious reason, but only as a good omen"! A conception that occurred during this phase of the moon was considered especially auspicious for the child; people moved into new homes in the first half of the lunar month. The day of the new moon was the most favorable for new enterprises, children were brought to school and courses of study begun on that day. A rational explanation of this last usage was offered, namely, "to give out-of-town students time to arrive," but even its author realized that it was not very convincing, and admitted "and also because it is a good omen." Cutting the hair or finger-nails on new moon day was frowned upon "because of the danger," for growth should not be checked on the day which is most auspicious for it. Such beliefs were very prevalent among German Christians, and though the rabbis often forbade these practices, their disapproval had little effect on their flock.[10]

The pagan veneration of the new moon, which had by no means disappeared in Biblical times, has no direct connection with the ceremony of blessing the new moon which was outlined in the Talmud and is observed to this day. But certain superstitious practices have been associated with the rite, pointing to its continued occult importance in human affairs. Some of these are first mentioned in a work composed during the post-Talmudic period, the *Masechet Soferim,* others are medieval accretions. In the first group are the practices of skipping three times at the close of the blessing, and addressing the moon three times: "As I skip before you and do not reach you, so, if others jump before me may they not strike me," and of then thrice bidding one's neighbor "Peace be unto you." The ceremony, as well as the threefold repetitions, are typical of magical acts. In the latter group are the practice of shaking one's clothes "to cast off the spirits," and the belief that one who has performed the full rite need not fear death during the ensuing month. In the sixteenth century the Safed school of Kabbalists instituted the custom of fasting on the eve of the new moon (the day of the new moon was a feast day). The practice was probably in vogue at an earlier time and may be connected with a Christian usage, deplored by a fifteenth-century German writer, but observed by "many people both laity and clergy, even including masters," who "bend the knee or bow the head at new moon or fast on that day, even though it be Sunday or Christmas when the church forbids fasting." A halting recognition that the fast was observed because of "the shrinking of the moon" is evidence of the persistence of primitive apprehensions.[11]

An interesting and obscure superstition attached to the four *Tekufot*, or "turnings of the sun," that is, the solstices and equinoxes. It was believed that during these periods a mysterious precipitation poisoned all water, which should therefore not be drawn or drunk at the crucial moment. The source of this Jewish superstition is very much in the dark. The solstices in particular, when the day attains its longest and shortest duration, have captured the imagination of primitive folk, and have induced sentiments of exaltation and despair. It was believed that at these times peculiarly potent supernatural forces are at work. During the Middle Ages, among the non-Jewish peoples of Europe, the advent of Midsummer Day was greeted with great festivities and bonfires, which, among other things, were supposed to drive off certain noxious dragons which polluted the wells and springs by dropping their seed into them as they copulated in the upper atmosphere.

It has been suggested that this late belief was derived from the Jewish superstition, which was first mentioned as far back as the tenth century; Grünbaum's contention that the Jews borrowed it from the Germans is certainly untenable. Hai Gaon, asked to explain the custom of not drinking water during the *Tekufot*, replied, "Although we do not know the reason, it should be meticulously observed, for not without good reason has it spread through Israel." Apparently it was already, in the tenth century, sanctioned by long usage. Then he proceeded to offer the prevailing explanation, to the effect that during the four quarters of the year the universe is guarded by specially appointed angels, but at the *Tekufot*, the time of the changing of the watch, when their supervision is momentarily relaxed, the powers of evil seize the opportunity to work havoc among men by poisoning their wells. Hai Gaon also suggested a rationalistic interpretation: the custom is an expression of man's dislike to begin a new season with so inconsequential an action as drinking water. This latter explanation was occasionally repeated during the Middle Ages, but without enthusiasm; the former was more often advanced as the true reason.[12]

A slight variant of this superstition is incorporated in the idea that it is blood, rather than poison, that pollutes the wells. An old legend, which made its first literary appearance in the *Maḥzor Vitry* (twelfth century), connects this belief with the following events: God turned the waters of Egypt into blood in the vernal equinox, and from then on at the time of the equinox a drop of blood is deposited in the waters and makes them unfit to drink; the same occurs at the summer solstice, when Moses smote the rock and blood flowed therefrom; at the autumnal equinox, when Abraham prepared to sacrifice Isaac, and blood appeared on his knife; and at the winter solstice, when Jephtha sacrificed his daughter in fulfillment of his vow. A Kabbalistic explanation has it that Lilit's menses are the source of these drops of blood. Still another legend is that the constellations Scorpio and Leo, or Cancer and Libra, engage in a bitter struggle at these four critical moments, and their blood taints our water. It is possible that there is some relation between this blood version of the *Tekufah* superstition and the medieval German belief that on Midsummer Day (St. John's Day) drops from the bleeding corpse of John the Baptist, which at that time hovers over the earth, are to be discerned on the leaves of the *Johanniskraut (Hypericum perforatum)*.[13]

Despite the reproof administered by Judah the Pious, and often repeated, that "the sincerely devout need fear no evil," there was a widespread indisposition to make use of water drawn during the *Tekufah,* or which had been left uncovered at that time. Maharil wrote that though he did not dispute Judah's dictum, "it is best not to count on miracles"! According to some, the danger was restricted to drinking water at the instant of the *Tekufah,* and did not apply within a city, but most people chose to play safe and accepted the broader view. Since the evil spirits were generally held responsible, it was possible to adopt certain preventive measures, which were first mentioned in Western Germany in the thirteenth century, and from there spread throughout the Jewish communities of Europe. These entailed the suspension of a piece of iron in the water, or the admixture of some salt, or the sealing of the vessel, all well-known anti-demonic devices. Thus ensured against contamination, the water could be imbibed without fear or danger.[14]

The notion that death would befall anyone who killed a goose during an undetermined brief period in the months of Tebet and Shebat (from about the middle of December to the middle of February) produced a general disinclination to slaughter geese throughout the two months. Some believed that it was possible to evade this consequence by eating immediately a bit of the dead fowl. The origin of this notion is obscure. There may be something to the opinion of a late commentator that it is based upon the belief that "the demons are at the height of their power in these months" (the period of the winter solstice) and for some reason resent the slaughter of a goose.[15]

As a final note to this chapter it should be pointed out that medieval medicine, Christian and Jewish, was strongly influenced by astrological considerations. The planets and stars were responsible for the functioning not alone of the universe, but of the human body as well; an exact and minute correspondence was drawn between the various heavenly bodies and the human organs. Even the foods that man consumes were related to the stars, and drew their peculiar natural and occult qualities from them. Therefore illnesses were often caused by astrological influences—we have seen how the waning and waxing of the moon can affect a man's mind (a non-Jewish surgeon advised against operating on a fractured skull at the full of the moon, because then the brain expands and fills the cranium)—and medical treatments took these factors into account.[16]

APPENDIX I

THE FORMATION OF MAGICAL NAMES

Whence came the multitude of new names that made its way into Jewish mysticism toward the end of the Geonic period and during the Middle Ages? Was it concocted out of pure fancy, or did it bear any discernible relation to the names already in use? Can we discover any method behind the mad luxuriousness of thirteenth-century invention? The material itself, as often as not, defies analysis; so many terms are obviously corrupted beyond all hope of restoration; many of the names actually look impossible, as though the scribe or typesetter had simply jumbled together a group of letters and dared the reader to make sense of them. It not seldom happens that the same name is written in two or three different forms in one and the same recipe. Gaster noted that the copyist of the text of *The Sword of Moses* which he published, "gives in many places what are intended to be different readings"; [1] the same is true of medieval manuscripts which I have examined. The lack of consistency in the names in a work like *Sefer Raziel* is exasperating—not only do varying forms of one name appear from page to page, but the same angel often bears so many aliases that one cannot keep up with him.

It is possible, however, to establish a set of rules according to which most of these names were created, so that we may observe the process at work even when the results in particular cases conform none too closely to our expectations. These rules were originally formulated in the Talmudic period and were extended and elaborated during the Middle Ages.

1. Following the model of such traditional angel names as Gabriel, Raphael, Michael, a large proportion of the new names was constructed of a root term and a theophorous suffix, *el* (God) being the commonest, with *yah, yahu* and other such particles of names of God also occurring often. The first part represented the characteristic attribute or function of the new angel. *Sefer Raziel* set down this principle in these terms: "The angels are named in accordance with the special activities over which they are appointed, as Raziel, who transmitted the mysteries (*raz*) to Adam; Yarḥiel, who rules

the moon (*yeraḥ*) ; Kochbiel, who governs the stars (*kochab*), etc." According to a later writer, "The names of the angels change constantly to conform with the missions to which they have been temporarily assigned, for the particular mission determines the name at the time." [2]

2. Another method widely employed involved the manipulation of traditionally received divine names or particles of these names: a. by combining them and alternating their component letters, such as יאהדונהי, which comprises יהוה אדני ; b. by combining a name with a word representing an attribute: שקדהוזי is שדי חזק ; the letters here are merely jumbled together; c. by dropping letters from, or adding new ones to such names, like the אני והו mentioned in the Talmud, which some scholars take to be shortened forms of אדני יהוה, or the Tetragrammaton plus inserted letters which may explain יכה יוסה ;[3] d. by transposing the letters of these names, e.g. אדני may assume 24 forms: אנדי, דאני, etc.

Other methods frequently applied were originally created to facilitate the allegorical and mystical interpretation of the Bible. According to the mystical view the entire *Torah* is made up of holy names which have been so skilfully secreted among the letters of the text that only an expert can ferret them out.[4] These systems provided the means of educing new names from the text of the Bible by a series of permutations, combinations and substitutions.

3. The simplest of these methods comprised merely the displacement of the letters of a word, so that the first word of the Bible, בראשית, might become שתיברא or אשרבית, etc.; letters were lifted out of a text; the words of a text were split up into three-letter units; words were read backwards, etc.

4. NOTARIKON [5]—originally this was employed as a method of abbreviation, to compose a word from the initial or final letters of several (e.g., שאו מרום עיניכם [Is. 40:20]= שמע, or ברא אלהים לעשות [Gen. 2:3]= אמת), or to decompose one word into several (e.g., אדם = אדם דוד משיח, or אפר דם מרה, פרדם = פשט רמז דרוש סוד) for purposes of anagogic homiletics. This method was later used to create some of the most important names in the entire mystical catalogue. One of these names,[6] guaranteed to protect its user against all weapons, is יהמהיה, which on examination turns out to be nothing more than an acrostic of the concluding letters of the first six (Hebrew) words of Ex. 15:11, "Who is like unto Thee among the mighty, O Lord?" The famous

name Agla (אגלא), whose awesome powers were set in operation even more often by Christian magicians than by Jews, is generally assumed to be composed of the first letters of the words, "Thou art mighty for ever, O Lord!" (from the second benediction of the *'Amidah*). That Christians who employed it understood the principle of its formation, if not its original source, is indicated by the fact that in Germany these four letters, inscribed on wooden platters which were then believed to be capable of extinguishing fires, were read as the initials of "Allmächtiger Gott, lösch' aus!" The interpretation, no doubt, varied with the use. One medieval Jewish writer traced this name to the initial letters of the four verses, Gen. 49:8-11.[7] Whether so or not in this particular case, the method of joining letters from various verses was widely used. The book *Shimmush Tehillim,* which assigns magical potencies to the Psalms, created a host of fantastic names from letters chosen more or less at random from each Psalm; for instance, the name that is hidden in Ps. 4 is *Yhyh,* made up of the final letters of verses 2, 3, 9 and 6; in Ps. 1 it is *Alḥd,* which consists of the initials of the first words in verses 1 and 4, the last letter of the last word in verse 3, and the second letter of the sixth word in verse 6. It is likely that there *was* a method to this madness, but if so it wholly escapes us now. The possibilities of combination were, of course, unlimited. The most celebrated example of this method is the use to which Ex. 14:19-21 was put to form the 72-particle name of God.

5. GEMATRIA [8]—The letters of the Hebrew alphabet also serve as numerals: א=1, ב=2, ג=3, etc. *Gematria* was a process of creating equivalences from the numerical values of words, and provided an ingenious method of reading novel and unexpected meanings into a text: רדו (Gen. 42:12)=210=the years of Egyptian bondage; ונושנתם (Deut. 4:25)=852=the duration of the Jewish state; etc. That Metatron is the demiurge was proved by the fact that numerically both Metatron and Shaddai equal 314. Sometimes only the simple units were employed (מספר קטן) so that י (10) and ק (100) were counted as 1, כ (20) and ר (200) were 2, etc. By this means it was possible to prove mathematically that *God* is solely *good* and the *first* of all beings, for יהוה=1(0)+5+6+5=17; טוב=9+6+2=17; and ראשון=2(00)+1+3(00)+6+5(0)=17.

This method was very popular and was elaborated in the course of time until it became an exercise in higher mathematics, which no doubt possessed intrinsic interest for its devotees in addition to its practical utility in interpreting the Bible—and in creating new names. Seven ways of figuring numerical values have been distinguished:[9] a. simple addition: א, ב, ג = 1, 2, 3 = 6; b. the sum of the letters plus 1 for the word: אבג = 6 + 1; c. the sum of the letters plus the number of letters in the word: אבג = 6 + 3. Sometimes b. and c. were joined, so that אבג = 6 + 1 + 3; d. addition of the values of the names of the letters: א = אלף = 111, ב = בית = 412, etc. Thus "Hear O Israel" is equated with the final "One" of the verse (אחד = 111 + 408 + 434 = 953 which is the equivalent of שמע ישראל, 410 + 541 + 2 = 953); e. addition of the cardinal numbers: א = אחד = 13, ב = שנים = 400, ג = שלשה = 635, etc. By a combination of d. and e. we get י = יוד = 20 = עשרים = 620 = כתר, therefore the letter *yod* represents the "crown" of glory; f. adding the values of all the letters in the alphabet that precede each letter of the word: אהיה = 1 + 15 + 55 + 15 = 86; g. adding the squares of the numerical values: אחד = 1 + 64 + 16 = 81. Once the numerical value of a Biblical word or verse, selected as especially significant for one reason or another, was arrived at, any number of words adding up to the same total could be concocted, and by their very obscurity and the "mystery" inherent in their character as epitomes of important Biblical statements could achieve the status of potent magical "names."

6. TEMURAH [10]—substitution or permutation, transposing the letters of a word (as in 2. above) or more frequently, replacing them with artificial equivalents obtained from one or another of a group of formal anagrams. Six of these proved the most popular:

a. By folding the alphabet in the center we get

א ב ג ד ה ו ז ח ט י כ
ת ש ר ק צ פ ע ס נ מ ל.

Corresponding letters on the upper and lower lines may be substituted for each other.

b. Reversing the lower line gives us

א ב ג ד ה ו ז ח ט י כ
ל מ נ ס ע פ צ ק ר ש ת.

c. א ב ג ד (ה) י כ ל מ (נ) ק ר ש ת (ך)
ט ח ז ו (ה) צ פ ע ס (נ) ץ ף ן ם (ך).

These three groups are respectively the combinations equalling 10,

100 and 1000. The five final letters (in the third group) have here their ancient numerical values, 500 to 900.

d. א ב ג ד ה ו ז
ח ט י כ ל מ נ
ס ע פ צ ק ר ש.

The alphabet is divided into three equal parts, the last letter, ת, not being used. Any one of the three letters in each column may be substituted for another.

e. א ב ג ד ה ו ז ח ט
י כ ל מ נ ס ע פ צ
ק ר ש ת ך ם ן ף ץ.

as in d. with the final letters included; these final letters, for purposes of *Gematria,* are here also given their ancient numerical values, as in c.

f. Each letter in a word is replaced by the letter immediately succeeding it in the alphabet: ב for א, ג for ב, ד for ג, etc.

While the above alphabetical permutations are those most frequently employed, they by no means exhaust the possibilities. The fourteenth-century manuscript *Sefer Gematriaot* [11] lists sixteen of them, and C. D. Ginsburg gives 24 in his work on the *Kabbalah.* Some Kabbalists went so far as to substitute for the letters of a word others resembling them in form, e.g., א = יוי, ה = דו, etc., and gave consonantal significance even to vowel points in this game.

It should be noted that several of these alphabets were often applied to one word or sentence in conjunction, as when the name Shaddai (שדי) was derived from the first verse of Genesis as follows: the שׁ is the equivalent of ב (בראשית) by method a, the ד comes from ה (אלהים) by f, the י from ש (השמים) by b.[12] While this, of course, was a forced reading of the name into the verse, these alphabets were also used for creative purposes; the Tetragrammaton (יהוה) appears as מצפץ (a), or כוזו (f), or שעפע (b), etc. The possible number of permutations and substitutions is endless, and when we realize that all of these methods, *Notarikon, Gematria* and *Temurah* (the three were usually lumped together as *Gematria* during the Middle Ages), may be used together, the possibilities are breath-taking. Is it any wonder that so many of these names defy unriddling?

7. Finally, words from foreign languages, names of pagan deities, even terms from the Latin liturgy, were transliterated into Hebrew, and in this guise became potent tools in the magician's hands.

APPENDIX II

MS. SEFER GEMATRIAOT, pp. 43a–44b, ON GEMS

(Notes on pp. 267–268)

This passage closely parallels Baḥya b. Asher's comment on Ex. 28:17, both apparently being derived from a common source. They were composed at about the same time, so that one could hardly have drawn from the other; each lacks passages present in the other; the language of the two is very similar, but Baḥya's text is longer and more wordy, while the present text contains several additional details about the use of the gems; and there are some interesting differences which illustrate the different environments (Spain and Germany) in which they were composed.

אדם לראובן על שם שאידמו פניו על שבילבל יצועי אביו (1) והודה ולא בוש. והוא אבן הנקרא רובינו. (2) ותועלתו אשה שנושאתו אינה מפלת נפלים. ועוד הוא טוב למקשה ובאכילה ובשתיה הוא טוב להריון כדודאים שמצא ראובן (3) ולכך כתי' אדם חסר וו' כי דודאים כדמות אדם (4) ולפעמ' אבן רובינו מעורב באבן אחרת ונק' רובין פלשט (5) לפי שראובן הציל את יוסף ונתערבבו יחד שנ' וישמע ראובן ויצילהו מידם (6) וכתי' ויען אתם ראובן לאמר הלא אמרתי אליכם לאמר אל תחטאו בילד וגו' (7) ויסר פרעה את טבעתו וכו' (8) ואותה טבעת היתה פלשט כלו' שהיו בו פלשין ולכך נמצאת אבן רובינו מעורבת בפלשט.

פטדה אבן שמעון היא פרזמא (9) ולי נראה סמרלא (10) וירוקה על שם זמרי בן סלאו (11) שהוריקו פניהם ושוב אין להם לא מלך ולא שופט וסימן לעבירה הדרקון והיא כהה שנתכרכמו פניהם ותועלתה ותולדותיה שמקררת את הגוף לכך כתו' לא יערכנה פטדת כוש. (12) כוש ומצרים שטופי זמה ולכך היא מצוייה שם לקור את הגוף. וגם לאהבה על שם כי שמע יי' כי שנואה אנכי (13) ונעשית אהובה בילידת שמעון.

ברקת היא קרבונקלא (14) נוצצת כברק ומאירה כנר והיא אבן טובה שתלה נח בתיבה שנ' צהר תעשה לתיבה (15) בגימ' לאור האבן. והיא אבן אקדח שבנביאים (16) וקודחת כגיחלים והיא אבן של לוי על שם ששבט לוי כולם היו בעלי תורה דכתי' יורו משפטיך ליעקב (17) וכתי' חכמת אדם תאיר פניו. (18) ומשה כשנולד נתמלא כל הבית אורה. (19) כי קרן עור פני משה. (20) ותועלת האבן טוב לנושאה מחכים האדם ומאיר

העינים ופותח את הלב ובאכילה ובשתיה נשחקה עם שאר סממנים (21) מחזרת הזקן לבחרות על שם לא כהתה עינו ולא נס לחה. (22)

נפך היא שמרגד (23) כדמתרגמינן איזמרגדין והיא ירוקה לפי שהוריקו פניו של יהודה כשנתגבר על יצרו והודה במעשה תמר. (24) וגם כשחשדו אביו על יוסף וכתי' חיה רעה אכלתהו (25) ונצטער עד שהפכו פניו לירקון וצלולה היא ולא עכורה כאבן שמעון לפי שנמצא נקי מן החשד דכתי' מטרף בני עלית (26) נעשו פניו צהובים מתוך שמחה ותועלת האבן מוספת גבורה לפי שנושאה נוצחת במלחמה (27) לפיכך היו שבט יהודה גיבורים. ולכך נקראת נופך שהופך האויב את העורף למי שנושאה דכת' ידך בעורף אויביך. (28)

ספיר אבן יששכר יודעי בינה לעתים (29) ובמתן תורה (?) ותכלת דומה לה וטובה לרפואות וטובה להעבירה על העינים שנ' רפאות תהי לשריך.(30)

יהלום היא אבן זבולן והיא מרגלית הנק' פירכה (read פירלה) (31) מצלחת בפרקמטיא יטיב לנושאה בדרך מפני השלום ומרבה אהבה ומביאה את השינה על שם יזבלני אישי. (32)

לשם היא אבן דן והיא טופציאה (33) ופרצוף אדם ניכר בה מהופך לפי שהפכו לסמל בפסל מיכה. (34)

שבו היא אבן נפתלי והיא טורקישקא (35) ונק' על שם שמושיב את האדם בחוזק וטוב שלא יכשל ויפול ונחמדה היא בעיני פרשים רוכבי סוסים ומחברת האיש על הרכב על שם נפתולי אלהים נפתלתי. (36)

אחלמה מתרגמי' עין עגלא והיא אבן הנקראת קרישטלו (37) והוא מצוי הרבה וניכר לכל והיא של גד על שם ששבט גד מרובים וניכרים לכל שנ' וטרף זרוע אף קדקד (38) ואבן אחרת הנקראת דיאמנטי (39) ודומה לקרישטלו אבל מראה אדמומית יש בה ואותה היו נושאין שבט גד והיא טובה למלחמה ומחזקת הלב שלא ירך לפי שהיו עוברין לפני אחיהם למלחמה והיא נקראת אחלמה על שם יחלמו בניהם (40) וכן ותחלימני והחייני (41) לשון חוזק (42) ואפי' מפני מזיקין ורוחות טוב לנושאה שלא יאחזנו מורך לבב שקורין גלוליר. (43)

תרשיש הוא יקינט (44) כדמתרגמי' כרום ימא גווניהם והוא אבן אשר ותועלתו שמעכלת המאכל. והאוכלה אין מאכל רע נשאר במעיו ונעשה שמן ועב והיינו דכתי' מאשר שמנה לחמו. (45) ובנותיהם נישאות למלכים ולכהנים גדולים כדכתי' בדברי הימים הוא אבי ברזית (46) לבני כהנים הנמשחים בשמן זית וארצו שמינה ומנשכת שמן ממעין ולפעמ' אבן ספיר מעורב באבן יקינט לפי שהיו שבט אשר מתערבין בנותיהן ל(ש)בט יששכר משום יפיין ויששכר על הספיר ותורה נמשלת למים. וזהו שפיר יקינט וספיר קורין שפיר מאשר שמינה לחמו לכל הבריאין והשמנים פניהם מאדימות וכן פעמים יקינט נמצאת אדומה.

שהם הוא אבן הנק' ניקלי (47) והיא אבן יוסף והיא מעלת חן ונקראת שהם אותיות השם על שם ויהי יהוה את יוסף ויתן וגו' (48) וטוב לנושאה במקום וועד ויהיו דבריו נשמעים ומצליחים לכך ויהי איש מצליח. (49)

ישפה לבנימין וכן נקראת דיאשפי (50) ובכל מיני גוונים תמצאנה ירוקה שחורה אדומה לפי שבנימין ידע במכירת יוסף. וכמה פעמים עלו מחשבות על לבו לגלות ליעקב ונשתנו פניו לכמה גוונים אם לאמרו אם להעלימו וגבר על יצרו וכסה הדבר ולא גילהו וזהו ישפה ולפי שהיה מעצור לפיהן ניתן לו כח לעצור את הדם. ישפה בגימ' בנימין בן יעקב.

NOTES TO APPENDIX II

1. Cf. *Gen. R.* ch. 98, 7; Rashi on Gen. 35:22.
2. *Rubino,* ruby; Baḥya continues with a long description of this gem which is lacking here.
3. Gen. 30:14.
4. See p. 182 above. From here to the end of the paragraph not in Baḥya.
5. *Fels,* mhd. *vels, velsch;* cf. Grimm, *Deutsches Wörterbuch,* s. v. *Fels.*
6. Gen. 37:21.
7. Gen. 42:22.
8. Gen. 41:42.
9. Perhaps this is the *prasinum,* a species of smaragd (cf. Ducange, s. v.); Baḥya: ונקרא פראש"מא והיא מין נופך שהוא מרק"די שהוא גם כן ירו' ככרתי.
10. Then this should read סמרלדא, *smiraldus, smeraldus,* another species of smaragd. This word does not appear in Baḥya.
11. Nu. 25:14.
12. Job 28:19.
13. Gen. 29:33.
14. Carbuncle.
15. Gen. 6:16.
16. Is. 54:12.
17. Deut. 33:10.
18. Ecc. 8:1.
19. Cf. *Sotah* 12a; *Pirke de R. Eliezer,* ch. 48.
20. Ex. 34:35.
21. From here to end of paragraph not in Baḥya.
22. Deut. 34:7.
23. Smaragd. Baḥya has here a discussion of the Arabic etymology of this word, and comments והוא ממין פראש"מא.
24. Cf. Gen. 38.
25. Gen. 37:33.
26. Gen. 49:9.
27. Preceding six words not in Baḥya.
28. Gen. 49:8.
29. I Chr. 12:32; Baḥya's name for this stone is שבי"לו.
30. Prov. 3:8; this paragraph is much longer in Baḥya.
31. *Perla,* pearl; the suggested reading is confirmed in Baḥya.
32. Gen. 30:20.
33. *Topazia,* topaz; Baḥya: אשטכסו'.
34. Cf. Jud. 18.

35. *Turkiska,* turquoise; Baḥya: טורקיזא.
36. Gen. 30:8.
37. *Cristalo,* crystal; Baḥya: קריסטא"ל.
38. Deut. 33:20.
39. *Diamanti,* diamond; Baḥya: ליאמן.
40. Job 39:4.
41. Is. 38:16.
42. From here to end of paragraph not in Baḥya.
43. I have not succeeded in tracing this word.
44. *Yakint,* jacinth; Baḥya: קריאוליק'.
45. Gen. 49:20; from here to end of paragraph not in Baḥya.
46. I Chr. 7:31.
47. *Nichilus, nichilinus lapis, achetae species* (Ducange, s. v.); Baḥya: אוניקלי.
48. Gen. 39:2.
49. Ibid.
50. Jasper; Baḥya: ישפיז.

ABBREVIATIONS AND HEBREW TITLES

The references under titles are to Bibliography B, The Hebrew Sources, Printed.

Agguda—*see* Alexander Süsslein HaKohen.
'Amude Shlomo—*see* Solomon Luria.
AR—Archiv für Religionswissenschaft.
A.Z.—Aboda Zara.
B.B.—Baba Batra.
Bek.—Bekorot.
Ber.—Berakot.
B'er Heteb—*see* Judah b. Simon Ashkenazi.
B.K.—Baba Kama.
B.M.—Baba Meẓia.
Brantspiegel—*see* Moses b. Ḥanoch Altschul.
Brit Abraham—*see* Horowitz, Abraham b. Shabbetai.
Da'at Zekenim—*see under title.*
Derech Ḥayim—*see* Judah Löw b. Beẓalel.
Eben Ha'Ezer—*see* Caro, Joseph b. Ephraim.
EJ—Encyclopedia Judaica.
'Emek Beracha—*see* Horowitz, Abraham b. Shabbetai.
'Emek HaBachah—*see* Joseph HaKohen.
'Emek HaMelech—*see* Naftali Herz b. Jacob Elḥanan.
'Erub.—'Erubin.
Git.—Gittin.
Güd.—Güdemann, M., Geschichte des Erziehungswesens und der Cultur der abendländischen Juden, 3 vols., Vienna 1880-1888.
Hadar Zekenim—*see under title.*
HaEshkol—*see* Yom Tob b. Solomon Lipmann-Mühlhausen.
Ḥag.—Ḥagigah.
Hagahot Maimuniot—*see* Meir HaKohen.
HaGan—*see* Isaac B. Eliezer.
HaḤayim—*see* Ḥayim b. Beẓalel.
HaManhig—*see* Abraham b. Nathan.
HaOrah—*see* Rashi.
HaPardes—*see* Rashi.
HaTerumah—*see* Baruch b. Isaac.
HaYashar—*see* Jacob b. Meir Tam.
HB—Hebräische Bibliographie, ed. M. Steinschneider.
HERE—Hastings, Encyclopedia of Religion and Ethics.
Ḥochmat HaNefesh—*see* Eleazar b. Judah.
Hor.—Horayot.
HUCA—Hebrew Union College Annual.
Ḥul.—Ḥullin.
Iggeret HaTiyul—*see* Ḥayim b. Beẓalel.
Jahrbücher—Jahrbücher für jüdische Geschichte und Literatur, ed. N. Brüll.
JE—Jewish Encyclopedia.
JJV—Jahrbuch für jüdische Volkskunde.
Joseph Omeẓ—*see* Joseph Yuspa Hahn.
JQR—Jewish Quarterly Review.
Kab HaYashar—*see* Ẓebi Hirsch Kaidanover.
Ker.—Keritot.
Ket.—Ketubot.
Kid.—Kiddushin.
Kiẓur Shelah—*see* Epstein, Jeḥiel Michel.
Kol Bo—*see under title.*
Lebush—*see* Mordecai b. Abraham Jaffe.
Leket Yosher—*see* Joseph (Joslein) b. Moses.
Lev Tov—*see* Isaac b. Eliakim.
M.—Mishna.
Ma'ase Book—*see under title.*
Ma'ase Rokeaḥ—*see* Eleazar b. Judah.

Maharil—*see* Jacob b. Moses Mölln.
Maḥ. Vit.—Maḥzor Vitry, *see under title.*
Mateh Moshe—*see* Moses b. Abraham Mat.
Meg.—Megillah.
Mek.—Mekilta.
Men.—Menaḥot.
MGJV—Mitteilungen der Gesellschaft für jüdische Volkskunde.
MGWJ—Monatsschrift für die Geschichte und Wissenschaft des Judenthums.
Miẓvat HaNashim—*see under title.*
MJV—Mitteilungen zur jüdischen Volkskunde.
M.K.—Moed Katan.
Mordecai—*see* Mordecai b. Hillel.
Ned.—Nedarim.
Neḥmad veNa'im—*see* Gans, David.
Netivot Olam—*see* Judah Löw b. Beẓalel.
Nid.—Niddah.
Nishmat Ḥayim—*see* Menasseh b. Israel.
Niẓaḥon—*see* Yom Tob b. Solomon Lipmann-Mühlhausen.
Oraḥ Ḥayim—*see* Caro, Joseph b. Ephraim.
Or Ḥadash—*see* Judah Löw b. Beẓalel.
Orḥot Ẓadikim—*see under title.*
Or Zarua—*see* Isaac b. Moses.
Pa'aneaḥ Raza—*see* Isaac b. Judah.
Pes.—Pesaḥim.
Pesakim Uketabim—*see* Israel Isserlein.
Pitron Ḥalomot—*see* Solomon b. Jacob Almoli.
R.—Midrash Rabbah.
Raben—*see* Eliezer b. Nathan.
Rabiah—*see* Eliezer b. Joel HaLevi.
Raziel—*see under title.*
REJ—Revue des Etudes Juives.
R.H.—Rosh Hashanah.
Rokeaḥ—*see* Eleazar b. Judah.
San.—Sanhedrin.
Semag—*see* Moses b. Jacob.
Semak—*see* Isaac b. Joseph.
Sha'are Ẓion—*see* Nathan b. Moses Hanover.
Shab.—Shabbat.
S. Ḥas.—Sefer Ḥasidim, ed. Wistinetzki, *see* Judah b. Samuel.
S. Ḥas. B.—Sefer Ḥasidim, Bologna version, *see* Judah b. Samuel.
S. Ḥas. Tinyana—*see* Moses Kohen b. Eliezer.
Sheb.—Shebuot.
Shelah—*see* Horowitz, Isaiah b. Abraham.
Shibbole HaLeket—*see* Ẓedekiah b. Abraham.
Shimmush Tehillim—*see under title.*
Shulḥan Aruch—*see* Caro, Joseph b. Ephraim.
Siddur Rashi—*see* Rashi.
Suk.—Sukkah.
Ta'ame HaMinhagim—*see under title* (Bibl. D).
Ta'am Zekenim—*see under title.*
Tashbeẓ—*see* Samson b. Ẓadok.
Terumat HaDeshen—*see* Israel Isserlein.
Teshubot HaGeonim—*see under title.*
Tishbi—*see* Elijah Levita.
Toledot Adam veḤavah—*see* Jeroḥam b. Meshullam.
Torat Ha'Olah—*see* Moses Isserles.
Tos.—Tosafot.
Toss.—Tossefta.
Yeb.—Yebamot.
Yereim—*see* Eliezer b. Samuel.
Yesh Noḥalin—*see* Horowitz, Abraham b. Shabbetai.
Yeven Meẓullah—*see* Nathan b. Moses Hanover.
Yore Deah—*see* Caro, Joseph b. Ephraim.
ZDMG—Zeitschrift der Deutschen Morgenländischen Gesellschaft.
Zera Kodesh—*see* Moses b. Menaḥem.
Ẓiyuni—*see* Menaḥem Ẓiyuni b. Meir.

NOTES

All Talmudic references are to the Babylonian Talmud except where a prefixed *J.* indicates the Jerusalem Talmud

CHAPTER I

THE LEGEND OF JEWISH SORCERY

1. See B. Monod, *REJ*, XLVI (1903), 237 ff., referring to Guibert de Nogent; Aronius, §757; according to Luther, "Ein Jüde stickt so vol Abgötterey und zeuberey, als neun Küe har haben, das ist: unzelich und unendlich" (*Werke*, LIII [Weimar 1920], "Vom schem Hamphoras," p. 602).

2. Lea, III, 429; Güd. I, 79. In 1254 Louis IX issued a decree commanding the Jews of his realm to abstain from the practice of magic. Philippe le Bel, in 1303, found it necessary, in order to retain control over "his Jews," to forbid the Inquisition to proceed against them on the charge of sorcery (Lea, III, 449). On the other hand, in 1409, Pope Alexander V ordered the Inquisitor of Avignon, Dauphiné, Provence and Comtat Venaissin to proceed against several categories of persons "including Jews who practised magic, invokers of demons, and augurs" (Thorndike, III, 37).

3. This is based on the contemporaneous account of Matthew Paris, *Hist. Angl.* ad An. 1188, f. 108b, cited by Prynne, I, 7-8; Schudt, IV, 2, p. 331; Jacobs, *Jews of Angevin England*, 342. The Hebrew version of this persecution in the account of Ephraim of Bonn, while not specifying the nature of the charge which prompted the attack, makes it clear that some such unwarranted accusation was responsible; see Neubauer and Stern, 69, and Wiener's edition of *'Emek Ha-Bachah*, Leipzig 1858, p. 9.

4. *Maḥ. Vit.*, §280, p. 247; see also *REJ*, III (1881), 9, n. 1. On Moses b. Jeḥiel see Gross, *Gallia Judaica*, 513, and Jacobs, op. cit., 225, 229.

5. *Maḥ. Vit.*, loc. cit.; Stössel, in *Kroner Festschrift*, p. 47; *Kol Bo*, §114; *Tos. M.K.* 21a; *Yore Deah* 387:2; *Pes.* 8b and Rashi, ad loc.; *Responsa* of Ḥayim Or Zarua, §144; Güd. III, 153; Zimmels, 82; *HaOrah*, II, 127, p. 219.

6. *Or Zarua*, II, §53, p. 12a; *S. Ḥas. Tinyana*, 7a; *Asufot*, 113b, cited in Güd. I, 136; *Maharil, Hil. Mez.; Yore Deah*, 291:2; but see pp. 146 ff. above.

7. On this subject see I. Münz, 45 ff., 107 ff.; S. Krauss, *Gesch. jüd. Ärzte*, 43, 54 ff.; *JE*, VIII, 417, Scherer, 41, §6.

8. S. Krauss, op. cit., 26 ff.; cf. E. Adler, *Jewish Travellers*, London 1930, pp. 2-3; Thorndike, III, 525-6.

9. Luther, *Werke*, LI (Weimar ed.), "Eine vermanung wider die Juden," p. 195; S. Dubnow, *History of the Jews in Russia and Poland*, I, 243 (Phila. 1916); Aronius, §724-5; *JE*, III, 233; Thorndike, III, 234; Scherer, 45, 53, 333,

369 ff., 577 ff. "So stand es im 13. und 14. Jahrhundert mit den Juden in der Nähe der Stadt Bonn. Hatte man früher die Juden mit den bösen Hexen in ursächlichen Zusammenhang gebracht, so mussten sie nunmehr für den Ausbruch ansteckender Krankheiten und Seuchen, wie die Pest, verantwortlich gemacht werden" (Joesten, 10-11); cf. Wickersheimer, *Les Accusations d'Empoisonnement,* etc., Anvers 1927. In some places the Black Death was attributed to the incantations as well as to the poisons of the Jews (Lea, III, 459).

10. Wuttke, 140; Strack, 59; Lowenthal, *A World Passed By,* 54-5; G. Caro, *Sozial- und Wirtschaftsgeschichte der Juden,* II, 196, 204; Aronius, §330; Scherer, 349 f., 411 ff.

11. I. Lévi, *REJ,* XXII (1891), 232 ff.; Aronius, §160.

12. See H. L. Strack, *The Jew and Human Sacrifice,* N. Y. 1909; I. Scheftelowitz, *Das stellvertretende Huhnopfer,* ch. 12: "Gibt es im Judentum Ritualmord?"; D. Chwolson, *Die Blutanklage und sonstige mittelalterliche Beschuldigungen der Juden,* Fkft. 1901; S. W. Baron, *A Social and Religious History of the Jews,* N. Y. 1937, III, 38, 106.

13. See the works cited in preceding note, and Thorndike, I, 62, 249, 418-19, 629, etc. This belief is not yet altogether dead. It was until recently (if not still today) believed by many people in the vicinity of Graz that the doctors of the local hospital annually executed a young patient, boiled his body to a paste and utilized this as well as the fat and charred bones in concocting their drugs (Summers, 161).

14. Aronius, §749; *JE,* III, 261; Strack, 174-5; Anton Bonfis, *Rerum Hungaricum decades,* Decad V, Book 4, ed. C. A. Bel, Leipzig 1771, 728, cited in Strack, 202; J. W. Wolf, *Beiträge zur deutschen Mythologie,* Leipzig 1852, p. 249, cited in Güd. III, 119, n. 1; Prynne, I, 30; Wiener, *Regesten,* pp. 236 f.; Graetz, *History* (Eng.) V, 177, quoting John Peter Spaeth of Augsburg; Summers, 195. Scherer, p. 435, quotes from an anonvmous fifteenth-century lampoon:

> Es wer vil mer zu schreiben not,
> Wie wir den christen tuen den tod
> Mit mancher wunderlicher pein
> An iren clein kinderlein.
> Wir fressen dann ir fleisch und pluet
> Und glauben, es kumb uns wol zu guet.

15. See Lea, III, 432 ff.; M. Summers, *History of Witchcraft* (see also the chapter on Germany in his work *The Geography of Witchcraft,* London 1927); M. A. Murray, *The Witch-Cult of Western Europe;* J. Français, *L'Église et la Sorcellerie;* Grimm, II, 890; cf. also Güd. I, 220 ff.

16. On Christian ritual and the host in the witch-cults see: Summers, 89, 145 ff.; Murray, 148; Lea, III, 500; on cannibalism and the use of blood: Summers, 144-5, 160, 161; Murray, 100, 129, 156, 158; Lea, III, 407, 468 ff., 502; on poison, Murray, 124, 125, 158, 279-80; and see also Thorndike under these items in his index. It is even recorded that "in the strife, waged at Bern in 1507, between the Dominicans and the Franciscans, the assertion was made that the Dominicans had used the blood and eyebrows of a Jewish child for secret purposes" (*JE,* III, 264).

17. Luther, *Werke* (ed. Jrmischer), 62, 375, cited in Güd. I, 225-6; *Yeven Mezulah,* 15.

CHAPTER II

THE TRUTH BEHIND THE LEGEND

1. On Biblical magic see J. G. Frazer, *Folk-Lore in the Old Testament,* 3 vols., London 1918; T. W. Davies, *Magic, Divination and Demonology Among the Hebrews and Their Neighbors,* London 1898; B. Jacob, *Im Namen Gottes,* Berlin 1903; A. Jirku, *Materialien zur Volksreligion Israels,* Leipzig 1914; on Talmudic magic see L. Blau, *Das altjüdische Zauberwesen,* Budapest 1898; D. Joel, *Der Aberglaube und die Stellung des Judenthums zu demselben,* Breslau 1881-3 (Part I devotes some space to the Biblical period); G. Brecher, *Das Transcendentale, Magie und magische Heilarten im Talmud,* Vienna 1850. Very little has been written on the magic of the Geonic period. See Joel's book, Part II, and J. A. Montgomery, *Aramaic Incantation Texts from Nippur,* Phila. 1913; J. Wohlstein, *Dämonenbeschwörungen aus nachtalmudischer Zeit,* Berlin 1894; M. Gaster, *The Sword of Moses,* London 1896; Cyrus H. Gordon, "Aramaic Magical Bowls in the Istanbul and Baghdad Museums," *Archiv Orientální,* VI (Praha 1934), 319-34.

2. *S. Ḥas.* 43, 1136, 1137, 1444; *Ḥochmat HaNefesh,* 12d;—*Hadar Zekenim* on Ex. 22:17; Moses Taku, *Ozar Neḥmad,* III, 61; cf. Grimm, II, 546. Gaster, *Ma'aseh Book,* II, 576 ff., has a typical German folk-tale about a magic ring that could be used to transform a person into a werwolf.—*Ziyuni,* 55a; *Ma'aseh Book,* II, 320 f.;—*S. Ḥas. B,* 1166; *Ḥochmat HaNefesh,* 12d; cf. Grimm, II, 898; Wuttke, 55;—*S. Ḥas.* 1453; *Ziyuni,* 26c; *Hadar Zekenim* on Ex. 8:12; *Da'at Zekenim* on Ex. 8:14; *HaḤayim,* IV, 10. Cf. Lea, III, 510: "One precaution, held indispensable by some experienced practitioners, was that the witch on arrest was to be placed immediately in a basket and thus be carried to prison, without allowing her feet to touch the earth, for if she were permitted to do so she could slay her captors with lightning and escape"; cf. also Grimm, II, 899, III, 444, §310.

3. *S. Ḥas.* 1463, 1465, 1466; Güd. I, 203, n. 8, 204, n. 5, 205, n. 3, II, 222, n. 3; *Pa'aneaḥ Raza* on Ex. 22:17-18, p. 69a; Hansen, 131; Lea, III, 405; *Ziyuni,* 7a, 49c; *Nishmat Ḥayim,* III, 23, 24.

4. *S. Ḥas.* 172, 1467; *Testament of Judah the Pious,* 5; *Rokeaḥ,* §316, p. 83a; *Toledot Adam veḤavah,* 28:1, p. 182b.

5. Blau, 18-19, 23 ff.; *HaḤayim,* IV, 10; *Nishmat Ḥayim,* III, 23.

6. Cf. *S. Ḥas.* 738, 1458, 1459, 1801, 1819, 1921; *Raziel,* 7b.

7. Cf. Scholem in *EJ,* IX, 717 ff.; *MGWJ,* LXIX (1925), p. 16.

8. Cf. A. Epstein, "Lekorot HaKabbalah HaAshkenazit," in *HaḤoker,* II (Vienna 1894), 1-11, 37-48; *JE,* III, 465 ff.; *EJ,* IX, 646 f.; Güd. I, 156 ff.; H. Gross, "Zwei kabbalistische Traditionsketten des R. Eleasar aus Worms," *MGWJ,* XLIX (1905), 692-700.

9. Cf. Kammelhar, 3, 4, 42, 43-5; *Ma'aseh Book,* II, 396 ff., 510 ff.; Scholem, *Kirjath Sepher,* IV (Jerusalem 1927), 317; Gaster, *Jewish Folk-Lore in the Middle Ages,* 9 ff.; N. Brüll ("Beiträge zur jüdischen Sagen- und Spruchkunde im Mittelalter," in *Jahrbücher,* IX [1889], 1-71) printed many legends from a sixteenth-century manuscript about the wonders performed by Judah the Pious and his disciples.

10. Joel, I, 85; Blau, 20; *San.* 67b and Rashi; *Yore Deah* 179:15.

11. *Hadar Zekenim* on Ex. 7:12; *S. Ḥas.* 211, 212, 1449, 1455; *Yereim,* 82; *Toledot Adam veḤavah,* 17:5, p. 127b; cf. *Lebush* on *Yore Deah* 179:15.

12. Rashi on *San.* 65b; *Nishmat Ḥayim,* III, 20; *Lebush* on *Yore Deah,* 179:1.

13. Cf. *B'er Heteb* on *Yore Deah* 179:1 (quoting *Naḥlat Shiv'ah* by Samuel b. David HaLevi, middle seventeenth century): "The *Torah* forbade only the magic of ancient times; nowadays there is no more 'magic' in the world, but it is all vanity."

14. *Torat Ha'Olah*, III, 77. See also Frazer, *The Magic Art*, I, 54, 119, and Thorndike, index, s. v. "Occult Virtue."

15. *Ẓiyuni*, 48d, 65d; cf. Bischoff, 31, 74, 169; Thorndike, II, 319, also I, 352.

16. *S. Ḥas. B* 477.

17. *S. Ḥas B* 1172; *S. Ḥas*. 210, 211, 379, 1455, 1456; Isserles to *Yore Deah* 179:16; *Piske Recanati* 563 (quoting Eliezer of Metz); Moses Taku, *Oẓar Neḥmad*, III, 82; Güd. I, 168 ff.

18. *S. Ḥas*. 1461; *Niẓaḥon* 309; *Orḥot Ẓadikim* 95b; Isserles to *Oraḥ Ḥayim* 664:1; Lauterbach, *HUCA*, II (1925), 353 f.

19. *S. Ḥas*. 163; cf. also 381.

20. Güd. I, 222, n. 1; Berliner, *Aus dem Leben*, 102; *Minḥat Kenaot*, by Abba Mari of Lunel, Pressburg 1838, p. 29.

21. *S. Ḥas*. 377; cf. *Pes*. 110b and Rashbam ad loc.

CHAPTER III

THE POWERS OF EVIL

1. Blau, 15-16; *JE*, IV, 514 ff.

2. *JE*, IV, 519, 520;—Jacob Mann, "New Studies in Karaism," *C.C.A.R. Yearbook*, XLIV (1934), 221;—see in particular, *Sefer Ḥasidim* and the works written by or ascribed to Eleazar of Worms: *Ḥochmat HaNefesh, Sefer Raziel*, the commentary on *Sefer Yeẓirah*, etc. For a characterization of his ms. *Sefer Malachim* see Güd. I, 162;—Rashi, Gen. 6:19.

3. Moses Taku, *Oẓar Neḥmad*, III, 97.

4. *Nishmat Ḥayim*, III, 12, 13, 14.

5. Deut. 32:17; Ps. 106:37. Gesenius interprets this word as "idols" (i.e., "lords" of the heathen, from the root *shud*, "to rule") which makes room for its later connotation of demon. It has, however, more properly been related to the Assyrian *šêdu*. "In function the *shed*," writes Montgomery (pp. 73-4), "is the Babylonian *šêdu limnu*, 'evil *šêdu*.' In the later Jewish demonology the *shedim* are the hobgoblins, the prevailing class of demons. They are the δαιμόνια of the Greeks."

6. Blau (pp. 14-15), discussing the Talmudic demonology, writes: "Wie sich Schedim, Mazzikin und die mannigfaltigen Ruchoth von einander unterscheiden, ist nicht leicht zu sagen; nur soviel scheint mir sicher, dass Ruchoth ursprünglich die Seelen Abgeschiedener bedeutet hatte, während Schedim eine eigene Gattung von Wesen bilden, welche . . . zur Hälfte Menschen und zur Hälfte Engel sind; . . . Mazzikin scheint beide nach ihren schädlichen Wirkungen zu benennen." Blau's attempt to distinguish among these categories, even in Talmudic literature, is forced; certainly, if any distinctions existed at that time, they had been completely lost by the Middle Ages; none appear already in Montgomery's incantation texts. Both Blau and Levy (*ZDMG*, IX, 482) regard the *ruḥot* as ghosts, but, as Montgomery points out, this view is unwarranted, "as the Rabbinic, Syriac and Mandaic use of the word shows. They are the πνεύματα

πονηρά, or ἀκάθαρτα of the New Testament, the equivalent of the Babylonian *utukki limnûti*. This development of *ruaḥ* we may trace in the Old Testament where 'a spirit of evil,' 'the evil spirit,' appears as an agent of Jahwe; like the Satan such potencies easily passed into malicious demons" (p. 75). Cf. also Bischoff, 41 ff., where, however, the *shedim* are defined as fallen angels.

7. *Ẓiyuni*, 49a; *Maḥ. Vit.*, p. 541, has a similar list, which differs in minor details. For *lilin* see *Erub.* 18b; cf. *S. Ḥas.* 1462.

8. *Kid.* 72a;—*S. Ḥas.* 1154, 1160; *Rokeaḥ* 216 and 337; *Asufot*, 157b (in Güd. I, 53); *Tashbeẓ*, 315. We also read infrequently of the *malach ra'*, "angel of evil," and *mashḥit*, "destroyer."

9. Cf. *Ber.* 6a and Rashi; also *Git.* 68a; *Pes.* 112b; *Mid. Tehillim*, ed. Buber, ch. 91, p. 398; Rashi on Nu. 22:23;—De Givry, 126; Reichhelm, abbot of Schöngau, c. 1270, who had received from God the gift of being able to see demons, "describes their number as so great that the atmosphere is merely a crowd of them; he often saw them as a thick dust, or as motes in a sunbeam, or as thickly falling rain" (Lea, III, 381-2).

10. Cf. *Abot*, 5:6; *Gen. R.* 7:7, etc.; *Hadar Ẓekenim* on Gen. 2:3. The word *la'asot* is understood to imply that there still remained something to complete when the Sabbath set in.

11. *Disputation of R. Jeḥiel*, 15; cf. *Erub.* 18b; *Gen. R.* 24:6; Rashi on II Sam. 7:14.

12. *JE*, IV, 520; *S. Ḥas. B* 1170; Ginzberg (*Legends*, V, 109) writes: "The view found in Josephus (Bell. Jud. VII, 6.3), as well as in Philo (De Gigant. 6-8 and De Somn. 1.133-36), that demons are the souls of the wicked reappears again in the Kabbalah (Zohar III, 70a), where it is borrowed from Christian sources, while it is entirely unknown to the earlier rabbis." This conception need not have been Christian in source; it may well have been current in the mystical tradition from which both *S. Ḥasidim* and *Ẓohar* drew, as a natural outgrowth of the prevalent view that the spirits of the dead remain on earth, at least for a time after death. Those who were evilly inclined in this life might be expected to remain so beyond the grave. In the later *Kabbalah* we find the view that "the sins of men are 'written' on their bones, and after their death the bones so inscribed are transformed into demons" (*Kiẓur Shelah, Inyane Ta'anit*, 153-4).

13. See M. Grünbaum, *Ges. Auf.*, p. 93.

14. *S. Ḥas.* 1950, p. 473; *S. Ḥas. B* 4; *Ẓiyuni*, 49b.

15. *S. Ḥas.* 140, 764; *S. Ḥas. B* 1145; *Ẓiyuni*, 27b; *Nishmat Ḥayim*, III, 23. When a donkey or horse snorts suddenly at night and refuses to go forward it should not be driven on, for a spirit or demon is blocking its path. All animals, and especially dogs, are sensitive to the presence of spirits; when a dog unaccountably whines and growls this is taken to be an indication that the Angel of Death is in town, and consequently is an omen of impending death. This belief occurs in German folklore also, cf. Grimm, III, 449, §454, 450, §493; Wuttke, 33.

16. Ginzberg, *Legends*, V, 108, where he cites the rabbinic literature; cf. *Maḥ. Vit.*, p. 507.

17. Rashi, *Erub.* 18b and *San.* 109a referring to *Nid.* 24b and tacitly to *Hag.* 16a; *Ẓiyuni*, 49b. Ẓiyuni's views may be compared with those of a contemporary German writer who maintained that demons are immortal, and cannot generate their kind or increase their number or eat and drink (Thorndike, IV, 281). Such opinions are common in medieval Christian thought. Prof. Thorndike suggests that the elemental character which is here attributed to the demons may well explain why brutes more readily sensed them.

18. *S. Ḥas. B* 1155; cf. also *Nishmat Ḥayim*, III, 16; Ginzberg, *Legends*, VI, 192, n. 58: according to *'Emek HaMelech* (by Naftali Herz b. Jacob Elḥanan,

a German Kabbalist of the sixteenth century) 140b, demons, both male and female, have their bodies and faces covered with hair, but their heads are bald.— Moses Taku, *Oẓar Neḥmad*, III, 61. The belief that demons could adopt animal and human forms played an important rôle in German folklore, which thus preserved the older Teutonic belief in gods who could invade the earth. It was especially prominent in the later witch-cults, in which, it was asserted, demons were worshiped in the shape of cat, goat, bull, dog, etc., or accompanied their witch-mistresses in these forms as "familiars"—cf. Grimm, II, 546; Summers, 101 ff., 134 ff.; Murray, 205 ff.; also N. Brüll, *Jahrbücher*, IX (1889), 40.

19. *S. Ḥas.* 373; *S. Ḥas. B* 1146; *Testament of Judah the Pious,* 23; *Hochmat HaNefesh,* 20b.

20. Cf. *Ber.* 60b and 62a; *Maḥ. Vit.* 81, 735; *Rokeaḥ,* 344; *Kol Bo* 21; *S. Ḥas. Tinyana,* 9a; *Oraḥ Ḥayim* 3:1.

21. *Kol Bo* 69; cf. *Shab.* 109a;—R. Tam in *Tos. Yoma* 77b and *Ḥul.* 107b, quoted by many later writers;—*Shab.* 108b; *Kol Bo* 69; *Semag,* I, 69; *Oraḥ Ḥayim* 4:3;—Abrahams, *Ethical Wills,* 37;—*Siddur Rashi,* §578, pp. 280-1.

22. *S. Ḥas.* 1871.

23. *Testament of Judah the Pious,* 17-20, 58; *Joseph Omeẓ,* 351; see Scheftelowitz, *Stell. Huhnopfer,* 20-21, where parallels from many peoples are given. Fear of inhabiting a new house built upon unoccupied land is universally felt, and similar devices resorted to.

24. *Yeb.* 64b; *S. Ḥas.* 370, 1122, 1870, 1871; *Toledot Adam veḤavah,* 1:2, p. 1c; *Terumat HaDeshen,* 211; *Joseph Omeẓ,* 350-1; Abrahams, op. cit., I, 47; *Jahrbücher,* IX (1889), 21; simulated burial of the patient is a fairly common therapeutic device, cf. Seligmann, *Mag. Heil- u. Schutzmittel,* 146 ff.; Samter, 108.

25. Rashbam, *Pes.* 111a; *Rokeaḥ,* 221; *S. Ḥas.* 1462; Güd. I, 206, referring to *S. Ḥas. B* 462, reads "like drops of blood" but I have not found such a text in any of the editions which I have consulted.—*S. Ḥas. B* 1153. The belief that demons dwell or assemble in trees was also strongly held among the Germans, cf. Grimm, I, 62 ff., II, 539 ff.; Wuttke, 41.

26. Cf. Lauterbach, *HUCA,* II (1925), 369, n. 31, where the Talmudic and Midrashic sources are cited; also *Hochmat HaNefesh,* 31c; *Orḥot Ẓadikim,* 95b. *Torat Ha'Olah,* II, 25, contains the view that certain sacrifices were slaughtered in the north of the temple area because they served to protect Israel from the demons who dwell in the north. According to *Raziel,* 15a, the north, which is the point of origin of cold and hail and sleet and tempests, was, like the demons, left uncompleted in the work of creation.

27. *Ẓiyuni,* 48d; a fifteenth-century German poet, Michael Behaim of Sulzbach, poked fun at a similar German belief:

> Auch sagt man wie daz trollen
> In Norwegen sein sollen.
> Nu hon ich verr durchvarn die lant,
> Das mir kein troll nie wart bekannt. (Hansen, 208)

28. Löwinger, *JJV,* II (1925), 166, n. 3, 168 ff.; see Grimm, I, 526 f., on the widely held belief in Northern Europe that a knife thrown into the heart of a whirlwind will produce a bloodstain—the blood of the spirit, or of the witch who inhabits the wind.—*S. Ḥas.* 379, 1463; Güd. I, 204, n. 5; this idea undoubtedly entered Jewish belief from the German. Thor (Donar), the Teutonic god of thunder and storms, was believed to fling wedge-shaped stones down from the heavens, a belief parallel to the classical and Oriental conceptions of gods who

rain shafts and bolts upon the earth during storms. The gradual transformation of the heathen gods into demons, under the influence of Christianity, did not affect such attributes, and we find them displayed by the spirits of a later age. "Uralter Glaube war es, dass von den Elben gefährliche Pfeile aus der Luft herabgeschossen werden"; cf. Grimm, I, 138 ff., 149, 381.

29. The demonology and Satan lore of the Christian peoples (especially in Northern Europe) were strongly colored by the residue of heathen mythology which popular Christianity incorporated. The old gods and heroes and spirits lived on as Satanic creatures, with their old attributes and characters unaltered. As Wuttke (p. 36) writes: "Der Teufel des Volksglaubens ist eine bestimmte, sinnlich wahrnehmbare, körperliche Gestalt, die in allen ihren Besonderheiten dem Heidentume entlehnt ist und in den christlichen Urkunden gar keinen Anknüpfungspunkt hat, und auch seine meisten geistigen Eigentümlichkeiten sind heidnischen Ursprungs." The Jews of the Middle Ages, on the other hand, were far distant in time from their heathen origins, and such elements had long since disappeared or had been so effectively disguised as to have lost their influence in popular belief. It is significant, in this connection, that a thirteenth-century gloss to Ezek. 9:3 identifies "the man clothed in linen" of the vision as the טובלא (*tiuvel, Teufel*) rather than by a Hebrew term (Perles, *Beiträge*, 150).

30. *Raben*, 271, confused Shibbeta with the demons of uncleanness, which rest on unwashed hands, rather than on foodstuffs. R. Tam, however (*Tos. Yoma*, 77b and *Ḥul.* 107b; cf. *Semag*, I, 69), stated specifically that Shibbeta is not such a spirit. In either case washing the hands destroys or removes the spirit. *Raben* says of Shibbeta that he twists and breaks children's necks. See also *Joseph Omez*, 349.

31. For the Talmudic references to these demons see Jastrow's *Dictionary* s. v.; cf. Abrahams, *Ethical Wills*, 48-9 and Rashi, Ps. 91:6.—See Grünbaum, *Ges. Auf.*, 97, and Löwinger in *JJV*, II (1925), 157 ff.;—Rashi, II Sam. 7:14; *'Emek HaMelech, Tikkune HaTeshubah* 6, *Kiriat Arba'* 126;—*S. Ḥas.* 1512.

32. *Shab.* 151b;—*San.* 96a; *Nid.* 16b;—Abrahams, op. cit., 48, "Do not leave an infant alone in the house by day or night, nor pass thou the night alone in any abode. For under such circumstances Lilit seizes man or child in her fatal embrace."—A similar conception of the seductive demoness is to be found in the *Avesta;* in Babylonia Lilit was called *ardad lili*, the "maid of the night." See Zoller, *Filologische Schriften*, III (1929), 122. One version of the Lilit legend has her deliver over to the prophet Elijah fifteen (or seventeen) of her names, which were to be used to keep off her unwelcome presence (cf. Gaster, *MGWJ*, XXIX [1880], 557 f.). These names of Lilit were not known, or at least not used, in the Middle Ages.

33. See the following for a discussion of the origin and development of the Lilit concept: I. Lévi, *REJ*, LXVIII (1914), 15 ff.; M. Gaster, *MGWJ*, XXIX (1880), 554 ff. and *Folk-Lore*, XI (1900), 157 ff.; I. Zoller, *Rivista di Antropologia*, XXVII (Rome 1926), and *Filologische Schriften*, III (1929), 121 ff.; Bamberger, *JJV*, I (1923), 320 ff.; and Ginzberg's comment in his *Legends*, V, 87, n. 40. These writers are mainly interested in the lady's origins and do not specifically tackle the problem of her change of character in post-Talmudic times. Lévi, however, does consider this question, and it is his opinion that the *lamia* aspect of Lilit is not part of the same tradition as the Talmudic version, and represents late borrowing from non-Jewish sources. While the germ of the later concept is unquestionably to be found in the Talmudic literature (Felix Perles, *Orientalistische Literaturzeitung*, XVIII [Leipzig 1915], 180, has pointed out two passages in the Midrash that imply the Lamaššu character of Lilit, one of them making her eat her own children), its development was fostered by outside influ-

ences, as Lévi suggests. Gaster (in *MGWJ*) also suggests that the later Lilit legend represents the fusion of two folkloristic streams, the Talmudic and an oriental source, which he considers to have been Manichæan. This last, he shows in a fascinating folkloristic excursion, was also utilized by Bogomil, who in the tenth century founded in Bulgaria the neo-Manichæan sect which influenced, in somewhat altered form, the Albigenses in Southern France, and became the fountain out of which sprang a whole series of Eastern European legends. Gaster, then, places the fusing of these two elements in the East, during the tenth century or somewhat earlier; it was during this period that Bogomil lived, and that the *Alphabet of Ben Sira,* which contains the earliest Jewish version of this legend, was composed. However, the Lilit legend makes a much earlier appearance, as Gaster himself later pointed out (*Folk-Lore*), in a passage in the *Testament of Solomon,* ch. 57 (*JQR, OS,* XI [1899], 16), and Montgomery (76 ff.) has published a series of Aramaic incantations dating from about the seventh century, which show clearly that Lilit was already, at that time, possessed of both the older Lilit and the Lamaššu characters. This is close enough to Talmudic times to make it fairly certain that the dual character of Lilit had already been fashioned during the late Talmudic period, and was beginning to assert itself in Midrashic texts. It is important to remember, however, that fertility spirits are indigenous among all peoples, and that psychologically it is natural to expect that a spirit that desires men for herself will be jealous of the women who displace her, and will seek to harm them and their children. Such a development is especially to be expected when the fertility spirit already possesses the attributes of a night- or wind-demon which attacks men, as in this case. My point is that it is possible to belabor unduly the search for origins outside of the folk-mind and the folk-tradition.

I have used the text of "The Alphabet of Ben Sira," version B, printed in Eisenstein's *Ozar Midrashim* (N. Y. 1915) I, 46-7; cf. also *Tishbi,* s. v. *Lilit.* Other conceptions of Lilit persisted in the Middle Ages, but we find no trace of them in Northern Europe. According to David de Pomis (*Zemaḥ David,* Venice 1587, p. 73), Lilit is a wild animal, or an evil spirit, or, as some say, a bird, which flits about alone at night and fills the air with its wailing. Solomon b. Abraham ibn Parḥon (in his *Maḥberet Ha'Aruch,* written in Salerno in 1160), while he followed the folk-etymology, deriving the name from *layil,* "night," approached closely the standpoint of modern scholarship which sees in Lilit a wind-demon, when he said that "Lilit grows out of the wind just as the salamander grows from the fire." See Zoller, *Filologische Schriften,* III, 128-9, and Ginzberg, loc. cit.

34. *Estrie,* Old French, from the Latin, *strix, striga,* cf. Grimm, II, 868. στρίξ originally signified the night-owl; in the early Middle Ages it came to mean the same as the German *Hexe,* "worunter man sich bald eine alte, bald eine junge Frau denkt." The word appears in various forms; cf. Rashi, *Git.* 69a; *S. Has.* 1465; *Ḥochmat HaNefesh* 17a; *Rokeaḥ* 316; Güd. I, 203, n. 4, and n. 8; *Toledot Adam veḤavah,* 28: 1, p. 182b; *Ziyuni* 9a.

Broxa, "maleficas et sortilegas mulierculas . . . quae vulgariter Broxæ nuncupantur" (Ducange, s. v.); Spanish, *bruxa;* Provencal, *bruesche;* originally denoted an unwholesome night-bird, and came like *strix* to mean "witch"; cf. Grimm, II, 869. It appears in *Toledot Adam,* loc. cit., and in Güd., loc. cit., n. 4.

Mare—the origin of this word is uncertain, cf. Grimm, I, 384; *S. Ḥas.* 1465; *Ḥochmat HaNefesh* 26c; Güd., loc. cit., n. 6 and n. 8; *Ziyuni,* 9a.

Werwolf—*S. Ḥas.* 1465; Güd., loc. cit., n. 4 and n. 8; cf. also Ginzberg, *Adolf Schwarz Festschrift,* Berlin 1917, p. 331.

35. *S. Ḥas.* 1465; *Ziyuni* 9a; Güd., loc. cit., n. 8. The following, from Ginzberg, *Legends,* V, 203-4, is also of interest here: "The German mystics (cf. *Ziyuni,*

end of Noah) identify the woodmen, werwolves and similar monsters, known in German folklore, with the builders of the tower of Babel, and further maintain that they were Japhethites, who were punished in this manner." The source of this view is *Midrash Aggadah,* Gen. 11:8, which "remarks that when the tower fell, some of the people found inside were thrown into the water, others into the forest, while still others into the desert; the first became water-sprites, the second apes, and the third demons." Here we have in essence an expression of the view that the wicked become demons.

36. Cf. *S. Ḥas.* 1465, 1466; *Rokeaḥ* 316; Güd., loc. cit.

37. *S. Ḥas.* 1465-7; *Testament of Judah the Pious,* 5; *Rokeaḥ,* loc. cit.

38. *Ẓiyuni,* 9a, which adds that some Kabbalists call these creatures "stones," "night wolves," and "Satans." *Ḥochmat HaNefesh* 30d speaks of "forest women," who travel in groups of nine (the *Waldfrauen, Waldweiber, Waldgeister,* were very popular characters in German mythology and folklore; cf. Grimm, I, 358f.; Wuttke 47). This passage also mentions a type of demon whose feet are constructed backward, heels in front and toes behind; the sense is not altogether clear.—*Ḥochmat HaNefesh,* 26c; Güd., loc. cit., n. 6; cf. Grimm, I, 384: "Dich hat geriten der mar"; Wuttke, 272 f.; cf. also Rashi's use of *caucher, calcare,* in his comment on Ex. 9:17.

39. Güd., loc. cit., n. 8; *Ẓiyuni* 7a; Perles, *Beiträge,* 125; cf. Wuttke, 277; *S. Ḥas.* 1465.

40. *Ḥochmat HaNefesh* 17a lists the following obscure types: זחולפו which Güd., loc. cit., n. 7, suggests may be an error for werwolf, which seems unlikely; this creature also preys on humans; בורוקולי (which in *Nishmat Ḥayim* occurs as בורקולאקאס; Güd. II, 366, thinks this may be a rendering of the old Slavic, *vlkodlak, vrkodlak,* which appears in Bulgarian and Slovakian as *vrkolak,* and in the White Russian dialect as *wowkolak*—"werwolf." But it is unlikely that this Slavic word should be found domesticated in Western Germany at the beginning of the thirteenth century); מיביארו and יקונופו; cf. Güd. I, 217, n. 5. Perles (*MGWJ,* XXIX [1880], 334) suggests that the former word is probably *megære* or *chimæra.* Güd. (II, 336) thinks it may be a corruption of the Italian *maliardo,* "sorcerer."

41. Schiller-Szinessy, *Cat. of Heb. Mss. in Cambridge,* 162; cf. Grimm, I, 414 f. and III, 145; Wuttke, 43 f.; Güd., *Quellenschriften,* 156;—Perles, *Graetz Jubelschrift,* 8-9; cf. Grimm, I, 363 f.

42. *Fae,* Old French; Güd. I, 294; *Maḥ Vit.,* 507-8; *Disputation of R. Jeḥiel,* 15.

43. Rashi, *Me'ila* 17b, and *Bek.* 44b; cf. Blondheim and Darmesteter, *Gloses Françaises . . . de Raschi,* Paris 1929, p. 102. *Tos. Me'ila,* loc. cit., has למ"טוך, "a spirit having the appearance of a child, which teases and annoys the women." This word may be a provincial term for one of the *lutins;* or, as Grünbaum (*Ges. Auf.,* 205) suggests, perhaps it should be read לעטוך, *Létiches, Letices,* which are "Petits animaux très blancs et très agiles; aussi les prend on pour des esprits doux et folâtres, les âmes des enfants morts sans baptême." (Am. Bosquet, *La Normandie,* 214). This corresponds closely with the description in *Tos. Me'ila.*

44. Perles, *Beiträge,* 146, 147 (from a thirteenth-century manuscript); cf. Grimm, I, 365 f. and Wuttke, 46.

45. *Responsa* of Meir of Rothenburg, ed. Cremona, 24; *Tos. Yoma* 54b; cf. Grimm, I, 404 f. The *nixe* was often pictured as a mermaid, cf. Wuttke, 48-9. According to ancient German myth the nixies drag people who unwarily go in swimming into the depths, where they drain their blood and then let their souls float up to the surface to take refuge under overturned pots and dishes; unless

someone turns these vessels right side up and releases the captive spirits, they force them to join the ranks of the water spirits. This must be the source of the belief, encountered among Germans and Jews, that in order to discover the spot where the body of a drowned person has come to rest one should let a wooden dish float freely until it stops of its own accord; directly beneath it the corpse will be found. The Jewish authority who calls this belief to our attention, while himself faintly skeptical, suggests that it is a godsend for all women whose husbands have been drowned, but who cannot remarry because proof of their widowhood is lacking (Wuttke, 50, 255; Grimm, I, 411; *Joseph Omez*, 352).

46. Rashi, *Bek.* 8a. The commentary on the *Targum* by David b. Jacob Szczebrzeszyn (Prague 1609) interprets the בני ימא of *Targum* II to Esther 1:2 as ווישר וויבר בל"א, *Wasserweib*, mhd. *wazzerwip*—"water-nymph, water-sprite" (see Perles, *Graetz Jubelschrift*, 9 and Grimm, I, 360 f.). Ginzberg (*Legends*, V, 53, n. 168) writes, "It is uncertain whether this statement of Rashi is based on a different text or whether, influenced by the belief in fays and naiads, prevalent in the Middle Ages all through Europe, Rashi ascribes to the Talmud something which is alien to it." Since Rashi writes, "There are fish in the sea which are half human and half fish, called in French שרוינ"א," he obviously has in mind the mermaids; we have seen that he does not hesitate to introduce other medieval spirits into his commentary. The *Tos.* on this passage interprets it in strict consonance with the text as we have it. The term "siren" occurs once or twice in Talmudic literature; see Jastrow, *Dictionary*, s. v. *sironi.* Lauterbach, *HUCA*, XI (1936), 214 ff., discusses Jewish beliefs concerning spirits that reside in bodies of water.

47. *S. Ḥas.* 1463; Güd. I, 205, n. 3;—*S. Ḥas.* 379. The dragon plays a dual rôle in medieval folklore, appearing in his more familiar form, as a fire-spitting serpent (which, however, is afraid of thunder), and as a demon who may enter a house in the shape of a man. (See, e.g., Thorndike, II, 562, and Wuttke, 45.) This account, incorporating elements of both rôles, is a transcription of some medieval folk-tale.

48. Cf. *JE*, II, 529, and Grünbaum, *Ges. Auf.*, 229; see also Wuttke, 27, 66, Grimm, I, 51.—S. Krauss (*MJV*, LIII [1915], 3 ff.) examined the evidence painstakingly and reached the following conclusions which invalidate this popular theory: the so-called plaits are not plaits at all, but really two intertwined arms; this particular shape was not universally required or utilized among German Jews; the name *Berches* has nothing to do with the goddess Perchta, but is derived from the Old High German *bergit, berchit,* which designated the loaf also known as *Brezel, Prezel,* from the Middle Latin *bracellus, brachellus,* which, in turn, meant "arms." Krauss is very persuasive. Cf. also B. Kohlbach, "Das Zopfgebäck im jüdischen Ritus," *Ztschr. Ver. Volksk.*, XXIV (1914), 265-71.

49. *Or Zarua*, I, 362; *Agguda*, 72b; *Mordecai, Niddah* 1086, p. 85c; cf. Güd. I, 215, n. 7 and Perles, *MGWJ*, XXIX (1880), 333.—Grimm, I, 384: "Der Nachthalb, Nachtmar, wickelt Haar der Menschen, Mähne und Schweif der Pferde in Knoten." In Tsarist Russia peasants kept a goat in the stable at night to frighten off demons from entangling the horses' manes.

50. Cf. Perles, in *Graetz Jubelschrift*, 25 ff., where the subject is examined in detail; also Landau, *MGJV*, IV (1899), 146; Grimm, I, 220 ff.

51. *Responsa* of Moses Minz, 19; also Perles, loc. cit.; Landau, loc. cit. and *Ztschr. Ver. Volksk.*, IX (1899), 72-77; Löw, *Lebensalter*, 105; Güd. III, 104-5; Bamberger, *JJV*, I. (1923), 328-9; Zoller, *Filolog. Schriften*, III (1929), 126; Samter, 63 ff. Perles suggested that the second element of the term, *kreisch*, was a corruption of the word *Kreis* (mhd. *kreiz*), "circle." The most potent protection against Lilit was afforded by a magic circle drawn around the bed of the

lying-in woman and her baby, a practice known and observed at an early time. Perles thinks that we have in the word *kreisch,* or *kreiẓ,* a reminiscence of a similar device employed against Holle. The facts, however, do not warrant this stretching of a point, and, indeed, favor the earlier interpretation which included the shouting in the title; moreover, noise is as orthodox and effective an anti-demonic measure as the magic circle, and there is no warrant in the ceremony for ruling out one in favor of the other.

52. Perles, loc. cit., 24-5; Grimm, I, 377 and II, 780. Prof. Ginzberg called my attention to the connection between the prescription that the egg must be laid on a Thursday and the creation of fowl on that day (Gen. 1:20); cf. also p. 129 above.

CHAPTER IV

MAN AND THE DEMONS

1. Ch. V, p. 7a.

2. *Ber.* 6a and Rashi; *Git.* 68a; Rashi on Nu. 22:23.

3. *Nishmat Ḥayim,* III, 27; Isserles to *Yore Deah* 179:16. Prof. Ginzberg considers the statement "they are more God-fearing than men are" to be essentially Islamic; Güd. I, 207, n. 3; *HaḤayim,* IV, 10; *Nishmat Ḥayim,* III, 27.

4. *Ber.* 43b—a man who walks alone is in danger of attack from demons; two walking together are safe, though they must be on guard; three walking together need have no fear at all; a torch may be considered the equivalent of one companion; Judah b. Bezalel's commentary, *Derech Ḥayim,* on *Abot* III, 5.—Ms. *S. Gematriaot,* 65b; *Netivot 'Olam,* 40c-d; *Joseph Omeẓ,* 94, §455; *Testament of Judah the Pious,* §43-4; cf. Grimm, III, 435, §14; *Kiẓur Shelah,* 75-7 (*Inyane Tefilat HaDerech*).

5. Cf. *Pes.* 112b, *Meg.* 3a, *San.* 44a; *Maḥ. Vit.* 507-8; Güd. I, 294; *S. Ḥas.* 239, 468, 939; *Maharil,* 86b; Solomon Luria, quoted in *B'er Heteb* on *Yore Deah* 116:5; *Nishmat Ḥayim,* III, 27;—*Derech Ḥayim* on *Abot* III, 5;—*Maḥ Vit.* 734; *Toledot Adam veḤavah,* 15:30, p. 112c; Abrahams, *Ethical Wills,* 48; Isserles, *Yore Deah* 116:5;—*Semak* 171; *Yore Deah* 116:5; *Orḥot Ẓadikim,* 32a; —*Ḥochmat HaNefesh,* 8c-d; *Leket Yosher,* II, 84; *Responsa* of Jacob Weil, 74a; cf. Samter, 131 ff.

6. *Pes.* 112b, *Maḥ. Vit.* 81, 83-4, *S. Ḥas.* 1909; Marmorstein, *JJV,* I (1923), 306, cites an early source which adds ובמוצאי שבת ובמוצאי יום טוב; see also H. Gollancz, *Clavic. Sal.,* 39;—cf. *Ber.* 6a and *Tos.,* ad loc.; Rashi, *Shab.* 24b; *Semag,* II, 19; *S. Ḥas. B* 1170; *HaTerumah,* 94b-c; *Rabiah,* §10, p. 8, and §196, pp. 240-1; *Mordecai, Shab.,* §564, p. 13c; *Kol Bo,* §35; *Maḥ. Vit.,* 280; *HaPardes,* 22a; Tyrnau, *Minhagim,* 4b. The original reason for introducing a shortened *'Amidah* in the Friday night service, as Prof. Ginzberg pointed out to me, was that at first this was the only evening service during the week; it was given this superstitious explanation when the *Ma'arib* became a daily service.

7. Cf. *Ber.* 54b—"Three require protection [from the demons]: an invalid, a bridegroom and a bride. Another version has it: an invalid, a woman in confinement, a bride and a groom. Some add, also a mourner." Cf. also Rashi, ad loc.

8. Cf. Landshuth, p. xx; Samter, 21 ff.; *JE,* IV, 92 ff.; Ginzberg, *Legends,* VI, 341, n. 118.

9. "Testament of Solomon," *JQR, OS,* XI (1899), 20; Marmorstein, *JJV,* II (1925), 355 f.

10. *Ziyuni,* 10c, 22b; *S. Ḥas.* 305, 327, 1544; *Ḥul.* 94a; Tyrnau's *Minhagim,* 7b, §61; *Nishmat Ḥayim,* II, 26; *Lebush, Yore Deah,* 179: 14; Grimm, II, 698 f., Samter, 79.

11. Ed. Gaster, 301 ff.; Prof. Ginzberg writes (p. 686): "This is to my knowledge the earliest story about a Dibbuk, which is first met with in the writings about Luria and his pupils. The nearest to that given in the *Ma'aseh Book* is the one told about Luria and Vital in the different versions of *Shibḥe HaAri,* which, however, were published later than the M. B." See, however, Scholem, *EJ,* V, 1099, where mention is made of a Safed protocol of 1571 containing reference to a Dibbuk. On Kabbalistic metempsychosis see Franck, 200 ff.; C. D. Ginsburg, 124 f.; Bloch, *MGWJ,* XLIX (1905), 160.

12. Gregory the Great, in his *Dialogues,* recounted the curious tale of a nun who ate a lettuce-leaf without making the sign of the cross, and was immediately possessed of a demon, which had been sitting on the leaf. (Lea, III, 381, Thorndike, I, 639.) The belief in demonic possession was so strongly held that the Catholic Church has a rite of "Ordination of Exorcists," *De Ordinatione Exorcistarum,* and a "Form of Exorcising the Possessed" (Summers, 207 ff., 211 ff.). This far the Synagogue certainly never went, though we have records of exorcisms utilized by individual Jews (cf. Scholem, loc. cit., 1099-1100). For the Talmudic view see Blau, 13, 31, 34, 55.

13. Ḥayim b. Bezalel expressed this view most clearly in his *Sefer HaḤayim,* IV, 10; Menasseh b. Israel (*Nishmat Ḥayim,* III, 10) again says the final word in the matter: "This is one of those traditions which require no proof."

14. *Zera' Kodesh,* by Moses b. Menaḥem of Prague, Furth 1696, end. The technique of exorcism among Jews and Gentiles shows a close relationship, even to such fine points as the requirement that the spirit make its exit through a specified spot on the body (in the case mentioned, the little toe of the right foot), and leave a sign of its departure, either on the body, or as here, in a tiny hole which it was to bore in the window-pane to permit egress. Cf. De Givry, 164 f.

15. See Ginzberg, *Legends,* V, 148, n. 47. This belief was equally widespread in medieval Christendom, and was accepted as literally true by the Church. In fact, physical relations between spirits and humans were believed to be the most characteristic feature of the witch-cults, and some medieval writers attributed the alarming development of witchcraft to the attractions of such a relationship. See Lea, III, 383 ff.; Summers, 90 ff.

16. Cf. *Erub.* 18b and Rashi. This theory was very popular with the later mystics and appears often in the writings of the Horowitz family, e.g., *'Emek Beracha,* II, §52, p. 60b, note by Isaiah; also p. 61b of the same work; *Yesh Noḥalin,* 18b, n. 17. It is because of this view that the avoidance of *keri* occupies such a prominent place in the mystical hygiene of this group.

17. *Disputation of R. Jeḥiel,* 15. Menasseh b. Israel (*Nishmat Ḥayim,* III, 16) discusses this question at some length, and with considerable erudition: one opinion has it that the demons, themselves without physical attributes of any kind, gather up the semen and use it to impregnate women and themselves; another, that demons do possess sex organs and are capable of physical union with men and women; a third admits of such a possibility only when demons temporarily assume human forms and seduce the children of men. Menasseh b. Israel draws here on Christian as well as Jewish sources; he forbears to commit himself to one or another of these views, but does not question the possibility of such unnatural carnal relations. These views find striking expression in medieval Christian thought. Thomas Aquinas explains how by acting alternately as succubus and

incubus, the demon could bear man offspring, while William of Auvergne "regards demons as incapable of sexual intercourse with human beings, but he thinks it possible that they may juggle with nature so as to produce the effects of sexual intercourse." The views of these two outstanding teachers of the thirteenth century were accepted and often repeated by their successors. Cf. Lea, III, 385, Thorndike, II, 358, IV, 310.

18. Such a story is to be found in the *Ma'aseh Book,* 383 ff.; Gaster suggests in his notes that this seems to be a German folktale, but the essential element, a demon marrying a girl, is as Jewish as it is German, or, indeed, of any other nationality.

19. *Ziyuni,* 49b. This is an interesting version of the well-known sociological phenomenon that when members of two races mate, their offspring are regarded as belonging to that race which is socially inferior, while within this group they tend to arrogate to themselves a superior position.

20. *Or Zarua,* I, §124, p. 22c;—*Responsa* of R. Meir b. Gedaliah (Maharam) of Lublin, 116.

21. *Kab HaYashar,* 69. Although the date of this event, 1681-2, is late, the passage is faithful to the beliefs of an earlier period. An interesting parallel to the episode of the forced separation between the demon and her human lover is afforded in an early Aramaic incantation in which a magical *get* (a bill of divorcement) achieves a like result; cf. Montgomery, 159.—That the proper habitat of demons is the desert and the mountain is an ancient and widely held belief (cf. Mat. 12:43). The banning of demons into these places occurs often in Babylonian-Assyrian, Hellenistic, and post-Talmudic Aramaic incantations and exorcisms. Cf. Montgomery, 78, n. 60.

22. The outstanding work on the subject is S. Seligmann's *Die Zauberkraft des Auges und das Berufen,* Hamburg, 1922; cf. also Elworthy, *The Evil Eye,* London 1895; Wuttke, 162 ff.; Bischoff, 50 ff.

23. Grünbaum, *Ges. Auf.,* 105 and *Nishmat Ḥayim,* III, 27.

24. See Blau, 152 ff.; A. Löwinger, "Der Böse Blick nach jüdischen Quellen," *Menorah,* IV (1926), 551-69; Grünbaum, loc. cit.; R. Lilienthal, " 'Ayin Hara'," *Yidische Filologye,* I (1924), 245 ff.; Montgomery, 89.

25. *Ziyuni,* 65c: according to the "scientists," "there are men who can work havoc with the merest glance," and also animals "whose roar spreads death a bow-shot away."

26. *Nishmat Ḥayim,* loc. cit.; Rashi on Nu. 12:1, *Suk.* 53a, and Ex. 30:12 (cf. II Sam. 24:1 ff.); *S. Ḥas.* 534; *Netivot 'Olam,* 107d;—*Rokeaḥ* 296; *Kol Bo* §74; Gaster, *Studies and Texts,* III, 228;—*Tashbez,* 190; *Leket Yosher,* II, 38; *Oraḥ Ḥayim* 141:6;—Isserles, *Eben Ha'Ezer* 62:3; Rashi, *B.B.* 2b. Since the seventeenth century belief in the evil eye has become very prominent in Jewish superstitions; the expressions "unbeschrieen," "unberufen," or, in Hebrew, "no evil eye," have become automatic accompaniments on Jewish lips of the slightest compliment. See Lilienthal, op. cit., for a detailed account of East-European Jewish beliefs.

27. Cf. Elworthy, 8; Thorndike, I, 217, II, 608; *Netivot 'Olam,* loc. cit.; *S. Ḥas.* 981, 1823.

28. De Givry, 92.

29. *Ber.* 19a, 60a; Preuss, *Berliner Festschrift,* 296 f.; Ginzberg, *Legends,* II, 95; Blau, 61 f.; *Yore Deah* 402:12; *Kol Bo* 114; Landshuth, p. xxxi; Rashi, *Ket.* 28a; *Kol Bo* 30; *Tashbez,* 551; *Yore Deah* 335:1 and *Ned.* 40a; *S. Ḥas.* 1446.

30. Schwab, *Vocabulaire,* 7; *Lev Tov,* 6:112, p. 67a; *Testament* of Shabbetai Horowitz, §11; Landau and Wachstein, *Jüdische Privatbriefe,* passim; etc.

31. Cf. *S. Ḥas.* 1, 1464, 1435, 1436, 688, 858, 705; *Kiẓur Shelah*, 149; *Leket Yosher*, II, 83. Not all rabbis were obsessed by this superstition. This same Isserlein, replying to a query as to whether the statement, "I'll be baptised before I let my mother-in-law put foot in my house!" was to be regarded as a vow, limited himself to the immediate question, and passed up an excellent opportunity for a homily on the evils of making such remarks (*Pesakim Uketabim*, §192).

32. *J. Meg.* I, 72b; *J. Yoma* I, 38d; *B.M.* 85a; *S. Ḥas. B* 416; *S. Ḥas.* 1287; cf. *Yesh Noḥalin*, §16 and n. 51, p. 39a;—*Ber.* 56a; *B.K.* 93a; Lea, III, 382; *S. Ḥas.* 129, 1436, 1439, 1727; *Joseph Omeẓ*, 354.

33. *S. Ḥas.* 101, 1504; Güd. I, 282; *HaḤayim*, I, 7; cf. *Tos. Meg.* 31b. It was customary not to call anyone to the *Torah* by name when the *Tochaḥah* was to be read, but the invitation was extended to "whoever wished" to accept it. In Mainz the practice was to stipulate, when employing a sexton, that he must read the chapter when no one else was willing to do so; cf. *Maharil, Hil. Keriat HaTorah*, Isserles, *Oraḥ Ḥayim*, 428:6; *JE*, XII, 175; E. N. Adler, *Jews in Many Lands*, Phila. 1905, p. 178. Reifmann wrote in 1841 (*Ẓion*, I, 184) that he himself saw a man refuse to eat bread which had been placed before him while he was reading the "chapter of maledictions."

34. *Paʿaneaḥ Raza* on Gen. 12:3, p. 16a; *Joseph Omeẓ*, loc. cit.; *Brantspiegel*, ch. 56, p. 100c.

35. *Kiẓur Shelah*, 202 (*Seder Hatarat Kelalot*); the *Kol Nidre* formula is dissimilar in purport and content; cf. *JE*, VII, 539 ff.

CHAPTER V

THE SPIRITS OF THE DEAD

1. *S. Ḥas.* 305; *Rokeaḥ* 313, p. 79b; Moses Taku, *Oẓar Neḥmad*, III, 88; *Nishmat Ḥayim* III, 3; *REJ*, XXV (1892), 4. On Jewish polypsychism see Ginzberg, *Legends*, V, 74, n. 18; *JE*, III, 458; Preis, 9-10; Franck, 192; Ginsburg, 114; Kammelhar, 60 f.; *Hochmat HaNefesh*, 6a ff. Among the multitude of proofs for the continued existence of the spirit after death, this one, for which "non-Jewish scholars" are cited as authority, is perhaps the most extraordinary: "Dice made out of the bones of a corpse will win a man as much wealth as he wishes"! *Ẓiyuni*, 21c, cf. also 29a.

2. *S. Ḥas.* 35, 63, 271, 1543, 1546, 1547, addendum on pp. 126 f., etc.; *Rokeaḥ*, 229 (quoted in *Taʿame HaMinhagim*, 112b); *Hochmat HaNefesh*, 17a; *Ẓiyuni*, 10d; Neubauer and Stern, 5, 52; Marmorstein, *MGWJ*, LXXI (1927), 43-4.

3. *S. Ḥas.* 266, 321, 322, 331, 1530, 1543; *S. Ḥas. B* 1163; *Testament of Judah the Pious*, 11 (cf. *Or Ẓarua*, II, 419, p. 85c); Kammelhar, 62; *Leket Yosher* II, 87; *Responsa* of Israel Bruna, 181, p. 66b; *Maʿaseh Book* 521 f.; Lowenthal, *Memoirs of Glückel of Hameln*, 12-13.

4. *S. Ḥas.* 265, 305, 1885; *Testament of Judah the Pious*, 1; *Rokeaḥ*, 316, p. 83a; *Toledot Adam veḤavah*, 28:1, p. 182b; *Ẓiyuni*, 21b, c; *Nishmat Ḥayim* II, 26; *Yore Deah* 362:6;—Landshuth, p. xlviii; *S. Ḥas. B* 25; *Responsa* of Meir of Rothenburg, Lemberg, 164; *Nimuke* of Menaḥem of Merseburg, 85b, 86a; *Orḥot Ẓadikim*, 78a.

5. *S. Ḥas.* 273, 323, 1537; *S. Ḥas. B* 1171; *Kol Bo* 114; *Yesh Noḥalin*, 3a;

I. Lévi, "Si les morts ont conscience de ce qui se passe ici-bas," *REJ*, XXVI (1893), 69-74.

6. *S. Ḥas. B* 1135; Lowenthal, op. cit., 27; Marmorstein, *JJV*, II (1925), 351 ff.;—Landshuth, pp. iv-vi (for Talmudic and medieval references); J. Mann, *CCAR Yearbook*, XLIV (1934), 231; *Testament of Judah the Pious*, 12; *Maharil*, 37a; *Oraḥ Ḥayim* 579:3, 581:4, 605:1; *Joseph Omez*, 956, p. 212, 986, p. 219; *Mateh Moshe*, 738, 789, 839; *'Emek Beracha*, II, 61, p. 74b; Grünbaum, *Jüdischdeutsche Chrest.*, 572. The practice has arisen, in fairly recent times, of measuring the grave of a pious man with wicks, when someone is ill, and presenting the candles made with them to the synagogue. Cf. *B'er Heteb* on *Yore Deah* 376:4.

7. *S. Ḥas.* 1723; *Testament of Judah*, 9; *Rokeaḥ*, 316, p. 83a; *Ziyuni*, 14b.

8. *S. Ḥas.* 269, 327; *S. Ḥas. B* 708; *Testament of Judah*, 13; *Rokeaḥ*, loc. cit.; *Ḥochmat HaNefesh*, 15b; *Toledot Adam*, loc. cit.; *MJV*, XLIV (1912), 135.

9. *Gen. R.* 11:5; *Maḥ. Vit.* 83-4, 113-4; *Rokeaḥ*, 362, p. 109a; *Ḥochmat HaNefesh*, 26c; *S. Ḥas. B* 1170; Marmorstein, *JJV*, I (1923), 305 f. A similar belief in the repose of the dead on the Sabbath is to be found in Christianity, which of course transferred the day of rest to Sunday. According to Israel Lévi (*REJ*, XXV [1892], 7-10) this Christian belief was borrowed from the Jews in the second half of the fourth century. See also Grimm III, 417.

10. *HaPardes*, 57a; *Siddur Rashi*, 521, p. 260; *HaManhig*, 65; *Mateh Moshe*, 391, 497; etc.—*HaPardes*, 7b; *Siddur Rashi*, 207, p. 95; *Tos. Beza* 33b; *Maḥ. Vit.* 151, p. 117; *Kol Bo*, 41; etc.—*Tashbez*, 14; *Leket Yosher*, I, 58.

11. The material has been discussed in an interesting essay by Israel Lévi, "Le Repos Sabbatique des Ames Damnées," *REJ*, XXV (1892), 1-13, XXVI (1893), 131-5. See also David Kaufmann, "Was the Custom of Fasting on Sabbath Afternoon part of the Early Anglo-Jewish Ritual?" *JQR, OS*, VI (1894), 954-6, and Ginzberg, *Legends*, V, 143 and VI, 22. In addition to the sources cited in these articles, see *Lev Tov*, 6:64, p. 63b, and Isserles, *Oraḥ Ḥayim*, 291:2. In medieval Lorraine the belief was current among Christians that on New Year's night the souls in purgatory bathe in the wells and streams, and water should therefore not be drawn then (Digot, III, 185).

CHAPTER VI

THE SPIRITS OF GOOD

1. The Bible speaks of great "hosts" of angels; see, e.g., Josh. 5:14, 15, I Kgs. 22:19, Job 25:3: "Is there any number of His armies?" etc. The Talmudic literature accepts unquestioningly this doctrine of an infinitude of angelic beings, which remained the prevailing view throughout the Middle Ages. Cf. Schwab, *Vocabulaire*, 6; *JE*, I, 583 f.; *Rokeaḥ*, 362.

2. *S. Ḥas.* 305: בריות בראשית יש ממונה עליהם; *S. Ḥas. B.* 1160: אין דבר שלא יהא מלאך ממונה עליו אפילו כל עשב ועשב; Eleazar of Worms wrote (Kammelhar, 53): על כל דבר מלאכים ממונים ואין לך פנה בעולם שפנוי מן המלאכים השומרים. Cf. also Güd. I, 162, n. 2, 169, and *Ḥochmat HaNefesh*, 18a. This notion was not unknown in contemporaneous German thought, as witness this statement from a sermon by Berthold of Regensburg (ed. Kling, p. 16), quoted by Güd. (loc. cit.): "Er [Gott] hat zu ieglichem künigriche einen engel gesetzet, der des künigriches da hütet, und danne zu ieglichem

hertzogetüme und zu ieglichem lande, daz ein lant mit sünderm namen ist, und danne zu ieglichem bistüme einen, und zu ieglicher stat einen, die in den landen und in den bistümen sint, und danne zu ieglichem dorfe einen, und zu ieglichem kloster einen, und zu ieglichem hüse einen, und zu ieglichem menschen einen sünderlichen, ez si jüng oder alt, getauft oder ungetauft, einem ieglichen christen menschen sünderlichen einen hüter und einen engel gegeben, und halt ieglichem heiden und ketzer und iüden und slafenen [Slav] und tatanen [Tartar]; ez sin iene oder diese, die nach menschen gebildet sind, der hat iegliches sinen engel, der sin hütet." Medieval Christianity shared with Judaism a very rich angelology, and put it to similar magical use in the so-called "Notory Art," which was not the most prevalent form of Christian magic. The specific concept of the "deputy," however, though intimated in the above quotation, seems to have made no inroads into Christian mysticism.

3. Cf. *Raziel,* 19b.

4. *Ẓiyuni,* 15c; cf. *Suk.* 29a; *Cant. R.* 8:14; *Mek. Beshallaḥ, Shirah,* II: even in the time of the Messiah God will not punish any nation until he shall have first punished its heavenly prince.—*Ẓiyuni,* 10c: המזל והמלאך המגינים על האדם; *S. Ḥas. B* 1157: שכל ענין שאדם עושה מלאך מזלו מראה באותו ענין למעלה. The terms "star" (*mazal*), "angel" (*malach*), "prince" (*sar*) and "deputy" (*memuneh*) are often used synonymously in this connection.

5. *S. Ḥas.* 1082, 133, 524, 1158, 826, 1461; *Joseph Omeẓ,* 351.

6. *S. Ḥas.* 1453; *Rokeaḥ* 201; *Raziel* 4a ff.

7. The thirteenth-century mystics were especially addicted to this doctrine; cf. *Ḥochmat HaNefesh* 16d, 18a, 29d; *S. Ḥas. B* 1162; *Ẓiyuni* 5c; Güd. I, 207, n. 2. William of Auvergne (thirteenth century) offered a similar explanation of such phenomena, with the important difference, however, that he attributed them not to angels but to the demons whom the sorcerer had invoked; cf. Thorndike, II, 350.

8. For a detailed exposition of rabbinic angelology see L. Blau, *JE,* I, 583 ff.; G. F. Moore, "Intermediaries in Jewish Theology," *Harvard Theological Review,* XV (1922), 41-85. Kaufmann Kohler's article (*JE,* I, 589 ff.) is especially valuable for its discussion of the early non-rabbinic sources. The Talmudic "princes" to whom particular provinces were assigned appear often in the mystical literature of the first Christian centuries, as well as in the writings of the Church Fathers (see Thorndike, I, 343, 453 f.) and were accepted by the medieval Church and Synagogue. See also *EJ,* VI, 626 ff.; Güd. I, 162 f.

9. *J. Ber.* 13a: "If trouble befall a man, let him not cry to Michael or Gabriel, but let him cry to Me and I will answer him at once." See, however, *Echah R.,* II, 6, and *JE,* VI, 203, for a Midrashic account of conjuration of angels.

10. Where the older Midrash (*Gen. R.* 10:6) reads: "There is not a blade of grass which does not have its *star* in heaven," the younger (*Mid. Tehillim,* ed. Buber, Vilna 1891, 104, p. 440) has, "Every single thing has its appointed angel (*memuneh*) over it." These quotations, with the substitution of a newer concept for an old, give us the clew to the confusion and combination of the two which I have noted. I don't think Ginzberg (*Legends,* V, 110, 159) is justified in reading the sense of the second into the first. The connotation of the one is astrological, of the other, theosophical. A closer rendition, in theosophical terms, of the Platonic concept is to be found in this Geonic statement: "There are those who maintain that for each species of living creature [that He was about to create] God first created a corresponding species of angel in heaven and asked them, 'How would you like it if I should create a replica of you on earth?' And according to their opinion and their wish did He go about the work of

creation." B. M. Lewin, *Otzar haGaonim,* V (Jerusalem 1932), Part II, p. 22 (cf. *Ḥul.* 60a).

11. Kammelhar, 53; Eleazar even agreed with the philosophers that the angels are "Intelligences," ibid. (cf. *More Nebukim,* II, 6).

12. Cf. *More Neb.* II, 42; Naḥmanides on Gen. 18, beg.; *Kuzari,* III, 11; Moses Taku, *Ozar Neḥmad* III, 61; Güd. I, 207, n. 1; Kammelhar 52; and Güd. I, 169, citing a ms. work of Eleazar of Worms.

13. Cf. *Shab.* 12b and *Sotah* 33a; *Maḥ. Vit.* §87, p. 54-5; *HaPardes,* 23a, 58a-b; *Yore Deah* 335:5; *Shelah* II, 146a; *S. Ḥas. B* 32, 1134. *HaPardes* 22d accounted for the Aramaic invitation to participate in the Passover meal, which serves as an introduction to the *Seder* service, on the ground that the demons, like the angels, speak Hebrew (cf. *Ḥag.* 16a), and an invitation in that language would overwhelm the proceedings with a host of these unwelcome guests.

14. *Tos. Shab.* 12b. See also *Tos. Ber.* 3a, which takes issue specifically with *Maḥ Vit.,* loc. cit.; *Teshubot HaGeonim,* ed. Harkavy, §373, 188 ff.

15. Eleazar of Worms divided these two types of service between two classes of angels, the angels (or messengers) proper, and the servants of God: מלאכים נקראים אותם הנשלחים לבני אדם ואותם של פניו נקראים משרתיו, Kammelhar, 53. The medieval *Kabbalah* distinguished ten classes of angels, but aside from one or two bare references to such a classification (cf. *Ziyuni,* 49a; H. Gross, *Gallia Judaica,* p. 411) they do not enter into North European speculations. Cf. Ginzberg, *Legends,* V, 23, n. 64, and 70, n. 22; *JE,* I, 591.

16. See Kammelhar, loc. cit.; *Teshubot HaGeonim,* ed. Harkavy, §373, p. 189; *Pa'aneaḥ Raza,* 23a and Ginzberg, *Legends,* V, 237, n. 154.

17. Moses Taku, *Ozar Neḥmad* III, 67:העולם כולו ביד הקב"ה ומינה מלאכים על כל אדם.

18. Cf. I. Elbogen, *Der jüdische Gottesdienst,* Leipzig 1913, p. 385; *Lebush* on *Oraḥ Ḥayim* 584:1; *Kol Bo* §67; *Yeven Mezulah,* 20. See *JE,* I, 592, for parallels in the apocalyptic and rabbinic literature.

19. *Rokeaḥ* §362; cf. *Ḥag.* 13b and *Tos.* ad loc. See Moore, *Harvard Theological Review,* XV (1922), 62 ff., for discussion of Metatron.

20. *Aramaic Incantation Texts,* 112.

CHAPTER VII

"IN THE NAME OF . . ."

1. See Prof. Lauterbach's essay, "Naming of Children," etc., *CCAR Yearbook,* XLII (1932), 316-60; *Ber.* 7b; *Ḥag.* 3b-4a; *S. Ḥas.* 363, 364, 366, 375, 377, 1118, 1551, 1552, 1871; *S. Ḥas. B* 477; *Testament of Judah,* 26, 28, 61; *Ḥochmat HaNefesh,* 24c; *Ziyuni* 17b; cf. Landshuth, p. xii f., for Biblical and Talmudic references; also Bischoff, 32 ff.

2. See Jacob, *Im Namen Gottes,* 72, 75 ff.; Frazer, *Golden Bough,* 1900, I, 403-47. Methusaleh advised Lamech, father of Noah, to delay naming his son "because the people of that generation were sorcerers, and they would have bewitched him if they had known his name" (*Da'at Zekenim* on Gen. 5:28).

3. *S. Ḥas. B* 1150; *Ziyuni* and *Pa'aneaḥ Raza* on Gen. 32:30.

4. *S. Ḥas.* 1452. However, the contrary opinion is inevitably implied in the practice; cf. *Ziyuni,* 22a: ראה כי אין טוב להשתמש בשמות ומכאן תבין גדול עונש המטריח את קונו. Even the invocation of angels involves a measure of coercion

upon God, who is ultivately responsible for their actions; cf. *Lebush* on *Oraḥ Ḥayim* 584:1: סגולת ההשבעות האמיתיות כן היא שהשם ית׳ יתן להם רשות לאותן מלאכים שיעשו דברי המשביעים בלא שום זכות.

5. Montgomery, 59; cf. also M. Gaster, *The Samaritans*, London 1925, p. 81.

6. Jacob, 73 f.; cf. also Grünbaum, *Ges. Auf.*, 120 ff.; De Givry, 109.

7. Rashi, *Sotah* 22a.

7a. Bischoff, 192 f., 195, offers an ingenious Hebrew derivation for this word.

8. *Ber.* 55a; cf. also *Men.* 29b.

9. *Joseph Omeẓ*, 73; Raziel, 4a; cf. also Gaster, *Sword of Moses*, 28, 48; *S. Ḥas.* 1458 (cf. *Kid.* 71a); *Joseph Omeẓ*, 279. The practice of altering the names of God in one way or another when writing them, or of substituting short-hand forms, grew up at a very early time. Eighty-three written substitutes for the Tetragrammaton have been listed. For fear of writing even the particle *Yah* proper names were abbreviated, so that Jehudah became Judah, the final "h" of Elijah and Isaiah was dropped, the number 15 was written ט״ו instead of י״ה, etc. See Lauterbach, *Proc. Amer. Acad. for Jew. Research*, 1931, 39-67; S. W. Baron, *A Social and Religious History of the Jews*, N. Y. 1937, III, 48;—*Raziel*, 2a.

10. See Gaster, *Ma'aseh Book*, pp. 357, 366, 370; *HaGan*, ch. 4; *S. Ḥas.* 1444, 1448, 1449. *Nishmat Ḥayim* III, 28, contains a general discussion of the powers that reside in the holy names, with quotations and proofs.

11. *San.* 67b and Rashi; Blau 27; *Hadar Ẓekenim* on Ex. 8:14, and Rashi on the same verse; cf. Güd. I, 169.

12. *San.* 67b, 65b and Rashi; Thorndike, II, 353, III, 139.

13. N. Brüll, *Jahrbücher*, IX (1889), 27; *JE*, VI, 37; *EJ*, VII, 501-7; Chayim Bloch, *The Golem*, Vienna 1925; cf. *Shelah*, III, 65a. In the seventeenth century the question was raised whether a *Golem* could be counted as one of a *minyan* (*JE*, loc. cit.).

14. *Commentary on Sefer Yeẓirah*, 4d, 15d ff.; *EJ*, loc. cit.

15. Steinschneider, *Cat. Munich*, p. 3; Grünbaum, *Jüdischdeutsche Chrest.*, 566. For a discussion of the *Golem* motif in German folklore see B. Rosenfeld, *Die Golemsage und ihre Verwertung in der deutschen Literatur*, Breslau 1934.

16. See Montgomery, 57 ff.; Gaster, op. cit., 7 ff.; Thorndike, I, 14, 360 ff.

17. Gaster, op. cit., 8-9; Blau, 133; Thorndike, I, 450.

18. The Aggadah has a few references to invocation of the names of God: Moses killed the Egyptian (Ex. 2:11) by merely speaking God's name; the name of God, engraved on Moses' staff, caused the sea to divide (Blau, 50, 60). The words *ehyeh asher ehyeh yah YHVH ẓebaot amen amen selah*, written on a staff, caused a stormy sea to subside (*B.B.* 73a).

19. Montgomery, 95 ff.; Wohlstein, 6-7, 9 ff.; *Ta'am Ẓekenim*, ed. Eliezer Ashkenazi, 54 ff. Cf. also J. Mann, *Texts and Studies*, II, 90 ff.

20. Lea, III, 412, 436; Thorndike, I, 729, II, 286 ff., IV, 170.

21. Cf. Lauterbach, loc. cit., 39, n. 1 and 2. On the meaning of the term שם המפורש concerning which there is considerable difference of opinion, see Grünbaum, *Ges. Auf.*, 190 and 238 ff.; Blau, 125; Grunwald, *MGJV*, V, 35 and X, 95; *JE*, XI, 262 ff.; L. Geiger, *Kebuẓat Maamarim*, ed. Poznanski, Warsaw 1910, p. 98, and Ginzberg's note, p. 394; H. H. Schaeder, *Esra der Schreiber*, Tübingen 1930, 53 ff. This term was applied in post-Talmudic times not alone to the Tetragrammaton, but also to the longer names; cf. Hai Gaon in Ashkenazi,

loc. cit.; Rashi, *San* 60a, *Suk.* 45a, *Erub.* 18b, etc. *Raziel,* 7a, has a *shem hameforash* which altogether defies classification.

22. The 12-letter name is mentioned once, in *Kid.* 71a, which also speaks of the name of 42 letters. The only other reference to this latter name in Talmudic literature is in *Lekaḥ Tov* to Ex. 3:15, p. 10a, ed. Buber. The name of 72 letters (or elements) is not mentioned in the Talmud, but does occur in one frequently repeated passage of the Midrash: *Gen. R.* 44:19, *Lev. R.* 23, beg., *Nu. R.* 1:11, etc.: ששמו של הקב"ה שבעים ושתים אותיות. *Cant. R.* to 2:2 has: ששמו של הקב"ה ע"ב שמות הן. Blau, 137 ff., suggests that the oldest mystical name is that of 12 letters; 42 and 72 developed out of it later. The name of 72 was known, at the latest, by the first half of the third century. The Talmudic literature, however, gives us no information about these names, what they were, what were their component elements, or how they were constructed.

23. This, in addition to the 4-, 12-, 42-, and 72-letter names, constitutes the list given in the ms. *S. Gematriaot,* 72b ff.

24. See, e.g., *Raziel,* 24b ff.; Jellinek, 40-41.

25. *Raziel,* 30b.

26. *Pesikta R.* ch. 21 (ed. Friedmann, 104a); see also Ginzberg, *Legends,* V, 5, n. 10. There were several theories as to just which name of God was responsible for the creation of the universe. The one most often advanced is that it was the Tetragrammaton alone, or in conjunction with the particle *yah,* that did the job. See Eleazar of Worms, *Commentary on S. Yezirah,* 1c; Jellinek, 33; Grunwald, *JJV,* I, 388, n. 4. *Raziel,* 12b, offers an interesting and original hypothesis: God had 73 of His names inscribed at His right hand when He was about to commence the work of creation. Out of the first name there came forth three drops of water which filled the universe; the second provided light; the third, fire; and so forth. When His task was completed He set the name of 42 to keep the celestial waters apart from the terrestrial; it was the removal of this name that caused the flood (p. 14a).

27. Cf. Thorndike, II, 407.

28. These particles were very popular. *Pes. R.,* loc. cit.: אפילו אות אחת משמו עושה צבא בכל שמו; Blau, 102 f.; Wohlstein, 30; Montgomery, 60; Jellinek, 33; Grunwald, *MJV,* XIX (1906), 112; etc.

29. *Ziyuni* 11a, 30b; see also *Raziel,* 24a-b, 33b.

30. An effort has been made by some scholars to reconstruct the three names known in Talmudic times, those of 12, 42 and 72, on the assumption that they were not the same as those employed in later times. Bacher (*Agada der babylonischen Amoräer,* 17-20) suggests that the 12-letter name was based on the three creative potencies חכמה תבונה דעת; and the 42 on the full ten: חכמה תבונה דעת כח גבורה גערה צדק משפט חסד רחמים with the addition of the Tetragrammaton. Franck (*Kabbalah,* 71) derives the name of 42 from the ten *Sefirot* (cf. also Bischoff, 35 ff., 107 ff.), which, as Ginsburg (*Kabbalah,* 183) points out, is an obvious anachronism. Robert Eisler (*REJ,* LXXXII [1926], 157-9) bases the names of 42 and 72 on the thirteen *Middot* of Ex. 34:6-7. Blau (p. 144), on the analogy of the Greek magical papyri, in which the seven Greek vowels play a great rôle, works out a triangular anagram which, beginning with one *YHVH* builds up by the addition of one letter at a time to three—this, he maintains, contains the 4-letter name in the first line, the 12 in the last, the 42 in the last four, and the 72 in its totality. Finally, A. Haffer (*HaZofeh,* II [1912], 127 ff.) derives the 12-letter name from the first three names of God that occur in the *Shema',* אל אלהינו יהוה, and to make up the 42-letter name he adds the final two words of the *Shema'* and the doxology ברוך שם כבוד מלכותו לעולם ועד. The name of 72 he derives from Deut. 4:34. See also Schwab, *Vocabulaire,* 28 ff.

These theories ring false, and certainly bear no relation to what was considered a potent magic name in the post-Talmudic period; in any event, such efforts are entirely a matter of conjecture and invention, which can in no way be substantiated from the available facts. It seems to me that there is a strong probability that the names of 42 and 72 employed in the Middle Ages were the same as those in use during the first few centuries of the Common Era. Hai Gaon (10th-11th century) (*Ta'am Zekenim,* 57) spoke of them in words which imply that they had been well known for a long time, and the tenacity of traditional lore, especially in a field such as that of mysticism and magic, in which letter-perfection is one of the prime requisites, is a well-known phenomenon.

31. See Appendix I.

32. Ms. *S. Gematriaot,* 74b: שם בן י"ב אותיות הוא יהוה יהוה יהוה והם ג' שמות של יברכך יאר וישא; *Ziyuni,* 60b: מאי יברכך ה' וישמרך וגו' שמו של הקב"ה והוא בן י"ב אותיות י"ד ו"ד י"ד ו"ד י"ד ו"ה; cf. L. Zunz, *Die synagogale Poesie des Mittelalters,* Berlin 1855, p. 146.

33. Ms. *S. Gematriaot,* 74b: שם בן י"ד אותיות יוצא משלש תיבות בפסוק שמע ישראל והם יהוה אלהינו יהוה והם י"ד אותיות מתחלפות באותיות שלפניהם.

34. Pp. 42b, 44b, 45a and 41b (in this last only the word פספסים occurs, intercalated between the second and third verses of the Priestly Blessing. The other three were probably originally included in the text, but dropped out before it was printed in the eighteenth century).

35. Cf. Bernard Heller, *REJ,* LV (1908), 60 ff., and LVII (1909), 105 f.; J. Perles, *MGWJ,* XXI (1872), 259-60; ibid., LXXVII (1933), 246; Schwab, op. cit., s. v.; Cordovero's *Pardes,* 21:14 (ed. Lemberg 1862, p. 113a), vocalizes the name as I have given it.

36. Cf. Albert Katz, *Allg. Zeit. des Jud.,* 1907, 312; S. Krauss, *REJ,* LVI (1908), 251-2; Nathan Hanover's *Sha'are Zion,* Vienna 1817, 34b, 35a, 28a, 60a, 63a; *REJ,* LXV (1913), 59-60, where Aptowitzer cites acrostics containing this name which are somewhat older than those in *Sha'are Zion.*

37. Ms. *S. Gematriaot,* 74b: שם בן עשרים ושתים אותיות הוא אנקתם וכו' ויוצא מחמש תיבות שעולות כ"ב אותיות והם יברכך יהוה וישמרך יאר יהוה; *Ziyuni,* 60d: אמרו בעלי העבודה כי שם של י"ב (read כ"ב) יוצא מיברכך על פי מסורת המקובלים מאלפא ביתות רבים וסידורם ופרושם (לא) אכחד כי הם אמרי קודש דע שהם ד' שמות הראשון אנקתם והשני פסתם וכו'. An incantation in a sixteenth-century manuscript employs "the 22-letter name of the Priestly Benediction" to conjure a divinatory spirit (Grunwald, *MJV,* XIX [1906], 106). By means of this name the dead will be recalled from their graves at the resurrection; cf. Gaster, *Studies and Texts,* III, 230; Gollancz, *Clavic. Sal.,* 42. The "Jerusalem" type of amulet-*mezuzah* (see p. 150 above) includes both benediction and name in a manner indicating their close relationship; cf. Aptowitzer, *REJ,* LXV (1913), 59. An additional item of evidence is provided by a late Italian ms. entitled *Sefer Ha-Razim* (Ms. D 146, J. T. S. Library) which (p. 18a) combines the name and the blessing in an amulet.

38. *Pardes,* loc. cit.; cf. also Joel, *Allg. Zeit. des Jud.,* XXXVIII (1874), 246, 351-2.

39. *Ta'am Zekenim,* 57; B. M. Lewin, *Otzar HaGaonim,* IV (Jerusalem 1931), *Ḥagigah,* 20 f. In connection with this name Maimonides launched a bitter denunciation of all these mystical names of God (cf. *More Neb.* I, 61, 62) which aroused only the faintest echo in Northern Europe.

40. Cf. *Raziel,* 24b, 45a-b; Ms. *S. Gematriaot,* 74b: ומכל אות ואות של זה השם יוצא שם אחד והם מ"ב שמות. There were other versions of the name

of 42, such as that which the *Zohar* constructed out of the ten divine names mentioned in the Bible (see Ginsburg, *Kabbalah,* 186-7), and the mnemotechnical signs for the ten plagues in the Passover *Haggadah* which a sixteenth-century ms. designated as this name because their numerical sum (by *mispar katan*) is 42 (Grunwald, *MJV,* XIX [1906], p. 119; see also *JE,* IX, 164); but these were "sports" which never challenged the position of the true name.

41. See I. M. Casanowicz, *Jour. Amer. Or. Soc.,* XXXVI (1917), 159. This prayer was made much of by the Kabbalists, who also composed other such prayers containing this name in acrostic; cf. Landshuth, p. xxv; *EJ,* II, 857.

42. Cf. *Tos. Ḥag.* 11b, s. v. אין דורשין: פי' ר"ת הוא שם ע"ב [read מ"ב] אותיות היוצא מבראשית ומפסוק של אחריו. (See also Bacher, *REJ,* XVIII [1889], 292-3, whose interpretation of this statement is far wide of the mark.) *Raziel,* 24b: זה השם . . . יוצא מן הפסוק הראשון שבתורה הוא מן ב' של בראשית עד ב' של בוהו; *Ziyuni,* 2c: פסוק בראשית לתיבות שש שש אותיות בשם של מ"ב; Ms. *S. Gematriaot,* 74b: שם בן מ"ב אותיות היוצא מפסוק בראשית עד ה' של בוהו ולא תחשוב ה' אחרונה של היתה; I may add that while the other works cited do not specify that the name of 42 to which they refer is the one of which I have been speaking, *Raziel* makes it clear that this is so. Cordovero (*Pardes,* 21:13, ed. Lemberg 1862, p. 112b) offers a complete exposition, through alphabetical permutations, of the derivation of this name from the opening verses of the Bible.

43. P. 43a: לא יוכלו למעבד שום כשוף אלא על ידי כלי ע"ב. Wohlstein, pp. 12 f., woefully misunderstood this passage when he stopped at the word כלי and translated it literally as "vessel," thus making the use of a vessel (he had in mind the many clay vessels that have been found inscribed with Aramaic incantations) obligatory upon the magician. The sentence quoted, and the context, make it unmistakably clear that the "vessel" or "tool" referred to is the name of 72.

44. *Ta'am Zekenim,* loc. cit.; Rashi, *M. Sukkah,* 45a; cf. also *Raziel,* 24b, 40b; ms. *S. Gematriaot,* 35a, 74b; Ginsburg, *Kabbalah,* 133 ff.; *JE,* IX, 164.

45. *Raziel,* 40b.

46. Ibid., 30b-31b.

47. Ms. *Raziel,* 74b-76a: 1. להכנים אהבה ולהוציא איבה ושנאה; 2. לשנאה; 3. לפתיחת הלב; 4. לשתק פה כל המדברים רעה; 5. להכנם אצל מלך או שלטון ולמצוא חן; 6. להפריד בין הנחברים; 7. לחבר הנפרדים ולהשלים ביניהם; 8. להפיל אימה; 9. לאדם שהוא טפש ושכחן; 10. לקפיצת הדרך לקפיץ ממקום למקום; 11. להריגה לאויבי'; 12. לקיום בני אדם; 13. לעקור אדם מעירו ולטלטלו; 14. יש בהם סוד גדול נסתר ונעלה וע"ז לא פירשו אותם, but in another hand we read: החלק י"ד לשד או לעקור איש מעירו או לכל דבר קשה.

48. P. 40b.

49. Ibid. 43a, 52b; on the 70 names of Metatron, cf. Steinschneider, *HB,* XIV (1874) 6-8, 33; *Kizur Shelah, Inyane Limmud,* p. 150. I have not attempted, by any means, to be exhaustive in this presentation of angelic and godly names, Hebraic and foreign. The material is far too vast to permit of anything more than a sampling here. Schwab has made the largest collection of such names, and if his etymologies are as often as not dubious, he presents a good survey of the entire field. The purpose of this discussion has been solely to illustrate the type of material under consideration.

50. See pp. 250 f. above.

51. Cf. *Raziel,* 21b, 34a-35a, 4a ff.

52. Grünbaum, *Ges. Auf.,* 122; *Raziel,* 5b.

53. Cf. *JE,* I, 130; Montgomery, 151, and Myrhman, *Hilprecht Anniversary Volume, Leipzig* 1909, p. 345; Gaster, *Sword of Moses,* p. xiv, l. 25; *Raziel,* 5a; Grunwald, *MJV,* XIX (1906), 112, and *Jahrb. für jüd. Gesch. und Lit.,* IV (1901), 130-31.

54. Cf. Güd. I, 218.

55. *Raziel,* 42a; *HaGan,* ch. 2, end; Grunwald, *MGJV,* V (1900), 66, §225; Lauterbach, *Proc. Amer. Acad. Jew. Research,* 1931, 40, n. 3; M. Gaster, *The Samaritans,* London 1925, p. 67.

56. Eisenstein, *Ozar Midrashim,* N. Y. 1915, I, 46; Schwab, *Vocabulaire,* 200, 201; Gaster, *MGWJ,* XXIX (1880), 554 ff., *Folk-Lore,* XI (1900), 157 ff., *Sword of Moses,* 19; cf. however, Grunwald, *MJV,* XIX (1906), 107, where these three terms are invoked not against Lilit, but to gain inspiration for the preparation of an amulet. See also Grunwald, *MGWJ,* LXXVII (1933), 241.

57. See J. Perles, *Etym. Studien,* 78; Heller, *REJ,* LV (1908), 69 ff.; Krauss, ibid., LVI (1908), 253-4; Heller, ibid., LVII (1909), 107-8; Brüll, *Jahrbücher,* I (1874), 154 ff.; Gaster, *Studies and Texts,* III, 228; Montgomery, 99.

58. *MGJV,* V (1900), 81.

59. See Güd. II, 333-4; Perles, *Graetz Jubelschrift,* 32 ff.; Grunwald, *MGJV,* V (1900), 79-84; E. Lévy, *REJ,* LXXXII (1926), 401 ff.; Steinschneider, *Cat. Munich,* p. 109.

60. Grunwald, *MJV,* XIX (1906), 112.

61. Steinschneider, *HB,* VI (1863), 121.

CHAPTER VIII

THE BIBLE IN MAGIC

1. *Joseph Omez,* pp. 277-8; *Yore Deah,* 179:9 and the commentaries; *S. Ḥas.* 818; *'Amude Shlomo* on *Semag,* I, §51; Landshuth, p. xx; Perles, *Graetz Jubelschrift,* p. 28. Wuttke, 144, writes of the Germans: "Gesang und Gebetbücher werden viel als Zauberschutz gebraucht, Wöchnerinnen und Säuglingen ins Bett gesteckt."

2. *S. Ḥas. B* 1140; Singer, *Proc. of Brit. Acad.,* 1919-20, 343; *Tashbez,* 256 (which attributes the statement concerning the manna chapter to the Jer. Talmud); *Yesh Noḥalin,* 10b, n. 9; *Or Ḥadash,* p. ix; *Yesh Noḥalin,* 13b, 14a.

3. *Maḥ. Vit.,* p. 510.

4. *Ber.* 56b; *Pes.* 112a, 111a; *JE,* III, 202; *HaḤayim,* IV, 10. Mention is also made of a verse which begins and ends with "lo" (the reverse of "el"), presumably Nu. 23:19. *Tos. Pes.* 111a refers this passage to a prayer by R. Ḥananel, beginning with "el" and ending with "lo," but Blau (70-71) considers that both statements refer to the same verses, Nu. 23:22-23, which begin and end with both "el" and "lo" when read forward and backward, respectively.

5. *M. San.* XI, 1; *San.* 101a and Rashi; *Sheb.* 15b; *S. Ḥas.* 818; *Toledot Adam veḤavah,* 17:5, p. 127b; *Yore Deah,* 179:10.

6. See, e.g., n. 8 below; *Shimmush Tehillim,* passim.

7. Ibid.; cf. Grunwald, *MGJV,* X (1902), 91 ff. for several ms. versions of this work; *JE,* III, 203 f.; *REJ,* XII, 315; *Kizur Shelah,* 111, 203. Schudt (II, 31:7, p. 191), in the 18th century, testifies to the popularity among German Jews of "das aberglaubische Büchlein Schimmusch Tillim, darin der gantze Psalter Davids zu lauter aberglaubischen Dingen verdreht wird." The use of hymns and psalms in incantations goes back to the ancient Babylonians, and was practiced by Christians as well as Jews. See Daiches, 41; C. Kayser, "Gebrauch von Psalmen zur Zauberei," *ZDMG,* XLII (1888), 456 ff.; Montgomery, 62 f.

8. See Bibliography C for a description of this ms. These quotations chosen at random will illustrate its style:
29a: ויהי יהוה את יוסף ויהי איש מצליח ויהי בבית אדניו המצרי (Gen. 39:2) דין
מעלי למימר להצלחה בשם יהוה יהוה יאה סוף יהוה ישא מצליח יהוה מנמין באנהר
כי תצא למלחמה על איביך ונתנו יהוה אלהיך בידך 66b: ;ידימי וכולא פסוק
ושבית שביו (Deut. 21:10) אמור כולא פסוקא בעידן קרבא ואת נצח והשם שלו שמשיאל
ש׳ מן י׳ כי בגי׳ י״ש כ״ת מ׳ מן ל׳ למלחמה למפרע ש׳ מן ב׳ איבך בגי׳ (א״ת) ב״ש
ויברכם ביום ההוא (Gen. 48:20) מעלי למימר על 31a: ;יו״ד מן יהוה א״ל מן אלהיך
הגידה לי (Cant. 1:7) נפיק מיניה 71b: ; כסא דמהולתא ויועיל לינוקא בשם . . . .
;יונתי (Cant. 2:14) מעלי בעת צרה והשם מלטיאל ; ענניאל ומעלי לשאילת חלם
.הנסתרות וגו׳ (Deut. 29:28) לשאילת חלום כתוב על ידך והב תחות רישך 68a:

9. Cf. *Shimmush Tehillim*, passim; Ms. *S. Gematriaot*, loc. cit.; pp. 122 f. above.

10. Cf. *Sheb.* 15b and Rashi; Blau, 95, n. 4; *Rabiah*, Aptowitzer's note, I, 4, n. 3; *Mordecai, Ber.* §19, p. 2a; *Kol Bo*, §29; *Joseph Omez*, §647, p. 143.

11. *Tashbez* 257; *HaManhig, Hil. Shab.*, 65; *Iggeret HaTiyul*, I, 3a, s. v. *zayin; Mateh Moshe*, §370; *'Emek Beracha*, II, 61, p. 77a; Perles, *Graetz Jubelschrift*, 28; Grunwald, *MJV*, XIX (1906), 114; *Testament* of Shabbetai Horowitz, §13.

CHAPTER IX

THE MAGICAL PROCEDURE

1. *Raziel*, 3a, 4a; cf. Gaster, *Sword of Moses*, 28, 48;—Ms. *S. Gematriaot*, 36a, 47a, 48b, 57a.

2. See Thorndike, I, 162; Montgomery, 46 f., 56; Marmorstein, *JJV*, I (1923), 295.

3. *Shab.* 66b; *Nishmat Ḥayim*, III, 25; Landshuth, p. vii; *Ta'ame HaMinhagim*, I, 46b, §353; Lauterbach, *CCAR Yearbook*, XLII (1932), 347 f.; Casanowicz, *Journal Amer. Or. Soc.*, XXXVI (1917), 165, n. 28; cf. Montgomery, 49; Grunwald, *MGWJ*, LXXVII (1933), 161; Frazer, *The Magic Art*, I, 65; Lewy, *AR*, XXIX (1931), 189 ff.

4. Blau, 147-49; Steinschneider, *Cat. Munich*, 109, and Grunwald, *MGJV*, V (1900), 80 ff.; cf. Gaster, op. cit., 35, 42; Wuttke, 183-4; *MGWJ*, loc. cit.

5. *A. Z.* 12b and Rashi; *Ta'ame HaMinhagim*, II, 44b; Perles, *Etym. Studien*, 78; Heller, *REJ*, LV (1908), 69-71; Gaster, *Studies and Texts*, III, 228; *Raziel* 33b, 40b; Gollancz, *Clavic. Sal.*, 36.

6. *Shab.* 66b.

7. Blau, 13, 77; *Tos. R. H.* 11b; Rashbam, *Pes.* 110a; Kaufmann, *JQR, OS*, IV (1892), 559; *Tashbez* 550; *S. Ḥas. B* 59; cf. Elworthy, 404 ff. R. Samuel b. Meir felt that while the fifth cup might be unnecessary so far as fear of demons was concerned, it might still be effective against magic (Rashbam and *Tos. Pes.* 109b, s. v. *Raba*).

8. *Testament of Judah*, 25, 29-36, 38-40; *S. Ḥas. B* 59, 477; *Kol Bo* 60; etc.

9. Rashi *Shab.* 66b; Gaster, *Sword of Moses*, pp. 35, 38, 43; *S. Ḥas.* 377, 815. See Franck, 134 f. and Ginsburg, 148 ff. on the Kabbalistic doctrine of numbers; cf. Aristophanes, *The Frogs*, trans. by Gilbert Murray, N. Y. 1925, p. 86:

> The man was talking to the dead, you dog,
> Who are always called three times—and then don't hear.

10. Blau, 73-4, 82; Gaster, op. cit., pp. 36, 37, 39; *Shimmush Tehillim*, Ps. 4, 19, 22, 121, 125; *Raziel*, 42a; Perles, *Graetz Jubelschrift*, p. 28.

11. *S. Ḥas. B* 1153; cf. Singer, *Proc. Brit. Acad.*, 1919-20, 353 f.; Wuttke, 90; Grimm, I, 503, 505, III, 469, §950; Löwinger, *Der Traum*, 30 f.; Kugler, *Hilprecht Anniversary* Volume, 308. There are many examples of nine in medieval Jewish magic and superstition; see, e.g., *S. Ḥas.* 1468; *B* 1146; Güd. I, 117, n. 7, 206, n. 2; Grunwald, *MJV*, XIX (1906), 114, 116.

12. E.g., numbers associated with the divine names, as 72 (*MJV*, XIX [1906] 114); 10, connected with the Ten Commandments (Gaster, *Studies and Texts*, III, 228; *MJV*, XIX, 116); 6 (*Shimmush Tehillim*, Ps. 8, 122); 21 and 24 (*MJV*, XIX, 114); etc.

13. *San.* 101a and Rashi; Blau 162 f.; Wellesz, *MJV*, XXXV (1910), 117; Thorndike, I, 93, 174; Wuttke, 184.

14. *Ta'anit* 19a and 23a ff. (*Yoḥasin*, Fkft. 1924, p. 63, contains a Geonic statement relating *Me'agel* to a town of that name); *Ẓiyuni* 22b; Levita, *Tishbi*, s. v. *Lilit;* cf. Daiches, p. 32; Scheftelowitz, *Stell. Huhnopfer*, ch. 6; De Givry, 104 f.; Knuchel, *Die Umwandlung*, Basel 1919; Bischoff, 76, 97, 182 ff.

15. Marmorstein, *JJV*, I (1923), 283.

16. *HeḤaluẓ*, XII (Vienna 1887), 96; *Kerem Ḥemed* VI (Prague 1841), 5; Marmorstein, *MGWJ*, LXXI (1927), 48; *JE*, V, 46; Güd. I, 52-3; Isserles, *Yore Deah* 340:3 (cf. Krauss, *MJV*, LIII [1915], p. 18);—*Shimmush Tehillim*, Ps. 2, 5, 7, 18, 19, 20, 21, 37, 92, 109, 119, 125; *Raziel*, 41b, 42a, 45a; Ms. *S. Gematriaot*, 56b, 70a. According to Schudt (II, VI, 6:5), Nu. 11:2, written on a bread-crust, was thrown into a fire to extinguish it.

17. *Raziel*, 45b;—Frazer, *The Magic Art*, I, 55 ff.; De Givry, 191 f.; Murray, 116 f.; Lea III, 451 ff.; Grimm III, 420, 430;—Gaster, *Sword of Moses*, 39, §68; Güd. I, 207, n. 2.

18. Ms. *S. Gematriaot* 27a-b, 55b, 68a, 71b (cf. Daiches, 21);—Grunwald, *MGJV*, V (1900), 82.

19. Güd. loc. cit.; *S. Ḥas. B* 1159, 1162; *Ḥochmat HaNefesh* 29d; *Ẓiyuni* 5c; Thorndike II, 350.

20. Samter, 121 ff.; *HERE*, VII, 747; Blau, 157 f., 164; Marmorstein, *JJV*, I (1923) 291 ff.; Rashi *Shab.* 57b; Gandz, *Isis*, XIV (1930), 194; Gaster, op. cit., 51; Wohlstein 16; *Rokeaḥ* §316, p. 83a; *Nishmat Ḥayim* III, 18; J. Lipez, 35; cf. Montgomery, 52; Grimm II, 983; Wuttke 461; I. Scheftelowitz, *Das Schlingen- und Netzmotiv im Glauben und Brauch der Völker*, Giessen 1912; cf. also *S. Ḥas.* 380, 1162, 1566, 1910; *Pa'aneaḥ Raza* 67a. For the use of *asar* with this special meaning in older Jewish literature see *Targum Jon.* Deut. 24:6; *Aggadat Bereshit*, Introd. 38; L. Ginzberg, *Geonica* (1909), p. 152.

21. Grunwald, *MGJV*, V (1900), 83; *MJV*, XIX (1906), 108, 110-111. Schudt, loc. cit., reports an interesting instance of sympathetic magic: to put out a fire, one would go to a spot where he could overlook the entire conflagration, and, while slowly reciting Nu. 11:2, pour with each syllable a drop of water into a pan of burning coals.

22. *Tos. Niddah* 17a; *S. Ḥas.* 683; Lipez 105; cf. *Shab.* 75b.

23. Frazer, op. cit., 148 f.; Strack 77 ff.; Wuttke 134 ff.; Scheftelowitz, *Stell. Huhnopfer*, ch. 9, 12; Grunwald, *JJV*, I (1923), 19; *JE*, III, 260;—*Raziel* 41a; *MGJV*, loc. cit., *MJV*, XIX (1906), 112; *Pa'aneaḥ Raza* 86b; cf. Gaster, op. cit., 39, §64, 46, n. 6; Gollancz, op. cit., 25-6. It should be noted that the inclusion of sweat in these prescriptions ran counter to a strong belief that human perspiration (except that of the face) is poisonous (cf. *Yore Deah* 116:4). On the "egg laid on a Thursday" see ch. III, n. 52, above. These lines from Hans

Vintler's *Blumen der Tugend* (Grimm III, 422) may be compared with the final recipe:

> ettlich legent des widhoffen hertze
> des nachtes auf die schlauffende lütt,
> das es in haimlich ding betütt
> vnd vil zaubry vnrain.

24. Grunwald, *MGJV*, V (1900), 25, §14; Perles, *Graetz Jubelschrift*, 29; Ms. *Raziel* 31a-b; cf. Gaster, op. cit., 47, §12. A few like recipes are also to be found in the Talmud; cf. e.g., *Ber.* 6a: "If one wishes to see the evil spirits, he must take the afterbirth of a first-born black cat, which is the daughter of a first-born black cat, burn it and grind it to a powder, and put the ash in his eye."

25. *Hadar Zekenim* on Ex. 22:17; *Raziel*, 3a-b, 6b; Ms. *Raziel*, 24b f.; cf. *Yore Deah* 179:19.

CHAPTER X

AMULETS

1. Cf. *JE*, I, 546 ff.; Blau 86 ff.; Ashkenazi, *Ta'am Zekenim*, 56; *S. Ḥas.* 367, 1455, 1457. An early Yiddish "Vrauen Büchlein" (*Mizvat HaNashim*, Venice 1552, ch. 47) reassured its pious readers that the woman who wears an amulet to the ritual bath "kein Sünde hat," and that it is no impediment to the performance of the rite and need not be removed.

2. Cf. *Shab.* 53a and Rashi; *Or Zarua* II, 18d, §83; *Oraḥ Ḥayim* 305:11; *Lev Tov* 6:129, p. 68b; *HaḤayim* IV, 3; Perles, *Graetz Jubelschrift*, 35. On the corals see *Tashbez* §60; *Responsa* of Meir of Rothenburg, ed. Lemberg, §140; Berliner, *Aus dem Leben*, 134; Zimmels, *Beiträge*, 118, n. 484.

3. *Shab.* 66a and Rashi (cf. A. Darmesteter and D. S. Blondheim, *Les Gloses Françaises de Raschi*, Paris 1929, 31, §246); *Maḥ. Vit.* 133, n. 35; *Rokeaḥ* §100; *Rabiah* 311, §221, and Aptowitzer's n. 10; Güd. I, 214; *Oraḥ Ḥayim* 303:24 and *B'er Heteb*, ad loc. A note in *'Amude Shlomo* to *Semag* I, 65 reads:
ואני המעתיק מצאתי בבאורי מהרר"ז שווינבר"ט וז"ל אבן תקומה אני ראיתי אבן חצץ שהיה בתוכו חלול ואבן קטן בתוכו כעינבל בזוג וכן נברא ואמרו שהוא אבן תקומה.
A thirteenth-century Latin ms. reports that "when the women of Salerno fear abortion, they carry with them the pregnant stone" (Thorndike, I, 740), and Wuttke (91-2) writes that a similar practice existed among the Germans.

4. *S. Ḥas.* 1463 and Güd. I, 204; cf. Frazer, *The Magic Art*, I, 187 f.; Grimm II, 729, III, 443; Lowenthal, *A World Passed By*, 115; *Kizur Shelah, In. Pes.*, 142 and *B'er Heteb* on *Orah Ḥayim* 477:2, n. 4; M. Schwab, *REJ*, XXIII (1891), 137. Berliner, op. cit., 102, suggests that the belief in certain German districts that a piece of *Judenmatz* in a house will protect it from fire, may be derived from this use of the *Afikomen* as an amulet. *Yore Deah* 305:15 and Lipez, 47; Grunwald, *MJV*, XIX (1906), 111, 112, 114; Perles, *Graetz Jubelschrift*, 35. A 14th century Archbishop of Aix, Richard Mauvoisin, had a Jewish astrologer named Moses carve some seals on his pastoral ring to avert disease and bring him fortune (Thorndike, III, 19).

5. Cf. Samter, 175 ff.; Seligmann, *Mag. Heil- u. Schutzmittel*, 200 ff., which discuss the anti-demonic virtues of red. These works and also Elworthy, *The Evil Eye*, contain much information on this general subject.

5a. *Leket Yosher* I, 9; cf. Berliner, op. cit., 92 f.; Grimm II, 920, III, 445, §333, 457, §656, 459, §708.

6. Cf. Thorndike I, 778 ff., etc., IV, 327; Grimm II, 996, 1017 ff.; *Toss. Shab.* V, 17; *B. B.* 16b; *JE,* III, 367 and V, 593 ff., 239 ff.; Steinschneider, *Kohut Memorial Volume,* 45, *Hebr. Uebersetzungen,* 964; Seligmann, op. cit., 208 ff.

7. Ms. *S. Gematriaot,* 43a-44b (cf. Baḥya b. Asher's comment on Ex. 28:17); see Steinschneider, *Kohut Mem. Vol.,* 69-70, for a Hebrew translation by Berachya haNakdan of a Latin treatise on 73 gems; also *Midrash Talpiot,* s. v. *Avanim Tovim,* and *Segulat HaAvanim.*

8. *Shimmush Tehillim,* passim; Grunwald, *MJV,* XIX (1906), 118.

9. *Raziel,* 42a.

10. There is an essential uniformity in all Jewish amulets, whatever the date or place of their origin; Talmudic (Blau, 93 ff., 117), modern Oriental (Casanowicz, *Journal Amer. Or. Soc.,* XXXVI [1917], 154, 156) and medieval, all are cut after the same pattern.

11. Cf. *Raziel* 41b; Rashi, *Git.* 67b; Grunwald, *MJV,* XIX (1906), 112.

12. Cf. *JE,* VIII, 251-2; Grunwald, *Jahrb. f. jüd. Gesch. u. Lit.* IV (1901), 119 ff.; *MGJV;* IX (1902), 137 ff.; Güdemann, *MGWJ,* LX (1916), 135 f.; Vajda, *MJV,* LIX (1918), 33 ff.; Grotte, *MGWJ,* LXVI (1922), 1 ff.; Grunwald, *JJV,* I (1923), 209; Grimm, I, 356, n. 4, III, 456, §644, 463, §812; Wuttke, 181-2; Montgomery, *Journal Amer. Or. Soc.,* XXXI (1911), 274, *Ar. Incan. Texts,* 259; *Raziel,* 42b, 44b; Gollancz, *Maphteaḥ Shelomo,* passim; the ms. *S. Gematriaot* is liberally sprinkled with hexagrams and pentagrams; Schwab, *Vocabulaire,* 21. See also "Testament of Solomon," *JQR, OS,* XI (1899), p. 16; Schudt, II, VI, 6:5.

13. *Raziel,* 44b; Montgomery, *Journal A.O.S.,* loc. cit., photographs facing pp. 272, 280; *Maphteaḥ Shelomo,* passim; Schwab, *Ms. No.* 1380, 29; Grunwald, *MJV,* XIX (1906), 108, 112; Scholem, *Kirjath Sepher,* IV (1927), 318-9.

14. See Grünbaum, *Ges. Auf.,* 217-8; de Gunzbourg, *REJ,* XXVII (1893), 145 and Grünbaum, ibid., XXIX (1894), 150 ff.; Steinschneider, *Cat. Hamburg,* Hamburg, 1878, 55 f. (cf. 99 f.); Grunwald, *MGJV,* V (1900), 60; Pilcher, *Proc. Soc. Bib. Archeology,* XXVIII (London 1906), 110-118; W. Ahrens, *Hebräische Amulette mit magischen Zahlenquadraten,* Berlin, 1916; Scholem (*MGWJ,* LXIX [1925], 101 f.) conclusively disposes of the contention that the astrological number-squares were Jewish. I have seen one magical number-square amulet in a late Italian ms. version of *Raziel* (*S. HaRazim,* J. T. S. Library, Ms. D. 146, p. 14a), which was no doubt copied from an earlier text. Cf. also W. Ahrens and A. Maas, "Etwas von magischen Quadraten in Sumatra und Celebes," *Ztschr. f. Ethnologie,* XLVIII (Berlin 1916), 232-253.

15. See *Toss. Shab.* V, 9, 10; *Shab.* 61a-b, 115b, and Rashi, 61a; *J. Shab.* 7c, 8b; *HaTerumah,* 90d-91b; *Maḥ. Vit.* 133, §35; *Rabiah,* I, 305; *Semag,* I, 9c, §65; *Raben,* §350; *Rokeaḥ,* 100; *Toledot Adam veḤavah,* 59d, 61a; *Lev Tov,* 6:112, p. 67a; *'Amude Shlomo* to *Semag* I, 65 and Solomon Luria's *Responsa,* §47; *Oraḥ Ḥayim* 301:25, 27, 334:14.

16. Cf. *Nishmat Ḥayim,* III, 25; Grunwald, *MJV,* XIX (1906), 107.

17. P. 41b. Grunwald, op. cit., 106, has a different table, from a 16th century ms.

18. See M. L. Rodkinson, *Tefilah LeMoshe,* Pressburg 1883, and *History of Amulets, Charms and Talismans,* N. Y. 1893; *JE,* X, 21 ff.; S. Gandz, "The Knot in Hebrew Literature," *Isis,* XIV (1930), 198; Blau, 152; Lauterbach, *HUCA,* II (1925), 362, n. 22; *'Amude Shlomo* to *Semag* I, 51.

19. *JE,* VIII, 532; Aptowitzer, *REJ,* LX (1910), 39 f.; Rashi on *Men.* 33b; *Responsa* of Meir of Rothenburg, ed. Cremona, §108; *'Amude Shlomo* to *Semag*

II, 23; *Shelah,* I, 187a (*Mas. Ḥullin*). Rashi and his grandson R. Tam illustrate two opposing views in their interpretation of a Talmudic remark to the effect that affixing the *mezuzah* improperly may be a source of harm; Rashi says, "This is dangerous because if it is not properly attached the house is not protected against demons"; R. Tam says, "If it is set up in an awkward place one may strike against it and hurt himself" (*Toledot Adam veḤavah,* 21:7, p. 143a).

20. *Shab.* 32b; *Yore Deah* 285:1; *Testament* of Shabbetai Horowitz, §9; *Kizur Shelah,* 69 (*Hil. Mezuzah*); Lipez, 72; Yoffie, *Journal of American Folklore,* XXXVIII (1927), 376.

21. Rashi, *Yoma* 11a. See p. 4 above.

22. Aptowitzer has assembled the information concerning the *mezuzah* in his very interesting articles in *REJ,* LX (1910), 39-52, LXV (1913), 54-60, and *HaZofeh,* II (1912), 100-102, upon which this presentation is based. See also Z. Nissan, in *Zion,* II (1842), 161-4; *JE,* VII, 532 f.

23. *HaZofeh,* loc. cit.; Rashi, *San.* 21b. *Raziel,* 42a, uses the identical term כתיבה גסה, "large writing," to describe the lettering of a magical inscription on a cake.

24. *REJ,* LX (1910), 41, n. 4, gives the sources; cf. especially Maimonides, *Mishneh Torah, Hil. Tefillin,* V, 4; *Kol Bo,* §90; *Raziel,* 8a; ms. *Ez Ḥayim,* p. 1024 (601 of original); *Kizur Shelah, Hil. Mezuzah,* p. 69.

25. Maimonides, loc. cit.; Asheri, *Halachot, Hil. Mez.,* §18; *Toledot Adam veḤavah,* 21:6, p. 142d; and the sources cited in *REJ,* LX (1910), 42, n. 5. Ms. *S. Gematriaot,* 62a, repeats the words of *Asufot,* cited in *REJ,* LXV (1913), 56, n. 3, but does not admit any indebtedness to Sherira Gaon.

26. *Maharil,* 87b. The power of awakening the dead was also attributed to this name of 14 letters; cf. Gaster, *Studies and Texts,* III, 230 and Gollancz, *Clavic. Sal.,* 42.

27. See Aptowitzer, op. cit.

28. Pp. 62b-64a.

29. Pp. 64a-b.

CHAPTER XI

THE WAR WITH THE SPIRITS

1. Moses Taku, *Ozar Neḥmad,* III, 88; *Ḥochmat HaNefesh,* 30c; *S. Ḥas.* 1512, 1566; Glassberg, 226; Güd. III, 100; Rabbinowicz, 21.

2. *R. H.* 16b; *Yoma* 20a; Rashi, *R. H.* 28a; *Raben,* 61; *Responsa* of Jacob Weil, § 191, p. 64b; *'Emek Beracha,* II, 61, p. 76b; cf. Finesinger, *HUCA,* VIII-IX (1931-32), 201 ff.; Lauterbach, *HUCA,* XI (1936), 256;—*Kol Bo* §35—*Pes.* 109b; *Mordecai, Pes.* §896, p. 21a; *Maḥ. Vit.* 280; *Kol Bo,* loc. cit.; *Or Zarua,* II, 56a; *Maharil,* 6b, 17a-b; Isserles, *Oraḥ Ḥayim* 481:2; etc. Prof. Ginzberg has called my attention to a statement in the *Mekilta* (ed. M. Friedmann, Vienna 1870, p. 16b) which turns the "night of protection" into a night when "all Israel requires protection." No echo of this view is to be found in the medieval sources.

3. *JE,* XI, 365; Tyrnau's *Minhagim,* 29b; *Mateh Moshe* 395; Landshuth, p. xxv; Brüll, *Jahrbücher,* IX (1889), 40;—*Ber.* 43b: "A scholar should not go out alone at night," originally a counsel against inviting gossip, as the *Gemara* explains, was later given a superstitious interpretation when it was attached to the passage (*Ber.* 54b) enumerating those who must fear demonic attack. Rashi (*Ber.* 62a) writes: "A scholar needs special protection against demons, because

they are more envious of scholars than of other men." Cf. also *Testament* of Shabbetai Horowitz, §24.

4. *S. Ḥas. B* 1154; *Rokeaḥ* 337; *Tashbeẓ* 315; Güd. I, 53.

5. *S. Ḥas.* 327; *Maḥ. Vit.* 70; *Joseph Omeẓ,* 102; *Testament* of Shabbetai Horowitz, §23; *Sha'are Ẓion,* 67a; etc.;—*Ber.* 5a; *Mordecai, Ber.* §6, p. 2a; *MGWJ,* LIX (1915), 242. The literature on the "*Keriat Shema'* at the bed" is too extensive to cite in full. No special insight is necessary to discern the import of its contents even in modern expurgated versions. Prayer, especially in the mystical sense favored by the "practical Kabbalah," enjoyed a fairly distinctive magical rôle, which has not yet been fully investigated. See J. Bergmann, "Gebet und Zauberspruch," *MGWJ,* LXXIV (1930), 457-463; H. G. Enelow, "Kawwana: The Struggle for Inwardness in Judaism," *Studies in Jewish Literature in Honor of Prof. Kaufmann Kohler* (Berlin 1913), 82-107; G. Scholem, "Der Begriff der Kawwana in der alten Kabbala," *MGWJ,* LXXVIII (1934), 492-518; *Major Trends in Jewish Mysticism,* Stroock Lectures for 1938, Lecture 4; *JE,* III, 465; Bischoff, 86 ff.

There is a curious statement that to leave a knife with its cutting edge upward is to court trouble. According to a German saying, "When a child falls into the fire, and at the same instant one notices a knife lying on the table sharp edge up, one should turn the knife over before saving the child." The explanation of this superstition is singular: "the blade turned upward cuts the face of the dear Lord and of the angels," who retaliate in consequence. This explanation is not found in the Jewish sources, but the injunction against bringing a knife into a synagogue, or leaving it on the table while grace is being said (it was either removed or covered) was probably based upon some such notion. The reasons that were offered are not very persuasive; "prayer lengthens man's days, but the knife shortens them" was a popular one; another told a gruesome tale of a man who, while saying grace, was so overcome with grief at the memory of the destruction of Jerusalem that he picked up a knife from the table and plunged it into his breast. But there was an ancient tradition that the *Shechinah,* the divine presence, hovers over men at prayer, and it is quite likely that we have here a fusion of Jewish and German beliefs. Cf. Güd. III, 129, n. 10; Wuttke, 312; Grimm, III, 454, §596; *Kol Bo* 17; *Mateh Moshe,* 304; *Orah Ḥayim* 180:5.

6. *Kol Bo,* 61, 67; Neubauer and Stern, 26; *Responsa* of Meir of Rothenburg (ed. Berlin 1891), 158-9; *HaḤayim,* IV, 7; ms. *Eẓ Ḥayim,* 516 (289 of original);—Marmorstein, *JJV,* I (1923), 289; *JE,* V, 347 f.

7. *Joseph Omeẓ,* 351.

8. Ibid., 466, p. 96; Rashi, *Men.* 35b; *Sha'are Ẓion,* 120b; Brück, 63; Löw, *Die Finger,* p. xiv. See also p. 175 above.

9. *S. Ḥas.* 211, 371, 1463 (cf. Güd. I, 205, n. 2); *Shimmush Tehillim,* Ps. 10; Blau, 91; *Ber.* 20a; *Raziel,* 43a; cf. Elworthy, 389 ff.

10. *Ber.* 43b; *S. Ḥas.* 325; cf. Bergmann, *MGWJ,* LXXI (1927), 162 ff.; Samter, 67 ff.; Seligmann, *Mag. Heil- und Schutzmittel,* 110 ff.; Wuttke, 93 f.

11. Blau, 158 f.; Rashi, *Ber.* 33a; *Pa'aneaḥ Raza,* 123a (cf. Grimm, I, 487, n. 4: "Ein Mensch von der Otter gebissen stirbt nicht, wenn er eher als die Otter, über das nächste Wasser springt").—Rashi, *San.* 67b; *S. Ḥas.* 1453; *B* 1144; *HaḤayim* IV, 10; *Nishmat Ḥayim* III, 20; *Shimmush Tehillim,* Ps. 15, 29. One is reminded of Washington Irving's "Headless Horseman" whose wild pursuit of poor Ichabod was halted at the bridge. Cf. Wuttke, 92 f.

12. Blau, 162 f.; *Orah Ḥayim* 328:20;—Berliner, *Aus dem Leben,* 96 f.; Elworthy, 412 ff.;—*S. Ḥas.* 326, 327; *HaGan,* ch. 2, end; *Testament* of Shabbetai Horowitz, §23.

13. *Ber.* 62a; *Pes.* 112b; Wuttke, 185; Samter, 60; Güd. III, 130.

14. *Hochmat HaNefesh*, 30d; Güd. I, 204, n. 4; *Brantspiegel*, ch. 66, p. 105d; cf. Blau, 159 f.; Seligmann, op. cit., 156 ff.; Elworthy, 221 ff.; Samter, 51; Wuttke, 95 f.; I. Goldziher, "Eisen als Schutz gegen Dämonen," *AR*, X (1907), 41-6.

15. Samter, 151 ff.; Otto Schell, "Das Salz im Volksglauben," *Ztschr. Ver. f. Volksk.*, XV (1905), 137-49; Seligmann, op. cit., 266 ff.; Wuttke, 95, 283; Lea, III, 511;—*Tos. Ber.* 40a; *Leket Yosher*, I, 34; *Joseph Omeẓ*, §88, p. 20; *Kiẓur Shelah*, 38; Isserles, *Oraḥ Ḥayim* 167:5; *Lipeẓ*, 50; cf. I. Löw, "Das Salz," *Jewish Studies in Memory of George A. Kohut*, N. Y. 1935, 454 ff.

16. Güd. I, 204, n. 4; *S. Ḥas.* 1465; *Pa'aneaḥ Raẓa*, 91a; Schudt IV, 2, p. 385;—cf. Samter, 153; Grimm II, 877, 923, III, 434, 440, 454; Wuttke, 129.

17. Jews have come to recognize the apotropaic virtues of garlic and onions in comparatively recent times (see I. Löw, *Die Flora der Juden*, II, 147). Cf. Samter, 159 f.; Grimm, II, 902; Scheftelowitz, *Stell. Huhnopfer*, 32.

18. *Ber.* 55b (cf. Blau, 155); *Nishmat Ḥayim*, III, 27 (cf. Grünbaum, *Ges. Auf.* 106-7); *S. Ḥas.* 327; Güd. I, 206, n. 5; *Joseph Omeẓ*, 351; Grunwald, *MGJV*, V (1900), 35, §55, 40, §81, 66, §225; cf. Gaster, *Sword of Moses*, 42, §111, 117; Elworthy, 151 ff., 241 ff.; Samter, 109 ff.; Schönbach, *Ztschr. Ver. f. Volksk.*, XII (1902), 7; Löw, *Die Finger*, p. xvii.

19. *Pithe Teshubah* on *Yore Deah* 179:3 mentions this Sephardic custom: before moving into a new home a hen and rooster were domiciled there for a while and then slaughtered on the premises; Scheftelowitz, op. cit., 20-1, 54; *Testament of Judah the Pious*, §50; cf. Marmorstein, *JJV*, II (1925), 361 f.; *S. Ḥas. B* 1145, 1146; Elworthy, 79 ff.; Strack, 31 f.; Grimm II, 956 f.

20. *Shab.* 67b; *Testament of Judah*, 51, 52, 59, 60; *S. Ḥas.* 171, 514; *Brantspiegel*, ch. 66, 105c; *Responsa* of Maharil, 118; *Yore Deah* 179:3; *Leket Yosher*, II, 6; cf. Marmorstein, *JJV*, II (1925), 364-5; Grünbaum, *Ges. Auf.*, 218; Schorr, *HeḤaluẓ*, VII (1865), 47-8; Scheftelowitz, *Ztschr. Ver. f. Volksk.*, XXIII (1913), 385 f.; Grimm, II, 949, III, 437, §83, 486, §23. In Austria, a Christian sells his crowing hen to a Jew! Wuttke, 118.

21. The literature on the *Kapparah* is fairly extensive; for a discussion of the rite see I. Scheftelowitz, *Das stellvertretende Huhnopfer*, Giessen 1914; I. Lévi, "Les Jardins d'Adonis, les Kapparot et Rosch Haschana," *REJ*, LXI (1911), 206-12; M. D. Hoffman, *Shibalim*, (Vienna 1876), 39-45; I. Löw, *Die Flora der Juden*, IV, 336 f.; J. Z. Lauterbach, "The Ritual for the Kapparot-Ceremony," *Jewish Studies in Memory of George A. Kohut*, N. Y. 1935, 413-22, and *HUCA*, XI (1936), 262 ff. The essential medieval Hebrew sources are: Rashi, *Shab.* 81b; *Mordecai*, *Yoma* §1181, p. 27c; *Sha'are Teshubah*, ed. Fischel (Leipzig 1858), §299 (cf. Joel, II, 27); *Responsa* of Solomon b. Adret (Vienna 1812) §395, p. 47a; *Orḥot Ḥayim* (Florence 1750), *Hil. Erev Kippurim*, §1; *Tur Oraḥ Ḥayim* 605; *Oraḥ Ḥayim* 605 (Venice 1564 ed. of *Shulḥan 'Aruch*); ms. *Eẓ. Ḥayim*, 289 (155 of original); *Toledot Adam veḤavah*, 7:1, p. 41a. All the codes contain descriptions, which embody minor variations; see, e.g., *HaOrah*, §95, p. 109; *Shibbole HaLeket*, 266; *Maḥ. Vit.* 373; *Kol Bo*, §68; *Tashbeẓ* 125; *Maharil* 43b-44a; Tyrnau's *Minhagim*, 22b-23a; *Leket Yosher*, I, 139-40; etc. For parallel customs from other cultures see Scheftelowitz, op. cit., Samter, 55 f., Grimm, III, 418, §44. Cf. also Aptowitzer, *Addenda et Emendationes ad Sefer Rabiah*, Jerusalem 1936, pp. 113 f.

22. *Maharil*, 38a; *HaḤayim*, IV, 5; *Torat Ha'Olah*, III, 56; *Shelah*, II, 145b (*Mas. Rosh Hashanah*); *'Emek Beracha*, II, 61, pp. 75a-b; cf. *JE*, XII, 66-7; Scheftelowitz, *AR*, XIV (1911), 383-4; Reifmann, *Zion*, I (1841), 184; H. Bodek, ibid., II (1842), 48, 54-7; Brück, 23-4; Grunwald, *JJV*, I (1923), 20; Samter, 65 f. Prof. J. Z. Lauterbach has treated this subject exhaustively in

his essay, "Tashlik—A Study in Jewish Ceremonies," *HUCA*, XI (1936), 207-340.

23. *San.* 92a (cf. Lauterbach, *HUCA*, II [1925], 358, n. 11); *Yore Deah* 178:3; *Oraḥ Ḥayim* 180:2;—*Lebush* on *Yore Deah* 178:3; *Kiẓur Shelah, Inyane Shabbat*, p. 119;—Bergmann, *MGWJ*, LXXI (1927), 170-1; Reifmann, *Ẓion*, I (1841), 184;—*Leket Yosher*, II, 15; *Ḥul.* 105b and Rashi;—Joel, II, 28-9; *Mordecai*, beg. *Yoma; Lev Tov*, VI, 66, p. 63c; *Mateh Moshe*, 306, 504; *Leket Yosher*, I, 57-8; cf. Grimm, I, 370, 422 f., II, 843 f.; Wuttke, 37, 67-8; *MGWJ*, loc. cit., 168.

24. *R. H.* 16b; *S. Ḥas.* 366, 367, 1136, 1519; *B* 247.

25. *Joseph Omeẓ*, 351; *S. Ḥas.* 1446, 1447; cf. Grimm, III, 451, §509.

26. *Yore Deah* 179:9 and *Pitḥe Teshubah* ad loc.

27. *Leket Yosher*, I, 49.

28. *Joseph Omeẓ*, loc. cit.; Schudt, IV, 2, p. 223.

29. *Tishbi*, s. v. *Lilit; HaḤayim* II, 8.

30. *Raziel*, 43b; cf. Scheftelowitz, op. cit., 8 f.; Zoller, *Filologische Schriften*, III (1929), 126.

31. Güd. I, 214; cf. Grimm, III, 417; Wuttke, 195; Digot, III, 181; cf. also A. Geiger, *Jüd. Ẓtschr.*, V (1867), 139 f.

32. Glassberg, 18, 61 (cf. L. Ginzberg, *Ginze Schechter*, II, 541); *Shelah*, I, 182a (*Mas. Ḥullin*).

33. Ibid.

34. *Kiẓur Shelah*, 73 (*Inyane Milah*); *Mateh Moshe* 118b (cf. Glassberg, 149, 179);—Glassberg, 65; *Ma'aseh Rokeaḥ*, 54; *HaManhig, Hil. Milah*, 129; *Yore Deah* 265:12; Perles, *Graetz Jubelschrift*, 23; Güd. III, 103; *B'er Heteb* on *Yore Deah* 178:3;—cf. Bergmann, *MGWJ*, LXXI (1927), 167; Goldberger, *HaẒofeh*, XI (1927), 166-7; *JE*, XII, 454.

35. *Toledot Adam veḤavah*, 17:5, p. 127b; *Yore Deah* 178:3, 179:17.

36. *Pirke de R. Eliezer*, ch. 29; *Rokeaḥ* 113; Gaster, *Ma'aseh Book*, II, 391; *MGWJ*, loc. cit., 169-70.

37. *Shelah*, loc. cit.; *Shibbole HaLeket*, 377; Glassberg, 59 f., 230; Bamberger, *JJV*, I (1923), 327.

38. See pp. 41 f. above.

39. *Rokeaḥ*, 353; *Tashbeẓ*, 465; *Responsa* of Moses Minz, 109, p. 100a; *Responsa* of Israel Bruna, 93, p. 40b; *Mateh Moshe*, 107b; Lauterbach, *HUCA*, II, 360; J. Reifmann, *Kochve Yiẓḥak*, XXXII (Vienna 1865), 31; cf. Grimm, III, 487, §31.

40. Lauterbach, *HUCA*, II (1925), 355; *Tashbeẓ*, loc. cit.; *Joseph Omeẓ*, 331-2; Isserles, *Eben Ha'Ezer* 64:1; *S. Ḥas.* 375.

41. *Raben*, 258b; *Tashbeẓ*, loc. cit.; *Maharil*, 64b; *Mateh Moshe*, loc. cit. A similar custom is observed by some Oriental communities.

42. Prof. Lauterbach has analyzed this custom as well as the other usages in the interesting essay already cited, "The Ceremony of Breaking a Glass at Weddings," *HUCA*, II (1925), 351-80; the sources are all painstakingly examined there. See J. Perles, "Die jüdische Hochzeit in nachbiblischer Zeit," reprint from *MGWJ*, IX (1860), for Talmudic material; cf. also Schudt, II, 25:6, p. 5; Grotte, *MGWJ*, LXVI (1922), 2; Grunwald, *JJV*, I (1923), 21; Glassberg, 149; Samter, 39 ff., 58 ff.; Grimm, III, 451, §514, 466, §884.

43. Lauterbach, op. cit., 368; *Rabiah*, I, 126; *Tashbeẓ*, loc. cit.; *Responsa* of Moses Minz, p. 101b;—*Rokeaḥ* 352, 353; *Maḥ. Vit.* 589; *Raben*, loc. cit.; *Maharil*, loc. cit.; Lauterbach, op. cit., 359; cf. A. Büchler, "Das Ausgiessen von Wein und Öl," *MGWJ*, XLIX (1905), 12-40; Bergmann, ibid., LXXI (1927), 166; Samter, 171 ff.; Scheftelowitz, 14 ff., ch. 3; Digot, III, 177.

44. *Maḥ. Vit.,* loc. cit.; *Kol Bo* §75; *Maharil,* loc. cit.; *Responsa* of Moses Minz, 79a, 99b; *Leket Yosher,* I, 113; Lauterbach, 359-60; Güd. III, 121 f. *Mitron* is a Hebraization of the French *mitre, mitra* (J. Perles, *Beiträge,* 59); the *sarganes* (a word which Prof. Ginzberg believes to be derived from *saracen,* denoting a wide, flowing garment) was originally worn on the Sabbath and holidays (*Rabiah,* I, 245-6), but came later to be identified as a mark of mourning; it was worn at weddings "to remind one of the day of death," in the words of Moses Minz. Seligmann, *Mag. Heil- und Schutzmittel,* 135, points out that ashes, the product of fire, are often employed as a means of protection.

45. *Rokeaḥ,* 353, 355; *Maharil,* loc. cit.; *Responsa* of Moses Minz, 99b; *Yereim,* 96; cf. Samter, 90 ff.; Grimm, II, 983 f.; Elworthy, 427 ff.; Prof. Ginzberg (*REJ,* LXVII [1914] 149 f.) interprets the transfer of the groom's garments to the bride as a token of possession.

46. Berliner, *Aus dem Leben,* 100; *Mateh Moshe,* 107c; Schudt, II, 25, p. 3; *Maharil,* 65a.

47. *Mateh Moshe,* 111c, citing *Kol Bo;* Landshuth, p. xxv; *Leket Yosher,* II, 96; *S. Ḥas.* 315, 317, 318; Isserles, *Yore Deah,* 339:1; cf. Grimm, III, 443, §281, 454, §593; Samter, 61 f. See, especially, "Beliefs, Rites and Customs of the Jews Connected with Death, Burial and Mourning," by A. P. Bender, *JQR, OS,* VI (1894), 317 ff., 664 ff., VII (1895), 101 ff., 259 ff.; and *JE,* III, 434 ff.; also Landshuth; J. Perles, "Die Leichenfeierlichkeiten im nachbibl. Judenthume," *MGWJ,* X (1861), 345-55, 376-94; and J. Rabbinowicz, *Der Todtenkultus bei den Juden,* Frankfort 1889.

48. See *Semaḥot* ch. 1; *Yore Deah* 353:2 and *M.K.* 25a;—Landshuth, p. xxxii; *Shelah,* II, 24b;—*Nishmat Ḥayim,* III, 26; *S. Ḥas.* 1542; *Testament of Judah the Pious,* §7; *Rokeaḥ,* 316; Löw, *Die Finger,* pp. xiv ff.; cf. Samter, 1 ff., 45 f., 80 f.; Bender, 102-3.

49. *Testament of Judah,* §2, 3; *Rokeaḥ,* 316, p. 83a; *Toledot Adam veḤavah,* 28:1, p. 182b (cf. Wuttke, 214, 215); Rabbinowicz, 27.

50. *Hadar Zekenim* on Nu. 20:1; *S. Ḥas. B* 851; *Kol Bo,* 114; *Pa'aneaḥ Raza* on Nu. 20:2; *Shibbole HaLeket,* p. 171; *Mordecai, Pes.* §896, p. 21a; *Tashbez,* 442, 447; *Or Zarua,* 56a; *Maharil,* 6b; *Brantspiegel,* ch. 74, p. 114a; Digot, III, 180; Cecil Roth, *History of the Marranos,* Phila. 1932, 101; *A.Z.* 20b. See also Rabbinowicz, 11; Landshuth, p. xxx; Bender, 106 ff.; Güd. I, 210; Grimm, III, 408, 422; Wuttke, 465; Samter, 83 ff.; Sartori, *Ztschr. Ver. f. Volksk.,* XVIII (1908), 362 f.; Seligmann, op. cit., 104.

51. Landshuth, p. liii; *Toledot Adam veḤavah,* 28:1, p. 182b; *Testament of Judah,* §8; *Rokeaḥ,* loc. cit.; *Joseph Omez,* 326; Isserles, *Yore Deah* 358:3;—*San.* 20a; Rabbinowicz, 31; *Tashbez,* 447; *Joseph Omez,* 327; *Yore Deah* 359:1; *Yesh Noḥalin,* 38a, n. 48; cf. *Ber.* 51a.

52. *Joseph Omez,* loc. cit.; *Mateh Moshe,* 112a; *Testament* of Shabbetai Horowitz, §3.

53. *Raben,* §11; *Kol Bo,* §114; Marmorstein, *JJV,* I (1923), 287; *Shibbole HaLeket,* §14, p. 345; *Or Zarua,* II, §422, p. 86b; *Maḥ. Vit.* 247; *Tashbez,* §447; ms. *Ez Ḥayim,* 542 (308 of original); *Rokeaḥ,* §316, p. 82b; *Responsa* of Israel Bruna, §181, p. 66b; cf. Güd. I, 211, n. 2; *JE,* XI, 599; Samter, 96, 150, 153-4; Seligmann, op. cit., 148 ff.; Grimm, III, 444, 446; Blau, 73.

54. *Toledot Adam,* 28:2, p. 182b; *Or Zarua,* loc. cit.; *Kol Bo,* loc. cit.; *Mateh Moshe,* loc. cit.; Isserles and *Lebush* on *Yore Deah* 376:4; *Kizur Shelah,* 61.

55. *Raben,* loc. cit.; *Maḥ. Vit.,* 248, §280; *Kol Bo,* loc. cit.; *Tashbez,* loc. cit.; *Maharil,* 84b; *Joseph Omez,* loc. cit.; *Mateh Moshe,* loc. cit.; *Kizur Shelah,* loc. cit.; cf. Bender, op. cit., 109 f.; Landshuth, p. lxviii; Sartori, op. cit., 368 ff.

56. *Rokeaḥ,* §313, pp. 77b, 79b; *Joseph Omeẓ,* 330;—*Yore Deah* 393:2, 3; —*Maharil,* 83; Tyrnau's *Minhagim,* 23b, n. 155; *Responsa* of Jacob Weil, 75b; *Kiẓur Shelah,* 61;—*Joseph Omeẓ,* 329, *Leket Yosher,* II, 96-7;—*Siddur Rashi,* §981, p. 281; *Shibbole HaLeket,* 353; *Maharil,* 83b-84a; *Yore Deah,* 386:1, 393:4. The custom of covering mirrors or turning them to the wall, which prevails among Jews nowadays, is not mentioned in the medieval sources, and is evidently a late borrowing. It is observed almost universally, arising, according to Frazer (*The Golden Bough,* I, 146), from the fear "that the soul projected out of the person in the shape of his reflection in the mirror, might be carried off by the ghost of the departed, which is commonly supposed to linger about the house till the burial." Cf. Bender, 117; *Ta'ame HaMinhagim,* III, 93b; Von Negelein, *AR,* V (1902), 22; Samter, 134.

CHAPTER XII

NATURE AND MAN

1. Eleazar of Worms, *Commentary on S. Yeẓirah,* 6c; *S. Ḥas. B* 1149; *Tishbi,* s. v. *bulmos;*—Güd. I, 213; *Raziel,* 15a;—*Maḥ. Vit.* 501;—Rashi on Ps. 103:5; Ginzberg, *Legends,* V, 51, n. 151; Güdemann, *Religionsgesch. Studien,* Leipzig 1876, 55-63.

2. Samson of Sens on *Kilayim* VIII, 5 (the man-plant is identified with the *adne* or *abne hasadeh* of Job. 5:23, and the *Yadu'a,* an animal employed in magic rites; Rashi, *San.* 65a), repeated in *Semag,* I, 39; ms. *Eẓ Hayim,* 991 (580 of original). See E. Fink, *MGWJ,* LI (1907), 173-82; L. Ginzberg, *A. Schwarz Festschrift* (1917), 329-33 ("Der Grundzug dieser Legende, die Pflanze, deren Berührung Tod bringt ist jüdisch und sehr alt. . . . Sehr jung dagegen und wahrscheinlich germanischen Ursprunges—findet sich daher nur bei den deutsch-französischen Autoren—ist die Umwandlung der todbringenden Pflanze in einen 'vegetabilischen Menschen,' die Raschi noch unbekannt ist"; p. 331), and *Legends,* V, 50, n. 148 and VI, 123, n. 720; cf. Thorndike, I, 597, 626, II, 142, III, 484, 566; Grimm, II, 1006 f.; Wuttke, 102-3; Frazer, *Folk-Lore in the O.T.,* II, 377 ff.

3. On the "barnacle goose" see these essays in which the literature is discussed in detail: I. Löw, *Flora,* IV, 347 ff.; Zimmels, *Minḥat Bikkurim* (Vienna 1926), 1-9; *JE,* II, 538 ff.; *JJV,* II (1925), 349; Ginzberg, *Legends,* V, 51, n. 150; cf. Jacobs, *Jews of Angevin England,* 54, 92; Thorndike, I, 491, II, 200, 386, 464-5.

4. *Shab.* 107b; *Ḥul.* 127a; *Tos. Shab.* 12a; *Rabiah,* I, 327, §236; *HaTerumah,* 80b, §217, 218; *Maḥ. Vit.* 123, §6 (cf. G. Schlessinger, *Die altfranzösischen Wörter im Machsor Vitry,* Mainz 1899, p. 35); *Raben,* 60; *Responsa* of Meir of Rothenburg (Lemberg), 160; Moses Taku, *Oẓar Neḥmad,* III, 78, 82; *Orḥot Ẓadikim,* 95a;—*Leket Yosher,* I, 104; *S. Ḥas. B* 1153; *Tashbeẓ,* 553; *Responsa* of Ḥayim Or Zarua, 146; *S. Ḥas. B* 589; *Ẓiyuni,* 48a; *Ḥochmat HaNefesh,* 14c; Rashi and *Tos. Shab.* 54b; *Or Ẓarua,* II, 19a, §83.

5. *S. Ḥas.* 1471; Thorndike, III, 34, 238.

6. *S. Ḥas.* 44, 49, 71, 798, 1161; *Rabiah,* I, 248, §197; *Maharil,* 44b; *Lev Tov,* ch. 10, p. 102b; *Oraḥ Ḥayim* 608:4. Garlic, in particular, enjoyed high repute as an aphrodisiac in the ancient world; see I. Löw, op. cit., II, 144. Maharil, loc. cit., refers to *Erdäpfel* (this was at the turn of the fifteenth cen-

tury, long before potatoes were introduced in Europe) which I have translated "melons"; see Grimm, *Deutsches Wörterbuch,* s. v.

7. Blau. 76-7; *JE,* IX, 301; *Rokeaḥ,* §317, pp. 85a, b, §318, p. 88b; *Responsa* of Meir of Rothenburg (Cremona), §124; *Lev Tov,* 101a; Isserles, *Oraḥ Ḥayim* 88:1. The concluding quotation is from *Ziyuni,* 50d; see also ibid. 50c.

8. *Nid.* 38a; *S. Ḥas.* 955, 1909; *Lev Tov,* 102b; *'Emek Beracha,* II, 52, pp. 62a-b, *Oraḥ Ḥayim,* 240:7.

9. *Nid.* 16b; *Pes.* 112b; Blau, 55, 56; *Rokeaḥ,* §317, p. 86b; *Joseph Omez,* §190, 191, p. 43.

10. *Ned.* 20a; *Sheb.* 18b; *S. Ḥas.* 952, 1908; *Lev Tov,* 100c-d; *Mizvat HaNashim,* ch. 65, 66; Grünbaum, *Jüdischdeutsche Chrest.,* 273-4, 276; *Ziyuni,* 15a.

11. *Rokeaḥ,* §317, p. 86b; *Ziyuni,* 78a; Abrahams, *Ethical Wills,* II, 209; *Mizvat HaNashim,* ch. 64; Gaster, *Ma'aseh Book,* I, 242-3, II, 648-9; cf. *Pa'aneaḥ Raza,* 133b; Thorndike, I, 177, IV, 136.

12. Ginzberg, *Legends,* V, 55, VI, 206; Scheftelowitz, *AR,* XIV (1911), 376 ff.; Krauss, *MJV,* LIII (1915), 20;—*Shab.* 111a; *Yeb.* 65b; *S. Ḥas.* 1918; —Gaster, *Studies and Texts,* III, 229-30; Güd. I, 216.

13. *Nid.* 31a; *Ber.* 60a; *Hadar Zekenim* and *Da'at Zekenim* on Ex. 1:16 and Lev. 12:2; Menaḥem Recanati, *Ta'ame HaMizvot,* 13b. and *Commentary on the Pentateuch,* beg. of *Tazri'a; Pa'aneaḥ Raza,* 87a; cf. Thorndike, II, 767.

14. *Hadar Zekenim* on Ex. 1:16; *S. Ḥas. B* 1141; *Lev Tov,* 100d; Güd. I, 212; in this last-mentioned place may be found a passage from Konrad von Megenberg which offers a striking parallel to the "signs" of Eleazar of Worms: cf. also Thorndike, I, 177, II, 329, 744, etc.

15. *Maharil,* 85a; ibid., 24b; cf. *Nid.* 27a; *Yeb.* 80b; Thorndike, III, 237, 238.

16. *Hor.* 13b; *S. Ḥas.* 1503; *Maḥ. Vit.* 720; *Tashbez,* 287, 558; *Maharil,* 86a; *Leket Yosher,* I, 45, II, 6, 15; *Joseph Omez,* pp. 45, 273, 343, 354; parallels to these beliefs may be found among other peoples, cf. I. Goldziher, "Muhammedanischer Aberglaube über Gedächtnisskraft und Vergesslichkeit, mit Parallelen aus der jüdischen Litteratur," *Berliner Festschrift,* 131-55; Grimm, III, 834, §463 and n. 1; Wuttke, 315.

17. *Maḥ. Vit.* 720; *Tashbez* 557; *S. Ḥas. Tinyana,* 11a; *Joseph Omez,* §575, p. 123; Isserles, *Oraḥ Ḥayim* 260:1; *'Emek Beracha,* II, 53, p. 64a; *Yesh Noḥalin,* 26a, n. 35; cf. Grünbaum, *Ges. Auf.,* 423, 424; Goldziher, op. cit., 133; Löw, *Die Finger,* p. xxii; *JE,* IX, 149; also *Oraḥ Ḥayim* 179:6.

18. *Maḥ. Vit.,* pp. 115-6; *Siddur Rashi,* §523, p. 261; Güd. I, 53; Grunwald, *MJV,* XIX (1906), 118; cf. Heller, *REJ,* LV (1908), 69 ff., and Krauss, ibid., LVI (1908), 253-4;—*Joseph Omez,* §73, p. 17; *Lebush* on *Oraḥ Ḥayim,* 299:10; *Kizur Shelah,* 134;—Goldziher, op. cit., 140 ff.; *HB,* VII (1864), 100, XIV (1874), 58; I. Löw, *Die Flora der Juden,* I, 203 f.

CHAPTER XIII

MEDICINE

1. See Güd. I, 197-8, 212, III, 130, 196 ff.;—Krauss, *Gesch. jüd. Ärzte,* 43, 52-3, 58-9; *JE,* VIII, 417;—Thorndike, IV, 126;—Steinschneider, *HB,* XVII (1877), 60-61; see Julius Preuss, *Biblisch-talmudische Medizin,* Berlin 1923, for the older material, and also Steinschneider, "Zur medicinischen Liter-

atur," op. cit., 56, 114, XIX (1879), 35, 64, 84, 105, 108, and L. Venetianer, *Asaf Judæus,* Strassburg 1916-7. Some physicians, in their experiments with chemistry, probably dabbled in alchemy also, but this branch of the magical arts had in general very little currency among Jews. Steinschneider says that "Hebrew literature contains remarkably little material on this subject"; I have not found any reference to or directions for the practice of alchemy in the literary works produced in Northern Europe, although Jews were popularly believed to be adepts. See G. Scholem, "Alchemie und Kabbala," *MGWJ,* LXIX (1925), 13-20, 95-110, 371-4, and LXX (1926), 202-9; R. Eisler, "Zur Terminologie u. Geschichte der jüd. Alchemie," *MGWJ,* LXIX (1925), 364-71, LXX (1926), 194-201; cf. Thorndike, I, 772-3.

2. *Leket Yosher,* II, 15, 17; *Brantspiegel,* ch. 15; *MJV,* XIX (1906), 111, 116.

3. Grimm, I, 486 f.; Ginzberg, *Legends,* III, 52-4, VI, 21-22; *HaOrah,* II, §158, pp. 230-1; *Kol Bo,* §41; Güd. I, 210, n. 6.

4. *Ber.* 43b; *Shab.* 113b and Rashi; *Teshubot HaGeonim* (ed. Musafia), §54; B. Lewin, *Otzar HaGaonim,* Haifa 1928, I, 97; *Tos. Pes.* 100b; *Rabiah,* II, 135-6; *Maḥ. Vit.* 83-4, §106; *Kol Bo,* 35a, §31; *HaManhig, Hil. Shab.,* §15; *'Emek Beracha,* II, 54, p. 65a; Strack, 58;—*Maharil,* 28a; *Kizur Shelah, In. Shab.,* p. 118;—*Pirke de R. Eliezer,* ch. 20; *Siddur Rashi,* §534, p. 267; *Maḥ. Vit.,* §150, p. 116; *HaManhig, Hil. Shab.,* §65; Tyrnau, *Minhagim,* 2a; *Oraḥ Ḥayim* 328:20;—*Rabiah,* I, 413, §383; Glassberg, 98; *Tos. A. Z.,* 29a; *Semag,* I, 45, end, and *'Amude Shlomo* on this passage; *Or Zarua,* IV, 22b, §151; *Yore Deah* 156:2; Preis, *Die Medizin in der Kabbala,* 19.

5. *Kol Bo,* §31, p. 31a; *Iggeret HaTiyul,* 6b; Thorndike, I, 728; Rivers, p. 82; the Talmudic regulations concerning phlebotomy (cf. *Shab.* 129b, etc.) were strictly adhered to during the Middle Ages.

6. *Brantspiegel,* ch. 4; Perles, *Beiträge,* 147; *S. Ḥas.* 345, 153; *Yore Deah* 179:6; cf. Thorndike, I, 654, IV, 126.

7. *M. Yoma,* VIII, 5; *Ta'ame HaMinhagim,* II, 41a (cf. *Tachkemoni,* I [Bern 1910] 71 for a similar opinion by Sherira Gaon);—Glassberg, 142; Grunwald, *MJV,* XIX (1906), 116; *Hadar Zekenim* and *Da'at Zekenim* on Gen. 32:32; *S. Ḥas. B* 59; *Nizaḥon,* 114; cf. Frazer, *The Magic Art,* I, 80 f.; Elworthy, 71.

8. Rivers, 7, 51; cf. *JE,* V, 426-7; Blau, 22-3, 55-6, etc.

9. 174.

10. *Rokeaḥ,* 221; *Tashbez,* 445; *Raben,* 271; Güd. I, 215; *Tos. Yoma* 77b; —*S. Ḥas.* 161; *Orḥot Ḥayim,* 53; *Oraḥ Ḥayim* 170:16; *Kizur Shelah,* p. 22; *Nishmat Ḥayim,* III, 27; cf. Montgomery, 89 ff., and Blau, loc. cit.

11. *S. Ḥas.* 1464.

12. *S. Ḥas. B* 1170; *Ḥochmat ḤaNefesh,* 26c.

13. Wellesz, *MJV,* XXXV (1910), 120; cf. Thorndike, I, 658-60, etc.

14. *Shab.* 67a; *Pesakim Uketabim,* 96; *Responsa* of Solomon Luria, §3; *B'er Heteb* to *Yore Deah* 179:1; *Joseph Omez,* 352.

15. *Yore Deah* 179:6; *Mordecai, Shab.* §527, p. 12d; *S. Ḥas.* 1468; cf. Thorndike, I, 582-3;—*Yore Deah* 155:1 and *Lebush;* Blau, 29; Wellesz, *MJV,* XXXV (1910), 117, 118, cites this gloss from a *Mordecai* ms. of the Paris Rabbinical School: ושמעתי שמורי הר"ר מרדכי ז"ל התיר להניח להם (לגוים) ללחוש ליודי על מכתו ואו' בשם הר"ר מנחם משפירא שאמ' כי החברות גורמים הרפואה ולא המילות לכן אין נפקותא מין אפילו אם מזכירים התלוי והקדשים.

cf. Jacobs, *Jews of Angevin England,* 153;—G. Caro, I, 136; *S. Ḥas.* 1352. Speaking of relics, it is related that "once a Gentile produced a shirt which he claimed had been worn by Jesus. 'If you don't believe me, just watch!' and he threw the shirt into a fire, but it didn't burn. The priests and monks turned to the Jews who were present and challenged them, 'Now you know that this shirt is holy.' But a Jew stepped forward with, 'Here, give it to me and I'll show you what it's all about.' Using strong vinegar and soap he scrubbed it vigorously before their eyes and then returned it, saying, 'Now throw it in the fire and see what happens.' They did so and it was instantly consumed. He then explained, 'It was smeared with a salamander extract which I washed off' " (*S. Ḥas.* 1809). The belief that the salamander was invulnerable to fire was very widespread in the Middle Ages, cf. Ginzberg, *Legends,* V, 52, n. 157, 158.

16. *Pa'aneaḥ Raza* on Lev. 19:26, p. 91b; Perles, *Beiträge,* 105; on the *Bärmutter* charm see Güdemann, *MGWJ,* XXIV (1875), 271, and ibid., LX (1916), 138; Staerk, ibid., LXVI (1922), 203; Perles, *Graetz Jubelschrift,* 28; Güd. I, 216, n. 10; A. Müller, *Ztschr. f. deutsches Altertum,* XIX (1876), 476; Grimm, II, 969;—Perles, *Graetz Jubelschrift,* 28-9; *S. Has. B* 1153. On numbers in medicine see Rivers, 88 ff.

17, Grunwald, *MJV,* XIX (1906), 111, 115, 116; Steinschneider, *HB,* XVII (1877), 60-61; cf. Gaster, *Sword of Moses,* p. xiii, ll. 2, 21; Thorndike, I, 730, IV, 129; Elworthy, 401.

18. *Sheb.* 15b; *Yore Deah* 179:8, 9; ms. *S. Gematriaot,* 47a, 49a, 54b, 63a; *Shimmush Tehillim,* Ps. 3, 6, 49, 119; Grunwald, *MJV,* XIX (1906), 116; cf. also pp. 105 f. above.

19. Strack, 19; Blau, 161 f.; *Rabiah,* I, 330; *Mordecai, Shab.* §523, p. 12c; Güd. I, 216; *Kol Bo,* §31, p. 31a; *Leket Yosher,* II, 15; *Oraḥ Ḥayim* 328:20;—*S. Ḥas.* 1218; *Mordecai, Pes.* §781, p. 19a; *Responsa* of Meir of Rothenburg (ed. Budapest), §160; *Tashbeẓ,* 555; *Or Zarua,* IV, 21d; *Maharil,* 75a; *Oraḥ Ḥayim* 328:25 and 48; cf. Wellesz, *MJV,* XXXV (1910), 119; Thorndike, I, 582, IV, 134; etc.

20. *San.* 101a and Rashi; Blau, 72, n. 1; *Responsa* of Meir of Rothenburg, (Budapest), §55; cf. Krauss, *Geschichte jüd. Ärzte,* 49; E. F. Knuchel, 69;—*Rabiah,* 285, 391; *Mordecai, Shab.* §499, p. 12a, §528, p. 12d; *Responsa* of Meir of Rothenburg (Lemberg), §175; (Budapest), §512; *Tashbeẓ,* 45; *'Amude Shlomo* to *Semag,* I, 65; *Yore Deah* 179:11; Wellesz, *MJV,* XXXV (1910), 118; Güd. I, 215; Zimmels, *Beiträge,* 66; cf. Grimm, II, 974 f., III, 343, 411; Wuttke, 339 f.

21. Blau, 73; *S. Ḥas.* 1523; cf. Azulai's note to *S. Ḥas. B* 445.

22. Professor Lauterbach has written a very interesting essay on this subject, "The Naming of Children in Jewish Folklore, Ritual and Practice," *C.C.A.R. Yearbook,* XLII (1932), 316-60, in which he discusses all the material in detail. The references that apply directly to this discussion are: *R. H.* 16b; *Semag,* II, 16; Samter, 98 f., 106 f.; *S. Ḥas. B.* 244; *Responsa* of Israel Bruna, §101; *Leket Yosher,* II, 83; *Kol Bo,* 76; *S. Ḥas.* 365. See also S. W. Baron, *Sefer HaYovel Le Professor Shmuel Krauss,* Jerusalem 1937, p. 218, for an instance of a change of name during illness, on the part of an Italian Jew, to Hezekiah ("YHVH strengthens").

23. *Shab.* 66b and Rashi; *Oraḥ Ḥayim* 301:24;—*S. Ḥas.* 211; *B* 205; Güd. I, 208, n. 1; Perles, *MGWJ,* XXIX (1880), 333; Glassberg, 139 and Introd. p. xix; Ducange, s. v. "boucage"; Grimm, II, 1016, III, 359; Wuttke, 105; Berliner, *Aus dem Leben,* 134.

24. Güd. I, 215;—*San.* 47b; *Raben,* 230d; *Yore Deah,* 368:1; cf. Seligmann, *Mag. Heil- u. Schutzmittel,* 149 ff.;—Gaster, *Studies and Texts,* III, 229-

30; *Shimmush Tehillim*, Ps. 19; cf. Samter, 145 f., 214; Seligmann, op. cit., 151 ff.; Wuttke, 89 f.

25. Güd. I, 214;—*Maharil*, 18b; Isserles, *Oraḥ Ḥayim* 453:1; cf. *Shimmush Tehillim*, Ps. 13; Krauss, op. cit., 49;—Grunwald, *MJV*, XIX (1906), 117; cf. Gaster, op. cit., III, 229. See also I. Löw, *Die Flora der Juden*, IV, 341 ff.

CHAPTER XIV

DIVINATION

1. Cf. *Niẓaḥon*, 57, 145; Eleazar of Worms, *Commentary on S. Yeẓirah*, 14c; *S. Ḥas.* 14, 391, 1950; *B* 33.

2. *Hochmat HaNefesh*, 7a, 25b f., 33c-d; Eleazar of Worms, *Commentary*, 21d-22a; *Torat Ha'Olah*, II, 2-3; *Orḥot Ẓadikim*, 94b ff.; Ginzberg, *Legends*, V, 64, n. 4; Franck, 190 f.; Ginsburg, 156.

3. Cf. *San.* 65b; *Ḥul.* 95b and the comments of Rashi and *Tos.;* these two passages were frequently repeated by the medieval writers, who, following Talmudic precedent, distinguished between the innocent "signs" fixed by Eliezer (Gen. 24:14) and Jonathan (I Sam. 14:9-10), and the taking of omens; cf. also *Hagahot Maimuniot* to *Hil. 'Akkum* 11:5. See Marmorstein, *JJV*, II (1925), 362 ff. for the Aggadic material. *Lebush* on *Yore Deah* 179:4 sums up the medieval view.

4. *Hochmat HaNefesh*, 25d; *S. Ḥas.* 14. Grimm, III, 411, quotes from a 14th century German ms., "du solt nit globen an zober . . . noch an die brawen un der wangen iucken"; see also II, 934 f.

5. *JE*, II, 255; Berliner, *Aus dem Leben*, 95; Marmorstein, *JJV*, II (1925), 372. A report that in the year 545, during a plague in Constantinople, every one who sneezed immediately died, was cited by a late writer to point the moral of responding "health!" to a sneeze (Grunwald, *JJV*, I [1923], 219); cf. Grimm, III, 430; Thorndike, II, 330; etc.;—*Ber.* 24b; *Oraḥ Ḥayim* 103:3; etc.

6. *JE*, IV, 632; *S. Ḥas. B* 1145, 1146; *Ẓiyuni*, 27b; *S. Ḥas.* 764; etc.; cf. Grimm, III, 450, §493; Wuttke, 33: "Die Hunde kündigen durch ihr Heulen einen Todesfall an u. sehen den Tod." Longfellow (*Golden Legend*, VIII, "The Village School") has put this belief into verse (cf. *B. K.* 60b):

> In the Rabbinical book it saith,
> The dogs howl when, with icy breath,
> Great Sammaël, the Angel of Death,
> Takes through the town his flight!

Güd. I, 201, n. 2;—*Ẓiyuni*, 49a, 75b; *Nishmat Hayim*, III, 22; Marmorstein, *MGWJ*, LXXI (1927), 44-5;—*Testament of Judah*, §50; *Orḥot Ẓadikim*, 95b (cf. *Suk.* 28a and Joel, II, 53 f.).

7. Grimm, II, 937 ff.; Wuttke, 208; Digot, III, 181; *Brantspiegel*, ch. 66, p. 105c; *Joseph Omeẓ*, 348; Berliner, op. cit., 83; cf. *San.* 65b-66a and Rashi.

8. *Raziel*, 20b-21a.

9. *Yoma* 88a; *S. Ḥas.* 1545; *Maharil*, 45b; *Responsa* of Maharil, 83a-b, etc.;—*Joseph Omeẓ*, 278; *S. Ḥas.* 395; Blau, 149; *S. Ḥas. B* 59; cf. Digot, III, 177; Grimm, III, 467, §889.

9a. *Kol Bo*, 41; *Lev Tov*, 6:66, p. 63c; Isserles, *Oraḥ Ḥayim* 296:1;—*Ker.* 6a; *Hor.* 12a; *Teshubot HaGeonim*, ed. Musafia, p. 7; *Mordecai*, beg. *Yoma;*

S. Ḥas. B 59; *Kol Bo,* 64; *Or Ẓarua,* II, 257, p. 60c; *HaManhig, Hil. Rosh. Hashanah,* 1; Isserles, *Oraḥ Ḥayim* 583:1, 2; *Shelah,* II, 145a; *'Emek Beracha,* II, 61, p. 75a; Güd. III, 136. The custom of eating special foods on *Rosh Hashanah* for their good influence upon the future was probably originally a reflection of Roman usage; it is found in medieval and modern Germany, perhaps derived from the Jewish practice, cf. Krauss, *MJV,* LIII (1915), 11; Güd. III, 131, n. 2; Scheftelowitz, *AR,* XIV (1911), 387-8; Wuttke, 65.

10. *S. Ḥas.* 1473.

11. Cf. Thorndike, II, 605, for the views of Thomas Aquinas; Grimm, I, 77 f., II, 927 ff.; *S. Ḥas.* 1139, 1450; even so enlightened a man as Mordecai Jaffe (16th century), who denounced most of the methods of divination as "vain and false things that have no reality," was obliged to admit that "astrologers and lot-casters sometimes disclose the truth"; see his *Lebush* on *Yore Deah* 179:1; see Blau, 45 f., for the Talmudic material.

12. *Horayot* 12a; *S. Ḥas.* 1516; *Mateh Moshe,* §849; cf. Grimm, III, 445, §325, 448, §421.

13. *Rokeaḥ,* §221, p. 50b; *Ḥochmat HaNefesh,* 14a; Naḥmanides on Nu. 14:9, and *Pa'aneaḥ Raza,* ad loc.; *S. Ḥas.* 1544; Güd. I, 206, n. 3; *Kol Bo,* §52; *Ẓiyuni,* 61d-62a; Marmorstein, *MGWJ,* LXXI (1927), 45; Tyrnau, *Minhagim,* 28b, §216; Isserles, *Oraḥ Ḥayim* 664:1; *Mateh Moshe,* §957; *Joseph Omeẓ,* 233, §1051; *Yalkut Reubeni,* 10d; cf. Elworthy, 78 f.; Von Negelein, *AR,* V (1902), 19; Digot, III, 182; Grimm, III, 436, §55; Wuttke, 221; Löwinger, *MJV,* XXXIV (1910), 53.

14. *Ḥochmat HaNefesh,* 24a; Güd. I, 206, n. 4; *Ẓiyuni,* 62a; *S. Ḥas.* 1516 and *B* 547; cf. Daiches, 26, 27; Grimm, III, 416; Jacob Weil (*Responsa,* §191, p. 64a, §192, p. 65b) wondered why "some people recite the *Vidduy* ('Confession') under water" on the eve of *Yom Kippur;* perhaps this was connected with the divinatory act.

15. *S. Ḥas.* 1059 and note; Ginzberg, *Legends,* V, 61, n. 310; *Ẓiyuni,* 64c.

16. *Ḥag.* 15a, b; *Git.* 58a; *Ḥul.* 95b; *Yore Deah* 179:4 and *Lebush,* ad loc.; —*S. Ḥas.* 285;—Berliner, op. cit., 24; Güd. III, 140, n. 1; *JE,* III, 202; Wuttke, 144; Steinschneider, *Heb. Uebersetz.,* 868, n. 120.

17. Thorndike, II, 266 f., IV, 190; De Givry, 249 ff., 256 ff.;—Ginsburg, 111-8; Franck, 183; Bischoff, 67 ff.;—Joel, II, 12; Güd. I, 219, n. 2; *Orḥot Ẓadikim,* 95b; *Joseph Omeẓ,* §180, p. 41; *Kol Bo* §41 (cf. *Teshubot HaGeonim,* ed. Musafia, §49).

18. *Semag,* I, §52; *Pa'aneaḥ Raza,* 128a; *Hadar Ẓekenim* on Deut. 18:10; *Nishmat Ḥayim,* III, 19; ms. *Eẓ Ḥayim,* 992 (581 of original); according to Grimm, III, 321, the Germans also used this device: "Losse mit schwarzen und weissen Stäbchen wurden von Slaven gebraucht"; Steinschneider, op. cit., 867 ff.; *HB,* VI (1863), 121-2; *Cat. Munich,* §235; cf. also ibid. §228,8; 294,3; 299,5; and Grimm, II, 929-30, III, 321; Güd. III, 139-40.

19. *Ḥochmat HaNefesh,* 30d-31a; cf. *Eshkol HaKofer,* by Judah Hadassi, ch. 31.

20. Thorndike, II, 110 ff.; ms. *Eẓ Ḥayim,* loc. cit.; *Toledot Adam veḤavah,* 17:5, p. 127b; cf. Albo's *Ikkarim,* IV, 4, and especially Husik's note, IV, 30.

21. *Shimmush Tehillim,* Ps. 16; Grunwald, *MJV,* XIX (1906), 108; Perles, *Graetz Jubelschrift,* 34; ms. *Raziel,* 21b f., 47a ff., ed. of Amsterdam 1701, 34b.

22. *Joseph Omeẓ,* 350; Grunwald, op. cit., 109; Perles, op. cit., 35 (cf. Gaster, *Sword of Moses,* 39, §65).

23. Lea, III, 422-3, 436; Thorndike, II, 168, 320, 365; Grimm, III, 432; *Mélusine,* II (1884), 483; Elworthy, 443 f.; Summers, 184-5; Daiches, *Babylonian Oil Magic in the Talmud and in the later Jewish Literature,* London 1913.

24. *San.* 101a and Rashi; cf. Daiches, op. cit., 7 ff.; Rashi, Gen. 42:14.

25. Güd. I, 208-9, n. 1, and Grunwald, *MGJV*, V (1900), 80-81. There are some minor differences between these two readings of the text; I have left the word which Grunwald reads as "Gerte" untranslated; Güdemann could not make it out. Grunwald took it to be the German word for "rod," that is, the hazel-rod which the Germans regarded as holy and which served so often as the magician's wand. But since the text speaks of no "rod" the word is best left in its obscurity. Passages in Dr. Johann Hartlieb's book on forbidden sciences, written in 1455, are strikingly similar to the text here translated: When the reflective medium (of which Hartlieb mentions several) has been prepared, "darnach nimbt er ain rain kind, und setzt das uf ainen schönen stul [elsewhere he writes, "etlich maister . . . setzen das kind in ir schoss'] . . . so stat der zaubermaister hinder im und spricht im etliche unerkante wort in die oren . . . und haisst im das rain kint die wort nachsprechen . . . so haisst er in sehen was er sech . . . darnach fragen sie den knaben, ob er icht sech ainen engel? wan der knab spricht ja, so fragen sie was varb er anhab? spricht der knab rott, so sprechen die maister ie, der engel ist zornig, und bäten aber mer . . . wan dan der tiüfel bedunkt, das er dienst genüg hab, so lasst er erscheinen den engel in weiss, so ist den der maister fro . . . so fragt er dan so lang bis er sicht puchstaben. die selben puchstaben sambent dan der maister und macht daruss wort, so lang bis er hat darnach er gefragt hat." Grimm, III, 428, 431-2; cf. alo Güd. III, 130-1. It might almost seem from these selections that one is a copy of the other, or that both are derived from a common source. It is probable, however, that they are independent accounts of a rite whose details were fixed and unvarying. The versions from late Oriental, North African and Spanish Jewish mss. which Daiches (14 ff.) printed differ very little from the medieval accounts. Rashi, in the eleventh century (*San.* 67b), mentions that a black-handled knife is required in invoking the "princes of the thumbnail"; three mss. from Spain, Tunis and the Orient, dating from the 16th to the 18th centuries (Daiches, 14, 18, 22), do not fail to include the black-handled knife! So tenacious and unalterable were the elements of the magic act! Other references to this method of divination are to be found in: *Ḥochmat HaNefesh,* 16d, 18a, 20c, 28d, 29a; *Ẓiyuni,* 10c; *Redak* on Ezek. 21:26; *Nishmat Ḥayim,* III, 19.

26. *Lev Tov,* 6:141, p. 69d; *Merdecai, B. K.* §227, p. 48a; *Responsa* of Meir of Rothenburg (ed. Budapest) §498; *Tashbeẓ,* §580; cf. *Yore Deah* 179:16. Daiches (p. 32) has suggested that the custom of looking at the nails during *Habdalah,* as well as other practices affecting finger-nails, may be connected with the frequent evocation of the "princes of the nail." The ceremony of looking at the nails can by no means be regarded as an act of onychomancy, as finger-nail divination is called (cf. Güd., *MGWJ,* LX [1916], 137). However, the late practice of enclosing the thumb within the other fingers during the course of this rite (cf. *Ta'ame HaMinhagim,* I, §415, p. 53a) may have been influenced by the belief that the "princes" inhabit the thumbnail in particular, since this nail was most often used in divination, and the finger should therefore be hidden from view. A medieval ms., giving directions for throwing lots, warns that one should not hold them with the thumb, "because demons, called 'princes of the thumb,' have power over that finger" and will defeat the purpose of the lot-caster; Steinschneider, *HB,* VI (1863), 121; cf. *Oraḥ Ḥayim* 179:6.

27. Thorndike, III, 429, II, 365 and I, 239; Grimm, III, 431.

28. See the references cited at the end of note 25.

29. Blau, 53; *S. Ḥas. B* 1132;—Ginzberg, *Legends,* VI, 237; *San.* 65b and Rashi; Rashi on I Sam. 28:12; *Pa'aneaḥ Raza* on Lev. 19:30, p. 91b; *Lev. R.* ch. 26; cf. also *Nishmat Ḥayim,* III, 7.

30. *San.* 65b; *S. Ḥas.* 324; N. Brüll, *Jahrbücher,* IX (1889), 39-40; *Yereim,* 90; *Yore Deah,* 179: 14 and comment of *Lebush;* J. Hansen, 208; *Ẓiyuni,* 10c.

31. *Ẓiyuni,* 10d, 55a; ms. *Ez Ḥayim,* 990-1, 994 (579 f. and 582 of original); ms. *Raziel,* 24b f.; cf. *San.* 65b, which speaks of spending the night on a grave "so that a spirit of uncleanness may rest on one"; Rashi interprets this "the spirit of the grave." Myrtle, hazel and hawthorn are the woods favored in magic, and most often prescribed for the indispensable magician's staff, the divining-rod, the witches' broomstick, etc.; cf. Summers, 121; Samter, 73 f.; A. Marmorstein, *The Doctrine of Merits in Old Rabbinical Literature,* London 1920, p. 18, n. 61.

32. Perles, *Graetz Jubelschrift,* 32-4; Grunwald, *MGJV,* V (1900), 79 ff.; Güd. II, 333-7; see also Perles, op. cit., 36 and Grimm, II, 813 ff. for German parallels. Prof. Ginzberg considers the only parallel in older Jewish literature to be the account of the raising of Joseph's coffin by Moses (see his *Legends,* III, 5 f.).

33. Perles, op. cit., 34.

34. *Raziel,* 6b; Grunwald, op. cit., 81.

35. *JE,* IX, 427 f; Graetz, *History* (Hebrew ed.) IV, 108; *S. Ḥas.* 1369, 172; see also Neubauer and Stern, 67.

36. Strack, 49; Wuttke, 209; Thorndike, IV, 404;—*S. Ḥas. B* 1143; *Nishmat Ḥayim,* III, 3; *Joseph Omez,* 351;—*S. Ḥas.* 291; Gaster, *Exempla of the Rabbis,* §391, p. 150; G. A. Kohut, "Blood Test as Proof of Kinship in Jewish Folklore," *Journal Amer. Or. Soc.,* XXIV (1903), 129-44; according to Franz M. Goebel (*Jüdische Motive im Märchenhaften Erzählungsgut,* Gleiwitz 1932, pp. 160 ff.) the legend of the blood-test in German folklore was derived from Jewish sources. The sympathy that prevails between close relations is further exemplified by the fact that when one twin is in pain, the other also suffers (*Ḥochmat HaNefesh,* 30c).

37. *Leket Yosher,* II, 50; Güd. III, 145; Berliner, *Aus dem Leben,* 93.

38. Scherer, 182, §20, 305 ff.; Jacobs, *Jews of Angevin England,* 176, 233; Abrahams, *Jewish Life in the Middle Ages,* 377; *MGWJ,* X (1861), 264-5; Zunz, *Zur Geschichte,* 173 f.

CHAPTER XV

DREAMS

1. Cf. Thorndike, I, 123; Güd. I, 81-2; *Semag,* Introd.; Gross, *Gallia Judaica,* 20; *Nishmat Ḥayim,* Introd.; see *JE,* IV, 654 ff. and A. Kristianpoller, "Traum und Traumdeutung," *Monumenta Talmudica,* IV, for the Biblical and Talmudic data on dreams; Bischoff, 63 ff., 158 ff.

2. *Or Zarua,* IV, 27d, §200; *Tashbez,* §352; *Mordecai, B.K.* §2, p. 40c and Introd. to Krakau ed. of *She'elot Uteshubot min HaShamayim* (see also *Shelah,* II, 201a); ibid., Livorno 1818 and Krakau 1895; *HB,* XIV (1874), 131; Malter, *Dreams,* 201-2; Güd. I, 81, n. 5; Löwinger, *Der Traum,* 20; Simon Duran (d. 1444) defended at length the reliability of dreams even in questions of strict science, as medicine and mathematics. Many questions in the science of medicine, he asserted, have been solved in dreams by the famous physicians Galen, Ibn Zohr, and others (Malter, op. cit., 203); cf. also Isidore Epstein, *The Responsa of Rabbi Simon b. Zemah Duran,* London 1930, 23 f., 39, 99.

3. Löwinger, op. cit., 6; the provision that a dream ban can be loosed only

by ten men is found in the Talmud, *Ned.* 8a; cf. *Leket Yosher,* II, 80; *Pitron Ḥalomot,* III, 3, p. 101; Löwinger, 34. The same provision affecting a dream vow was ascribed to the Geonim: *Kol Bo,* 109d; *Yore Deah,* 210:2.

4. Thorndike, II, 605; *Ber.* 57b; *S. Ḥas.* 382, 1138; *Leket Yosher,* I, 41; *Pitron Ḥalomot,* Introd., p. 3, and I, 2, pp. 14 ff.; cf. also *S. Ḥas.* 634, 1522, etc.; *Nishmat Ḥayim,* III, 5.

5. *S. Ḥas.* 382; *Ẓiyuni,* 20a; *Nishmat Ḥayim,* loc. cit.; cf. also Löwinger, op. cit., 8, for a similar opinion of Saadia. The *spiritus* theory of dreams was popular in Europe, cf. Thorndike, II, 298.

6. *Ẓiyuni,* loc. cit.

7. Ibid., 19d; *Ḥochmat HaNefesh,* 4a-b, 6b; *S. Ḥas. B* 1131;—Raben, 26; *Responsa* of Ḥayim b. Isaac Or Zarua, §164; Löwinger, op. cit., 20; *Ma'aseh Book,* II, 517, cf. *Shab.* 152a, b; *Ta'anit* 24b; *S. Ḥas.* 591, etc.

8. *Ḥag.* 5b; *Nishmat Ḥayim,* loc. cit.

9. Rashi, *San.* 30a and *Yeb.* 24b; *S. Ḥas.* 382, 1550; *Ḥochmat HaNefesh,* 4a-b, 6b; *Orḥot Ẓadikim,* 63a; cf. Hai Gaon's remark (*Ta'am Ẓekenim,* 58): "Concerning what you have said, that every man has his own genius of dreams who appears as an old man to one, as a youth to another, we have heard that this is so, but we have not ourself beheld such an apparition, nor have we spoken with anyone who has."

10. *S. Ḥas.* 382; *Ma'aseh Rokeaḥ,* §130, p. 31; *Nishmat Ḥayim,* III, 27. Similar explanations of the causes of dreams are to be found in medieval Christian works; see Thorndike, II, 412, where the theories of Bartholomew of England (13th century) are given; he believed that dreams are produced by divine inspiration, by angelic administration, by diabolic illusion, or by natural and bodily causes. See also Löwinger, op. cit., 8, and *Pitron Ḥalamot,* I, 1:1, pp. 6-7, for slightly different analyses of the causes of dreams, and Thorndike, I, 358, for the view of Philo Judæus.

11. *S. Ḥas.* 382, 383; *J. Maaser Sheni,* 55c; *Ber.* 55b (cf. Bacher, "Une Ancienne Altération de Texte dans le Talmud," *REJ,* XXVII [1893], 141 ff.), *Ber.* 55a; *S. Ḥas.* 1189, 1522; *Maḥ. Vit.,* 48.

12. *Pitron Ḥalomot,* I, 7, pp. 43 ff.; *Tos. Ber.* 55b; *She'elot Uteshubot min HaShamayim,* §22; *S. Ḥas.* 389; *B* 440. According to Tyrnau, *Minhagim,* 22a, §133, Meir of Rothenburg was "expert in interpreting dreams."

13. Lea, III, 447; Thorndike, II, 162, 290 ff.; Steinschneider, "Das Traumbuch Daniels und die Oneirokritische Litteratur des Mittelalters," *Serapeum,* XXIV (1863), 193-201, 209-16; *JE,* I, 433; *Pitron Ḥalomot,* Introd. to Part II, p. 56.

14. *Pitron Ḥalomot,* pp. 6, 57-8, 82.

15. Löwinger, op. cit., 29 ff.; *Ber.* 56b-57b. See *Pitron Ḥalomot,* Part II; for Christian parallels see De Givry, 324; Thorndike, II, 290 ff., IV, 303, etc.; Grimm, II, 958 f.

16. Ms. *Ez Ḥayim,* 264-6 (141-2 of original); *Ḥochmat HaNefesh,* 8b-c; cf. *S. Ḥas.* 180, 1550, 1563, etc.

17. On this and the following paragraphs see *Pitron Ḥalomot,* I, 3, 5, 6, 8; *Ḥochmat HaNefesh,* loc. cit.; *HaḤayim,* II, 6; as to the determination of the reliability of dreams according to the time of night, see *Ber.* 55b; *S. Ḥas.* 390, 958; *Ḥochmat HaNefesh,* 4b; Löwinger, op. cit., 8-9; Thorndike, II, 330, III, 554.

18. I Sam. 28:6; Löwinger, op. cit., 22; *Ta'am Ẓekenim,* 57-8 and Introd. to Krakau ed. of *She'elot Uteshubot min HaShamayim,* p. 3;— *S. Ḥas.* 211, 80; Güd. I, 207, n. 4; *She'elot,* etc., §9; *Maharil,* 63b; cf. also *S. Ḥas. B* 949; A. Neubauer, *REJ,* XII (1886), 92.

19. *S. Ḥas.* 1723; *Testament of Judah,* §9; *Rokeaḥ,* §316, p. 83a; *Yereim,* §90; *Yore Deah,* 179:14; *S. Ḥas.* 324; Grimm, III, 425, ll. 237 ff.

20. *S. Ḥas.* 1556.

21. Ibid., 1456.

22. A. Marx, *Proceedings Amer. Acad. for Jewish Research,* IV (1932-3), 153; *She'elot,* etc., §5, 3, etc.; *Shimmush Tehillim,* passim; ms. *S. Gematriaot,* 68a, 75a; *Nishmat Ḥayim,* III, 6; Löwinger, op. cit., 23 f.

23. *Responsa* of Meir of Rothenburg, §5 (ed. Berlin 1891); Grunwald, *MGJV,* V (1900), 82; *Raziel,* 40a-b; ibid., 33b, 40a, 3a-b; cf. also Grunwald *MJV,* XIX (1906), 106, 108.

24. *Siddur Rashi* §429, p. 214; *Maḥ. Vit.,* §78, p. 47; *Mateh Moshe,* 397, 401; *Kiẓur Shelah, Inyane Shabbat,* p. 130; see also *S. Ḥas.* 1522.

25. *S. Ḥas.* 1523; *Ḥochmat HaNefesh,* 8b; ms. *Eẓ Ḥayim,* 264 (141 of original).

26. *Shab.* 11a; *Pitron Ḥalomot,* III, 1:1, pp. 82-3; Issarles, *Oraḥ Ḥayim* 429:2; *Leket Yosher,* I, 41, 42; *S. Ḥas.* 1521; cf. also *Tashbeẓ,* 3; *Raben,* 179; *S. Ḥas.* 281; *Oraḥ Ḥayim* 220:2; *JE,* V, 348; Löwinger, op. cit., 32 f.

27. *Pitron Ḥalomot,* III, 1:2, pp. 83-4.

28. *Mordecai, Shab.* §318, 321, p. 8b; *Maharil,* 37a;—Tyrnau, *Minhagim,* 15a, 32a; *Leket Yosher,* I, 41; *Mateh Moshe,* 760; *Joseph Omeẓ,* 944, p. 210; *Shelah,* II, p. 7b (*Mas. Shabbat*); cf. *Oraḥ Ḥayim* 288:5; *S. Ḥas.* 1776.

29. *Ber.* 31b; *Maharil,* 2b, 27b, 36a, b; *Responsa* of Marahil, §168, p. 72a; *Leket Yosher,* I, 42, 104, 124; Tyrnau, *Minhagim,* 23a, 25b, 32a; *Oraḥ Ḥayim* 288:4, 418:1, 5, 597:3; cf. *S. Ḥas.* 281, 287.

30. *Ber.* 55a; Löwinger, loc. cit.; ms. *Eẓ Ḥayim,* 263 (140 of original) cites the three-fold repetition attributed to R. Isaac, which is also found in *Tos. Ber.* 55a and *Maḥ. Vit.* 48; *Leket Yosher* I, 24, 42; *Toledot Adam veḤavah* 13:2, p. 83c; *Pitron Ḥalomot,* III, 2:1, pp. 93-5; cf. also *Mateh Moshe,* 368.

CHAPTER XVI

ASTROLOGY

1. Thorndike, II, 973, IV, 317; Maimonides, *Mishneh Torah, 'Akkum,* 11, 8; *Nishmat Ḥayim,* III, 21; Moses of Tachau lent his support to this Maimonidean position in his anti-Maimonidean polemic (*Oẓar Neḥmad,* III, 82), and severely criticized "those men to whom the spirit of *Torah* is foreign, who busy themselves with astrology and believe in it and make it their creed, and thereby bring harm to others." See *JE,* II, 243 ff. and *EJ,* III, 578 ff., for a general survey of the rabbinic material. The use of the word *mazal,* "star," "constellation," to signify "luck" may be seen in the Talmud; in the Middle Ages it was more frequent. "We call good fortune, good *mazal,* and the reverse, bad *mazal* . . . in German it is *Glück* and in Italian *ventura*" (Levita, *Tishbi,* s. v. *mazal*). This usage of the word did not displace its astrological sense in the vernacular until modern times.

2. The literature is too extensive to be cited in full. See D. Feuchtwang, "Der Tierkreis in der Tradition und im Synagogenritus," *MGWJ,* LIX (1915), 241-67; L. Löw, *Gesammelte Schriften,* II, 115-31; *JE,* II, 241-5; A. Marx, "The Correspondence between the Rabbis of Southern France and Maimonides about Astrology," *HUCA,* III (1926), 311-58; A. Z. Schwarz, "Iggeret R.

Abraham b. Ḥiya HaNassi," *Ad. Schwarz Festschrift*, Berlin 1917, 23 ff. (Hebrew section); "Beraita de Mazalot," *Oẓar Midrashim*, ed. S. A. Wertheimer, Jerusalem 1913, pp. 1-7 (Introd.) and 1-28 (from which *Raziel* seems to have borrowed extensively); Abraham b. Hiya HaNassi, *Megillat HaMegaleh*, ed. Julius Guttman, Berlin 1924; Raphael Levy, *The Astrological Works of Abraham ibn Ezra*, Paris 1927; Bischoff, 124 ff.; see also pp. 69 f., 208 above. Some of the more important references are: *Shab.* 156a-b and Rashi, *M.K.* 28a; *Teshubot HaGeonim* (ed. Harkavy) 206 ff.; *S. Ḥas.* 989, 1447, 1453, 1516; Eleazar of Worms, *Commentary on S. Yeẓirah*, 14c; *Niẓaḥon*, 145; *HaḤayim*, I, 3, III, 6, IV, 10; Isserles, *Yore Deah*, 179:2; *Neḥmad veNa'im*, §298, 303, which enumerates the cities and countries governed by each Zodiacal sign. See also Thorndike I, 306, 353 f., II, 6, 42, 183, etc. According to one view, God "appointed" a star for each man before even the earth was created; *Raziel*, 21a; Eleazar of Worms, op. cit., 1b; Kammelhar, 41. As was pointed out in the chapter on angelology, the stars were personalized by associating angels with them, so that each planet had its own archangel, and each man "an angel of his star." See the references there cited, and also Rashi, *Meg.* 3a; *Ḥochmat HaNefesh*, 8c, 16d; *Pa'aneaḥ Raza* on Ex. 13:3, p. 73b; Yom Tob Mühlhausen, *HaEshkol* (ed. Judah Kaufman), 145.

3. Cf. Ginzberg, *Legends*, V, 164; *Raziel*, 17b, 34b; Eleazar of Worms, *Commentary on Sefer Yeẓirah*, 12a; Montgomery, 97-8; Thorndike, II, 900.

4. Eleazar of Worms, loc. cit.

5. *Suk.* 29a; *S. Ḥas. B* 1148, 66;—Neubauer and Stern, 65, 76; Kammelhar, 14;—Thorndike, IV, 413 f.; *Leket Yosher*, II, 17-18; Güd. III, 128-9; cf. *Neḥmad veNa'im*, §295, 297.

6. *Raziel*, 17b ff., 34b, 41b; *S. Ḥas.* 1549; Eleazar of Worms, op. cit., 8d ff., 20c ff.; *Ḥochmat HaNefesh*, 17b; *Rokeaḥ*, 353; *HaḤayim*, V, 6; *Iggeret HaTiyul*, 8a, 9a-b; *Or Ḥadash*, 15; Grunwald, *MJV*, XIX (1906), 109-10; Güd. I, 154; Thorndike, I, 113, 679, II, 582 ff., etc.; Wuttke, 58 ff.; cf. *Neḥmad veNa'im*, §8, 98, 107, 301.

7. Ibid., §299; Rashi, *Shab.* 75a; *Raziel*, 20a-b; ms. *S. Gematriaot*, 84a; Eleazar of Worms, *Commentary*, 12a; *MGJV*, VIII (1901), 114; ms. *S. Gematriaot*, 84b; cf. Wuttke, 63; Grünbaum, *Ges. Auf.*, 227; Thorndike, III, 103 ff.

8. *Shab.* 129b and Rashi;—*Kol Bo* 58; *Tashbeẓ*, 554; *Responsa* of Jacob Weil, 74b; Tyrnau, *Minhagim*, 28a; *Mateh Moshe*, 965; *Joseph Omeẓ*, §739, p. 165; *Lebush* on *Yore Deah*, 116:5;—*Rabiah*, I, 348-9; *Raben*, 371; *B'er Heteb* on *Yore Deah* 116:6;—*Yore Deah* 179:2 and the comment of *Lebush*; *Joseph Omeẓ*, 349; Eleazar of Worms, *Commentary*, 21d; a 16th century ms. (N. Brüll, *Jahrbücher*, IX [1889], 5) accounts for the prejudice against beginning undertakings on Monday and Wednesday on the ground that *bed* (the two Hebrew consonants which designate these days) in Persian signifies "bad," but this explanation is far-fetched; cf. Ginzberg, *Legends*, V, 39, n. 109. Parallels to this Monday-Wednesday superstition may be found in German belief (see Berliner, *Aus dem Leben*, 90-1): "Montags Anfang hat keinen guten Fortgang"; "Was man Montags beginnt wird nicht Wochenalt"; Grimm, III, 463, §821; see also Thorndike, I, 672 ff.; Grim, II, 953 ff.; Wuttke, 88; Steinschneider, *Ueber die Volkslitteratur*, 15-16.

9. Landsberger, "Der Brauch in den Tagen zwischen dem Pessach- und Schabuothfeste sich der Eheschliesung zu enthalten," *Jüd. Ztschr. f. Wiss. u. Leben*, VII (Breslau 1869), 81-96; I. Lévi, "Le mariage en Mai," *Mélusine*, VII (1895), 105 ff., VIII (1896), 93 f.; Abrahams, *Jewish Life in the Middle Ages*, 184; Güd. I, 276, n. 1;—*Rokeaḥ*, 355; Tyrnau, *Minhagim*, 14b; *Mateh Moshe*, 686-8; *Oraḥ Ḥayim* 493:1-4; *Leket Yosher*, I, 97-8.

10. *Ḥochmat HaNefesh*, 6b; *Commentary on S. Yeẓirah*, 9b;—*Yore Deah* 179:2; Isserles, *Eben Ha'Ezer*, 64:3; *Joseph Omeẓ*, 349; *'Emek Beracha*, II, 52, p. 62a;—*S. Ḥas. B* 59; *Semak*, 136; Grünbaum, *Jüdischdeutsche Chrest.*, 260; *Joseph Omeẓ*, 348;—*Testament of Judah*, §56, 57; *B'er Heteb* on *Oraḥ Ḥayim* 260:1; cf. Abrahams, op. cit., 185; Berliner, op. cit., 91; Digot, III, 184; Grimm, II, 595; Wuttke, 57-8.

11. *JE*, IX, 244; *'Emek Beracha*, II, 61, p. 75b; cf. Wuttke, 14: "Wenn man dem Vollmonde drei Verbeugungen macht, bekommt man etwas geschenkt"; *Kiẓur Shelah*, 136; *JE*, XII, 618; Lipez, 130 (cf. *S. Ḥas. B* 97); *Ta'ame Ha-Minhagim*, I, 55a, §432; Thorndike, IV, 282.

12. See Aptowitzer, "Issur Shetiat Mayim B'sh'at HaTekufah," *HaẒofeh*, II (1912), 122-6 and Ginzberg, "Arba' Tekufot," ibid., III (1913), 184-6, for a survey of the Jewish material; *Teshubot HaGeonim* (ed. Musafia) §14; Joel, II, 24-5; *HaManhig, Hil. Seudah*, §18; cf. Wuttke, 63 f., 78 f., 301, also 85: "Am Georgi-Tage, 23 Apr., soll niemand Brunnenwasser trinken, dann öffnet sich die Erde und lässt ihr Gift aus"; Grimm, II, 590, III, 454: "Bei Sonnenfinsterniss decke man alle Brunnen, das Wasser wird sonst giftig." Grünbaum, op. cit., 144, mentions a Coptic belief that on Midsummer Day or near it, the archangel Michael discharges a drop into the Nile which makes its water undrinkable. There is also a remark that during Nisan (the month in which the Spring Equinox occurs) a poisonous, jelly-like substance falls on vegetation (*HaPardes*, 23a).

13. Ginzberg, *Legends*, VI, 204, n. 109; Perles, *Etym. Studien*, 73; Grunwald, *MGJV*, V (1900), 84 ff.; *JJV*, I (1923), 217; *Schudt*, II, 29:13, p. 108; Güd. I, 206; Wuttke, 104. In Northern Italy the peasants went out into the fields on Midsummer Day to seek "the oil of St. John," which had wonderful properties, on oak leaves. Brück, 45 ff., suggests that the Jewish belief may be connected with the Phoenician Adonis rites, celebrated during the midsummer season at a river near the Syrian Byblos, when the river ran red with the blood of the dying god.

14. Aptowitzer, op. cit., 122, 126; *S. Ḥas.* 562; *Ẓiyuni*, 62b; *Rokeaḥ*, 275; *Mordecai, Pes.* §894, pp. 20d-21a; *Maharil*, 6b; *Leket Yosher*, I, 70; *Responsa* of Israel Bruna, §36, p. 16b; Isserles, *Yore Deah*, 116:5; *Oraḥ Ḥayim* 455:1;—*Hagahot Maimuniot, Hil. Pes.*, 458:9; Tyrnau, *Minhagim*, 8a; *Shibbole Ha-Leket*, 211, p. 171. An attempt was made to explain the use of iron on the ground that Ex. 7:19, speaking of the first plague, predicts that all the streams and all water stored "in vessels of wood and in vessels of stone" will turn to blood, omitting metal receptacles; another, Kabbalistic, explanation was that the consonants of the Hebrew word for iron, *barzel*, are the initials of Jacob's wives, Bilhah, Rachel, Zilpah, and Leah, and that these ladies protect the water against the spirits (Isserlein's supercommentary to Rashi, Ex. 7:19; Brück, 41-2). *Ẓiyuni*, 42a, has the note that "in many places they call the *Tekufah* 'Wasserkalb'"; Güdemann's suggestion (III, 130) that this ailment, dropsy ("Wassersucht, ahd. auch wazarchalp") may have been traced to the *Tekufah* is borne out by Schudt (IV, 2, p. 270): "so jemand in solchen Augenblick [of the *Tekufah*] auch nur das gerinste von Wasser trincke, so bekomt er Wassersucht und andere Kranckheiten."

15. *Testament of Judah*, 48, 49; Isserles and *B'er Heteb* on *Yore Deah*, 11:4.

16. Eleazar of Worms, *Commentary on S. Yeẓirah*, 10 ff., 15b; *Ẓiyuni*, 4c-d; *Pitron Ḥalomot*, I, 8:1; Thorndike, IV, 134 and index, s. v. "Astrological Medicine."

APPENDIX I

THE FORMATION OF MAGICAL NAMES

1. P. 21.

2. *Raziel,* 21b; *Pa'aneaḥ Raza,* 37b, note.

3. *M. Suk.* 45a; *San.* 56a; see on these Blau, 134, n. 2; Gaster, *Sword of Moses,* 12; L. Geiger, *Kebuẓat Maamarim,* ed. Poznanski, Warsaw 1910, Ginzberg's notes, pp. 394, 395.

4. Cf. Naḥmanides, Introd. to his *Commentary on the Pentateuch; Raziel,* 24a-b: וידוע שכל התורה כולה שמותיו של הקב"ה יתברך; Isaiah Horowitz (*Shelah,* III, 87a) writes: הענין נודע כי כל התורה כולה היא שמותיו ית' בצירוף אותיותיה המתפשטים לאין תכלית. According to Eleazar of Worms (*Rokeaḥ* 311), the *Kaddish* is recited after the reading of the *Torah* because every single word in the *Torah* conceals the Ineffable Name of God, and therefore each word merits the recital of the prayer which sanctifies that Name.

5. Νοταρικόν; Latin, *notaricum,* from *notarius,* "a shorthand writer," see *JE,* IX, 339 f. This exposition is derived mainly from Schwab, *Vocabulaire,* 14 ff.

6. Cf. Grunwald, *MJV,* XIX (1906), 114.

7. Cf. Grünbaum, *Ges. Auf.,* 123; Grunwald, loc. cit.; Güd. II, 336-7.

8. The etymology of this word is in doubt; see *JE,* V, 589 ff.; Schwab, *Vocabulaire,* loc. cit.; Ginsburg, *Kabbalah,* 131 ff.; Gaster, op. cit., 11 ff.; Dornseiff, 133 ff.,

9. These seven were the most frequently employed. *JE,* loc. cit., lists almost twice as many.

10. Cf. the references in note 8; a. is referred to in *Nu. R.* ch. 18, ch. 13; b. in *Shab.* 104a, *Nu. R.* ch. 18; c. in *Suk.* 52b; d. in *Shab.* 104a.

11. Ms. *S. Gematriaot,* 71a.

12. Ibid., 22a

BIBLIOGRAPHY

A.—A NOTE ABOUT THE SOURCES

Although this book is concerned primarily with the Jewish Middle Ages (c. 1000–1600),* it has been necessary to pay considerable attention to source material originating in earlier periods, particularly to the Talmud. This encyclopedia of Jewish law, customs and beliefs was accepted as the final word on all matters appertaining to Judaism, and Jewish life was deliberately patterned after its dicta. It would therefore be impossible to comprehend any phase of medieval Jewish life without giving due weight to the influence of the Talmud in shaping it.

The same is true, to a lesser degree, of the Geonic writings, especially the responsa, which were frequently accepted as authoritative. Still another type of material originating in the Geonic period is of importance for us, namely, the mystical and magical literature and inscriptions which have been edited by such scholars as Gaster, Montgomery, and others. The *Sword of Moses* has a great deal in common with the Aramaic incantation texts derived from magical bowls. This material represents the transition between Talmudic and medieval magic and superstition, and is extremely useful in tracing the process of development. Incidentally, the interesting problem of how the transference of the Greek-Egyptian magical tradition, the influence of which this material clearly displays, occurred by way of Babylonia rather than Palestine warrants investigation.

So far as the medieval sources themselves are concerned, it must be said at the outset that very few indeed have any direct bearing upon our subject. There is hardly any Jewish literature in the north of Europe devoted specifically to magic. *Sefer Raziel,* probably compiled in the thirteenth century and containing much Geonic mystical material (so potent were its contents considered that mere possession of the book was believed to prevent fires), and the anonymous *Shimmush Tehillim,* "The (Magical) Use of the Psalms," were

* See S. W. Baron, *A Social and Religious History of the Jews,* N. Y. 1937, III, 116; and Abrahams, *Jewish Life in the Middle Ages,* Introd., for a discussion of the application of the term "Middle Ages" to Jewish history.

all, besides some of the works of Eleazar of Worms and his school, such as *Ḥochmat HaNefesh,* which contain more or less pertinent material. In recent years several scholars, most notably Professor Max Grunwald of Vienna, have published extracts from manuscript works dealing with this subject, which lead one to believe that additional material of this nature is hidden away in European libraries.

A good deal of information is disclosed by the popular works on ethics and manners, of which the thirteenth-century *Sefer Ḥasidim,* attributed to Judah the Pious, is the best and most fertile example. It is a veritable mine of folklore and superstition. Other such books, as *Orḥot Ẓadikim,* Moses b. Ḥanoch's *Brantspiegel,* the several versions of the *Vrauen Büchlein,* etc., though less important, have proved informative. Collections of legends and folk-tales (e.g., Gaster's translation of the *Ma'aseh Book,* and N. Brüll's collection in the *Jahrbücher*) also reveal many beliefs and practices of the period.

Again, there are three works whose primary purpose is legalistic, but which have a degree of personal orientation, so that it is possible to glean from them much valuable information. These are Samson b. Ẓadok's *Tashbeẓ,* the *Maharil,* and Joseph b. Moses' *Leket Yosher,* which attempt to present the opinions and decisions and practices, with much personal comment, of three leading authorities, Meir b. Baruch of Rothenburg, Jacob Mölln, and Israel Isserlein, respectively. The last contains a great amount of personal and biographical material, and is therefore the most interesting and most useful for our purpose.

Most of the literature, however, is legalistic or exegetical, attempting to codify and interpret Jewish law and precepts. We may distinguish among these: 1. the large number of codes and expositions of customs (*Minhagim*), which contain many personal reminiscences and observations on current usage (such works as Isaac b. Moses' *Or Ẓarua,* Eliezer b. Nathan's *Raben,* Moses b. Jacob's *Semag,* Eliezer b. Joel's *Rabiah,* and Tyrnau's *Minhagim,* are outstanding in this respect); 2. works such as Eleazar b. Judah's *Rokeaḥ,* and *HaḤayim,* by Ḥayim b. Beẓalel, which combine ethical and legalistic subject-matter; 3. the commentaries on Bible and Talmud (notably Rashi, the *Tosafot,* Isaac b. Judah's *Pa'aneaḥ Raza, Ẓiyuni*); 4. the glosses and notes on Codes, such as Solomon Luria's *'Amude Shlomo* on *Semag* and the very important additions of Moses Isserles in the *Shulḥan 'Aruch,* as well as Mordecai Jaffe's notes thereto; 5. the codifications of matter pertaining primarily to the ritual, such as

Siddur Rashi and *Maḥzor Vitry,* the latter being especially useful; 6. and finally, the vast responsa literature, containing rabbinic decisions and opinions upon a great variety of disputes and queries relating to law, ritual, custom, morals, etc.

These works contain a great deal of valuable information, though it is far from a simple task to ferret it out. Naturally, the direct references to contemporary conditions are most significant. But they present also a perplexing problem, namely, to distinguish between mere recapitulation of old legislation and tradition, and reporting of contemporaneous practice. The mere fact that Talmudic prescription was baldly quoted is no indication that it was still observed. It is necessary, therefore, to weigh carefully internal evidence; these works, after all, were composed primarily for public use, they were not mere encyclopedic compendia. Therefore the fact that certain Talmudic material is included, while other is omitted, that certain matters are gone into in some detail, and others glossed over, that a degree of freedom is evidenced in discarding time-worn practices with the observation that they are no longer observed because of altered circumstances, that disputes arise concerning proper observance and occasional notes and anecdotes illustrate differences in observance of old customs, all help us the better to evaluate what might otherwise appear to be merely mechanical repetition of Talmudic injunctions. It must be noted, moreover, that many of the superstitious practices enumerated in Talmudic and Geonic literature are still observed today, so that we may not doubt that reference to them in the Middle Ages represents a true reflection of current observance.

There is little material of a more general nature which is of help, but the anti-Maimonidean polemic of Moses Taku, *Ketab Tamim,* the *Disputation of R. Jeḥiel,* and a few other works, contain interesting information.

I have also used some material later in date than 1600, such as the writings of the Horowitz family, the commentaries on the *Shulḥan 'Aruch,* and Menasseh b. Israel's *Nishmat Ḥayim,* as well as a few books emanating from Southern Europe (Solomon Almoli's *Pitron Ḥalomot,* Levita's *Tishbi,* Ẓedekiah b. Abraham's *Shibbole HaLeket, Kol Bo,* Menahem Recanati's works) because they reflect more or less directly upon the period and region we are studying.

Unfortunately, none of the interesting pictorial material to be found in periodicals and the encyclopedias can be definitely ascribed to our period, and I have therefore refrained from using it.

The Bibliography of Hebrew Sources includes all the Hebrew source material which has been utilized; the Bibliography of Modern Literature contains only the material which is more or less directly relevant to the study of medieval Jewish magic and superstition. Other literature referred to in the notes is fully indicated there.

B.—HEBREW SOURCES, PRINTED

Abraham b. Nathan (c. 1300), *Sefer HaManhig,* Warsaw 1885.
Alexander Süsslein HaKohen (d. 1349), *Sefer HaAgguda,* Krakau 1571.
Baruch b. Isaac (c. 1200), *Sefer HaTerumah,* Warsaw 1897.
Caro, Joseph b. Ephraim (1488–1575), *Shulḥan 'Aruch,* comprising *Yore Deah, Oraḥ Ḥayim, Eben Ha'Ezer,* and *Ḥoshen HaMishpat.*
Da'at Zekenim, Leghorn 1783.
Eleazar b. Abraham Altschul (c. 1600), *Sefer Kne Ḥochmah Kne Binah,* Krakau 1894.
Eleazar b. Judah b. Kalonymos of Worms (d. c. 1238),
Sefer HaRokeaḥ, Warsaw 1880.
Ḥochmat HaNefesh, Lemberg 1876.
Ma'ase HaRokeaḥ, Sanok 1912.
Perush al Sefer Yeẓirah, Przemysl 1883.
Sefer Ma'asim Yain HaRokeaḥ, Lublin 1608.
Sha'are HaSod veHaYiḥud veHaEmunah, in *Kochve Yiẓḥak,* XVII (1862), 7–15.
Account of persecutions in Mainz 1187–8, in Neubauer and Stern, *Hebräische Berichte,* No. 5.
Eliezer b. Joel HaLevi (d. c. 1235), *Sefer Rabiah,* ed. V. Aptowitzer, Berlin and Jerusalem 1912–1936.
Eliezer b. Nathan of Mainz (1st half 12th century), *Sefer Eben Ha'Ezer* (*Raben*), Simleul-Silvanici 1926.
Eliezer b. Samuel of Metz (d. 1198), *Sefer Yereim,* Vilna 1881.
Elijah Levita (1468–1549), *Sefer HaTishbi,* Grodno 1805.
Epstein, Jeḥiel Michel (middle 17th century), *Kiẓur Shne Luḥot Ha-Brit* (*Kiẓur Shelah*), Warsaw 1874.
Gans, David (1541–1613), *Neḥmad veNa'im,* Jessnitz 1743.
Hadar Zekenim, Leghorn 1840.
Hebrew Ethical Wills, ed. Israel Abrahams, 2 vols., Philadelphia 1926.
Horowitz, Abraham b. Shabbetai (16th century),
Yesh Noḥalin, Amsterdam 1701.
'Emek HaBeracha, Amsterdam 1729.
Brit Abraham, Lemberg 1875.

Horowitz, Isaiah b. Abraham (c. 1555–c. 1630),
Shne Luḥot HaBrit (*Shelah*), 3 vols., Lemberg 1860.
Horowitz, Shabbetai b. Israel, *Ẓevaah,* at end of *Yesh Noḥalin,* Amsterdam 1701.
Ḥayim b. Beẓalel (d. 1588), *Sefer HaḤayim,* Warsaw 1876.
Iggeret HaTiyul, Lemberg 1864.
Vikuaḥ Mayim Ḥayim, Amsterdam 1712.
Ḥayim b. Isaac Or Zarua (13th century), *Responsa,* Leipzig 1860.
Isaac b. Eliakim of Posen (16th century), *Lev Tov,* Amsterdam 1723.
Isaac b. Eliezer (15th century), *Sefer HaGan,* Diehrenfurt 1808.
Isaac b. Joseph of Corbeil (second half 13th century), *Sefer Miẓvot Katan* (*Semak*), Kopys 1820.
Isaac b. Judah HaLevi (second half 13th century), *Paʿaneaḥ Raza,* Tarnopol 1813.
Isaac b. Moses of Vienna (c. 1200–70), *Or Ẓaruaʿ,* Pt. I and II, Zitomir 1862, Pt. III and IV, Jerusalem 1887–90.
Isaac Tyrnau (14th-15th century), *Sefer Minhagim,* Warsaw 1869.
Israel Bruna (15th century), *Responsa,* Stettin 1860.
Israel Isserlein (d. 1460), *Terumat HaDeshen,* Furth 1778.
Pesakim Uketabim, Fürth 1778.
Sefer Biure Maharai, Piotrkov 1908.
Jacob HaLevi of Marvège (13th century), *She'elot Uteshubot min HaShamayim,* Livorno 1818, at end of *Responsa* of David ibn Abi Zimra (Radbaz); and
Kuntras She'elot Uteshubot min HaShamayim, ed. A. Marcus, Krakau 1895.
Jacob b. Meir Tam (1100–1171), *Sefer HaYashar,* ed. F. Rosenthal, Berlin 1898.
Jacob b. Moses Mölln (c. 1365–1427), *Sefer Maharil,* Warsaw 1874.
Responsa, Krakau 1881.
Jacob Weil (first half 15th century), *Responsa,* Hanau 1630.
Jeroḥam b. Meshullam (1st half 14th century), *Toledot Adam ve-Ḥavah,* Kopys 1808.
Joseph HaKohen (1496–1580), *ʿEmek HaBachah,* ed. M. Wiener, Leipzig 1858.
Joseph (Joslein) b. Moses (c. 1420–1488), *Leket Yosher,* ed. J. Freimann, Berlin 1903-4.
Joseph Yuspa Hahn (d. 1637), *Joseph Omeẓ,* Frankfort 1928.
Judah (Löw) b. Beẓalel (d. 1609), *Or Ḥadash,* Leipzig 1859.
Derech Ḥayim, Warsaw 1833.
Netivot ʿOlam, Zitomir 1867.
Judah b. Samuel of Regensburg (the Pious; d. 1217), *Sefer Ḥasidim* (attributed to him, but composed after his death).

Sefer Ḥasidim—Das Buch der Frommen (nach der Rezension in Cod. de Rossi, No. 1133), ed. J. Wistinetzki, 2nd ed., with Introd., etc., by J. Freimann, Frankfort 1924.

Sefer Ḥasidim, Lemberg 1863, 1867 (Bologna version).

Ẓevaat R. Jehudah HeḤasid, in above editions of *Sefer Ḥasidim.*

Judah b. Simon Ashkenazi of Tiktin (1st half 18th century), *B'er Heteb,* notes on *Shulḥan 'Aruch.*

Klausner, Abraham (2nd half 14th century), *Sefer Minhagim,* Riva di Trento 1559.

Kol Bo (14th century), Lemberg 1860.

Ma'aseh Book, trans. by Moses Gaster, 2 vols., Philadelphia 1934.

Maḥzor Vitry, ed. S. Hurwitz, Berlin 1889–1893.

Meir b. Baruch of Rothenburg (13th century),

Responsa, Cremona 1557.

Responsa, Lemberg 1860.

Sefer Sha'are Teshubot Maharam bar Baruch, ed. M. Bloch, Berlin 1891.

Responsa, ed. M. Bloch, Budapest 1895.

Sefer Maḥneh Leviyah, Livorno 1819.

Meir b. Gedaliah (Maharam) of Lublin (d. 1616), *Responsa,* Warsaw 1881.

Meir HaKohen (end 13th century), *Hagahot Maimuniot,* in editions of Maimonides' *Mishneh Torah.*

Menaḥem of Merseburg (15th century), *Nimuke R. Menaḥem,* at end of *Responsa* of Jacob Weil, Hanau 1630.

Menaḥem Recanati (Italian rabbi, 13th–14th century, frequently quotes German authorities), *Sefer Recanati,* Warsaw n. d.

Perush 'al HaTorah, Venice 1523.

Ta'ame HaMiẓvot, Basle 1581.

Menaḥem Ẓiyuni b. Meir of Speyer (middle 15th century), *Sefer Ẓiyuni,* Lemberg 1882.

Menasseh b. Israel (1604–1657), *Nishmat Ḥayim,* Leipzig 1862.

Miẓvat HaNashim, Venice 1552.

Mordecai b. Abraham Jaffe (c. 1530–1612), *Lebush,* 5 parts, Venice 1620.

Mordecai b. Hillel (13th century), *Sefer HaMordecai,* Riva di Trento 1559.

Moses b. Ḥanoch Altschul (16th century), *Brantspiegel,* Frankfort 1703.

Moses Kohen b. Eliezer (15th century), *Sefer Ḥasidim Tinyana,* Piotrkov 1910.

Moses Isserles (1530–1572), *Responsa,* Hanau 1710.

Torat Ha'Olah, Lemberg 1858.

Torat Ḥatat, Piotrkov 1903.

Notes in *Shulḥan 'Aruch.*

Moses b. Jacob of Coucy (1st half 13th century), *Sefer Miẓvot Gadol (Semag),* Kopys 1807.

Moses b. Abraham Mat (2nd half 16th century), *Mateh Moshe,* Warsaw 1876.

Moses b. Menaḥem of Prague (17th century), *Zera' Kodesh,* Fürth 1696.

Moses Minz (15th century), *Responsa,* Lemberg 1851.

Moses Taku (or of Tachau; d. c. 1290), *Ketab Tamim,* in *Oẓar Neḥmad,* III (1860), pp. 54–99.

Müller, Joel, *Teshubot Ḥachme Ẓarfat veLotir,* Vienna 1881.

Naftali Herz b. Jacob Elḥanan (16th century), *'Emek HaMelech,* Amsterdam 1648.

Nathan b. Moses Hanover (d. c. 1663), *Yeven Meẓulah,* Piotrkov 1902.
     Sha'are Ẓion, Jassy 1843.

Orḥot Ẓadikim, Königsberg 1859.

Rashi (Solomon b. Isaac) (1040–1105), Commentary on Bible and
     Talmud. Works attributed to Rashi, but composed by his
     pupils:
     Sefer HaPardes, Constantinople 1807.
     Sefer HaOrah, ed. Solomon Buber, Lemberg 1905.
     Siddur Rashi, ed. Solomon Buber, Berlin 1910–11.

Raziel HaMalach, Amsterdam 1701.

Samson b. Ẓadok (d. 1312), *Sefer Tashbeẓ,* Warsaw 1924.

Shimmush Tehillim, Sabbionetta 1551.

Solomon b. Aaron Luntschitz (d. 1619), *'Amude Shesh,* Amsterdam 1772.

Solomon b. Jacob Almoli (16th century), *Pitron Ḥalomot,* Warsaw 1879.

Solomon Luria (1510–1573), *Responsa,* Fürth 1768.
     'Amude Shlomo, at end of *Semag,* Kopys 1807.

The Sword of Moses, ed. M. Gaster, London 1896.

Teshubot HaGeonim, ed. Jacob Musafia, Lyck 1864.

Teshubot HaGeonim, ed. Abraham Harkavy, Berlin 1887.

Ta'am Ẓekenim, ed. Eliezer Ashkenazi, Frankfort 1854.

Yeḥiel of Paris, *Vikuaḥ Rabenu Yeḥiel mi Paris,* Thorn 1873.

Yom Tob b. Solomon Lipmann-Mülhausen (14th–15th century), *Sefer Niẓaḥon,* Amsterdam 1827.
     HaEshkol and *Kavvanat HaTefilah,* ed. Judah Kaufman, N. Y. 1927.

Ẓebi Hirsch Kaidanover (d. 1712), *Kab HaYashar,* Sulzbach 1805.

Ẓedekiah b. Abraham HaRofeh (Rome, middle 13th century), *Shibbole HaLeket,* ed. Solomon Buber, Vilna 1886 (contains many citations from German authorities).

C.—HEBREW SOURCES IN MANUSCRIPT

Eẓ Ḥayim, Jewish Theological Seminary Library, N. Y., modern copy of the original by Jacob b. Judah Ḥazan of London, written in 1287; see, for description, *Catalogue of Adler Mss.,* 4055–7, p. 30; D. Kaufmann, *JQR, OS,* IV (1892), 20-63, 333-44, 550-61, V (1893), 353-74, VI (1894), 754-6; S. Neubauer, ibid., VI, 348-54; and the partial edition by Hermann Adler, *Steinschneider Festschrift,* Leipzig 1896, pp. 187-208.

Sefer Gematriaot, also alternatively entitled *Sefer Eliyahu,* Jewish Theological Seminary Library, N. Y., German-rabbinic characters, 14th century; on p. 84b there is a notation that the מחזור רס"ט, the 269th calendar cycle, began in 1333, and בשנת ה' למחזור ובשנת י"ו
למחזור אנו עושים פסח חדש ימים אוג' שבועות קודם פסקווא שלהם.

Sodot HaTefilah, J.T.S. Library, bound with and in same hand as preceding; ascribed to Naḥmanides, but really by Eleazar of Worms. "This commentary is an excellent illustration of the statement of R. Jeḥiel b. Asher (quoted in *Tur Oraḥ Ḥayim,* No. 113) that the *ḥaside Ashkenaz* had the custom to count the number of words in the prayers and to investigate why this number was chosen." (A. Marx, *JQR, NS,* II [1911], 263.)

Sefer Raziel, J.T.S. Library, German-rabbinic script; does not correspond throughout with the printed text, but often contains a more complete text.

Sefer HaRazim, J.T.S. Library, ms. D 146, Italian script, 17th–18th century; pp. 1–9a correspond with 15a–30b of above ms. of *Sefer Raziel,* with interesting variations.

D.—MODERN LITERATURE

Abelson, J., *Jewish Mysticism,* London 1913.

Abrahams, Israel, *Jewish Life in the Middle Ages,* Philadelphia 1896.
Hebrew Ethical Wills, 2 vols., Philadelphia 1926.

Ahrens, W., *Hebräische Amulette mit magischen Zahlenquadraten,* Berlin 1916.

Aptowitzer, V., "Les Noms de Dieu et des Anges dans la Mezouza," *REJ,* LX (1910), 39–52, LXV (1913), 54–60.
"Tikkun Mezuzah lefi Ba'ale HaSod," *HaẒofeh,* II (1912), 100–2.
"Issur Shetiat Mayim Besha'at HaTekufah," ibid., 122–6.

Aronius, J., *Regesten zur Geschichte der Juden in fränkischen und deutschen Reiche bis zum Jahre 1273*, Berlin 1902.

Bacher, W., "Une Ancienne Altération de Texte dans le Talmud," *REJ*, XXVII (1893), 141–3.

Bamberger, M. L., "Aus meiner Minhagimsammelmappe," *JJV*, I (1923), 320–32.

Bender, A. P., "Beliefs, Rites and Customs of the Jews, Connected with Death, Burial and Mourning," *JQR, OS*, VI (1894), 317 ff., 664 ff., VII (1895), 101 ff., 259 ff.

Bergmann, J., "Zur Geschichte religiöser Bräuche," *MGWJ*, LXXI (1927), 161–171.

"Gebet und Zauberspruch," *MGWJ*, LXXIV (1930), 457–63.

Berliner, A., *Persönliche Beziehungen zwischen Christen und Juden im Mittelalter*, Halberstadt 1881.

Aus dem Leben der deutschen Juden im Mittelalter, Berlin 1900.

Bischoff, Erich, *Die Elemente der Kabbalah*, II, Praktische Kabbalah, Magische Wissenschaft, Magische Künste, Berlin 1914.

Blau, Ludwig, *Das altjüdische Zauberwesen*, Budapest 1898.

Bloch, Chayim, *The Golem*, Vienna 1925.

Bloch, Philipp, *Geschichte der Entwickelung der Kabbalah*, Trier 1894.

"Die Kabbalah auf ihrem Höhepunkt und ihre Meister," *MGWJ*, XLIX (1905), 129–66.

Brecher, Gideon, *Das Transcendentale, Magie und magische Heilarten im Talmud*, Vienna 1850.

Brück, Moses, *Rabinische Ceremonialgebräuche in ihrer Entstehung und geschichtlichen Entwickelung*, Breslau 1837.

Brüll, Adolf, "Beiträge zur Kenntniss der jüdisch-deutschen Literatur," *Jahrbücher*, III (1877), 87–119.

Brüll, N., "Beiträge zur jüdischen Sagen- und Spruchkunde im Mittelalter," *Jahrbücher*, IX (1889), 1–71.

Büchler, A., "Das Ausgiessen von Wein und Öl als Ehrung bei den Juden," *MGWJ*, XLIX (1905), 12–40.

Caro, Georg, *Sozial- und Wirtschaftsgeschichte der Juden im Mittelalter und der Neuzeit*, Vol. I, Leipzig 1908.

Casanowicz, I. M., "Jewish Amulets in the United States National Museum," *Journal of the American Oriental Society*, XXXVI (1917), 154–67.

"Two Jewish Amulets in the United States National Museum," ibid., XXXVII (1917), 43–56.

Chajes, H., "Gleibungen un Minhagim in Farbindung mitn Toyt," *Filologische Schriften*, II (1928), 281–328.

Daiches, Samuel, *Babylonian Oil Magic in the Talmud and in the later Jewish Literature*, London 1913.

Digot, Aug., *Histoire de Lorraine,* III, Nancy 1856, pp. 169–217.
Dornseiff, Franz, *Das Alphabet in Mystik und Magie,* Leipzig 1925.
Eisenstein, J. D., *Ozar Dinim Uminhagim,* N. Y. 1917.
Eisler, Robert, "Le Mystère du Schem Hammephorasch," *REJ,* LXXXII (1926), 157–9.
"Zur Terminologie und Geschichte der jüdischen Alchemie," *MGWJ,* LXIX (1925), 364–71, LXX (1926), 194–201.
Elworthy, Frederick Thomas, *The Evil Eye,* London 1895.
Enelow, Hyman G., "Kawwana: the Struggle for Inwardness in Judaism," *Studies in Jewish Literature issued in honor of Professor Kaufmann Kohler,* Berlin 1913, pp. 82–107.
Epstein, Abraham, "LeKorot HaKabbalah HaAshkenazit," *HaḤoker,* II (Vienna 1894), 1–11, 37–48.
Feuchtwang, D., "Der Tierkreis in der Tradition und im Synagogenritus," *MGWJ,* LIX (1915), 241–67.
Finesinger, Sol B., "The Shofar," *HUCA,* VII–IX (1931–32), 193–228.
"The Custom of Looking at the Fingernails at the Outgoing of the Sabbath," *HUCA,* XII–XIII (1938).
Fink, Elias, "Über das angeblich fabelhafte Tier *Adne HaSadeh* der Mishna," *MGWJ,* LI (1907), 173–82.
Français, J., *L'Église et la Sorcellerie,* Paris 1910.
Franck, Adolph, *The Kabbalah,* N. Y. 1926.
Frazer, J. G., *The Magic Art,* Vol. I, London 1920.
Gaidoz, H., "Le Mariage en Mai," *Mélusine,* VII (1894), 105–11.
Gaidoz, H., and Rolland, E., "Les Ongles," *Mélusine,* II (1884), 481–92.
Gandz, Solomon, *The Knot in Hebrew Literature,* reprint from *Isis,* XIV (1930).
Gaster, Moses, "Lilith und die drei Engel," *MGWJ,* XXIX (1880), 553–65.
Jewish Folk-Lore in the Middle Ages, London 1887.
The Sword of Moses, London 1896.
"Two Thousand Years of a Charm against the Child-Stealing Witch," *Folk-Lore,* XI (1900), 129–61.
"The Wisdom of the Chaldeans: An Old Hebrew Astrological Text," *Proceedings of the Society of Biblical Archaeology,* XXII (1900), 329–51.
The Exempla of the Rabbis, London 1924.
Studies and Texts, 3 vols., London 1925–8.
Ma'aseh Book, 2 vols., Philadelphia 1934.
"The Maassehbuch and the Brantspiegel," *Jewish Studies in Memory of George A. Kohut,* N. Y. 1935, pp. 270–8.
Ginsburg, Christian D., *The Kabbalah,* London 1925.

Ginzberg, Louis, *The Legends of the Jews,* 7 vols., Philadelphia 1909–38.
"Arba' Tekufot," *HaZofeh,* III (1913), 184–6.
Article "Cabala," *JE,* III, 459–79.
de Givry, Grillot, *Witchcraft, Magic and Alchemy,* London 1931.
Glassberg, A. J., *Zichron Brit laRishonim,* Krakau 1892.
Goebel, Franz M., *Jüdische Motive im märchenhaften Erzählungsgut,* Gleiwitz 1932.
Goldenweiser, Alexander A., *Early Civilization—An Introduction to Anthropology,* N. Y. 1922.
Goldmann, Arthur, "The Wachnacht among Vienna Jews," *Filologische Schriften,* I (1926), 91–94.
Goldmerstein, L., "Magical Sacrifice in the Jewish Kabbala," *Folk-Lore,* VII (1896), 202–4.
Goldziher, Ignaz, "Muhammedanischer Aberglaube über Gedächtnisskraft und Vergesslichkeit, mit Parallelen aus der jüdischen Litteratur," *Festschrift z. siebzigsten Geburtstage A. Berliners,* Frankfort 1903, 131–55.
"Eisen als Schutz gegen Dämonen," *AR,* X (1907), 41–6.
"Wasser als Dämonen abwehrendes Mittel," *AR,* XIII (1910), 20–46.
Gollancz, Hermann, *Clavicula Salomonis,* Frankfort and London 1903.
Sepher Maphteah Shelomo, Oxford 1914.
Gordon, Cyrus H., "Aramaic Magical Bowls in the Istanbul and Baghdad Museums," *Archiv Orientální,* VI (Praha 1934), 319–34.
Grimm, Jacob, *Deutsche Mythologie,* 4th ed., 3 vols., Berlin 1875–8.
Gross, Heinrich, *Gallia Judaica,* Paris 1897.
"Zwei kabbalistische Traditionsketten des R. Eleasar aus Worms," *MGWJ,* XLIX (1905), 692–700.
Grotte, Alfred, "Eine neue Hypothese über den Ursprung des Magen David," *MGWJ,* LXVI (1922), 1–9.
Grünbaum, Max, *Jüdischdeutsche Chrestomathie,* Leipzig 1882.
"Un Prétendu Talisman Arabe d'Origine Juive," *REJ,* XXIX (1894), 150–2.
Gesammelte Aufsätze zur Sprach- und Sagenkunde, Berlin 1901.
Grunwald, Max, "Aus Hausapotheke und Hexenküche," *MGJV,* V (1900), 1–87; *MJV,* XIX (1906), 96–120; XXIV, 118–45; *JJV,* I (1923), 178–226.
"Ein altes Symbol in neuer Beleuchtung," *Jahrbuch für jüdische Geschichte und Literatur,* IV (1901), 119–31.
"Bibliomantie und Gesundbeten," *MGJV,* X (1902), 81–98.
"Fünfundzwanzig Jahre jüdischer Volkskunde," *JJV,* I (1923), 1–22.

"Jüdische Mystik," ibid., 371–93.
"Zur Vorgeschichte des Sukkothrituals und verwandter Kultformen," ibid., 427–72.
"Neue Spuk- und Zauberliteratur," *MGWJ,* LXXVII (1933), 161–71, 241–52, 467.

Güdemann, Moritz, "Vermischungen von Jüdischem und Heidnischem aus neuer und alter Zeit," *MGWJ,* XXIV (1875), 269 ff.
Religionsgeschichtliche Studien, Leipzig 1876.
Geschichte des Erziehungswesens und der Cultur der abendländischen Juden, 3 vols., Vienna 1880–8.
Quellenschriften zur Geschichte des Unterrichts und der Erziehung bei den deutschen Juden, Berlin 1891.
"Der 'Magen David' oder Davidsschild," *MGWJ,* LX (1916), 135–9.

de Gunzbourg, David, "Un Talisman Arabe," *REJ,* XXVII (1893), 145–6.

Hansen, Joseph, *Quellen und Untersuchungen zur Geschichte des Hexenwahns und der Hexenverfolgung im Mittelalter,* Bonn 1901.

Hebrew Characteristics, N. Y. 1875.

Heller, Bernard, "Le Nom Divin de Vingt-Deux Lettres," *REJ,* LV (1908), 60–71.
"Autre Note sur le Nom Divin de Vingt-Deux Lettres et sur le Démon de l'Oubli," *REJ,* LVII (1909), 105–8.

Hoffer, Abraham, "Interpretation of 12-, 42-, and 72-Letter Names" (Hebrew), *HaZofeh,* II (1912), 127–32.
"Yesodo Umekoro shel Yom Mitat HaAb veHaEm mide Shanah beShanah," ibid., X (1926), 116–21.

Hoffman, Moses David, "Minhag Kapparot veTashlich," in his *Shibalim,* pp. 39–45, Vienna 1876.

Jacob, B., *Im Namen Gottes,* Berlin 1903.

Jacobs, Joseph, *The Jews of Angevin England,* London 1893.
Jewish Diffusion of Folk-Tales, London 1888.

Jellinek, Adolf, *Auswahl kabbalistischer Mystik,* Leipzig 1853.

Joel, David, *Der Aberglaube und die Stellung des Judenthums zu demselben,* 2 parts, Breslau 1881–3.

Dr. Joesten, *Zur Geschichte der Hexen und Juden in Bonn,* Bonn 1900.

Kammelhar, Israel, *Rabenu Elazar miGermizah,* Rzeszow 1930.

Kaufmann, David, "Was the Custom of Fasting on Sabbath Afternoon part of the Early Anglo-Jewish Ritual?" *JQR, OS,* VI (1894), 754–6.

Kaufman, Judah, *R. Yom Tob Lipmann Mühlhausen,* N. Y. 1927.

Kayser, C., "Gebrauch von Psalmen zur Zauberei," *ZDMG,* XLII (1888), 456–62.

Knuchel, Eduard Fritz, *Die Umwandlung in Kult, Magie und Rechtsbrauch,* Basel 1919.

Kohlbach, Berthold, "Feuer und Licht im Judentume," *Ztschr. Ver. f. Volkskunde,* XXIII (1913), 225–49.

"Das Zopfgebäck im jüdischen Ritus," ibid., XXIV (1914), 265–71.

Kohler, Kaufmann, "The Tetragrammaton and its Uses," *Journal of Jewish Lore and Philosophy,* I (Cincinnati 1909), 19–32.

Kohut, Alexander, *Ueber die jüdische Angelologie und Daemonologie in ihrer Abhängigkeit vom Parsismus,* Leipzig 1866.

Kohut, George Alexander, "Blood Test as Proof of Kinship in Jewish Folklore," *Journal of the American Oriental Society,* XXIV (1903), 129–44.

Krauss, Samuel, "Engelnamen," *MGJV,* VII (1901), 75–83.

"Note sur le Nom Divin de Vingt-Deux Lettres et sur le Démon de l'Oubli," *REJ,* LVI (1908), 251–4.

"Aus der jüdischen Volksküche," *MJV,* LIII (1915), 1–40.

Geschichte der jüdischen Ärzte, Vienna 1930.

Kugler, F. X., "Die Symbolik der Neunzahl bei den Babyloniern," *Hilprecht Anniversary Volume,* 1909, 304–9.

Kynass, F., *Die Juden im deutschen Volkslied,* Greifswald 1934.

Landau, A., "Hollekreisch," *Ztschr. Ver. f. Volkskunde,* IX (1899), 72–7.

Landau, A., and Wachstein, B., *Jüdische Privatbriefe aus dem Jahre 1619,* Vienna 1911.

Landsberger, "Der Brauch in den Tagen zwischen dem Pessach- und Schabuothfeste sich der Eheschliesung zu enthalten," *Jüdische Ztschr. f. Wissenschaft und Leben,* VII (Breslau 1869), 81–96.

Landshuth, Eliezer Lazar b. Meir, *Seder Bikur Ḥolim,* Berlin 1867.

Lang, Andrew, *Magic and Religion,* London 1901.

Lauterbach, Jacob Z., "The Ceremony of Breaking a Glass at Weddings," *HUCA,* II (1925), 351–80.

"Substitutes for the Tetragrammaton," *Proceedings of the American Academy for Jewish Research,* Philadelphia 1931, 39–67.

"The Naming of Children in Jewish Folklore, Ritual and Practice," *Yearbook of the Central Conference of Amer. Rabbis,* XLII (1932), 316–60.

"The Ritual for the Kapparot-Ceremony," *Jewish Studies in Memory of George A. Kohut,* N. Y. 1935, 413–22.

"Tashlik—A Study in Jewish Ceremonies," *HUCA,* XI (1936), 207–340.

Lea, Henry Charles, *A History of the Inquisition of the Middle Ages,* Vol. III, N. Y. 1911, pp. 379–549.

Lévi, Israel, "Le Juif Sorcier," *REJ*, XXII (1891), 232 ff.

"Le Repos Sabbatique des Ames Damnées," *REJ*, XXV (1892), 1–13; XXVI (1893), 131–5.

"Si les morts ont conscience de ce qui se passe ici-bas," *REJ*, XXVI (1893), 69–74.

"La commémoration des âmes dans le Judaïsme," *REJ*, XXIX (1894), 43–60.

"Le mariage en Mai," *Mélusine*, VII (1895), 105 ff.; VIII (1896), 93–4.

"L'Intercession des vivants en faveur des morts," *REJ*, XLVII (1904), 214.

"Les Jardins d'Adonis, les Kapparot et Rosch Haschana," *REJ*, LXI (1911), 206–12.

"Lilit et Lilin," *REJ*, LXVIII (1914), 15–21.

Levy, Ernest, "Hokuspokus," *REJ*, LXXXII (1926), 401–10.

Levy, Ludwig, "Die Schuhsymbolik im jüdischen Ritus," *MGWJ*, LXII (1918), 178–85.

Lewy, Heinrich, "Zum Dämonenglauben," *AR*, XXVIII (1930), 241–52.

"Beiträge zur Religionsgeschichte und Volkskunde," *AR*, XXIX (1931) 187–99.

Lewysohn, Abraham, *Mekore Minhagim*, Berlin 1846.

Lifschitz-Golden, M., *Les Juifs dans la Littératur Française du Moyen Age*, N. Y. 1935.

Lilienthal, Regina, "Das Kind bei den Juden," *MJV*, XXV and XXVI (1908), 1–24, 41–55.

"'Ayin HaRa'," *Yidische Filologye*, I (Warsaw 1924), 245–71.

Lipez, J., *Sefer HaMeta'amim*, Warsaw 1890.

Loewe, Heinrich, *Die Juden in der katholischen Legende*, Berlin 1912.

Löw, Immanuel, "Die Finger in Litteratur und Folklore der Juden," *Gedenkbuch zur Erinnerung an David Kaufmann*, Breslau 1900, 61–85.

Die Flora der Juden, 4 vols., Vienna 1926–1934.

"Das Salz," *Jewish Studies in Memory of George A. Kohut*, N. Y. 1935, 454 ff.

"Ha'iddana," *HUCA*, XI (1936), 193–206.

Löw, Leopold, *Die Lebensalter in der jüdischen Literatur*, Szegedin 1875.

Lowenthal, Marvin, *The Memoirs of Glückel of Hameln*, (trans.) N. Y. 1932.

A World Passed By, N. Y. 1933.

The Jews of Germany, N. Y. 1936.

Löwinger, Adolf, *Der Traum in der jüdischen Literatur,* Leipzig 1908.
"Der Schatten in Literatur und Folklore der Juden," *MJV,* XXXIII and XXXIV (1910), 1–5; 41–57.
"Die Himmel in nachbiblischer Auffassung," *MJV,* XLI (1912), 12–37.
"Rechts und links in der Bibel und Tradition der Juden," *MJV,* LV (1916), 1–69.
"Der Windgeist Keteb," *JJV,* II (1925), 157–70.
"Der Böse Blick nach jüdischen Quellen," *Menorah,* IV (Vienna 1926), 551–69.

Malter, Henry, "Dreams as a Cause of Literary Compositions," *Studies in Jewish Literature in honor of Prof. Kaufmann Kohler,* Berlin 1913, 199–203.

Marmorstein, A., "Beiträge zur Religionsgeschichte und Volkskunde," *JJV,* I (1923), 280–319; II (1925), 344–83.
"David ben Jehuda Ḥasid," *MGWJ,* LXXI (1927), 39–48.

Marx, Alexander, "The Correspondence between the Rabbis of Southern France and Maimonides about Astrology," *HUCA,* III (1926), 311–58.

Maury, L. F. Alfred, *La Magie et l'Astrologie dans l'Antiquité et au Moyen Age,* 4th ed., Paris 1877.

Monod, Bernard, "Juifs, Sorciers et Hérétiques au Moyen Age," *REJ,* XLVI (1903), 237 ff.

Montgomery, James A., "Some Early Amulets from Palestine," *Journal of the American Oriental Society,* XXXI (1911), 272–81.
Aramaic Incantation Texts from Nippur, Philadelphia 1913.

Moore, George Foot, "Intermediaries in Jewish Theology," *Harvard Theological Review,* XV (1922), 41–85.

Müller, Alois, "Ein mit hebräischen Buchstaben niedergeschriebener deutscher Segen gegen die Bärmutter," *Ztschr. f. deutsches Alterthum,* XIX (1876), 473–8.

Münz, I., *Die jüdischen Ärzte im Mittelalter,* Frankfort 1922.

Murray, Margaret Alice, *The Witch-Cult in Western Europe,* Oxford 1921.

Nacht, Jacob, *The Symbolism of the Shoe with Special Reference to Jewish Sources,* 1915 (Reprint from *JQR, NS,* VI).
"Der Fuss. Eine folkloristische Studie," *JJV,* I (1923), 123–77.

Nash, W. L., "A Hebrew Amulet against Disease," *Proceedings of the Soc. of Biblical Archaeology,* XXVIII (London 1906), 182–4.

von Negelein, Julius, "Bild, Spiegel und Schatten im Volksglauben," *AR,* V (1902), 1–37.

Neubauer, A., and Stern, M., *Hebräische Berichte über die Judenverfolgungen während der Kreuzzüge,* Berlin 1892.

Nissan, Zalman, "Mekor HaMinhag Lichtov al Aḥore Gevil HaMezuzah," *Zion,* II (Frankfort 1842), 161–4.
Oppenheim, D., "Die Bernikel-Gans," *MGWJ,* XVIII (1869), 88–93.
Perles, J., *Die jüdische Hochzeit in nachbiblischer Zeit,* reprint from *MGWJ,* IX (1860).
"Die Leichenfeierlichkeiten im nachbibl. Judenthume," *MGWJ,* X (1861), 345–55, 376–94.
Etymologische Studien zur Kunde der rabbinischen Sprache und Alterthümer, Breslau 1871.
Beiträge zur Geschichte der hebräischen und aramäischen Studien, Munich 1884.
"Die Berner Handschrift des kleinen Aruch," *Jubelschrift zum siebzigsten Geburtstage des Prof. Dr. H. Graetz,* Breslau 1887, 1–38.
Pick, Bernhard, *The Cabala,* Chicago 1913.
Pilcher, E. J., "Two Kabbalistic Planetary Charms," *Proceedings of the Soc. of Biblical Archaeology,* XXVIII (London 1906), 110–18.
Preis, Karl, *Die Medizin in der Kabbala,* Frankfort 1928.
Preuss, Julius, "Bon malan bei Raschi," *Festschrift zum siebzigsten Geburtstage A. Berliners,* Frankfort 1903, 296–300.
Prynne, William, *A Short Demurrer to the Jewes,* London 1656.
Rabbinowicz, Jacob, *Der Todtenkultus bei den Juden,* Frankfort 1889.
Reifmann, J., "Mekor Minhag Ẓom Ḥatan veKallah beyom Ḥatuntam," *Kochve Yiẓḥak,* XXXII (Vienna 1865), p. 31.
Rivers, W. H. R., *Medicine, Magic and Religion,* London 1924.
Rodkinson, Michael L., *Tefilah leMoshe,* Pressburg 1883.
History of Amulets, Charms and Talismans, N. Y. 1893.
Rosenfeld, B., *Die Golemsage und ihre Verwertung in der deutschen Literatur,* Breslau 1934.
Rydberg, Viktor, *The Magic of the Middle Ages,* N. Y. 1879.
Samter, Ernst, *Geburt, Hochzeit, und Tod,* Leipzig 1911.
Sartori, Paul, "Feuer und Licht im Totengebrauche," *Ztschr. Ver. f. Volkskunde,* XVII (1907), 361–86.
"Das Wasser im Totengebrauche," ibid., XVIII (1908), 352–78.
Scheftelowitz, Isidor, "Das Fischsymbol im Judentum und Christentum," *AR,* XIV (1911), 1–53, 321–92.
Das Schlingen- und Netzmotiv im Glauben und Brauch der Völker, Giessen 1912.
"Tierorakel im altjüdischen Volksglauben," *Ztschr. Ver. f. Volkskunde,* XXIII (1913), 383–90.
Das stellvertretende Huhnopfer, Giessen 1914.
Schell, Otto, "Das Salz im Volksglauben," *Ztschr. Ver. f. Volkskunde,* XV (1905), 137–49.

Scherer, J. E., *Die Rechtsverhältnisse der Juden in den deutsch-österreichischen Ländern,* Leipzig 1901.

Scholem, Gerhard, "Alchemie und Kabbala," *MGWJ,* LXIX (1925), 13–30, 95–110, 371–4; LXX (1926), 202–9.

"Bilar Melech HaShedim," in *Madae' HaYahadut,* I (Jerusalem 1926), 112–27.

Bibliographia Kabbalistica, Leipzig 1927.

Perakim leToldot Sifrut HaKabbalah, Jerusalem 1931.

Einige kabbalistische Handschriften im Britischen Museum, Jerusalem 1932.

"Der Begriff der Kawwana in der alten Kabbala," *MGWJ,* LXXVIII (1934), 492–518.

Articles "Golem" and "Kabbala," *EJ,* VII, 501–7, IX, 630–730.

Major Trends in Jewish Mysticism, Hilda Stich Stroock Lectures for 1938 (unpublished).

Schönbach, Anton E., "Zeugnisse zur deutschen Volkskunde des Mittelalters," *Ztschr. Ver. f. Volkskunde,* XII (1902), 1–14.

Schorr, O. H., "Malachim, Shedim Umazzikim," *HeḤaluẓ,* VII (Frankfort 1865), 16–22, VIII (1869), 3–16.

Schudt, J. J., *Jüdische Merckwürdigkeiten,* 4 parts, Frankfort 1714–1718.

Schwab, M., *Vocabulaire de l'Angélologie,* Paris 1897.

Le Ms. No. 1380 . . . Supplément au Vocabulaire, Paris 1899.

Seligmann, M., *Die Zauberkraft des Auges und das Berufen,* Hamburg 1922.

Die magischen Heil- und Schutzmittel aus der unbelebten Natur, Stuttgart 1927.

Singer, Charles, "Early English Magic and Medicine," *Proceedings of the British Academy,* London 1919–20, pp. 341–74.

Spoer, Hans H., "Notes on Jewish Amulets," *Journal of Biblical Literature,* XXIII (Boston 1904), 97–105.

Staerk, W., "Zwei alte jüdische Beschreiungsformeln," *MGWJ,* LXVI (1922), 200–3.

Steinschneider, Moritz, "Das Traumbuch Daniels und die oneirokritische Litteratur des Mittelalters," *Serapeum,* XXIV (Leipzig 1863), 193–201, 209–16.

"Loosbücher," *HB,* VI (1863), 120 ff. (also *Die Hebraeischen Uebersetzungen des Mittelalters,* Berlin 1893, 867–72).

Ueber die Volkslitteratur der Juden, Berlin 1872 (reprint).

"Zur medicinischen Literatur," *HB,* XVII (1877), 56 ff., 114 ff.; XIX (1879), 35, 64, 84, 105, 108.

"Medicinische Handschriften," *Magazin für die Wissenschaft des Judenthums,* X (Berlin 1883), 101–12, 157–69.

"Lapidarien," *Semitic Studies in Memory of Rev. Dr. Alexander Kohut,* Berlin 1897, 42–72.

Der Aberglaube, Hamburg 1900.

Stobbe, Otto, *Die Juden in Deutschland während des Mittelalters,* Berlin 1923.

Stössel, D., "Von den Abänderungsmöglichkeiten im rabbinischen Schrifttum unter besonderer Berücksichtigung des *ha'iddana* Prinzips," *Festschrift zum 70. Geburtstage des Oberkirchenrats Dr. Kroner, Stuttgart,* Breslau 1917, 27–66.

Strack, Hermann L., *The Jew and Human Sacrifice,* N. Y. 1909.

Summers, Montague, *The History of Witchcraft and Demonology,* London 1926.

Ta'ame HaMinhagim, by "Ish Shuv," 4 parts, Lemberg 1906–11.

Thorndike, Lynn, *The Place of Magic in the Intellectual History of Europe,* N. Y. 1905.

A History of Magic and Experimental Science, 4 vols., N. Y. 1923–34.

Vajda, Bela, "Menora, Davidsschild und Salomos Siegel," *MJV,* LIX (1918), 33–42.

Wellesz, J., "Volksmedizinisches aus dem jüdischen Mittelalter," *MJV,* XXXV (1910), 117–20.

Wickersheimer, Ernest, *Les Accusations d'Empoisonnement portées pendant la première moitié du XIVe siècle contre les Lépreux et les Juifs; leurs relations avec les Épidémies de Peste (Communication faite au Quatrième Congrès International d'Histoire de la Médecine [Bruxelles, avril 1923]),* Anvers 1927.

Wiener, M., *Regesten zur Geschichte der Juden in Deutschland während des Mittelalters,* Hanover 1862.

Wohlstein, Joseph, *Dämonenbeschwörungen aus nachtalmudischer Zeit,* Berlin 1894.

Wuttke, Adolf, *Der deutsche Volksaberglaube der Gegenwart,* 3rd ed., Berlin 1900.

Yoffie, Leah Rachel, "Popular Beliefs and Customs among the Yiddish-Speaking Jews of St. Louis, Mo.," *Journal of American Folk-Lore,* XXXVIII (1927), 375–99.

Zimmels, H. J., *Beiträge zur Geschichte der Juden in Deutschland im 13. Jahrhundert, insbesondere auf Grund der Gutachten des R. Meir Rothenburg,* Vienna 1926.

"Ofot Hagedelim beIlan," in *Minḥat Bikkurim,* Vienna 1926, 1–9.

Zoller, Israel, *Lilith,* Rome 1926 (reprint from *Rivista di Antropologia,* XXVII).

"Lilit," *Filologische Schriften,* III (1929), 121–42.

GLOSSARY OF HEBREW TERMS

Afikomen—a cake of unleavened bread eaten at the end of the Passover meal.

Aggada—non-legal portion of Talmudic literature.

Amora (pl. *Amoraim*)—post-Mishnaic authorities cited in the Talmud (c. 220-500 C.E.).

Dibbuk—spirit of deceased person which has entered body of living person.

Gaon (pl. *Geonim*)—heads of Babylonian and Palestinian academies after the sixth century.

Gehinnom—realm in which the wicked expiate their sins.

Gemara—portion of the Talmud containing Amoraic commentary on the Mishna.

Gilgul—transmigration of souls.

Habdalah—ritual marking the close of Sabbath and holidays.

Halacha—legal portion of Talmudic literature; legal tradition, generally.

Ḥazan—precentor.

Hashba'ah—invocation.

Hoshana Rabbah—seventh day of the Feast of Tabernacles.

Jahrzeit—annual commemoration of death.

Kaddish, more specifically, *kaddish yatom*—prayer for mourners.

Kiddush—blessing over wine at inception of Sabbath and holidays.

Kosher—ritually pure.

Keri—seminal pollution.

Lag B'omer—thirty-third day in the counting of the *Omer;* 18th of Iyar.

Malach—angel.

Mazal—star or constellation.

Mazzah—unleavened bread.

Mazzik—demon.

Memuneh—"deputy" angel.

Mezuzah (pl. *Mezuzot*)—a Biblical inscription attached to the doorpost.

Midrash—commentary on the Bible, mainly of an Aggadic nature.

Minyan—minimum of ten men required to constitute a congregation.

Mishna—the "Oral Law" forming basis of the Talmud; edited c. 220 C.E. by R. Judah HaNassi.

Rosh Hashana—New Year.

Ruaḥ—spirit.

Sar—prince.

Seder—Passover meal and service.

Sefirot—the ten creative attributes of God, according to the *Kabbalah*.

Shechinah—the divine Presence.

Shed—demon.

Shema'—the verse beginning, "Hear, O Israel" (Deut. 6:4), and the prayer composed of Deut. 6:4-9, 11:13-21, Nu. 15:37-41.

Sukkot—Feast of Tabernacles.

Tanna (pl. *Tannaim*) — authorities cited in the Mishna and coëval writings.

Targum—Aramaic translation of the Bible.

Tefillin—phylacteries.

Tekufah—"turning of the sun," i.e., the solstices and equinoxes.

Torah—the Pentateuch.

Yom Kippur—Day of Atonement.

INDEX

B

C

D

E

bols of, 173; Teutonic goddess of, 40.
Fever, 110, 117, 119, 197, 198, 203, 204.
Fig (a gesture), 161 f., 175.
Figures, magical, 141 f., 148, 151.
Finger, 7, 158, 161, 175.
Finger-nails, 128, 129, 217, 255, 256, 308, n. 26; divining by, 219; order of cutting, 191.
Fire, 31, 72, 118, 125, 159, 181, 182, 196, 198, 226, 233, 252, 262, 289, n. 26, 298, n. 5, 301, n. 44, 305, n. 15; as dream symbol, 239; as omen, 213; on Sabbath, 3, 143; ordeal by, 227; protection against, 295, n. 4; quenched by name, 96; *Sefer Raziel* prevents, 315; to extinguish, 294, n. 16, n. 21.
Fires, of *Gehinnom,* 66, 67.
First encounter, 212.
First things, 122.
Fish, 165, 166, 173, 183, 185, 188, 213, 230; as dream symbol, 239. *See also* Sturgeon.
Flame, spirit is like, 61.
Flight, power of, attributed to sorcerers and witches, 14.
Flood, removal of name caused the, 289, n. 26.
Folk biology, 184–190.
Food, effect of, on procreation, 184 f.; incantations inscribed on, 122 f.; left overnight, 46; not eaten on Saturday evening, 68; strewn at wedding, 173 f.; token of good fortune, 213. *See also* Corn; Garlic; Honey; Liquids; Manna; Meat; Milk; Nuts; Oil; Olives; Onion; Pepper; Salt; Spices; Water; Wheat; Wine.
Forgetfulness, actions affecting, 190 f.; charm against, 102; spirit of, 117, 191.
Forgetting and remembering, 190–192.
Formula, for change of name, 205; for creating *Golem,* 85; for negating curse, 60; for ordeal, 227.
Four, 142.
Fowl, 162, 163, 164, 173, 174, 183, 184, 245; as omen, 212; creation of, 281, n. 52. *See also* Feathers, chicken; Hen; Goose; Rooster.
Fox, 133.
France, 6, 68, 148, 176, 178, 249.
Frankfort, 113, 202.
Frazer, J. G., 21, 124, 126, 302.
Frederick I, of Austria, privilege issued by, 228.
Free will, problem of, 208 ff.
Freiburg, city council of, requests expulsion of Jews, 8.
Friday, 145, 253, 254; night, 47, 67, 68, 166, 186, 195, 281, n. 6. *See also* Sabbath, eve of.
Fright, as remedy, 196.
Fulda, Jews of, accused of murder, 7.
Funeral, 49, 106, 113, 121; rites, 176 ff. *See also* Hands, washing, after funeral.
Future, foretelling the. *See* Divination.

G

Gabriel, 98, 126, 142, 151, 156, 251, 260, 286, n. 9.
Galen, 120, 230, 309, n. 2.
Garlic, 46, 185, 194, 299, n. 17, 302, n. 6.
Gaster, Moses, 72, 89, 100, 101 f., 260, 316.
Gehinnom, 66, 170, 234; angel of, 66, 68, 76. *See also* Hell.
Gematria, 94, 99, 262 f., 264.
Gems, 136–138, 265–268.
Generation, spontaneous, 182 f.
Genethlialogy, 252.
Genii, 40.
Genitalia, 112. *See also* Sex organs.
Geomancy, 217 f.
George of Podiebrad, 252.
Gerald of Wales, cited, on barnacle goose, 183.
Germany, 8, 48, 68, 72, 85, 86, 120, 134, 141, 148, 164, 171, 176, 178, 201, 216, 249, 258, 262, 307.
Gershon b. Ḥiskiya, 230.
Gerson, Jean, 193.
Gerte, 220, 308, n. 25.
Ghost, 49, 62, 175, 176, 223, 274, n. 6, 302, n. 56. *See also* Dead, the, spirits of.
Ghoul, 37.
Gilgul, 50. *See also* Metempsychosis; Soul, transmigration of.
Gilles de Rais, 9.
Ginsburg, C. D., 264.
Glass, breaking of, at wedding, 172.
God, 44, 45, 65, 66, 104, 107, 112, 139, 146, 157, 158, 165, 175, 211, 226, 228, 247, 250, 257, 262; agents of, 69, 71, 72, 74, 75, 76, 204; anger of, 23, 60; appeal to, 155; attributes of, 90, 98; the creator, 29, 286; dreams come from, 232, 234; fear of, 208; the healer, 30; language of, 74; name of, 15, 80, 83, 84, 85, 90–97, 98, 100, 107, 108, 109, 113, 143, 151, 201; protection of, 46; root of magic, 21;

K

L

M

R

S

T

U

V